The Gun Digest Book
of the
.22 RIMFIRE

By John Lachuk

DBI BOOKS, Inc., Northfield, Ill.

Editorial Staff

Editor
Robert S.L. Anderson

Production Manager
Pamela J. Johnson

Cover Photography
John Hanusin

Associate Publisher
Sheldon L. Factor

ISBN 0-695-81197-5   Library of Congress Catalog Card Number 78-70509

CONTENTS

Introduction

AN INFORMAL poll of fellow shooting enthusiasts of my acquaintance revealed that all but one had begun their shooting careers with a .22 rimfire rifle or pistol. All had "graduated" into bigbore shooters in adulthood, but a goodly number (about 85 percent) had at least one rimfire gun that still witnessed frequent use. Many had two, three, or more rimfire rifles and/or handguns, in more or less continual service. Obviously, some smallbore target competitors were numbered among my sampling. However, a large proportion were not target buffs at all, but rather everyday hunters and informal shooters whose only target activity consisted of merely plinking.

The apparent conclusion to be drawn from this pint-sized poll is that the youthful affection for the .22 rimfire that lighted up our formative years, persists throughout our adult lives. That sometimes slumbering sentiment often experiences a resounding resurgence with advancing years, when the attributes that made rimfire guns so attractive to our youth again reassert themselves with the enfeebling effects of old age. Then the muted report, near absence of recoil, and overall gentle character of the rimfire round become, once more, compelling assets.

The usual frothy treatment, designed more to entertain than inform, was avoided in order to reach a greater depth of rimfire knowledge than has been presented in print before. Most of the chapters could very likely be expanded to book-length without becoming redundant, but that would present an impractical printing project. Hopefully, the most important points are adequately covered.

It is the fond hope of the author, that this volume will enrich your enjoyment of the .22 rimfire and engender a fuller appreciation for its many talents. If the information presented helps you to realize increased performance from your favorite .22 rimfire, I will have realized my goal.

John Lachuk
Southern, California
October, 1978

CHAPTER 1

The .22—Everyone's Gun

THE .22 RIMFIRE IS indeed "everyone's gun!" Young boys and girls have carried on a love affair with the .22 for generations. And this kind of romance can last a lifetime, as yours truly can attest!

Admittedly, the .22 holds an irresistible appeal for the very young because it fits their dimensions and abilities far better than any centerfire cartridge; but, it's a fallacy to believe that the .22 rifle or handgun is merely a stage in the evolution of a marksman or hunter—a stepping stone to bigger and better things. Far from being "just a boy's gun," it provides positive benefits for every age group.

In the middle years, the .22 rimfire offers restful recreation in the form of plinking at random targets at nominal cost and without requiring a month-long safari in search of an area remote enough to absorb the noise. Because of the rimfire's hushed voice and requirement for no more than a 100-yard shooting range, .22 target facilities can be found in or near most cities and towns. Anyone who seriously enters into smallbore competition will quickly discover that this is a game that in truth separates the men from the boys. To become a winner, you will need precision equipment and total dedication to the sport!

Senior citizens often take refuge in the rimfire smallbore because it reduces the ravages of recoil and racket at a time in life when excesses of both can prove discomforting. A mature friend of my own youth was the late Burt Koeppe, of South Gate, California. Burt loved life, and he loved to shoot. Although slight of stature, he gloried in the muzzle blast of a bigbore revolver. He even displayed a distinct affection for his 4-inch barreled Smith & Wesson Model 29 .44 Magnum that delivered enough concussion and recoil to curl your hair—which was OK because Burt didn't have much hair left! As what remained began to gray, I noticed that Burt's regard for the short-barreled .44 Magnum ebbed apace. There came a time when the stubby revolver was left to grace a bureau drawer, and a classic Smith & Wesson K-22 replaced it in Burt's working battery. He took no less pride in striking the mark with his rimfire handgun. Inasmuch as the target was more often than not an itinerant tin can, the effect of the .22 was just as convincing as that of the .44 Magnum.

As for me, I burned many a cylinder-full of .22 Long Rifles in my Harrington & Richardson Sportsman, demolishing uncountable numbers of empty ammo boxes, cans and bottles. (Today, bottles are *verboten* and rightly so! Who needs all of that broken glass cluttering up what little remains of our virgin areas?) Burt and I were into informal fast-draw competition (shooting blanks) many years before it became a national craze. Lacking the exotic electonic timers that were to come later, we vied to see who could beat the coin on the back of the wrist, held at shoulder height, to the ground. Since the outcome was always in doubt, we never tired of the game.

My very first gun was a rusted relic resurrected from the city dump at about age 10—it was *sans* stock and sights. I improvised a stock for this bolt action Winchester single shot .22 rifle from a worn-out Benjamin pump air rifle, and rigged up a blade-and-notch sight duo from scrap metal. Scrub the rusty barrel as I might with brass brushes and steel wool, I couldn't restore its shiny, smooth surface! But it *shot,* and it *was* my *first honest-to-goodness firearm.* I treasured that old Winchester despite the fact that it was balky about extracting empty cases and that excess headspace caused frequent ruptured case heads, to the accompaniment of flying brass and powder particles. Accuracy was poor—less than I had come to expect from my air rifle. So when a schoolmate offered to sell me his "Western Field" 5-shot, clip-loading, bolt action rifle for $5, I skipped lunch until I could afford it! Skinny as a rail but deliriously happy, I repaired to the Great Owens Valley where desert denizens came to respect that rifle. The rattle of the bolt during reloading never disturbed game, because the animal was dead by the time I had to recharge the chamber.

The teaching talents of the .22 have never really been disputed. The diminutive rimfire round has been the career-launching platform for many of the well-known members of today's shooting fraternity. For example, Roy Weatherby, "The High Priest of High Velocity," famed for his magnum cartridges and quality guns, began his hunting career in Kansas. He walked the furrows that his tenant-farmer father had sown, picking off an occasional unattentive crow that lingered too long for a last bite before winging away 'midst raucous scolding and the *crack* of Roy's Stevens "Crackshot" .22. As a stripling in tattered jeans and ankle-high "clodhoppers," Roy would have been hard to recognize as the merchant of magnums that we know and respect today. As the sun descended and the birds flew to roost, young Roy hurried to a nearby grove of cottonwoods, there to guard songbird nests from raiding blue jays. Later, as a teenager, Roy poled a small boat alone through the forbidding silence of the Florida Everglades, potting deadly alligators and water moccasins with a pump action .22—the hides were sold to nearby tanners to buy more ammunition.

Another highly successful entrepreneur of the firearms field who is also a graduate of the smallbore school is Neale A. Perkins, founder and president of Safariland Leather Products, maker of premium-quality holsters and leather goods. Neale's father presented him with a Winchester Model 63 "Speed King" auto with an appropriately shortened stock to accommodate his 12-year-old arms. Young Neale used it to clip the heads off of grouse that roosted on rail fences near his Pasadena, California home. With time and practice, he reached the point where he could drop them in flight! The stock of that Winchester autoloader was twice lengthened as Neale grew up, and it accompanied him to Africa when he was 18. There, Neale kept the camp in meat by shooting some of the numerous, small oribi antelope that roamed the plains. All but one were one-shot, behind-the-shoulder kills—the 38-grain hollow point slugs invariably ending up as perfect mushrooms under the skin on the opposite side of the chest cavity. At last count, Neale had fed in excess of 30,000 rounds through his faithful Winchester, and it is still going strong! Today, Neale probably wouldn't recommend taking oribi antelope with a .22 rimfire; however, this example of the .22's ability to down even medium-sized game proves a point—the little .22 Long Rifle *can be* a lethal game taker when used by someone who knows that cartridge's capabilities.

A boy's attraction to a .22 simply will not be denied. Even Elmer Keith, well known for his firm affinity to big, *BIG*bore rifles and handguns, began life on a Montana ranch where he made life precarious for

The .22 rimfire holds irresistable appeal for youngsters because it fits their dimensions and abilities better than a centerfire round, but the .22 is not "just a boy's gun!" It provides benefits for every age group.

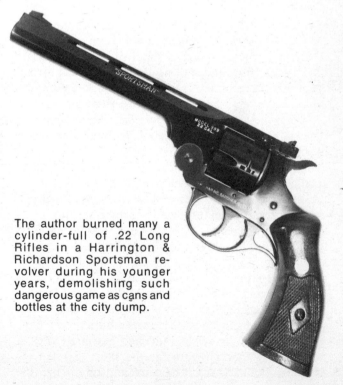

The author burned many a cylinder-full of .22 Long Rifles in a Harrington & Richardson Sportsman revolver during his younger years, demolishing such dangerous game as cans and bottles at the city dump.

The biggest bigbore buff of all time, Elmer Keith on the left, with the author on the right. Sandwiched in between is movie actor Clint Eastwood. Even Elmer, with all of his commitment to big-bore handguns and rifles, used and still uses the .22 rimfire for much of his small game hunting.

Actor James Arness, shown here with the author, is most famous for firing blanks on the streets on Dodge City, but he is equally at home with live ammo, having begun with a .22 rimfire early in life.

neighboring ground squirrels, woodchucks and jack rabbits, using a succession of rimfire rifles and six-guns. To this day, he still finds occasion to exercise one of his many smallbore guns.

To an exhibition shooter, the .22 rimfire is an indispensable tool of his profession. He requires a cartridge that is accurate but not overpowering, allowing him to perform in relatively confined spaces with crowds of people at every quarter. Annie Oakley, dubbed "Little Miss Sure Shot," by Indian chief Sitting Bull, made her reputation with a lever action .22 Marlin Model 1897 (available in its current configuration as the Model 39). Other Marlin marksmen of yore were, Frank E. Miller, Captain A. H. Hardy, Gus Peret and Tom Mix. Adolph Topperwein and his wife "Plinky," spread the fame of Winchester .22's with their remarkable shooting prowess. Adolph made history in 1907, when he began a marathon shoot, firing 8 hours a day for 10 successive days, eventually punching .22-sized holes through 72,500 airborne wooden cubes measuring 2½ inches on a side. That record stood for 52 years, until it was decisively shattered by present-day exhibition shooter Tom Frye, but more on that later!

Certainly unique among exhibition shooters was my old friend Rodd Redwing, a full-blooded Chickasaw Indian. To the genuine sorrow of all who knew him, Rodd has gone to the "Happy Hunting Grounds," where doubtless the angels have prevailed upon him to demonstrate his magic with .22 rimfire six-guns and rifles! Rodd used to perform with live ammo in close quarters, with people pressing in, using nothing more than a 2-foot square steel backstop. Only a man as certain of his marksmanship as Rodd would or *could* have done it! He was doubtless the greatest single con-

With a .22 Long Rifle, you can hunt everything from brush rabbits to bobcats.

sumer of Necco candy wafers anywhere in the world. He shattered literally thousands of these tiny, white candy discs, firing a pair of Colt Single Action Army revolvers (sleeved down to .22 rimfire) from the hip, or "point" shooting (no sights) a Marlin Model 39 lever action. To make it more interesting, Rodd would have a pendulum swinging across in front of the target, with a 2-inch hole in its center. Rodd had to time his shots to go through the hole as it swung past. He would also shoot through the tiny hole of a "Lifesaver" mint, shattering the Necco wafer behind it.

Rodd Redwing was the technical firearms director on virtually every important Western filmed in Hollywood during his lifetime, beginning with Howard Hughes' *The Outlaw,* through such classics as *Shane, Duel In The Sun, High Noon, Vera Cruz, One-Eyed Jacks,* etc. He taught stars such as Marlon Brando, Glenn Ford, Dean Martin, et al, how to handle six-gun and rifle with convincing dexterity.

Not all movie cowboys needed coaching. Some grew up with guns in their hands. Would you believe Matt Dillion with a .22? James Arness received his first gun, a Remington Model 241 "Speedmaster" autoloader, as a gift from his father when he was only 12 years of age. His first 18 years were spent in his birthplace of Minneapolis, but school vacations found him in a woods cabin on his father's 5-acre island in the center of Ox Lake, located in northern Minnesota. Brother Pete, better known to TV viewers as Peter Graves, often went along on these combination hunting/fishing vacations. The two evenly-matched brothers competed with each other in everything including marksmanship.

Should you take up formal target competition, you'll soon find that it demand the best equipment, such as this Model 52 Winchester with Unertl scope, and absolute dedication from the shooter!

The Marlin 39 is the modern generation of Marlin lever action .22 rimfire rifles. It and its forebearers have been the favorites of thousands of shooters, young and old.

Shortly after Jim got his own .22 rifle, they chanced to walk up on four crows perched on a fence rail. The birds were alert to their presence, but not yet alarmed enough to fly. As Jim tells it, "I rashly bet Pete that I could get all four of them with my new automatic rifle." His younger brother jeered back, "I'll bet you 5 bucks you can't!" Jim raised his rifle slowly to avoid alarming the already restless birds and carefully took aim. "I managed to pick off two of them before they got off of the rail. The third was just lifting when I nailed it. The fourth black bandit was in full flight by that time. I swung out ahead of it and caught it with a lucky shot! I never let on to Pete that I was more surprised than he was. I collected that $5 too, and spent it on ammunition." (The compact bottom-ejecting Model 241 was licensed to Remington by John M. Browning. They ultimately dropped the fine little rifle from their line; however, it is still available as the Browning Automatic from the Browning Company, Morgan, Utah.)

Roy Rogers, cinema's famed "King of the Cowboys," grew up on an Oklahoma cattle ranch, where a lever action Marlin .22 was as much a part of his daily wearing-gear as were boots and chaps. His early addiction to the Marlin lever rifle was reflected in his later choice of a deer/varmint rifle, a Marlin Model 336 .30-30. While on a varmint hunting trip together, he pointed out to me its obvious advantages of handiness, quick action, and compactness in a saddle boot, whether on horseback or a motorcycle (both favored modes of transportation for the cowboy movie star.) Roy certainly could afford the latest magnums, but he hewed to his familiar lever action! He personally felt my own custom made .240 Page "Sooper Pooper" was rather exotic for his tastes.

By now, you probably think that I own stock in the Marlin company. Not so! Americans have been in love with lever action rifles ever since the Henry demonstrated how much fun it was to shoot more than one shot at a time! Marlin made one of the first, and for many years, the *only*, .22 lever action. With but minor modifications over the years, it is still one of the best!

Star Steve McQueen began his career as a celluloid cowboy, playing the role of bounty hunter Josh Randall

Actor Steve McQueen numbers several .22 rimfire handguns and rifles among his collection. Here he is sighting his Marlin 39. The target on the shelf indicates that he can hit with it after he gets it sighted in to center the bull's-eye!

on the highly successful TV series, *Wanted—Dead or Alive*. He was later a standout as one of *The Magnificent Seven*. It's no accident that Steve handles a gun with convincing reality. During his early teens, Steve lived for a time with his great-uncle on the latter's Ozark farm. Steve had a single shot Stevens "Crackshot" rifle, and the "old man" would dole out a few rounds of ammunition and instruct Steve to go out and "bring back their dinner." "The bore was pitted," says Steve, "and it was far from accurate. I pretty near had to poke the thing into a squirrel's ear, but it furnished many a pot of squirrel stew. With that gun, it wasn't so much a matter of marksmanship as it was of stalking!" The battered Stevens disappeared during Steve's subsequent wanderings from seaman aboard a Caribbean tanker, to Texas oil field worker, to lumberjack in Canada, and finally a stint in the Marine Corps; but, he never forgot the enjoyment it gave him. His current battery includes a Marlin lever action Model 39A.

Cinematic gunplay is not confined to westerns. Robert Stack is still best remembered for his role as the poker-faced Elliot Ness on the TV series, *The Untouchables*, where he handled a Thompson submachine gun like a pro. Bob *is* in fact a gun pro. At just 16 years of age, he became an official member of the All-American Skeet Team. During 1936 and 1937, this Skeet prodigy won virtually every major tournament held in America. He got his start with firearms years before, hunting small game with a .22 rimfire in the company of his father.

The year of 1978 marked the centennial of John M. Browning's invention of his first gun, a falling block single shot of wondrous simplicity and reliability, marketed by Winchester for only $15, in calibers large and small, *including the .22 rimfire Short!* Browning went on to prove that this display of genius at the tender age of just 23 years, was no flash in the pan—he was granted a total of 128 separate and distinct firearms patents during his lifetime. John M. Browning, the unchallenged, unassailable *giant* of firearms development devoted much of his inventive talent to the .22 rimfire

1978 marked the centennial of John M. Browning's first gun, the Winchester High Wall Rifle. He is shown here holding the original model of his incomparable .22 rimfire autoloading rifle, from whence all others since have sprung. Many of his inventions were devoted to the rimfire cartridge.

cartridge. He recognized it as a tremendously important sporting cartridge in the United States, as well as overseas. Tens-of-thousands of American boys have had reasons aplenty to be grateful to the great John M. for his contributions to rimfire smallbore sporting and target arms, beginning with his classic pump action repeater, the Model 1890 Winchester. Browning followed a decade later with his Model 1900 bolt action single shot (my first gun!), and climaxed his rimfire rifle designs in 1913 with his Remington Model 24 bottom-ejecting autoloader. (Please, let's not forget the ever faithful Colt Woodsman in 1914! Inexplicably, Colt

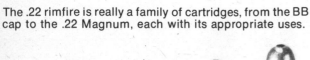
The .22 rimfire is really a family of cartridges, from the BB cap to the .22 Magnum, each with its appropriate uses.

abandoned the Woodsman, but its basic design has been kept alive in the Browning Challenger II.)

When my own son Michael outgrew his BB guns, I bought him a Winchester Model 69 clip-fed bolt action and a shooting jacket that was a tad too large for him. He soon grew into, then out of that jacket! While he was doing it, we both had a lot of fun, and he learned the basics of marksmanship and gun handling.

Why have so many people, from so many walks of life, used the .22 rimfire for a significant part of their lives? Like all of us, they realized its potential for range or field, for offering challenge and providing enjoyment. The .22 rimfire is all things to all men.

The .22 cartridge knows no class distinction. It is loved alike by peasant and potentate, and graduating from one estate to the other does nothing to diminish the

The closer you look at the tiny .22 rimfire, the better it looks! It weighs but 52.5 grains and measures no more than 1-inch in length yet weighed and measured in terms of utility and pleasure derived, it looms 10 feet tall!

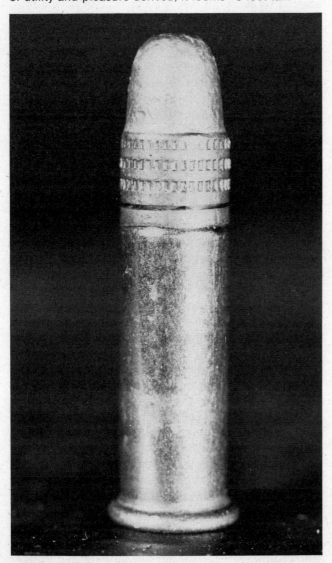

popularity of the compact cartridge. Definitive sales figures are lacking, but reliable estimates place the annual consumption of all types of .22 rimfire ammunition in excess of 5 billion rounds!

The .22 cartridge as we know it today (in all of its configurations), had its beginnings in the days of muzzle loading firearms, an early outgrowth of the percussion cap. Except for a relatively small, but growing group of black powder shooters, muzzle loaders have long since been relegated to collector's shelves and museums. Yet the tiny .22 remains forever the envy of those who have a yen for immortality—it remains forever young! More than a century of unrelenting refinement has made the .22 the most accurate (and most reasonable in cost) of all ammunition.

The closer you examine a .22 Long Rifle cartridge, the better it looks. This miniscule energy cell is a miracle of efficiency and effectiveness. It weighs but 52.5 grains overall—less than the projectile alone from most centerfire rounds—and measures no more than 1 inch in length. Yet weighed and measured in terms of utility and pleasure derived, it looms 10 feet tall!

The .22 rimfire is indeed a family of cartridges with many members. In addition to the Long Rifle, there is the Long, the Short, the CB Cap and the BB Cap, plus a relative newcomer, the .22 Winchester Magnum Rim Fire. Each represents a different power range, and each has its most appropriate uses.

You can do anything with a .22 rimfire that you can do with a centerfire gun, providing you scale down the range and target accordingly. You can hunt anything from brush rabbits to bobcats, with a .22 Long Rifle hollow point, and even stretch that a bit with the .22 Magnum and the new high-performance Long Rifle loadings that I will describe in detail later on. As the book unfolds, you will learn how to enjoy your .22 rimfire rifle or handgun to the maximum. You'll be introduced to the mighty smallbore as a tool for survival and even defense, as well as the instrument of what I call, ''Advanced Plinking,'' encompassing such challenging games as silhouettes offhand, and instinctive aerial target shooting, in which you allow your mind's own built-in radar to direct your bullets.

I shoot the .44 Magnum revolver (as well as the .357 and .41 Magnums) often, and I have hunted with the same .300 Weatherby Magnum rifle for over 15 years. While my writing over this same period has touched upon nearly every caliber available, the .22 rimfire still holds a special niche in my heart, carved before I was old enough to realize that it was not the best cartridge for hunting elephants. My long association with .22 rimfires via magazine articles and books has prompted many people to call me ''Mr. Twenty-Two.'' That's their appellation, of course; however, the more I shoot the tiny .22 the more I realize my readers (and editors) might be right! When it comes right down to it, the .22 is like an old friend—you never tire of its company.

CHAPTER 2

Choosing Rimfires for Recreation

TODAY'S PROLIFERATION of models and options in the automotive industry has made the choice of a new car something akin to a nightmare. The situation is only slightly less hectic in the field of firearms. From a market that was highly stable—often for decades at a stretch—the gun companies have lately taken to emulating the auto makers, with new models coming and going with dizzying rapidity.

Some defunct models can be written off as simply unsuccessful experiments. However, others were well designed and executed and deserved the opportunity to prove themselves in the field. Whether their untimely demise resulted from disappointing customer response or what-have-you, we will likely never know. It seems probable that many fine guns died with the stroke of a pen in the hands of an anonymous auditor in the accounting department, who considered them "uneconomical" to produce.

To list just a few casualties of the accounting department: Colt abandoned their fine little Colteer, Courier, and Stagecoach Carbine autoloading rimfire rifles several years back. They then followed with a handgun housecleaning that virtually wiped out their entire .22 inventory, save for the Diamondback, a scaled-down Python sub-caliber police training revolver parading as a sporting gun. Who would have dreamed a couple of years back that an institution such as the incomparable Colt Woodsman could get the axe? Or that the cunning Colt .22 caliber New Frontier single action six-shooters would suffer the same fate without so much as a, "By your leave?"

Retrenchment seems to be the order of the day. Mossberg has cut back from 12 rimfire models a few years ago to just seven. One of those, however, is their striking new Plinkster, a novel approach that should prove popular. About 1972, Winchester introduced their bolt action .22 Model 310 single shot and Model 320 clip-loaded rifles, with well designed stocks and

actions. Both were beautifully made and accurate. A few years later, these models were unceremoniously yanked from the market. The year of 1974 witnessed Winchester's introduction of the well-proportioned autoloading Model 490. By 1978 it had already vanished from their catalog. That's a life span of only 3 years, hardly a fair test! As of this writing, a good inventory remains in the Winchester warehouse, and shipping will continue until present stocks are exhausted. If you want a really fine firearm likely destined to become a much sought after collector's item in the not-too-distant future, better act now!

As a matter of fact, if there is *any* rimfire rifle or handgun that you are seriously planning to buy, *get it now!* Like a beautiful girl with many suitors, it can't be kept waiting too long! If you delay, the particular make and model that you want may not be waiting on the dealer's shelf when you decide to call.

Points to Ponder
Before You Purchase

Recognizing that rimfire rifles come in a dozen or more makes, a half-dozen action styles, an infinite variety of stock configurations, barrel lengths, types of sights, magazine styles, finishes, etc., and with pistol options only slightly less bewildering, what criteria do we use to sort out an intelligent choice? Certainly the basic consideration is the purpose to which the rifle or pistol will be put. If your new rimfire rifle is to become a constant trail companion or a huntsman's tool, it must be relatively light and handy, highly reliable, and capable of accuracy sufficient to nail down your intended target out to the practical limits of a rimfire's humane killing range. On the other hand, if you plan to bag bull's-eyes, your choice is necessarily restricted to specialized target rifles, which are about as handy and free-swinging as Olympic barbells! If you're purchasing a first rifle for your offspring, you must match it to his or her stature and strength. Adult size and musculature vary too. A long-armed, goose-necked bloke like myself needs a longer-than-normal stock, while a stocky, bull-necked wrestler might be tempted to saw off part of a standard stock. So step one in your choice should include putting a prospective purchase to your shoulder to see how well it fits!

A person's predilections play no small part in his choice of a rimfire rifle or handgun. I have a fondness for lever action rifles and single action revolvers. I always thought that the Good Lord had misplaced me by about a century—thus I missed the days of the western frontier. With carbine in my saddle boot and a thumb-buster in my holster, I can sometimes escape the jet age for a time and play at being cowboy!

Top-ranking factors in the choice of a rimfire rifle are basic quality of design and workmanship. Regardless of action style, it should be smooth-working without any hitches in its movement. If a clean action grates as if it were full of sand, or it feels like you're dragging a stick across a picket fence, something is drastically out of kilter! Bolts, levers, etc. shouldn't rattle in the frame. A snug fit is generally a mark of quality. Good design entails an ample safety margin also. One test that you can usually perform at the dealer's (but ask first) is to cock the gun, place it on safety, and strike the heel (not the toe) of the stock smartly against the wooden floor. You may be startled to hear the firing pin fall! A safety that

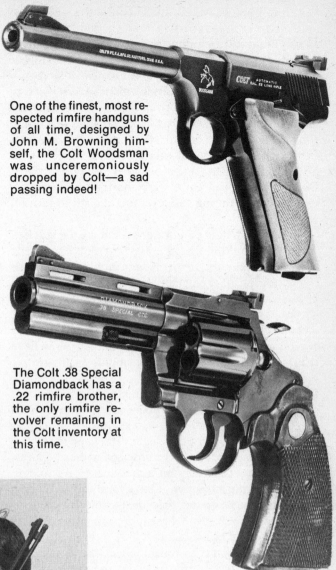

One of the finest, most respected rimfire handguns of all time, designed by John M. Browning himself, the Colt Woodsman was unceremoniously dropped by Colt—a sad passing indeed!

The Colt .38 Special Diamondback has a .22 rimfire brother, the only rimfire revolver remaining in the Colt inventory at this time.

Personal predilections play a large part in determining which rifle will best suit your needs. Here we find fans of the bolt action Remington 541-S (left) and the Browning BAR autoloader (right), engaging in some good natured arguments for their choices. Good trigger pull and superior accuracy are the usual claims of the bolt afficionado, however that is less valid today with guns like the BAR which excel in both aspects.

13

locks the firing pin rather than just the trigger is to be preferred whenever possible. Some action styles, such as an autoloader, preclude this design feature. Safety demands a solid lockup with an enclosed head. Double extractors and a strong bolt stop are also desirable.

A smoothly polished exterior with deep, brilliant bluing, plus an interior free from coarse tool marks are indications of good workmanship. Flat areas of any gun *should be flat,* not buffed off round at the edges or exhibiting a washboard effect. Holes shouldn't be buffed out into dishes on an otherwise flat surface. Burred screw heads, plus scratches and dings apparently acquired during assembly are enough to turn off any deal.

Ask your friendly gun dealer to remove the stock of any bolt action rifle that interests you, so that you can examine its innards. In this hidden area, you'll see the true character of the maker. If the trigger mechanism and magazine look like refugees from a tin can factory, reconsider your choice. All factory stocks today are machine inletted, but if the wood looks like it was carved with a hatchet, look for another gun. You have the right to expect inletting to be smooth, with positive contact points along the action and at the tip of the forend, unless the barrel is intended to be free-floating.

Today, the majority of rimfire stocks are made of what the advertisers call, "walnut-finished American hardwood," usually birch, a light yellow, plain-grained wood, which is nonetheless sturdy and with tight pores. Functionally, it is every bit as serviceable as walnut, lacking only the attractive grain of true walnut. Walnut will normally be found only on the more expensive rimfire rifles. Makers of these more expensive rimfires are justly proud of the fact that they went to the added trouble and expense to bring their customers nothing but the best, and loudly proclaim the same in their advertising. Impressed checkering is almost a foregone conclusion these days, although I often feel that the gun would look far better if simply left plain rather than embossed with a gaudy waffle/flower design! Hand-checkering, to be found only on the most expensive rimfire rifles, should be well executed. However, it's unrealistic to expect it to be totally free of error, as some gun writers would have us believe. The cost of hand-checkering a *custom* rifle today runs around $100 to $150, depending upon the pattern. With today's labor costs and generally poor level of individual workmanship, a production-line rifle can't be held to such high standards. Regardless, the stock should be sanded smooth, without coarse spots where end grain is visible and should be finished with a moisture-resistant material, hopefully with the pores well filled. Grip caps, forend tips, et al, are frosting on the cake—nice to have if the balance of the gun is acceptable.

Speaking of "balance," heft the gun and see if it has a "feel" that you like. Is it muzzle heavy, muzzle light, or somewhere in between? If you plan to hand-carry the gun on the trail, does the point of balance fall somewhere near the receiver, so that it hangs conveniently in a one-hand carry? I'm a firm believer in sling straps, but remember that our ancestors, from Daniel Boone to Kit Carson, hand-carried their rifles over countless miles!

The younger generation doesn't bridle over the absence of walnut and steel the way we old-timers are apt to. They accept alloy substitutes and plastic components on everything from automobiles to dishwashers as a fact of modern life. For my own part, I have to take away points from any gun that exhibits an abundance of plastic components with the exception of the Remington Nylon 66, which is molded entirely of Du Pont structural nylon. (Somewhat lacking in esthetic appeal, it is nonetheless a practical field rifle.) Modern makers have turned almost entirely to die cast metals for trigger guards. So long as they are smoothly finished, without blowholes or that "painted" look and the bluing matches the barrel and receiver, such cast parts shouldn't detract from the appearance or serviceability of the gun. Some such trigger guards are so well integrated that they can be detected only with a magnet. Plastic grips on a handgun are acceptable if they fit well.

During the years prior to World War II, "quality control" consisted of hiring and retaining competent craftsmen, who took personal pride in the products they turned out. Now it consists of trying to train desultory workers and motivate them with pension plans and paid vacations. The results are rather spotty. Inspectors at various stations along the route of fabrication can weed out only the really bad examples of incompetence. Thus workmanship is seen to vary widely, even among rifles from the same manufacturer.

After you have decided on a given make and model of rifle or handgun, it pays to shop for workmanship and materials. "Aren't materials the same from one gun to another in a given make and model?" you may ask. To a certain extent, yes. However, the wood used in one stock might be reasonably well figured, while a sister rifle in the same rack looks homely as a mud fence. Examine the finish on the metal in good light, with a wary eye for ripples and dished holes, as well as rounded edges that should be crisp and sharp. Fit between mating metal parts should be without discernible gaps. Wood-to-metal fit should be snug and tight. Trigger pull should be checked as it can vary in both weight of pull and degree of creep from gun to gun.

In general, you can expect to encounter the best trigger pull on bolt action rifles, the worst on autoloaders. The latter results from efforts by the makers toward attaining the greatest possible safety factor, avoiding accidental discharge or multiple shots from a single pull of the trigger. For the most part, modern handguns have overall excellent trigger pulls, *especially,* the autoloaders! Ideally, a trigger pull should require no more than 4 pounds, preferably between 2½ and 3½ pounds; and feel crisp with a minimum of takeup and backlash.

In loading a tubular magazine rifle, you have to have a long reach to get the inside tube out far enough to permit insertion of the ammo into the keyhole slot in the bottom of the external tube. Tubular magazines are vulnerable to bending if carelessly handled.

If you're teetering between two rifles of roughly equal merit, you might be influenced one way or the other by the style of magazines employed. Perhaps most widely used today on rimfire rifles is the tubular magazine, located either in the butt stock or running parallel under the barrel. The other favorite is the detachable box magazine. There are pluses and minuses to both types. The tubular magazine requires some slight gymnastics to load. The muzzle must be pointed up to load an under-barrel tubular magazine, in order for gravity to move the ammo toward the receiver as it is inserted in the small keyhole slot found midway along the outer tube. The inside tube, which holds the follower and spring, and ultimately the ammo itself, must usually be held up by one hand, otherwise it responds to the pull of gravity and follows the ammo down before you're through loading. A brightly colored follower is handy to let your eyes know when the loading slot is indeed clear to receive ammo. Otherwise, you may be trying to push rounds in against the unseen follower. Of course, it takes longer to insert 15 or so rounds into the tubular magazine than it does to load five or even 10 into a clip, but the time between loadings is longer with the former. So, you pays your money and you takes your choice!

Many malfunctions, especially with autoloaders, are attributable to poorly formed or bent lips on detachable box magazines. On the other hand, tubular magazines can be put out of action by blowing sand, grit, lint, and accumulations of bullet lubricant that can cause the follower to hang up, etc. They are also prone to denting or bending if carelessly handled. Then there is the danger of a cartridge hanging up inside of a tubular magazine. The shooter believes that his rifle is empty,

only to have the errant round pop back at some later date and be chambered unawares with possible tragic results. It does no good to say that a shooter should be more careful—watch the chamber when you work the action, be careful of the direction the muzzle is pointed, etc. The fact remains that there is a threat there that must be considered.

Let me be quick to add that I have *never* had any trouble with tubular magazines! I do take the precaution of cleaning them from time to time, pushing an oiled patch through both tubes every now and again. I use the slotted tip on my cleaning rod to avoid leaving a patch lodged in the tube. Of course, cleaning the inner tube requires that the follower be forced back by the cleaning rod. It's a good idea not to leave the tubular magazine loaded to capacity for long periods of time—this avoids weakening the follower spring. If the spring reaches the point where it is hard pressed to get that last round or two back to the feeding ramp, don't bother trying to stretch it out, just replace it immediately!

A point in favor of the clip-loader is that spare loaded magazines can be carried for quick reloads when in the field. Most makers offer optional 10-shot magazines, as well as the standard (usually five-shot) clips that fit flush with the bottom of the stock. The longer ones aren't much to look at, but they do stretch the time between loadings!

While modern rimfire ammunition minimizes the need for frequent cleaning of your rifle or handgun, it still pays to clean and oil the bore before setting a gun aside for any lengthy period of inactivity. Also, autoloading arms long and short should be subjected to a thorough action cleaning now and then, just to keep them from becoming sluggish from a buildup of gunk in the working parts. Therefore it pays to consider the ease of field stripping any given gun. Can the rifle/pistol be cleaned from the breech, or must it be cleaned from the muzzle—with the inevitable wear that results? Look through the bore with a strong backlight. Don't take for granted that a new bore is necessarily bright and shiny. I have seen new rifles that were apparently test-fired and left uncleaned. Their bores were festooned with red rust! If the bore looks a bit murky, ask the dealer to run a *dry* patch through it, then look again. If there *is rust* or even perhaps some pits, *pass!*

Barrel length, as with weight, is important primarily as it relates to projected use. Chronographs tell us that ordinary .22 Long Rifles, either standard or high velocity, gather about all of the momentum they are going to from rifle barrels 16 to 18 inches in length. Some tests even indicate that barrels longer than 20 inches tend to slow the muzzle velocity somewhat. For a fast-handling field rifle, choose a 20-inch or shorter tube. If you like a slightly muzzle-heavy feel, take the 24-incher. Certainly a longer barrel hangs steadier for offhand shooting, especially on those long-range targets. In my experience, barrel length is not a factor in accuracy. With open or receiver sights, the sighting radius could have an effect upon your group size, but given equal quality, a scope-sighted rifle with a 16-inch barrel should shoot as well as one with a 24-inch tube.

Sight radius is infinitely more important with a handgun. Thus the longer the barrel, the more precise the sight alignment should be. Although mechanical accuracy should be about equal, few shooters can group as well with a 2-inch barreled pistol as they can with one 6 inches or longer. You'll soon discover that a revolver with a 6- or even 7½-inch barrel is just about as fast from an open holster and tracks game about as quickly as a stubby revolver and with a lot more assurance!

The one factor that you have no way to assess even in small measure at the dealer's is the inherent accuracy of a given gun. Many years of accuracy testing a wide range of rimfires of every make has taught me that even guns of a single make and model can vary to no small degree from one to another and for no apparent reason. The only exception to which I can attest without equivocation is the Weatherby Mark XXII. I have fired a large number of these guns from early production and late. They were uniformly very accurate! However, I can't guarantee that any other given brand of gun that I test and report on will necessarily do as well from one example to another. I have received some excoriating letters from time to time from irate shooters who claim that ''Brand X'' won't shoot for them, and they bought it just because I said the gun was accurate. I usually advise them to return the gun to the gunshop where they bought it for checking, or to return it to the factory for service. Often it turns out that the fault lies not with the gun but with the shooter. We'll have more to say about getting the best accuracy out of your own gun later.

If you can talk the dealer into letting you test fire the gun, or perhaps borrow a like number from a friend, you can get an idea of what to expect. First, mount a good scope on the gun! You can't get a good reading with iron sights. Shoot from a bench rest, preferably in the early morning before the wind rises. Use sandbags fore and aft to steady the gun and remember breath control and trigger squeeze! To be fair, try at least half a dozen brands of ammo. Most guns have their ammo preferences. You can reasonably expect 1½- to 2-inch 10-shot groups at 50 yards from a good quality field rifle. A heavyweight target rifle should do about as well at 100 yards.

Holding a handgun with both hands across a sandbag should tell you about what it can deliver at 25 yards. The average field gun is normally capable of putting 10 shots inside a 2-inch circle at 25 yards. A target arm should just about halve that.

Burning up a couple of boxes of ammo should point up any action malfunctions such as failures to feed, particularly in autoloaders. Often the solution is as simple as changing brands of ammo, or perhaps inserting a new magazine.

If a particular gun appeals to you greatly, but it has some less than desirable attributes, such as a lousy trigger pull, or perhaps a stock that received a lick-and-a-promise finishing job, don't reject the gun out-of-hand. In a later chapter, we'll help you learn the tricks of trigger improvement, plus stock refinishing routines. Personally, I would sooner take an attractively grained stock with a poor finish than a dull looking piece with a flawless finish!

Sad as it seems, *cost,* intrudes as a factor of importance into a decision that sould be based upon merit alone. With the exception of a few true-blue bargains, which we will point out as we go along, the old saw, ''You get what you pay for,'' applies to guns as well as to most other attributes of the good life. The so-called, ''Dealer's recommended retail price,'' is in a shambles since the courts shot down the Fair Trade Act. Some companies even refuse to set such standards.

Available Action Types

Getting back to basics, let's consider each action style in turn, its advantages and poor points. Historically, the single shot rifle in its various forms, tip-up, falling block, rolling block, and turning bolt, was first to chamber the .22 rimfire. Such names as Ballard, Hamilton, Hopkins & Allen, Remington, Stevens and Winchester emblazoned the barrels of countless single shot rifles around the turn of the century. Those guns were proudly carried by a fortunate generation of young Americans who knew where they were going and never doubted for a moment that they were born into the finest nation ever to grace the earth! Our current crop of would-be marksmen and nimrods can taste a little of that glorious past by shooting the revived Stevens

Crackshot falling block single shot. One-shot-at-a-time rifles are excellent "teacher" guns both from the aspect of utmost safety, and also in terms of engendering full appreciation for the importance of each and every shot!

Bolt Action

The familiar turning-bolt action dates all the way back to the introduction of the Nicholas Dreyse *Zündnädelgewehr,* or needle gun, which actually predated the enclosed metallic cartridge! The turning-bolt was first applied to the .22 rimfire by gun genius John Moses Browning when he patented his single shot in 1899. It was licensed to Winchester for production but many other companies soon copied the basic design, which included a manual cocking knob at the rear of the bolt. Nearly all modern bolt action rimfires cock on

opening by camming the sear rearward as the bolt handle is raised. Some rimfire rifles possess concealed hammers, which are cocked as the bolt is pulled rearward to extract the empty case.

Bolt actions with internal strikers have distinct advantages. Powerful coil springs can impart such great force to the firing pin that striker travel can be reduced to a bare fraction of an inch. This leads to virtually instantaneous lock time, hence greater accuracy. (There is less time after trigger release for the gun to waver off-target.) All quality bolt action target rifles and many of the better field rifles feature high-speed locks. Trigger mechanisms can also be highly sophisticated on bolt action rifles. For example Remington's 580 series and the various Savage/Anschutz bolt guns possess triggers that break like the proverbial "glass

The pump action Browning BPR has a locked breech, a feature not shared by the BAR. Thus the BPR only is offered in .22 Magnum chambering. The look and most parts are shared by both rifles. The sharp-humped receiver is a family characteristic which looks better in hand than in a photo!

Once a shooter learns to lower the lever without dropping the rifle from his shoulder, he finds that it delivers repeat shots in rapid succession.

rod!" Bolt actions are justly famed for superior accuracy. Their tubular receivers can be made thick and stiff; headspace is easier to control in production and not subject to changing with wear; and the entire assembly is easy to bed in a one-piece stock, for proper barrel support. Although repeat shots come slower from a bolt action rifle than from a pump, lever, or autoloader, it remains highly popular because of its utter dependability and generally high value received per dollar expended.

Pump Action

In terms of rapid-fire capability, the pump action takes second place only to the autoloader. The Colt Lightning Magazine rifle introduced America to the pleasures of .22 rimfire pump action guns in 1887. The Lightning's under-barrel tubular magazine loaded easily and quickly with either Shorts or Longs, through a swinging block, accessible on the right side of the receiver. This is more complicated to produce, but is a simpler-to-use system than that in vogue today! Today's trombone rimfire rifles have their greatest appeal to users of slide action shotguns and bigbore rifles. Port-side shooters like myself often choose pumps over bolt actions because they don't have to reach over the top of the receiver to work the action.

Lever Action

If your electronic baby sitters were Hopalong Cassidy, Rex Allen, and Roy Rogers, rather than Captain

Kirk and Mr. Spock, of *Star Trek* fame, you likely lean toward the lever action rather than the "now-generation" autoloader. If you date back *before* TV as I do, the chances are even more in favor of the lever. Anyone who still pines for the days of the Old West just can't resist the attraction of a rimfire rifle that reflects the romance of the frontier like a sun-drenched desert reflects the broad blue sky! However, true frontiersmen knew that it was no mirage when they first laid eyes upon the bright brass receiver of the Henry rifle in 1860. This first successful repeating cartridge rifle began the love affair with levers that lingers still! The lever action is as American as turkey dinners, apple pie, and "The Stars and Stripes Forever." It was favored by such stalwarts as Teddy Roosevelt, and Buffalo Bill, not to mention the Texas Rangers! Such able marksmen as Colonel Larson and Annie Oakley used it.

Current examples of this enduring design are uniformly excellent. The original rimfire version, the Marlin Model 1891, is still going strong as the Model 39, and it has been joined in recent years by new offerings from Ithaca, Browning, and Winchester. Aside from nostalgic appeal, the lever action has practical pluses in its favor. No other rifle rides with such aplomb on the side of a horse, making it by far the best saddle carbine for a rancher. The visible hammer is reassuring to careful hunters, providing positive evidence of a cocked condition or a gun on safe. Once a shooter learns the technique of lowering the lever without lowering the gun from the shoulder, he will find it delivers repeat shots in rapid succession, without taking the sights off the target.

Autoloaders

Autoloader advantages are obvious on the surface of it. Not only does the gun remain at the shoulder when firing a rapid-fire string, the hands remain in place on pistol grip and forend, the eye and mind remain on the target. If the target happens to be a bouncing bunnie, lead can be compensated quickly according to impacts marked by flying sand or snow. On the target range, the autoloader flicks out the empty and plugs the chamber with a new round without requiring the shooter to shift his position one iota. No shuffling around to get the sandbags rearranged and the cross hairs again quartering the bull's-eye. The inevitable result is tighter groups with less effort and time expended. Thus far, no target rifles have been designed with auto actions, but some autos, notably the Weatherby Mark XXII deliver near-target accuracy.

Major Gun Manufacturers

Browning

In general, the heavier the barrel, the more accuracy you are likely to realize from it. However, heavy barrels make for heavy guns, less than desirable in the field, and poor sellers across the counter. One maker's method of attacking that problem revealed some canny conniving! When Browning designed their new autoloading BAR-22, they recognized the need for both accuracy and relatively light weight. Their answer was to shave 4 inches from the muzzle of the accepted standard 24-inch barrel and pack that weight into the rear half of the barrel, then taper steeply down to the muzzle. The result was accuracy little short of phenomenal! They coupled that with the best trigger pull that I have yet found on an autoloader for an overall winner. The slab-sided receiver is sharp-shouldered top/rear, resembling the centerfire bigbore Browning BAR and the Browning B-2000 autoloading shotgun. The resemblance results in a unique family appearance that carries over to the lookalike brother Browning BPR-22, a pump-actuated rimfire rifle.

Both Brownings share most of their parts. Exceptions include the pump which has a forearm that is cutaway to clear the ejection port when the slide is pulled rearward, the breechblock which lacks an operating handle, and the trigger guard which has a slide release left/forward inside the trigger guard. Shared is the under-barrel tubular magazine holding 15 Long Rifle cartridges. The BPR by virtue of its locked breech, is also available in .22 Magnum with a magazine capacity of 11 rounds. Stock and forearm on both are of handsome selected French walnut, finished to tabletop smoothness, tightly mating to metal that is also highly polished and blued to a deep luster. A ramp-mounted gold bead and folding leaf rear sight (adjustable for elevation) round out these rifles. Generous well-executed hand-checkering sets off the overall ex-

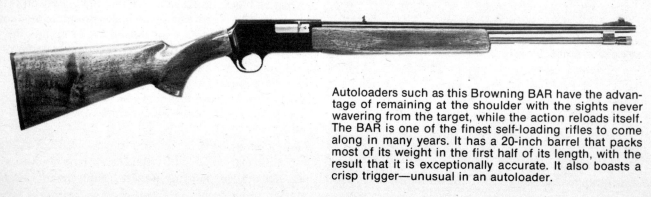

Autoloaders such as this Browning BAR have the advantage of remaining at the shoulder with the sights never wavering from the target, while the action reloads itself. The BAR is one of the finest self-loading rifles to come along in many years. It has a 20-inch barrel that packs most of its weight in the first half of its length, with the result that it is exceptionally accurate. It also boasts a crisp trigger—unusual in an autoloader.

tremely high quality appearance of the Browning BAR/BPR twin rimfires. A .22 Magnum version of the BPR-22 is also available. Both of these fine rifles effectively perpetuate the tradition of John Moses Browning, founder of the firm.

The year 1978 marked the centennial celebration of Browning's first invention, a single shot falling block devised when he was but 23 years of age. John grew up in the gunshop of his father, Jonathan, in the town of Ogden, Utah, where his inventive genius received full rein. In 1880, he and his brothers began manufacturing the single shot falling block in what they laughingly labeled, "The largest arms factory between Omaha and

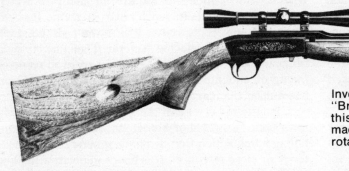

Invented by Browning in 1913, this slender, fast-handling "Browning Automatic .22" autoloader remains popular to this day. It has the quickest takedown of any rimfire made—press a button on the bottom of the receiver and rotate the barrel a quarter turn.

the Pacific." Browning's present corporate headquarters, sharing a 646-acre tract of canyon land with resident mule deer, cradled in the same Wasatch Mountains that saw John Browning's beginnings, still hews to that same motto. John's own son, Val A. Browning, steered the destiny of the firm for 47 years and remains as honorary chairman of the board. A grandson, Bruce, developed the BAR and major components of other modern Browning designs.

In the beginning, John licensed most of his designs out to established arms makers rather than attempt production on his own. His original single shot became famous as the Winchester High Wall. His first rimfire design, a pump action with under-barrel tubular magazine, was marketed as the Winchester Model 1890, and was followed by the single shot bolt action Winchester Model 1900. In 1913, John developed his slender, lightweight, bottom-ejecting autoloading rifle, which he took to Fabrique Nationale in Belgium. Browning did this as a result of his earlier "split" with Winchester, and because it was said that European rimfire ammunition burned cleaner than its American counterpart, thus didn't foul the mechanism. When Remington developed their non-fouling .22 Kleanbore ammunition, they took up production of the Browning auto and sold it as their Model 24. They revised it in 1935 with a thicker, longer barrel and renamed it the Model 241. It continued in production until 1951.

This heritage of the world's greatest gun genius survives to this day, with a modernized, beefed-up stock and forend—it is sold by Browning by the prosaic name, "Browning Automatic .22." It features the fine finish

for which Browning is well known, plus hand-checkering front and rear. A quick quarter-turn of the 19¼-inch barrel separates it from the interrupted threads of the steel receiver, allowing easy disassembly of action parts for cleaning. A concealed tubular magazine in the butt stock loads 11 Long Rifles through a funnel-shaped port on the right side. (The original Browning design called for loading through a small hole in the top of the pistol grip, but that proved to be too tedious.) Typical Browning open sights grace the barrel, and a barrel-mounted scope mount is available. The Browning Automatic .22 is available in three grades, Grade I, Grade II with tasteful but simple engraving, and the Grade III with highly ornate engraving. The Short-chambered version that was once the darling of shooting gallery operators the world around is still available.

Although John Browning never developed a .22 rimfire lever action rifle, he did originate the Winchester 1886, 1892 and 1894 centerfire lever guns, greatly strengthening and improving the overall design. While not a direct product of John M.'s genius, the present-day Browning BL-22 certainly is true to his spirit, innovative and up-to-date in design, yet religiously reflecting the spirit of the frontier. The most startling attribute of the BL-22 is its abbreviated lever throw of only 33 degrees, barely a flick of the fingers, without even having to move the hand from the pistol grip. And no chance of ever pinching the trigger finger with this lever gun; the trigger travels *with* the lever, down and up. Empties spit out at the right through a small rectangular port, leaving the top of the receiver solid to accept a low-mounted scope on its dovetail grooves. The tubular magazine running full length under the 20-inch barrel opens with the press of a button. It snaps closed without regard to rotation of the knurled tip, feeding 15 Long Rifles, 17 Longs, or 22 Shorts, separately or intermingled. The BL-22's visible hammer has the traditional half-cock safety notch, but it may seem somewhat redundant in view of the fact that the firing pin is shorter than the breechblock. Thus the hammer could be left resting upon the inertia firing pin in complete safety. As with all Browning firearms, stock and forend are of the finest obtainable walnut, finished to perfection, a fitting accompaniment to the deep bluing on the all-steel rifle.

If you're interested in a lever action trail companion or merely a plinking rifle with the accuracy required to bag small game when the occasion arises, take a searching look at this one! The BL-22 is available in a plain Grade I and a Grade II with tasteful scroll engraving on the receiver, plus hand-checkered grip and forend.

Hard on the heels of his development of the Browning Automatic .22, John Browning invented the first successful autoloading rimfire handgun, the famed Colt Woodsman, based upon the same principle of delayed blowback. It sounds simple enough now. All he had to do was balance the weight of the breechblock and its return spring against the energy in the tiny .22 case that was trying mightily to escape from the chamber, in such a way that the bullet would already be on its way before the case won its struggle with inertia and spring tension. Then have another cartridge waiting conveniently in a magazine ready for the breechblock to pick it up on the return cycle and ram it into the waiting chamber. Yes, it sounds simple—after someone else thought of the idea and ironed out all of the bugs!

As noted earlier, the Colt Woodsman is no longer with us. Perhaps the spirit of this wonderful gun has joined its maker in that special corner of Valhalla reserved for the world's greatest all-time mechanical geniuses! Meanwhile, back at the ranch in Morgan, Utah, in 1976, one of Browning's present-day gun developers evolved a variation upon the theme, the Browning Challenger II, autoloading pistol, externally resembling the original, but inwardly new. Offered with a 6¾-inch barrel only, it boasts adjustable Patridge sights, with the rear one riding high and dry, completely independent of the recoiling slide, thus more steady than the original. A conventional 10-shot clip fills the grip, which is covered by thin slabs of resin-impregnated walnut, smooth and eye-catching. A gold trigger helps set off the rich blue of the all-steel autoloader. As with everything originating at the Browning plant, this one's a winner! For field or range it represents a sound investment.

Charter Arms

Small, independent arms firms generally have a high rate of terminal cash flow problems unless they have something really worthy to offer, and exhibit some canny management as well! Charter Arms Corporation of Stratford, Connecticut, first saw the light of day in 1964. Gun designer and the firm's founder, Doug McClenahan, supplied the product. Partner, Dave Ecker, collaborated in the management. The original Charter Arms offering was its Undercover snub-nosed revolver, billed as, "The lightest all-steel .38 Special made." When an optional 3-inch barrel proved more popular than the original 2-incher, the slightly longer tube became the standard. The .38 Special cylinder could hold no more than five rounds in its circumscribed circumference, but a later .22 rimfire version was able to squeeze a full six holes into the same diameter. Thus was born a marvelous palm-sized-plus kit gun, weighing only 18½ ounces, in standard or Magnum.

Latest from Charter is their AR-7 Explorer takedown-and-stow-in-the-stock .22 rimfire survival rifle, which weighs only 2½ pounds and measures but 16½ inches when stowed. We'll have more to say about both of these Charter products later.

Ithaca

Adding an exclamation point to the perennial popularity of lever action rimfire rifles is the latest from Ithaca, their Model 72 Saddlegun, with 18½-inch barrel, over the traditional tubular magazine that accepts 15 Long Rifles (only). Plain, well-finished stock and forend are of selected American walnut. Hooded ramp and leaf sights are backed by a grooved receiver for tip-off mounted scopes. The .22 Magnum version has a magazine capacity of 11 rounds.

A long-time favorite of the youngsters is the Ithaca lever action single shot Model 49, with Martini-styled falling block action that demands neither manual dexterity or close attention. It is about the fastest loading single shot around these days. The 18-inch barrel is underscored with a dummy magazine, for that grown-up Western look, accentuated by the barrel band and straight stock. The hammer must be manually cocked for each shot, adding further to the safety factor for young shooters. It is light enough for sub-teeners at 5½ pounds and is available in a short-stocked "youth model."

Rossi

On June 26, 1888, John M. Browning was issued Patent #385,238, on a handy top-ejecting .22 rimfire pump rifle that later became known as, "the most popular .22 caliber pump action rifle ever made." Winchester made untold thousands of these utterly reliable takedown rifles, marked as were all of Browning's rimfire designs by perfect balance and light weight, before it died an uneasy death. Thanks to Amadeo Rossi & Co., Sao Leopoldo, Brazil, a leading arms maker in South America, the Winchester Model 62 has been revived, and is currently being imported by Interarms of Alexandria, Virginia, in two models, a 23-inch barreled rifle and a 16½-inch barreled carbine. The under-barrel tubular magazines hold 13 Long Rifles, 16 Longs, or 20 Shorts separately, or intermingled in the Model 62SA rifle. Capacity for the carbine Model 62SAC is 12, 14, and 18 rounds, respectively. Weights are 5½ and 4¾ pounds. Note that these guns will not permit mounting a scope over the action, because the breechblock rises out of a locking mortise at the front and slides back along the top of the receiver. However, either gun makes a premium plinker with its bead front and open leaf rear sight.

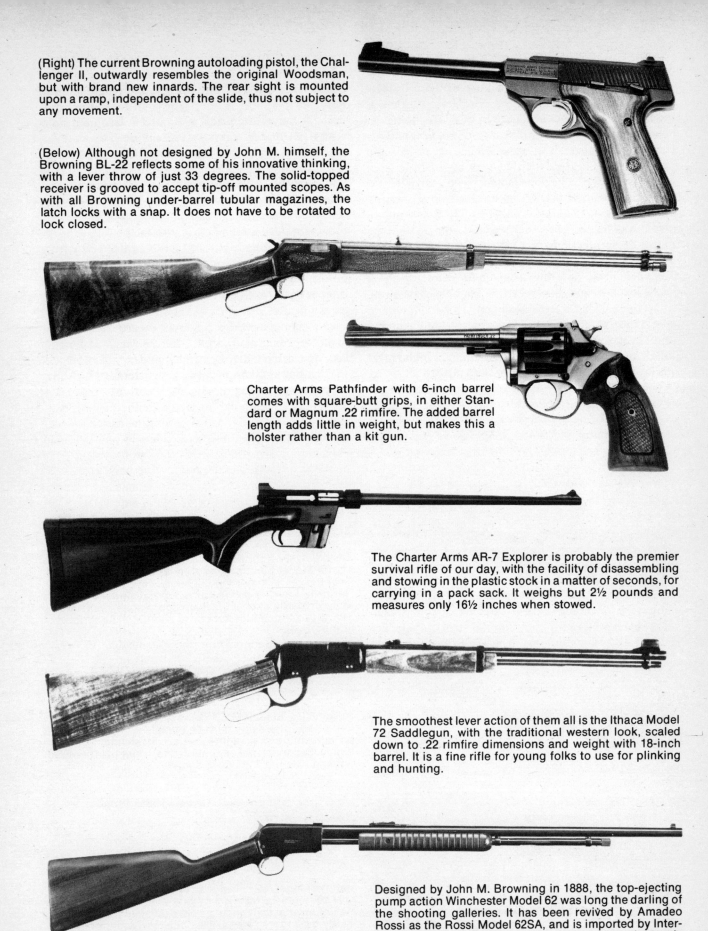

(Right) The current Browning autoloading pistol, the Challenger II, outwardly resembles the original Woodsman, but with brand new innards. The rear sight is mounted upon a ramp, independent of the slide, thus not subject to any movement.

(Below) Although not designed by John M. himself, the Browning BL-22 reflects some of his innovative thinking, with a lever throw of just 33 degrees. The solid-topped receiver is grooved to accept tip-off mounted scopes. As with all Browning under-barrel tubular magazines, the latch locks with a snap. It does not have to be rotated to lock closed.

Charter Arms Pathfinder with 6-inch barrel comes with square-butt grips, in either Standard or Magnum .22 rimfire. The added barrel length adds little in weight, but makes this a holster rather than a kit gun.

The Charter Arms AR-7 Explorer is probably the premier survival rifle of our day, with the facility of disassembling and stowing in the plastic stock in a matter of seconds, for carrying in a pack sack. It weighs but 2½ pounds and measures only 16½ inches when stowed.

The smoothest lever action of them all is the Ithaca Model 72 Saddlegun, with the traditional western look, scaled down to .22 rimfire dimensions and weight with 18-inch barrel. It is a fine rifle for young folks to use for plinking and hunting.

Designed by John M. Browning in 1888, the top-ejecting pump action Winchester Model 62 was long the darling of the shooting galleries. It has been revived by Amadeo Rossi as the Rossi Model 62SA, and is imported by Interarms in all of its former glory. It's a fine open-sight-only plinker and hunting arm.

Marlin

John Mahlon Marlin began making revolvers in 1870, after the Rollin White patent ran out. His first rifle was the Ballard single shot produced in 1875. His first lever action rifle, introduced in 1881, was one of large caliber with an open-top receiver in the Winchester style. Eight years later, he devised the side-ejecting solid-top lever action for which he became famous. The year 1891 saw the introduction of the Marlin lever action .22 rimfire that led directly to today's Model 39. The first standard takedown version was the Model 1897, which continued in production until World War I. Following "The War to Save Democracy," the Marlin Model 39 was introduced, differing mainly in its pistol grip stock and 24-inch octagon-only barrel. The leaf mainspring and trigger spring were abandoned in 1939 in favor of more modern coil springs, and the butt stock acquired a shotgun-styled plate, plus beavertail forend. Finally, in 1954, the 39M Mountie was added with 20-inch barrel and straight stock that harked back to the Model 1897.

The Marlin Model 39 is the oldest in point of lineage of any .22 rimfire rifle made, and it has survived because it has timeless virtues—a never-bobble lever action, the solid-topped frame which allows easy scope mounting, simple takedown and rigidly maintained quality standards.

Marlin doesn't confine itself to the manufacture of only lever action rimfire rifles. In fact, they have perhaps the widest array of rimfires available from an American maker today, beginning with a quartet of autoloaders, topped by the Model 49 DeLuxe. This gun is a 5½-pound, 22-inch barreled beauty, with two-piece American black walnut stock checkered fore and aft, split by a flat-sided steel receiver that's set off by scrollwork, a damascened bolt, and a gold trigger. The tubular under-barrel magazine holds 18 Long Rifles. A ramp-post front sight is backed by an elevator-adjustable leaf rear, and the receiver is grooved for tip-off scope mounting. In the guard behind the trigger is an easy-to-reach crossbolt safety. The Model 99C is mechanically identical, but the stock continues in a single uninterrupted piece from forend tip to white-lined black butt plate. In the military image resembling the M1 Carbine, are the Model 99M1 and 989M2 with 18-inch barrels, hand-guard stocks, sling swivels, and fully adjustable and removable rear sights. The 99M1 has a nine-shot tubular magazine, and the 989M2 has a seven-shot clip. All four rifles, for that matter, *all* Marlin *and* Marlin/Glenfield autoloaders have a bolt hold-

The oldest .22 rimfire rifle in continuous production is the Marlin Model 39, direct descendant of the Marlin 1891. Over the years, minor modifications have been made, but basically the rifle is the same as that devised by John Mahlon Marlin almost 90 years ago. Shown is the Model 39A with 24-inch tapered barrel and full pistol grip.

Resembling the .30 M1 Carbine, the Marlin Model 99M1 has a hand guard and barrel band, plus sling swivels and an adjustable rear sight, making for a fine, compact, highly functional trail or hunting rifle. It is shown here with optional Glenfield 200C 4X scope.

Marlin's Model 782 delivers .22 WMR punch with the accuracy required to take on rabbits and chucks out to its maximum effective range of approximately 150 yards. The handy detachable magazine holds seven big ones! The stock is well formed for adult shooters, with a comb high enough to accommodate a scope on the grooved receiver.

open device for added safety.

Marlin offers two bolt action .22 Magnum rifles, with 22-inch Micro-Groove barrels topped by open sights, backed by grooved steel receivers and mounted in American black walnut stocks. The Model 782 uses a convenient seven-shot clip, while the Model 783 loads into a 12-shot under-barrel tubular magazine.

Marlin's bolt action Models 780 and 781 are spitting images of the .22 Magnum models, but in .22 Short, Long and Long Rifle. Both feature Marlin's Wide-Scan removable front sight hoods, on ramped brass beads, backed by traditional-appearing, semi-buckhorn rear sights with the usual step-adjustment for elevation, but cleverly contrived to fold flat to facilitate scope mounting.

Marlin's Glenfield line of rimfire rifles represent real bargains in terms of value received per dollar expended! They retain all of the mechanical assets of the standard Marlin line, but with some sacrifice in finish, coupled with a substantial dollar savings. The Glenfield rifles also use birchwood stocks, totally functional and certainly not unpleasing to the eye, albeit less expensive. The Glenfield Model 60 is the counterpart of the Marlin Model 99C. The Glenfield 20 is an economy mate to the Marlin 780. The Glenfield 10 stands alone as a budget-priced single shot bolt action trainer for any youth lucky enough to have a doting dad in the wings. The gun cocks manually, via a "T" knob at the rear of the bolt.

Mossberg

At just 20 years of age, Oscar F. Mossberg emigrated from his native Sweden to the United States to make his fortune. Not long after, he landed a job with Iver Johnson Arms, and because of his apparent mechanical aptitude, he was set to gun designing. It was Mossberg who designed the hammer block action that enabled Iver Johnson to adopt the motto, "Hammer the Hammer," with its memorable illustration of the hand with a hammer banging away at the rear of an Iver Johnson revolver. Oscar was to work for several arms and machine manufacturers and dabble at gun making himself for a time, before he began manufacturing in earnest in 1919, in partnership with his two grown sons, Harold and Iver. Their first gun was a .22 rimfire four-shot pistol. The first Mossberg .22 rifle, a hammerless pump was produced in 1922. During World War II, they produced the Model 44 .22 training rifle used for preliminary marksmanship training by both the Army and the Navy.

The firm of O.F. Mossberg has always been noted for

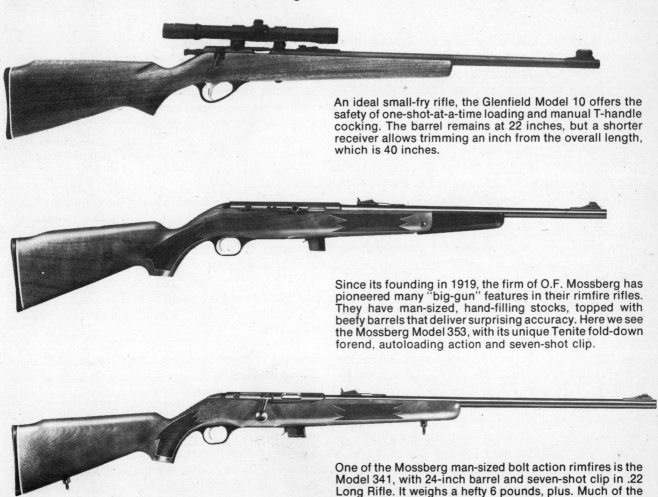

An ideal small-fry rifle, the Glenfield Model 10 offers the safety of one-shot-at-a-time loading and manual T-handle cocking. The barrel remains at 22 inches, but a shorter receiver allows trimming an inch from the overall length, which is 40 inches.

Since its founding in 1919, the firm of O.F. Mossberg has pioneered many "big-gun" features in their rimfire rifles. They have man-sized, hand-filling stocks, topped with beefy barrels that deliver surprising accuracy. Here we see the Mossberg Model 353, with its unique Tenite fold-down forend, autoloading action and seven-shot clip.

One of the Mossberg man-sized bolt action rimfires is the Model 341, with 24-inch barrel and seven-shot clip in .22 Long Rifle. It weighs a hefty 6 pounds, plus. Much of the weight is in its fully-proportioned stock.

The Mossberg Model 144 is the only one that retains a once-upon-a-time trademark of Mossberg rifles—the plastic finger grooves at the front of the pistol grip. Featuring ultimate accuracy at a price, it makes an excellent starter rifle for the neophyte target shooter.

The Mossberg Model 340B lacks some of the target refinement of the 144, but offers high accuracy in a somewhat lighter, smaller package. It features a seven-shot .22 Long Rifle clip and target-styled front and receiver sights.

Most recent and most novel offering from Mossberg is their Model 377 Plinkster, with thumb-hole stock of polystyrene foam with the look and feel of walnut. The autoloader with such a high comb needs stilts to hold the scope. The elevating device comes with each gun. Note that this is a right-hand-only rifle!

rather beefy .22 rifles, but the bulk was always more muscle than fat. Their man-sized stocks and hand-filling forends are apparent in today's offerings, along with the extraordinary accuracy of their AC-KRO-GRUV rifling. The lightest weight Mossberg is the Model 353, 5-pound autoloading carbine, with unique two-position stock extension of black tenite, which folds down to provide a positive grip, especially handy in prone position. The clip that extends slightly below the Monte Carlo stock holds seven Long Rifles and the abbreviated 18-inch barrel totes traditional open sights, backed by a grooved receiver. A carbine-styled sling and swivels are included.

Mossberg's look-alike Models 341 (seven-shot clip) and 321 (single shot) are bolt actions with 24-inch barrels, scaling 6 pounds-plus. Both boast Monte Carlo combs and impressed checkering, plus sling swivels. *Every Mossberg .22 rimfire rifle has sling swivels!* That's a feature I would highly commend to the other makers who often charge twice as much money for their products! The Mossberg 640K echoes the above features, only in .22 Magnum caliber, as does the 340B, but with a click-adjustable receiver sight and a globe front sight.

As a youngster, I had a brief acquaintance with a Mossberg target rifle. It shot like gangbusters! Modern-day kids can have the same thrill of hitting what they aim at using a Mossberg Model 144 .22 Long Rifle target rifle with seven-shot clip, high-comb target stock, Mossberg receiver sight with ¼-minute micro-

meter click adjustments, and adjustable forend stop with 1¼-inch sling swivels. The bolt action is Mossberg's smoothest and finest, with a heavyweight barrel, snugged at the forend by an adjustable barrel band. A globe sight with inserts tops the crowned muzzle. The Model 144 retains a feature that was once a trademark of Mossberg rimfire rifles—the finger groove plastic insert along the front of the pistol grip. The accuracy of this rifle will make your hair stand on end! If you can handle 8 pounds in the field, it makes a crackerjack varmint rifle. With a scope mounted upon the grooved receiver, you should be able to pick off chucks a football field away with firm assurance. If the weight seems a bit awesome for a field companion, you might try having that 27-inch barrel trimmed back about 5 inches. The bullets will never know it's gone, but you'll have less trouble keeping the muzzle up. The same cure might help your youngster get an early start at genuine target competition.

There's one more Mossberg to mention, a novel creation called the "Plinkster." This semiautomatic with 20-inch barrel, looks pretty straight-forward from the pistol grip to the muzzle, but the back end is mind-boggling. Up to now, a thumbhole stock was something only the guy who could afford a custom rifle was apt to have, but here you can get the feel of the thing for small bucks. You don't really expect a selected walnut stock for that kind of money, but it sure looks like the real thing. Actually, the entire stock is molded from high-impact modified polystyrene.

Remington

You don't need any historical resume on Remington Arms. The company execs were down at Plymouth Rock, waiting to greet the Pilgrims! Despite the staid, old company image, Remington brass have always displayed a willingness to gamble on innovative ideas. And their batting average is well up around 800! For example, back in 1959, they had the courage to create an all-plastic .22 rimfire autoloading rifle—well *almost* all plastic! The barrel, action parts, and stamped action cover are all steel, but the body of the rifle, stem to stern is composed of molded nylon. It's not an heirloom maybe, but *rugged it is!* In a sort of overkill attempt Remington PR guys drove trucks over Nylon 66's and went back to shooting them without a hitch.

In 1972 Remington went out on the limb again by introducing what remains the finest .22 rimfire sporter made in America, the Model 541-S. With bigbore stock and full-bodied 24-inch target quality barrel, plus an action lifted from the Remington match-winning 540X target rifle, the 541-S proved popular from the outset.

Even Remington's run-of-the-mill bolt action rimfires are pretty impressive in terms of stoutness and accuracy. Their .22 trio of Models 580, 581, and 582 all share the same 24-inch open-sighted barrels, with grooved steel receivers, riding in bigbore configuration plain walnut-finished stocks. In order of their appearance, they are, #1 a single shot, #2 a five-shot clip-loader, and #3 an under-barrel tubular magazine rifle holding 14 Long Rifles, 15 Longs, or 20 Shorts, mixed or interchangeably. The 580 is available with 1-inch trimmed from the butt stock for youthful shooters. In 1978, Remington began including in the box with all of their Model 581 rifles a single shot adapter that can be inserted by removing the stock, thus discouraging casual removal by eager lads and lasses. The gun can thus be issued as a single shot until you're convinced that your budding marksman has learned enough to handle a repeater. Then out comes the adapter and in goes the normal clip. If you're casting a backward glance at that 580 with the optional short stock, just buy the 581 and turn to Chapter 14 for instructions on stock shortening. Other assets of the 580 series are their rotary locking lug actions, styled after the system used in field artillery, and their superbly crisp, single-stage trigger mechanisms. The weights of all three hover around the 5-pound mark. The Model 581 is available as a lefthand version with a port-side handle, but it still loads and ejects from the right.

Still popular are Remington's conventional autoloading Models 552A and 552BDL Deluxe—both share the same 21-inch barrels and newly slenderized stock configurations. Both have under-barrel tubular magazines that handle 15 Long Rifles, 17 Longs, and 20 Shorts, mixed or otherwise. This remarkable facility, shared by no other autoloading rifle, results from Remington's exclusive floating chamber. When fired with a Long or Long Rifle cartridge, the full-length case covers the chamber opening. When a Short is fired, part of the

Remington's Nylon 66 represents a new and revolutionary approach to gun making. The entire body of the gun is molded of structural nylon. Only the action cover, barrel and action parts are steel.

The finest bolt action .22 rimfire rifle made in America today is the Remington Model 541-S, with genuine walnut stock, checkered fore and aft, with plastic rosewood-grained forend tip and grip cap. It comes sans sights, but the receiver is grooved for tip-off mounts, and drilled and tapped for standard mounts. The barrel is drilled and tapped for open sights.

The Remington Model 552 BDL Deluxe .22 rimfire autoloading rifle boasts a unique floating chamber, it will fire Shorts as well as Longs and Long Rifles. The stock is genuine walnut with impressed checkering and high gloss finish. The southpaw will welcome the gas diverter abaft the ejection port, which keeps flying brass and powder granules out of his face.

expanding powder gas is diverted to the front of the floating chamber, imparting a greater rearward thrust than the Short could exert upon the breechblock unassisted. Also new in 1978 is the Williams Guide-style fully adjustable open rear sight on the 552BDL, a welcome adjunct to its checkered genuine American walnut stock, finished in bright and beautiful Du Pont RK-W coating. The plain-Jane butt stock and forend of the 552A is walnut-finished hardwood. All of the above applies to Remington's Model 572A and 572BDL Deluxe, except that these two are pump actions.

Savage

With a jaundiced eye on our dubious future, Americans are increasingly reaching back into our proud past searching for something to feel good about. The rebirth of the Savage/Stevens Model 72 Crackshot with unique lever-lowered falling block action is a barometer of our need for nostalgia. Around the turn of the century, this lightweight, trim, no-nonsense single shot provided endless hours of diversion for a happy generation of young Americans who fortunately never heard of TV. The modernized version has some safety features lacking in the original. A hammer block similar to that found on a revolver prevents firing unless the trigger is deliberately squeezed, and an interlock device drops the hammer to half-cock if the lever is lowered when the manual hammer is at full-cock. Thus the most famous "teacher" rifle of all time has been made even more goof-proof. The Crackshot is also a handsome rifle just hanging on the wall, with its color casehardened receiver and oil-finished walnut stock and forend. Weighing only 4½ pounds with its 22-inch octagon barrel topped by bead

and leaf sights, it can serve your youngster for a lifetime.

The Stevens bolt action single shot .22 rimfire Model 73 with 20-inch barrel, weighs a quarter-pound more in its standard configuration, a ¼-pound less in its stock-shortened 18-inch barreled Youth Model. It boasts a safety that automatically engages when the bolt is raised for loading and has an advantage over the Model 72 in that its grooved receiver will accept a tip-off mounted scope. In addition, you save about one-third on cost.

Still another youth-oriented rifle from Savage is the Model 89 Martini-styled falling block single shot .22 with manual hammer. This Western-styled lever action carbine carries a dummy tubular magazine under the barrel to promote the image. As with the Crackshot, this one is a purely open sight affair, with the usual post and elevator-adjusted rear leaf. With 18½-inch barrel, it weighs a hefty 5 pounds.

More adult directed is the Savage/Stevens Model 34 bolt action .22 rimfire with 20-inch barrel, open sights, and grooved steel receiver. The 34 utilizes the concealed hammer rather than the more common internal striker, thus requiring a somewhat longer-than-usual receiver. The five-shot clip can be augmented with an optional 10-shot model. The Monte Carlo stock is that ubiquitous walnut-finished hardwood.

With similar features, the Savage Model 65-M chambers the .22 Magnum behind a 22-inch barrel with a stock upgraded to genuine walnut. Both have impressed checkering and black plastic butt plates, and weigh 5 pounds-plus.

The more stylish Savage Model 80 semiautomatic

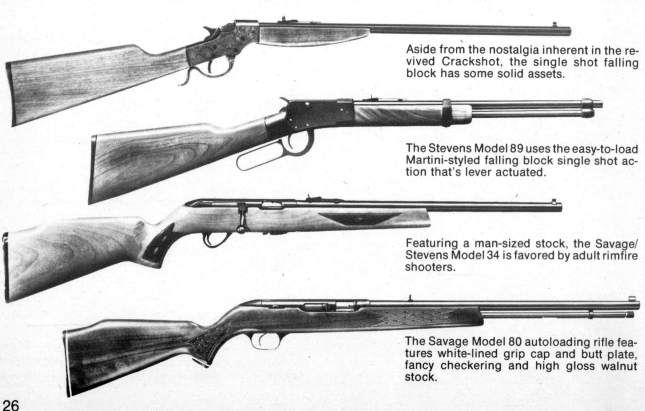

Aside from the nostalgia inherent in the revived Crackshot, the single shot falling block has some solid assets.

The Stevens Model 89 uses the easy-to-load Martini-styled falling block single shot action that's lever actuated.

Featuring a man-sized stock, the Savage/Stevens Model 34 is favored by adult rimfire shooters.

The Savage Model 80 autoloading rifle features white-lined grip cap and butt plate, fancy checkering and high gloss walnut stock.

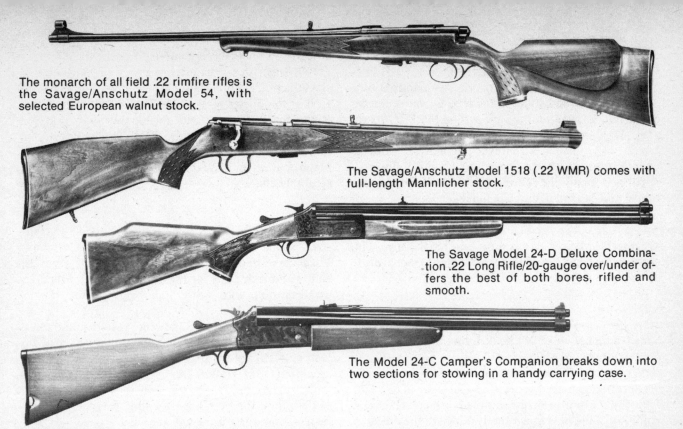

The monarch of all field .22 rimfire rifles is the Savage/Anschutz Model 54, with selected European walnut stock.

The Savage/Anschutz Model 1518 (.22 WMR) comes with full-length Mannlicher stock.

The Savage Model 24-D Deluxe Combination .22 Long Rifle/20-gauge over/under offers the best of both bores, rifled and smooth.

The Model 24-C Camper's Companion breaks down into two sections for stowing in a handy carrying case.

rifle with 20-inch barrel has a tubular magazine suspended under the barrel, holding 15 Long Rifles only. It sells in the same general price range as the Model 65-M. Any one of the Savage man-sized rifles would make companions for plinking or small game hunting.

Consummate quality and superior design are still available in .22 rimfire rifles, but at a price! The Savage/Anschutz line of rimfire sporting rifles are expensive *but they are worth every penny of it!* In terms of boundless personal satisfaction derived and last-forever quality, all of the Savage/Anschutz sporters fall well within the "bargain" category! Top billing goes to the Model 54 Sporter, a formidable 6¾-pound bolt action with gracefully tapered 24-inch barrel, topped by a tall ramped bead front and adjustable folding leaf rear sight. The flawless action with target-crisp trigger is in fact borrowed from the Anschutz Match 54, which has dominated international competition for years. Microsecond lock time and super smooth action mark this five-shot clip-loader, with optional 10-shot clip available. As the 54-M, chambered in .22 Magnum, it utilizes a four-shot-only magazine.

The Model 164 borrows its bolt action from the more modestly-priced Anschutz 64 target rifles, but it is nonetheless a beautiful and effective rifle, also with an excellent trigger pull. In general appearance, it resembles its more expensive cousin, with stylish schnabel forend, hand-checkering and white-lined black plastic butt plate. For other southpaw shooters in my audience, I recommend the 164, because it lacks the rollover comb of the 54, although the bolt remains on the right. The 164 is available chambered for either the standard or magnum .22 rimfire.

Utilizing the same action as the 164, the Models 1418 (standard .22) and 1518 (.22 Magnum) are styled in the trim Mannlicher tradition, with forend gently tapered clear to the rifle muzzle 19¾ inches from the bolt face. The butt stock is down-curved in the European style for an altogether fetching appearance. If you want a rifle guaranteed to arouse utter envy in your friends, and to decorate the mantle, plus shoot up a storm in the field or on the range, try this jewel! All three Savage/Anschutz models share that richly grained European walnut, with its deep, dark luster!

For virtually infinite versatility, it would be hard to beat the Savage Model 24-D, Deluxe Combination .22 Long Rifle/20-gauge over/under, with 24-inch barrels. For outings that promise both feathers and fur, you are prepared with both smooth and rifled barrels. The rugged field-styled gun has a two-way opening lever abaft of the breech and manual cocking hammer with integral barrel selector. It is also available with the top barrel chambered for .22 Magnum. The lower barrel will accept 3-inch magnum shells. The dual barrel band and post front sight is backed by a folding leaf and grooved receiver—an ideal setup for Weaver's Qwik-Point red-dot sight! It weighs a hefty 7½ pounds.

A plain-Jane scaled-down version is the Model 24-C Camper's Companion with 20-inch barrel, weighing a more acceptable 5¾ pounds. Unique with the 24-C is a butt stock trap that accepts 10 .22 Long Rifles and two shotshells. Chambering is standard .22 and 20-gauge 2¾-inch only. A plastic case is included that allows stowing the Camper's Companion in a handy 5 x 22-inch package with thongs for tying to pack or saddle. Cost is only slightly less than for its bigger brother.

Weatherby

In 1964, Roy Weatherby, a man accustomed to doing everything in grand style, introduced the most elegant auto ever! Styled after the pace-setting Mark V Weatherby Magnum bigbore rifle, the Weatherby Mark XXII rifle is man-sized in every dimension, from its 24-inch tapered sporter barrel to its tastefully pro-portioned hand-checkered selected walnut stock, tipped and capped with white-lined genuine rosewood. Originally offered as a clip-loader, it later became avail-able as an under-barrel tubular magazine rifle. The Weatherby Mark XXII is a bargain for the man who appreciates beauty in all things and takes personal pride in owning the best!

Winchester

In 1978, the Winchester Model 9422 received the added designation of XTR, denoting the use of Win-chester's new ultra high luster finish on both metal and the American walnut stock. Styled after the all-time favorite Winchester Model 94 .30-30 lever action car-bine, the .22 rimfire 9422 was already a handsome arm. Addition of the new finish surely added to the image of excellence. The 9422 is a grand new rifle in a grand old tradition!

With the 9422 taking the rimfire world by storm, Winchester has pared down the remainder of their .22 stable to one lone autoloader, the Model 190, with 20½-inch barrel, studded with open sights and backed by a scope-grooved alloy receiver. Butt stock and forearm of American walnut bear an attractive pattern of impressed checkering and the under-barrel tubular magazine accepts either 17 Longs or 15 Long Rifles, separately or mixed. At a relatively light 5 pounds, the 190 makes a good small game or plinking rifle for any age.

As already noted above, some Winchester Model 490 semiautomatic .22 Long Rifle clip-loaders are still in inventory. If you like the lines of this 6-pound, all-steel, bigbore-styled rifle as I do, get your order in pronto!

Ruger

In 1961, Sturm, Ruger & Company introduced a handy 18½-inch barreled autoloading carbine cham-bered for the .44 Magnum. The yard-long gas-operated carbine was an instant success, leading Bill Ruger to produce the 10/22 Carbine just 3 years later. The 10/22 a dimensionally identical .22 rimfire, features a unique 10-shot rotary magazine that blends smoothly into the bottom of the stock.

The original launching pad for Ruger's Horatio Alger success story was his Luger-look .22 autoloading pistol. Utilizing modern production methods such as stamp-ings and welded parts enabled a highly functional, accu-rate pistol to be offered at an unheard of low price. The original Ruger and the later target-style Mark I still

outsell and undersell the competition.

Bill Ruger deserves credit for reviving the sinking single action revolver after it was quietly interred by Colt at the outset of WW II. The introduction of the Ruger Single Six met with unanimous approval from shooters across the nation in 1953. The updated New Model Super Single Six Convertible continues to sell better than ever, available in both blued and stainless steel models.

Hawes

Hawes, of Van Nuys, California, imports five Scout-sized single action revolvers from West Germany. They come in a variety of finishes ranging from all blue with black grips for the Hawes Deputy Marshal, to all chrome with white stag strips for the Hawes Deputy Texas Marshal. Mixing grips, cylinders and barrels of brass, chrome, and blue, results in the three other Deputy revolvers. The frames appear to be of die cast metal, as are the trigger guard and backstrap. The exception is the Hawes Deputy Denver Marshal with solid brass frame. It appears likely that the brass frame model offers the best hope for long wear. Cylinders, barrels, and inner workings are steel.

Harrington & Richardson

Long noted for delivering exceptional quality at an affordable price, Harrington & Richardson, Inc., was founded in 1871 by Gilbert H. Harrington and William A. Richardson. It was Gilbert's invention of the top-break action that eventually led to introduction of the H&R Sportsman revolver in 1933, in both single and double action. Famed competition shooter and gunwrit-er, Walter F. Roper, collaborated with John W. Har-rington (both deceased) on the original design. With the result that the Sportsman leaped ahead of the then competition by several giant steps! Notable among the Roper innovations were a selection of six styles of hand-checkered walnut grips, each designed in accord with Roper's anatomical analysis of the human hand as it related to the use of one-hand guns. Roper was a pioneer in the effort to make grips fit the hand rather than attempting to make the hand fit the altogether unfit grip configurations of the day. Roper was also among the first to perform in-depth studies of pistol sights, resulting in the bold, clean-cut Patridge sights used on the Sportsman, with the front blade click-screw adjust-able for elevation and the rear readily adjustable for windage. The 6-inch steel barrel was milled with a solid sight rib, another pioneer design concept inspired by Roper, as was also the extension tang behind the trigger guard, which gave the revolver a place to rest upon the second finger. The cylinder was shortened from the standard .38 Special length down to 1¼ inches, all but eliminating the long leap from chamber to barrel for the .22 slug. The nine-shot cylinder not only provided more shooting per loading, but reduced the degree of rota-

Noted for its fine accuracy, the Weatherby Mark XXII clip-loader is also high in eye appeal.

The Winchester Model 9422's action is rugged, goof-proof and smooth-working. It's available for both Standard and Magnum .22 rimfire.

Winchester's budget-priced autoloading Model 190, with 20½-inch barrel and under-barrel tubular magazine, holding 17 Longs and 15 Long Rifles.

The little brother to Ruger's .44 Magnum carbine is the 10/22 Ruger Carbine, with barrel band and carbine-style butt plate.

(Left) Ruger's Luger-look autoloading pistol—quality at a price.

(Right) The Ruger Mark I target-directed auto pistol with adjustable sights is available with tapered 6⅞-inch barrel or with 5½-inch bull barrel.

The New Model Super Single Six comes with both .22 Long Rifle and .22 WMR cylinders.

The Hawes Deputy Silver City Marshal mixes chrome-plated frame with blued cylinder and barrel, and brass-plated guard.

Hawes imports five different versions of the single action rimfire revolvers. Shown is the top-of-the-line Deputy Denver Marshal, with solid brass frame.

tion, allowing a shorter hammer travel for the first, and for many years, the *only* short action on the market!

The Sportsman action was revised in 1973 to incorporate a fail-safe transfer bar which rises to transmit the hammer impact to the firing pin only when the trigger is deliberately held to the rear, absolutely eliminating any possibility of accidental discharge. With but one other alteration, the addition of attractive milled slots that result in a ventilated rib, the Harrington & Richardson Sportsman is still available today. Many of its pioneer design features have been copied by other makers, but it still stands out as a fine, accurate revolver for informal target or small game shooting. It represents one of those very few real bargains that I promised to point out as we go along!

In addition to their top-of-the-line Sportsman, H & R offers a broad spectrum of revolvers reaching down to fit the most modest budget, yet every one a practical pistol for the plinker/Nimrod. The Model 926 is in the image of the Sportsman, but with solid rib and 4-inch barrel, plus manual ejection—a fine compact kit or trail gun. The Model 676, a side-ejecting double action styled in the frontier tradition, comes with unfluted dual .22 Long Rifle/.22 Magnum cylinders, in barrels of 4½-, 5½-, 7½-inch and 12-inch lengths. With color casehardened frames and walnut grips, they make handsome trail companions. Identical in design is the Model 650, with rust resistant nickel finish and 5½-inch barrel, the 5½-inch blued Model 649, and the 5½-inch barreled Model 950 in nickel *sans* magnum cylinder.

H & R also makes a number of swing-out cylinder double action revolvers in a wide variety of finishes and barrel lengths. Representative are the Model 939 with ventilated rib on a 6-inch heavy barrel, and thumb-shelf target walnut grips, and the Model 930 nickel-finished revolver with either 2- or 4-inch barrel.

Bottom-budget offerings are the dual-cylinder Model 666, with 6-inch barrel, and the Model 622 with either 2½- or 4-inch barrel. Both revolvers are double action and each requires the cylinder be removed and the base pin used to manually eject fired cases.

In 1976, H & R introduced their Model 700 autoloading rifle in .22 Magnum, with 22-inch barrel, topped by conventional open sights, backed by a long cylindrical steel receiver holding the simple blowback action. Ammo feeds from a five-shot detachable box magazine. The plain walnut stock has a Monte Carlo scope-height comb, and the receiver is factory drilled and tapped for conventional mounts. This man-sized 6½-pound rifle is obviously aimed at the small game hunter who desires an autoloading .22 Magnum. Both the ammo and the gun are too expensive for plinking. H & R also markets two modest-priced bolt action rimfire rifles, the single shot Model 750, and the Model 865, five-shot cliploader.

The Harrington & Richardson Sportsman revolver introduced in 1933 was far ahead of its time in shooter-oriented features.

Outwardly identical to the Sportsman, the H&R Model 926 comes with 4-inch barrel.

H&R Model 676 comes with dual .22 LR/.22 WMR cylinders.

Also a double action, the Model 649 has high luster bluing on cylinder and barrel, with satin blue on the frame.

The swing-out cylinder Model 939 features ventilated rib and heavy barrel, with slab-sided look. The rear sight is adjustable, making this a budget-priced target revolver.

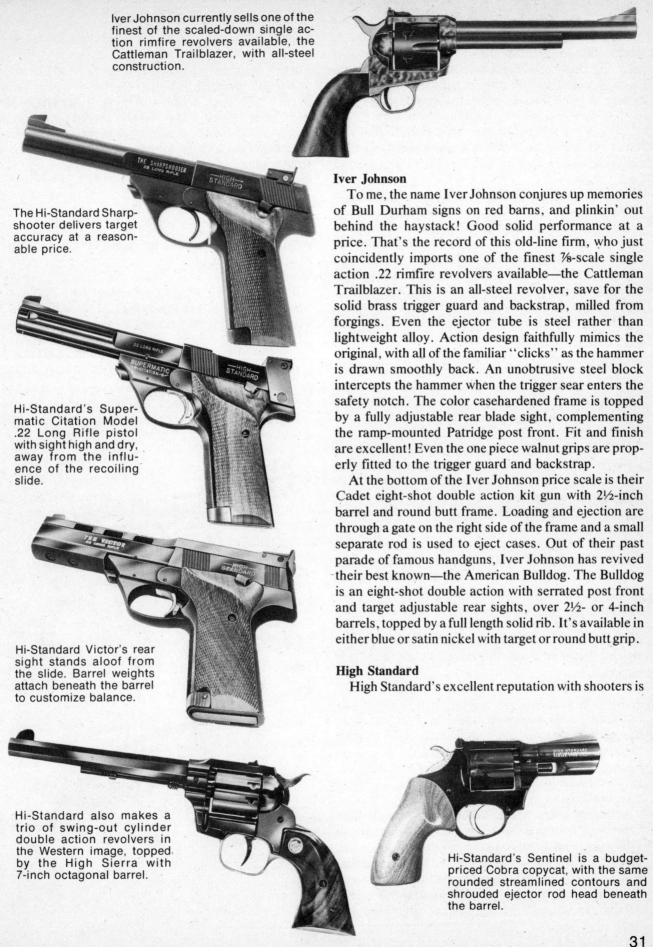

Iver Johnson currently sells one of the finest of the scaled-down single action rimfire revolvers available, the Cattleman Trailblazer, with all-steel construction.

The Hi-Standard Sharpshooter delivers target accuracy at a reasonable price.

Hi-Standard's Supermatic Citation Model .22 Long Rifle pistol with sight high and dry, away from the influence of the recoiling slide.

Hi-Standard Victor's rear sight stands aloof from the slide. Barrel weights attach beneath the barrel to customize balance.

Hi-Standard also makes a trio of swing-out cylinder double action revolvers in the Western image, topped by the High Sierra with 7-inch octagonal barrel.

Hi-Standard's Sentinel is a budget-priced Cobra copycat, with the same rounded streamlined contours and shrouded ejector rod head beneath the barrel.

Iver Johnson

To me, the name Iver Johnson conjures up memories of Bull Durham signs on red barns, and plinkin' out behind the haystack! Good solid performance at a price. That's the record of this old-line firm, who just coincidently imports one of the finest ⅞-scale single action .22 rimfire revolvers available—the Cattleman Trailblazer. This is an all-steel revolver, save for the solid brass trigger guard and backstrap, milled from forgings. Even the ejector tube is steel rather than lightweight alloy. Action design faithfully mimics the original, with all of the familiar "clicks" as the hammer is drawn smoothly back. An unobtrusive steel block intercepts the hammer when the trigger sear enters the safety notch. The color casehardened frame is topped by a fully adjustable rear blade sight, complementing the ramp-mounted Patridge post front. Fit and finish are excellent! Even the one piece walnut grips are properly fitted to the trigger guard and backstrap.

At the bottom of the Iver Johnson price scale is their Cadet eight-shot double action kit gun with 2½-inch barrel and round butt frame. Loading and ejection are through a gate on the right side of the frame and a small separate rod is used to eject cases. Out of their past parade of famous handguns, Iver Johnson has revived their best known—the American Bulldog. The Bulldog is an eight-shot double action with serrated post front and target adjustable rear sights, over 2½- or 4-inch barrels, topped by a full length solid rib. It's available in either blue or satin nickel with target or round butt grip.

High Standard

High Standard's excellent reputation with shooters is

31

well deserved. They have produced the most varied and certainly some of the best designed of American-made autoloaders. High Standard was founded in August of 1926, by Gustave A. Beck and Carl Gustav Swebelius (a watchmaker's son who emigrated to the United States in 1879). During WW II, they were deeply involved with production of machine guns both for the British and American governments. Plant facilities established during the conflict enabled High Standard to enter the commercial marketplace after the war in viable volume.

Today, High Standard offers shooters a veritable smorgasbord of fine autoloaders. They range from the field-styled Sport King, with fixed sights on either a 4½- or 6¾-inch barrel to the top-of-the-line target-intended Victor, with full-length ventilated rib on either a 4½- or 5½-inch barrel. All High Standard autos are currently constructed upon the "Military" frame, with grip angled to match the Model 1911 .45 ACP. All are stocked with deeply checkered genuine walnut, straight-sided on the Sport King, with target thumb-shelf on the target models. All share the exclusive High Standard button-removable barrels, the basic crisp trigger mechanism and wide-serrated trigger. All, save for the Sport King, have micro-adjustable target sights. The Sharpshooter, a real bargain for the beginning target shooter, has the rear sight mounted upon the slide. However, the slide fits so tightly, that there is no danger of the sight shifting position from shot to shot. Given a comfortable, secure hip holster such as the Safariland Model 75 with its kangaroo-style clip pouch, the 42-ounce Sharpshooter makes a superior field pistol, rugged, reliable and exquisitely accurate! With its bull barrel it hangs steady as an anvil! The rear sight on the Trophy and Citation models rides upon a frame-mounted bracket, free and clear of the slide. Both guns are offered with either 5½-inch bull barrel or 7½-inch fluted barrel. Note that you can order with one or the other, then buy the added barrel as an accessory, interchanging them at will as befits the need. The Citation, Trophy and Victor all share a trigger adjustable for travel, weight of pull and backlash.

The short-firing Hi-Standard Olympic ISU Model with the bulbous muzzle brake, which won the gold medal at the Olympics in Rome in 1960, has been dropped for the time being, but with the NRA increasingly interested in International style shooting competition, it may be revived later, either as a complete gun or as a kit including barrel, slide and magazine to attach to existing High Standard frames.

In recent years, High Standard has brought their expertise to bear upon wheel guns, resulting in a trio of Western-styled double action revolvers. The High Sierra is distinctively marked by its 7-inch octagonal barrel. The Double Nine sports a 5½-inch round barrel while the Longhorn has a 9½-inch round tapered barrel. All share the same steel frame with swing-out nine-shot

cylinder, micro-adjustable sights and smooth walnut grips. Each comes with a dual cylinder in .22 Magnum chambering, instantly interchangeable. All are finished in High Standard's high luster Trophy Blue.

The Hi-Standard Sentinel is a revolver of modern mien, with either a 2- or 4-inch barrel, with integral rib and ejector shroud, round butt checkered walnut grips and target-adjustable sights. All of the above applies to the Camp Gun, except that it has a 6-inch round barrel. Both double action revolvers share the same frame/grip configuration. Both come with dual .22 Magnum nine-shot cylinders.

Smith & Wesson

Would you believe that the Smith & Wesson .22/32 Kit Gun was a spinoff of the only "heavyweight frame" target revolver of its day? Introduced in 1911 at the instigation of their West Coast representative, Phil B. Bekeart, the .22/32 Target was the first .22 rimfire to use a frame adapted from a larger caliber, in this case, the .32 Hand Ejector. With a slender 6-inch barrel topped by a tall Patridge post, backed with an adjustable target rear sight, the .22/32 Target won many a match in its day! When still heavier frame revolvers displaced the .22/32 from the firing lines, Smith & Wesson cleverly changed their tack, cut the barrel to 4 inches, rounded

The Smith & Wesson .22/32 Kit Gun with rounded butt and 4-inch barrel slips into any kit with ease and delivers premium accuracy.

Smith & Wesson's precision K-22 Masterpiece is available as a standard .22 rimfire, or as the M.R.F., chambering .22 Magnum ammo.

the butt, and renamed it the "Kit Gun." In that day, the word "kit" didn't designate a do-it-yourself project in a box. Rather, it meant the gun was something to pack with your camping or traveling gear, as in, "Pack up your troubles in your old *kit* bag."

After WW II, the Kit Gun was revised with new improved target sights, and the barrel was beefed up and given a full length rib, which added a little welcome heft to the lightweight .22 revolver. My own .22/32 Kit Gun was among the first produced after the war. For years, I limped along with the original walnut round butt grips and a Mershon adapter, because I never could get a good hold on the tiny handle. Recently, I discovered Frank Pachmayr's Presentation/Compac SJ/C-Small rubber grips, and my Kit Gun suddenly acquired a whole new personality. It was as if we had never met before! For the first time I was able to group my shots into acceptable clusters instead of all around the target frame. I was amazed, gratified, ecstatic! It's like a second honeymoon! Incidentally, those self-same grips make a Smith & Wesson Chief's Special totally controllable, even with dynamite loads!

The Smith & Wesson K-22 Masterpiece was introduced in 1940 as a revised version of the old K-22 Outdoorsman. Improvements included a short action with backlash adjustment, micrometer sights, and a straight-tapered barrel with full-length rib. The Masterpiece lives up to its name. If you want the finest rimfire revolver going and can afford to invest almost two bills, this one's for you! It's available with either a 6- or 8⅜-inch barrel. Have that barrel trimmed to 4 inches and add a Baughman-styled forward-slanting front sight, and you've got the .22 Combat Master-

piece, a fine field gun. The Model 48 K-22 Masterpiece M.R.F. is a .22 Magnum chambered version, with all three barrel lengths offered.

Stoeger

In 1968, Luger owners and those who wished they were Luger owners were pleased to discover that Stoeger Arms was manufacturing a .22 Long Rifle version of the famed toggle-top that served the German armed forces in two wars. Innumerable examples were "liberated" after both conflicts came to an end, and numberless more commercial Lugers were imported into America. You might say it was more popular here than in Europe. Which is rather ironic because the inventor was American Hugo Borchardt, who found American makers cool to his design concept, thus sold it in Germany.

The .22 Luger is now being manufactured in the States, by Stoeger, with the same heft and balance, the same natural-pointing grip, the same unhandy safety as the original! The safety can, however, be installed either right- or left-handed. To keep the weight within an ounce of the original, Stoeger was obliged to use a lightweight alloy. They chose for strength as well as reduced weight, using 7075 T6 aluminum alloy forgings, not castings, milled to finished contours. This material, used for aircraft structural components and landing gear, will withstand 82,000 psi. The totally revised action boasts an improved trigger squeeze and an easy takedown that allows cleaning from the breech end. The standard model is available with a 4½-inch barrel only. A target-sighted version offers the option of 4½- or 5½-inch tube, all hammer-forged, with the familiar

Stoeger imports the Finnish Sako Model 78 .22 rimfire rifle, sold with open sights, but with grooved receiver for scope mounting. The Model 78 is marked by superb European craftsmanship that is only a fond memory here in the States.

Stoeger is now manufacturing a .22 rimfire version of the Luger with an improved action and high tensile alloy frame, that brings it within 1-ounce of the original weight. It is available with a target adjustable rear sight, and the safety lever is reversible for left-handed use.

Stoeger imports the Llama Automatic, shown here in satin chrome finish, with adjustable sights, ventilated rib, and grip safety, in the image of the .45 ACP.

knob at the muzzle, dovetailed for a military-styled blade. Wooden grips are plain on the fixed-sight model, checkered on the target gun.

Also from Stoeger come the compact Llama autoloading pistols in .22 Long Rifle, looking rather like scaled down .45's with adjustable sights, ventilated ribs and thumb-rest plastic grips. The sub-sized pocket pistols carry eight-shot clips, weigh 23 ounces, have 3$^{11}/_{16}$-inch barrels and come in satin chrome or blued finish.

Another Stoeger import is the Llama Comanche .22 rimfire revolver with 6-inch barrel, ventilated rib and target sights. You have to look close to tell this one from the K-22, and it's priced about the same.

The matchless Finnish Sako rifle is also being imported by Stoeger in .22 Long Rifle and .22 Hornet. The Model 78 action with a 22½-inch barrel mounts firmly in a European walnut stock, finely hand-checkered, with Monte Carlo comb. A detachable box magazine holds five rounds. The Model 78 has open sights and a grooved receiver.

Thompson Center

Many of you may regard a single shot pistol as a rather specialized tool, reserved for the long-range shooting "pro." I thought that myself until I actually tried a Thompson/Center Contender. Barrels are available in .22 Long Rifle chambering (which also chambers all of the smaller rounds down to BB Caps), .22 Magnum, or in 5mm Remington. Any or all of these can be fun investments for confirmed pistol buffs or .22 handgun nimrods interested in seeing just how far away they can actually hit. The Contender can pick off squirrels about as far as a rifle and just as convincingly! If you have bigbore centerfire aspirations, T/C backs up every receiver with about 24 various-caliber barrels, all of the way up to such boomers as the .30-30 Winchester and .44 Magnum!

Colt

Colt Industries has become so enamored of diversification in recent years that they have just about forgotten where old Sam planted the tree! Talk about forgetting your roots—Colt has virtually resigned from rimfires. However, they deserve at least a mention here for retaining a single .22 rimfire—the Diamondback revolver—in one barrel length, 4 inches. The Diamondback is a .38 Special scaled down from the popular Colt Python .357 Magnum. It became a rimfire merely as an afterthought, with the idea of supplying law enforcement with a sub-caliber training handgun for either of the centerfire arms. It takes a really dedicated Colt buff to choose this one over the many other makes selling at more reasonable prices.

Revolvers vs Autos

Note that some firms, such as Iver Johnson, make

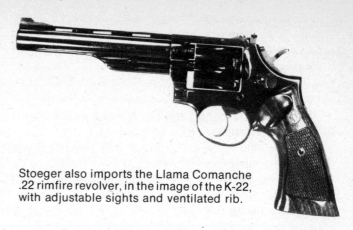

Stoeger also imports the Llama Comanche .22 rimfire revolver, in the image of the K-22, with adjustable sights and ventilated rib.

both single and double action revolvers, thereby assuring sales to advocates of both action styles. An enduring controversy has raged over the relative merits of single action versus double action revolvers, ever since the days of Billy the Kid, who preferred the latter at a time when most of his contemporaries carried Frontier Colts. Billy is supposed to have run up quite a score, but he never made it past 21 years of age—and he died by a single action!

The rapid-fire potential of a double action is seldom used unless two adversaries face each other at arm's length. For aimed fire at a distant target, the double action revolver must be used in single action mode anyway. Ergo, no advantage! The swing-out cylinder double action revolver dumps empties in one quick motion, whereas a single action requires dexterity, finesse, *and time,* to remove the spent cases. Score one for the DA. One seldom-mentioned problem with the DA revolver is the fact that a few flakes of unburned powder under the ratchet/ejector will freeze the cylinder, requiring painstaking cleaning to restore function. However, this situation arises most often with hot-loaded bigbores, so is not a factor with rimfire revolvers. Until a few years ago, SA six-shooters were often carried as five-shooters by seasoned veterans who realized that the safety notch was something less than totally reliable. The only sure-fire way to be safe was to lower the hammer over an empty chamber. However, today most SA revolvers are equipped with fail-safe

A single shot pistol designed for the field shooter and hunter, the Thompson/Center Contender is really a "system gun" with a single receiver backed by a couple dozen barrels in every imaginable caliber.

devices to prevent accidental firing, even if you hammer on the hammer. In the final analysis, it all boils down to finding out which one best fits your hand and pleases your eye!

To carry the discussion a point further, how do revolvers score against autoloading pistols? You can whip up a pretty heated debate if you'll drop this around the campfire some night! Some revolver partisan will certainly point out that despite modern quality control, an occasional dud will find its way under the hammer of your pistol, perhaps just as you draw a bead on a nervous furry critter. A wheel gun goes, "click," then cycles to the next round without a stutter. The auto requires a two-handed fumble to yank back the slide and jack another round into the chamber. Meanwhile your dinner-on-the-hoof has fled!

The auto afficionado will counter that his machine is quicker to load—true, given a spare loaded clip. But what if you start even, with both guns fully fired? The auto shooter must remove the magazine, feed it seven to 10 rounds, replace the magazine, and finally drop the slide. Our revolver buff, if firing an SA, must push out six individual cases through the loading gate, then refill with six loaded hulls, and close the gate. If using a DA, he swings out the cylinder and dumps the brass, drops in six, and closes the cylinder. I timed these cycles with a friend of average dexterity and came up with the following numbers: 5 seconds to drop an empty magazine from a Hi-Standard Sharpshooter and push home a loaded one; 25 seconds to pull, load, and replace an empty magazine; 36 seconds to empty a Ruger Single Six and reload; 15 seconds to empty and reload a Smith & Wesson K-22. Conceding that the Sharpshooter once loaded, has 10 rounds at the ready, as opposed to six for the K-22, it looks like a standoff be-

tween the DA and the auto. The SA comes in a poor last, but I love 'em just the same!

Neither revolver nor autoloader are jam-proof when dunked into mud or sand, but the revolver, especially the SA can stand more dirt without requiring major surgery. On the other hand, most autos can be field stripped, cleaned and assembled in minutes, without the aid of tools. Try that with a K-22 sometime! Honors for versatility go to the revolver, chambering anything from CB Caps to shot cartridges. SA's with dual cylinders offer the further capability of shooting .22 Magnum ammo, no small thing if you're all by yourself in the wild sometime!

Generally autos have the accuracy edge, but the difference is so slight that the average shooter would never know it. At one time, autos were marked by soda-straw barrels, spindly grips, mushy triggers and GI-styled sights. Thanks to firms like High Standard, who made an intelligent effort to upgrade the breed, autos now come from the factory with crisp, light triggers, hand-filling grips, big bold target-adjustable sights, and barrel options to suit any desired balance, even to the point of movable weights. Autos like the Hi-Standard Victor have driven revolvers completely off the target ranges that they once dominated.

The alleged velocity loss occasioned by the gap twixt cylinder and barrel of a revolver is more imagined than real. During chronograph testing, a Hi-Standard Victor clocked 1162 fps from a 5½-inch barrel. Using the same ammo, a 6-inch barreled K-22 registered 1196 fps. No clear advantage demonstrated there, even in light of the ½-inch barrel difference.

If the above leaves you still wondering what gun to buy, read on! I have other elucidating information to follow.

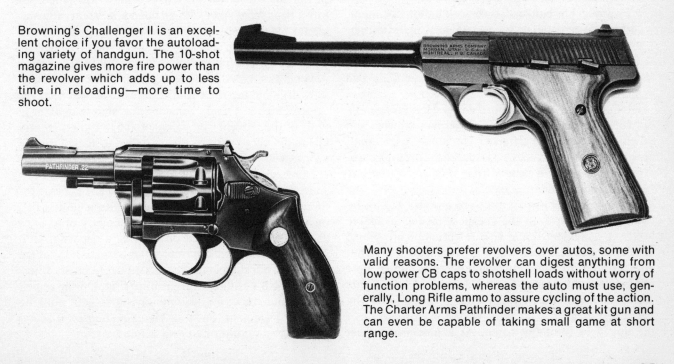

Browning's Challenger II is an excellent choice if you favor the autoloading variety of handgun. The 10-shot magazine gives more fire power than the revolver which adds up to less time in reloading—more time to shoot.

Many shooters prefer revolvers over autos, some with valid reasons. The revolver can digest anything from low power CB caps to shotshell loads without worry of function problems, whereas the auto must use, generally, Long Rifle ammo to assure cycling of the action. The Charter Arms Pathfinder makes a great kit gun and can even be capable of taking small game at short range.

CHAPTER 3

Iron Sights vs Glass Sights

WE MET ATOP A UTAH mountain during deer season. He stood tall and lank, in faded blue Levi's jacket and tattered jeans, as if he had just stepped out of a Gary Cooper movie. He politely examined my bolt action .300 Weatherby topped by a 3X-9X variable scope of imposing dimensions. "Personally, I'm 'spicious of them newfangled telescope sights," he drawled. "They'd just slow me down!" He peeled back a weathered Stetson, revealing a shock of graying hair. "Here's what I use." He handed me a Savage Model 99 lever action .30-30, a caliber long since discontinued by that company. It looked as if it doubled for a fence post during the winter! The bead was completely worn off of the front sight from many a long mile riding in a saddle boot. The open notch rear sight was rounded off at the corners, and the step elevator had fallen out years before. Apparently it was never missed.

I returned his battered carbine without comment, wondering if he could hit his Stetson at 10 paces with it. Later that same day, *I watched him put three bullets through the chest cavity of a running deer at more than 100 yards,* so rapidly that I looked to see if he had switched to an autoloader!

Obviously, this old-timer had no need for a scope. An optical sight probably would have just slowed him down! His comments reflected a lingering suspicion of scope sights that had been widespread during my youth. I remember when a scoped rifle was as rare as one *without* a scope today!

Hunting scopes of that era were a pretty sad lot by comparison with even the cheapest models available today. I remember lining up a selection of pre-World War II scopes on a rock wall one evening to settle a bet with a friend, Leland Crow, an inveterate hunter, now of Hamilton, Montana. As dusk approached, the lights went out on all but the Lyman Alaskan. Leland won the bet! The Lyman was the only American-made scope of the day worthy of the name. At a time when most domestic scopes were dim and murky, the Alaskan delivered a 9mm exit pupil!

On the other hand, iron sights of that day were every bit as good as current issue if not better. The Lyman Number 48 series of micrometer receiver sights, now discontinued, were jewels of precision. Open sights were of traditional design, but with superior workmanship and finer machining.

Open Sights

My young eyes had no difficulty taking a "fine bead" across an open notch rear sight. I could light kitchen matches at 15 feet with my .22 rifle using only the sights provided by the factory. With the exception of the Remington Model 541-S, modern rimfire field rifles are delivered from the factory with open sights installed. Sights range from adequate to excellent. Most incorporate a bead front sight with an open notch rear, adjustable for elevation by means of a wedge-shaped elevator with steps or notches along its upper edge. Windage is adjusted by driving the sight from side to side in the dovetail slot milled in the barrel. Some makers thoughtfully drill and tap their rimfire rifles to accept receiver "peep" sights. Others consider that step redundant in view of the current popularity of scope sights. Nearly all are delivered with receivers milled to accept rimfire scopes with tip-off mounts.

Iron sights possess some obvious advantages. For starters, they don't add to the cost of the rifle, being for the most part factory issue. Open sights seem to "fit" on a rifle. They don't destroy the symmetry of its lines as does a scope perched on top like a papoose. Iron sights are light in weight, more rugged than the average scope and not subject to the vicissitudes of the weather. Weather isn't critical with a rimfire rifle. During a spell of rain and snow, you can merely move your plinking into the basement, but to a big game hunter, a scope crippled by weather can ruin his entire trip.

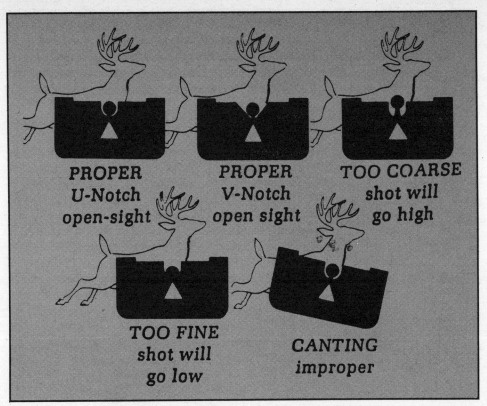

PROPER
U-Notch
open-sight

PROPER
V-Notch
open sight

TOO COARSE
shot will
go high

TOO FINE
shot will
go low

CANTING
improper

Open sight notches come in a variety of "V" and "U" configurations, teamed with bead front sights. One of the main problems of sight alignment results from holding the bead too high in the notch during the excitement of hunting. Another difficulty is the ease of canting the rifle which will direct the bullet low and to one side.

(Right) Patridge style sights with square notch and post offer positive elevation alignment and improved windage as well.

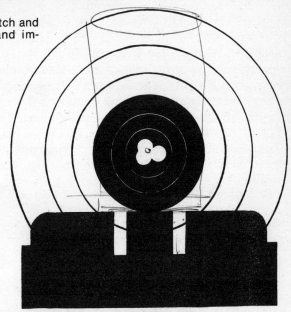

The notches in rear sights come variously cut with a "V" or "U" coupled with a brass or ivory bead front sight. Contrary to general belief, a large bead with a wide notch that allows plenty of light on both sides, is more accurate and faster to use on running game than a narrow notch and small-diameter bead. Better still are the square post front sight and square-notched rear Patridge sights, again with the rear notch wide enough to admit considerable light alongside the post. Patridge sights provide a positive elevation factor which is missing with the "U" and bead combination The average shooter is apt to take a fine bead, held low in the notch when sighting in or shooting at a target. Then when shooting at moving game, hold the bead higher in the notch

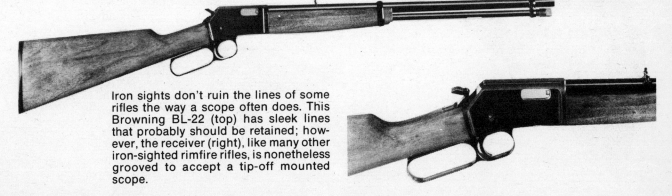

Iron sights don't ruin the lines of some rifles the way a scope often does. This Browning BL-22 (top) has sleek lines that probably should be retained; however, the receiver (right), like many other iron-sighted rimfire rifles, is nonetheless grooved to accept a tip-off mounted scope.

where it's more easily seen, leading to overshooting.

Beads *must* be flat-faced to avoid "shooting away from the light!" A round-faced bead inevitably picks up a highlight on the side toward the sun. The shooter's eye unconsciously ignores the dark side of the bead and moves the bright portion to the middle of the notch, resulting in a miss.

The best front sight ever to come down the pike was the old Redfield Sourdough Patridge post with 45-degree angled flat face inset with a .070-inch square block of phosphor bronze. I shed buckets of tears when Redfield abandoned the sight a few years back. Fortunately Burris is currently making a passable copy in a variety of heights to match almost any rear sight. Burris also offers the usual round bead front sights, along with dovetailed ramps, plus step-adjustable and folding leaf rear sights. A similar selection is available from Lyman, Marbles, and Williams Gun Sight.

Marbles' sights are marked by precision and fine finish. They are famed for their exclusive "Sheard Bead" front sights in white, red or gold. Their folding rear sights offer screw-adjustable windage and allow elevation adjustment via a "notch piece," riding in vertical grooves. The notch piece is reversible, to provide either a "V" or "U" notch. As an aiming aide, a white diamond points out the center of the notch.

Williams Gun Sight Company, founded by Harvey Williams in 1926 and still operated strictly as a family company by five of his seven sons, is the darling of the gunsmiths because of the imaginative design incorporated into their sights. The Williams "Streamlined" front sight ramp is a joy to install because it fits correctly and always results in a satisfied customer. The Williams "Shorty" ramp can be used on virtually any rifle and looks at home even on a short carbine barrel, as well as pistol barrels. Williams' bead front sights are

(Above left) Marble has long been famed for their exclusive "Sheard Bead" front sight. All of their sights are marked with excellent workmanship.

(Above right) Marble's rear sights offer a unique windage adjustment via a screw in the base, as well as elevation adjustment of the notch piece, which moves vertically in a slot. The notch piece is reversible, to offer either "U" or "V" notch. The sight also folds down to accommodate a scope.

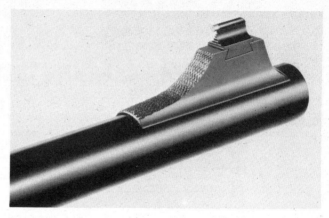

The Williams Shorty ramp looks in proper proportion even on short-barreled carbines or on handgun barrels

The Ruger 10/22 illustrates the typical rimfire open sight setup, with U-notched rear and bead front sights. The rear notch is adjustable for elevation by means of two screws holding the slotted rear blade. Although not grooved, the receiver has factory drilled and tapped holes to accept a dovetail mount base that is included with the rifle.

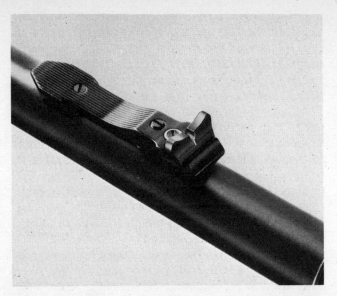

The Williams Dovetail Open Sight slips easily into place and is locked into the dovetail with a "Gib Lock" underneath, tightened by a screw on top. Windage and elevation adjustment are simple and precise.

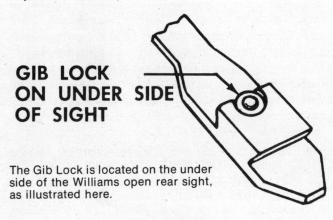

GIB LOCK ON UNDER SIDE OF SIGHT

The Gib Lock is located on the under side of the Williams open rear sight, as illustrated here.

Williams sights offer the option of four different sight blades, any one of which slides into a dovetail slot in the sight.

"SQ"   "U"   "V"   "B"

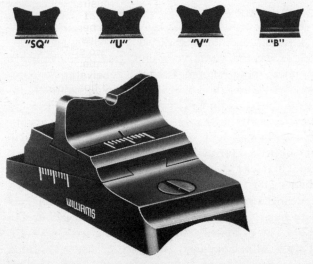

Williams Guide Open Sight consists of three pieces, dovetailed for positive windage and elevation adjustment.

available in white, gold or fluorescent. The latter has the quality of reflecting brightly in almost any light. If you're in the market for a new front sight, I heartily recommend it! Williams' dovetail open rear sight slips smoothly into any standard dovetail notched barrel and is locked there firmly by Williams' exclusive "Gib Lock," a cam on the bottom, tightened from above via a slotted screw head. Elevation is screw adjustable with infinite precision, instead of rough adjustment with a stepped wedge. Windage is affected by moving the male dovetailed blade in the female slotted base, locking it into place with a screw. Four interchangeable blades are offered, with square notch, "V," "U," or with a shallow wide "V," in a variety of heights. When it comes to open rear sights, however, hands down winner is the Williams "Guide," with screw-on base topped by two other dovetailed sections offering easy, positive windage and elevation adjustment. Milled from high tensile alloy and hard-anodized, the unit is compact, lightweight, and offers the same four choices of rear notch shape.

There is no denying that open sights have their disadvantages. They force the shooter's eye to perform some rather unlikely gymnastics, attempting to focus upon three objects at one time, the rear sight usually about 14 to 16 inches away, the front sight from 28 to 34 inches distant, and the target located anywhere from a few feet to a 100 yards away. Young eyes can just about hack it, but if some silver is staining your locks, you know all too well that the rear sight becomes furry as a mad cat's back with advancing age and the onset of farsightedness. Even some younger shooters never advance beyond the stage of mediocrity, because they allow an undisciplined eye to skip from rear sight to front, to target and back again. The result—getting a proper sight picture is impossible. The alternative is to let the sights blur and focus on the target, or focus somewhere between the sights and let everything appear in varying grades of fuzziness. Sounds like a pretty grim prospect, especially if you happen to be pushing 40 or beyond!

Receiver or "Peep" Sights

You may find a happy solution in the aperture or "peep" sight mounted upon the receiver near the eye. The eye looks *through* a receiver sight, *not at it*. Thus the weary eye is obliged to focus only the front sight (which after all is pretty far away even if you're holding your newspaper at arm's length these days), and the distant target—a far easier chore! There is, however, a natural temptation to start skipping again from rear sight to front "just to be sure" that everything is properly lined up. You'll finally learn to accept the fact that your eye will indeed center that front bead or post in the middle of the aperture, allowing you to concentrate upon lining up front sight with the target. About 30 percent increase in sighting radius (the distance from rear sight to front), results in marked improvement in accuracy, as well. Add to this, the fact that a rear peep sight doesn't cover up half of the target as does a notched blade rear, and you begin to realize what an advantage a receiver sight can be.

As mentioned previously, the Lyman 48 receiver sight, designed by the late Townsend Whelen, one of the most revered men in shooting, has been discontinued. However, Lyman continues to manufacture their Series 57 and 66 receiver sights, identical except that the former fits rounded receivers, and the latter fits flat-sided autoloaders, pumps and lever action rifles. Both feature

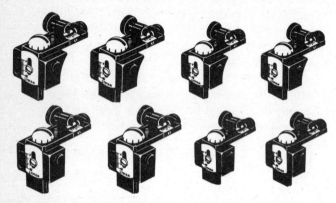

Lyman's Series 57 (top) and 66 (bottom) come with tamper-resistant coin-slotted "Stayset" knobs. The T-slotted base has a quick release button, allowing the male-matching slotted sight bar to slip straight up and out to accommodate a scope or use of open sights.

The Williams Foolproof Receiver Sight is named for the fact that it is easily adjusted with a screwdriver when sighting in, but the countersunk screw heads discourage casual tampering by bystanders when on the range or in the field.

If your eyes aren't quite up to the chore of aligning three objects on widely disparate planes of focus, try a receiver (peep) sight such as this Williams Foolproof mounted on a Remington Nylon 66. Note that the sight is mounted well back, as close to the eye as possible. Sighting radius is also increased.

audible click quarter-minute micrometer screw adjustments for windage and elevation, with either serrated target knobs or finger-proof coin-slotted "Stayset" knobs. The latter are a real boon if you have friends who just can't refrain from tampering with anything that turns. Lyman's series 57/66 are all milled steel, with T-slotted sight bases and adjustable zero plates on the side to help return to the same zero after the sight bar has been removed and replaced. A quick-release button on the side allows instant removal of the sight bar in order to use a flip-up open sight or scope if desired. Both the 57 and 66 come with a pair of interchangeable screw-in aperture discs, a 5⁄8-inch outside diameter disc with a .040-inch opening for target, and a 1⁄2-inch O.D. with .093-inch peep for hunting.

There is widespread sentiment among veteran shooters to remove any and all aperture discs and file them away in a drawer somewhere in the fond hope that they will eventually get lost altogether! That premise is not without merit, except that aging eyes sometimes find that the narrow remaining rim disappears along with the disc. Williams Gun Sight again comes to the rescue with their "Twilight Aperture," with smaller 3⁄8-inch O.D. and .125-inch opening, which is large enough to allow ample light transmission, but still has a sharpening effect upon the target and front sight, much as a smaller diaphragm opening increases depth of field in a camera lens. A bright golden ring is inset around the circumference of the disc, clearly outlining it even under poor lighting conditions. These discs are available as accessories for their FP "Foolproof" receiver sights, which feature countersunk screwdriver-slotted micrometer adjustments for elevation and windage. At right angles to both adjusting screws Williams thoughtfully inserts set screws. Once you sight in the Foolproof it *stays* sighted in! Milled from 85,000 psi alloy, the FP is sturdy, yet weighs only 1½ ounces.

For economy-minded shooters, Williams offers the 5D receiver sight, lacking the micrometer screws, but readily adjustable all the same, and positive locking. It will also accept the Twilight Aperture.

Lighting conditions can vary widely during a day in the field. A day that starts out brightly sunlit might well turn to cloudy before noon. Taking this fact into account, the Merit Gunsight Co. devised their ingenious "Merit Iris Shutter Sighting Disc," which fits all standard receiver sights, with a variable diameter diaphragm like that of a camera lens, only miraculously miniaturized to fit within the Merit #4 disc only ½-inch in diameter and ¼-inch thick! A twist of the knurled disc instantly changes the iris opening from a pinhole .025-inch to a yawning .155-inch, with infinite click-stop adjustments between, allowing the hunter to adjust to bright or dim light. The extremely thin edge of the iris delivers a sharply defined opening. The Merit #3 disc is 11⁄16-inch in diameter, offering apertures from .022-inch to .125-inch. It is available with insert lenses ground to your own prescription, in clear, yellow or Calobar green. A special target version comes with a 1½-inch flexible neoprene light shield and a special steel cup that protects the iris from any stray light that might possibly enter from the rear, resulting in an absolutely black, clear aperture.

When you go to the range to sight in your newly installed receiver sight, you will make the horrifying discovery that even with the sight bar touching the receiver, your front sight just isn't high enough to center your group on the target. The only cure is a higher front sight. But *how much* higher? Thanks to Lyman we have a chart to aid you. Adjust your receiver sight to leave about ⅛-inch of clearance above the receiver, in case you want to lower your point of impact at some future date. Then carefully fire a 10-shot group at 100 yards. Measure the distance from the center of the group to your aiming point. Measure the sight radius. With those two facts at hand, consult the Lyman chart for the proper sight height. (The Lyman chart appears further on in this chapter.)

Scope Sights

It could be argued that a good micrometer receiver sight costs about as much as some scopes. True, some scope sights may sell for just half as much as a Redfield receiver sight, but is it actually better? Small tube cheapie scopes are to my way of thinking, no bargain! They could serve as training scopes for youngsters, but they would soon be outgrown, eventually requiring the purchase of a good scope anyway. Better to start with a quality product!

The primary advantage of any scope over iron sights lies in its ability to pull both essential elements of the sight picture, reticle and target, together, focused into one optical plane. The eye is allowed to "rest," focused on infinity, which is actually its "cruising range." The target is magnified, thus easier to see, and the narrow reticle obscures little if any detail, especially useful when holding high for long-range shots. A scope gathers light rays at the large front objective lens and compresses them into a tight little bundle called the "exit pupil," emerging at the rear ocular lens. Thus the image appears brighter than real life, opening up those deep shadows in woods and brush, and stretching a hunter's day from early light to dusk, when unaided eyes can only peer in puzzlement!

A scope's exit pupil can be clearly seen by holding the scope at arm's length toward a strong light and observing the bright spot visible on the ocular lens. The size of that bright spot provides one definitive way of judging the quality of a scope. If you're at a gun dealer,

Merit Gunsight Co. manufactures a line of variable iris sighting discs. Rotating the knurled rear ring of the discs changes the opening from tiny to large, to meet the needs of varying lighting conditions often encountered afield.

The Williams 5D receiver sight offers high quality at reasonable cost — a consideration that's especially important to the rimfire rifle owner.

Many veteran shooters prefer to remove the sight disc from any receiver sight and use the threaded ring in the sight bar for the rear sight, as you see here.

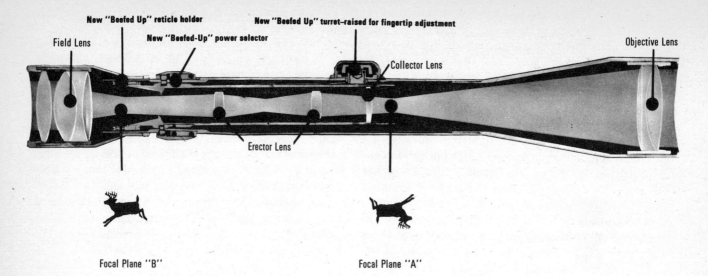

New "Beefed Up" reticle holder
New "Beefed Up" turret—raised for fingertip adjustment
New "Beefed-Up" power selector
Field Lens
Objective Lens
Collector Lens
Erector Lens

Focal Plane "B"
Focal Plane "A"

The primary advantage of a scope over iron sights is that it places the target and the reticle in the same image plane, clearly focused and brighter than life. This diagram shows the path of light from the target, through the lenses to the eye. The target image is focused upside down at focal plane "A," Erector lenses rotate the image 180 degrees at point "B." This image is magnified by the eyepiece lenses before it passes to your eye.

trying to select from two or more scopes, compare the sizes of their exit pupils. All else being equal, choose the one with the largest exit pupil! You can make the same judgement by comparing specifications of various scopes. The diameter of the exit pupil will be listed in the charts in millimeters and represents approximately the *clear* or unobstructed diameter of the objective lens, divided by the scope's *true* (not advertised) power. It is important to have an exit pupil larger than the approximate 5mm pupil diameter of the human eye at dawn or dusk light, or the scope image will begin to fade before it should. During bright midday, the human eye closes down to about 2.5mm, but a large exit pupil is helpful even under these ideal conditions, because it allows you to see the full field of the scope, even if your eye is slightly off center. With the coming of night, the iris of the human eye opens to its maximum of about 7mm, thus a scope with an exit pupil of 7mm or even larger could prove beneficial under extremely poor lighting conditions. Sometimes makers will list a "luminosity" factor, or "relative brightness" rather than the exit pupil. Don't be confused. Just whip out your handy calculator, take the square root, and you're back to the exit pupil again.

Other important factors in comparing scopes are the eye relief and field of view. Eye relief isn't as critical for a rimfire rifle as it is for a bigbore, with its ever-present threat of recoil burying the scope in your forehead. However, you don't want a scope that must repose in your eye socket before you can see through it! Field of view or width of field, is normally listed in feet at 100 yards distance. Again, all else being equal, the wider the field, the better. When tracking running game, a wide field is essential to keep the animal from simply leaping out of the scope, leaving you to wonder, "which way'd he go?"

A good scope aids your eye in yet another way, by improving definition. Under ideal light conditions, the average eye unaided by optics can distinguish detail subtending about 1 inch at 100 yards. Assuming quality optics, a scope will divide this by its own magnification. Thus, you should see ¼-inch detail with a 4X scope and ¹/₆-inch with a 6X, etc.

The term, "resolution," refers to a scope's ability to deliver crisp detail edge-to-edge throughout its entire viewing range, with little or no curvature or distortion at the fringes of its field. An excellent way to check this is to point the scope toward a brick wall, firmly anchored to eliminate shake or trembling, and look to see if the bricks appear to curve inward at the edges, or tend to blur. Also, note if the color appears to fade at the edges. None of these failings should be present in a well-made scope.

Today, nearly all scopes are purged of air and moisture by the factory, then filled with dry nitrogen to eliminate the problem of fogging on inside lens surfaces. However, the effectiveness of the sealing is inversely proportional to the cost of the scope! You can help your scope exclude moisture by leaving the caps off of the adjusting turrets only as long as absolutely necessary to make required sighting-in changes, then replacing them snugly.

On the face of it, you might imagine that the higher power a scope possesses the better it will reveal tiny targets such as ground squirrels at the outer fringes of your rifle's reach, say 100 to 125 yards. Not so! Every

One of the better scopes designed primarily for rimfire rifle use is the Weatherby Mark XXII — it's housed in a graceful ⅞-inch alloy tube, with integral tip-off mount. It's designed to fit most brands of rimfires.

The remarkable Bushnell Custom 22 variable 3X-7X comes with their unique "Bullet Drop Compensator," and two dials, computer calibrated to the trajectories of the standard velocity .22 Long Rifle, and the high velocity loading. The dials are instantly interchangeable by loosening the coin-slotted screw atop the elevation turret.

additional X added to your scope's power subtracts feet from the width of field and dims the light passing through. These factors can be offset to a degree by, in the first instance, enlarging the rear ocular bell and, in the second, enlarging the front objective bell with commensurate increases in lens diameters. Scope designers soon reach a practical limit to these solutions, imposed by the excess bulk that results. Current "wide-field" scopes with oval bell housings fore and aft represent an effort to enjoy the best of both worlds and are fairly successful at it. However, a rimfire rifleman has little need of a fixed-power scope with more power than 4X, or a variable with a higher top value than 6X, unless you want to count the hairs on a woodchuck a football field away!

As you shop for a scope sight to fit your own pet .22 rimfire rifle, bear in mind that it's pretty difficult to go very far wrong. Optically, the cheapest of today's scopes are so much improved over those of my youth, that comparisons are in truth, "odious!" World War II brought with it what seemed to those of us that lived through it, many technical miracles. Notable among these was magnesium fluoride lens coatings, molecularly deposited on the glass-to-air surfaces. At first they were relatively soft and easily scratched, but soon the presently used "hard" coatings came along and cured that problem. Lens coatings had the effect of trapping errant light rays that had previously bounced around merrily inside of our old scopes, reflected from one glass surface to the next and back again, to the point where only about 55 percent of the light was ever allowed to exit the rear. Lens coating increased light transmission to better than 90 percent.

There remains a signifcant gap between what is being done and what could be done. The camera industry is pointing the way with multi-coated lenses, further enhancing image clarity and contrast. Even they are far behind *the state of the art,* as represented by satellite lenses that can virtually read a newspaper from outer space by the light of moon!

Scoping the Rimfire

A rimfire nimrod is just as much in need of a quality scope as a big game hunter, but he balks at spending the same kind of money. Top-of-the-line scopes currently cost as much or more than many rimfire rifles. However, there is happily a middle ground. The Weatherby 4X Mark XXII scope sight is currently the highest in price among scopes designed primarily for rimfire use; however, it is also the tops in quality, sharp and brilliant edge-to-edge of its ample field of 25 feet at 100 yards, with an impressive 7mm exit pupil, boasting big game scope eye relief of 3½ inches, all housed in a streamlined high tensile ⅞-inch diameter alloy tube with graceful integral tip-off mounts that fit most rimfire rifles. For an extra few dollars, you can have Weatherby's exclusive "Lumi-Plex" reticle of electro-formed nickel alloy, luminescent against dark backgrounds. Dual-diameter cross hairs are bold at the sides, fine at the center. Clearly marked windage and elevation adjustment knobs have positive ¼-minute click stops.

Bushnell

Noted for aggressively pursuing the latest technology is Bushnell Optical Company, makers of the fixed-power 4X Custom .22 scope and the variable 3X to 7X

Custom .22. Both scopes feature quality coated optics, plus Bushnell's latest innovation, their "Bullet Drop Compensator." Built right into the elevation adjustment turret, it automatically compensates for bullet drop from 50 yards to 200 with 25-yard increments between. Two dials come with each scope, computer calibrated for the standard velocity .22 Long Rifle, and one for high velocity. A .22 Magnum dial is in the works. In practice, the rifle is simply sighted in at 50 yards. Then for any range out to 200, the shooter dials in the proper reading and holds dead-on. No more holding over one-and-a-half woodchucks to pick off that unwary *hoary marmot* in the next pasture! Bushnell achieves remarkable versatility in mounting their rimfire scopes, courtesy of a male dovetail extruded full length along the base of the black, hard-anodized, high-tensile alloy tubes. Each scope is delivered with a 2¾-inch long alloy mounting block, with back-to-back female dovetails which simultaneously grasp the scope tube and the rifle's grooved receiver, with two opposing Allen head screws cinching the assembly firmly in place. Because the block can be shifted to any spot along the bottom of the scope tube, and/or rifle receiver, it allows complete freedom to choose the best possible position to suit your own requirements for eye relief and scope position.

Many of the higher quality rimfire rifles match the weight and proportions, not to mention the price of comparable big game rifles. Such guns as the Savage/Anschutz Model 54 and Model 164, the Marlin Model 39A or the Weatherby Mark XXII, and the Remington Model 541-S all cry out for 1-inch diameter tube scopes which contain optics of quality commensurate with that of the rifles. Bushnell, Redfield, Weaver, B-Square, etc., offer attractive, secure mounting rings for attaching 1-inch scopes to grooved .22 receivers. Some rimfire rifles such as the Remington Model 541-S, Savage/Anschutz 54, 164, etc., have factory drilled and tapped screw holes in the receiver, as well as the customary male dovetail grooves, to accept conventional screw-on mounts from Buehler, Conetrol, Redfield, etc. This capability opens up a wide array of high quality optics to the rimfire nimrod who wants to match a fine rifle with an equally fine sight.

Because he does much of his shooting at ranges from 25 to 60 yards, the rimfire rifleman may be plagued by positive parallax, in which the image seen in the scope moves side to side or up and down in the same direction when the shooter's eye moves. Most big game scopes are adjusted at the factory to be free of parallax at 100 or 150 yards, depending upon the power. Rimfire scopes are usually parallax-free at 75 yards. During the writing of this book, I polled all of the major scope makers, asking first, "can you set a big game scope to be parallax free at 75 yards, if special ordered through a dealer?" The answer was universally, "Yes!" All of them stated that there would be no additional charge on a new scope so ordered. To the question, "Will you change a used scope to be parallax-free at 75 yards?" Again the answer was a wholehearted, "Yes!" Some stated that a nominal handling charge would be required. Some said that there would be no charge. Thus, if you have a good 1-inch tube scope that you would like to shift to your favorite rimfire rifle, send it back to the maker, with a note explaining that Mr. Twenty-Two sent you!

The Bushnell Banner line of scopes holds some bargains for the smallbore buff. The foot-long fixed-power 4X weighs only 10 ounces; the variable 1.5X to 4X has the same weight, but is 1½ inches shorter while the 11½-inch long 3X to 9X weighs in at just 11 ounces. The ultimate, Supreme Model, is a variable 4X to 12X, with rotating objective bell to adjust for ranges from 50 feet to 1,000 yards (infinity). The Supreme should be saved for those *big* rifles, such as the Savage/Anschutz Model 54, Remington Model 541-S or Weatherby Mark XXII, all of which possess the fine accuracy required to make use of those high X's. This big bell Banner from Bushnell will enable you to shoot the eyes out of a squirrel at 100 yards. None of the standard tip-off mounts are solid enough for mounting this relatively heavy scope. In any case, it must be high enough to clear the rifle barrel at the objective lens. George V. Miller, ramrod at Conetrol Scope Mounts, Sequin, Texas, has thoughtfully come up with excellent rimfire mounts. His streamlined mount bases and cleverly contrived projectionless rings have long been favorites with owners of fine centerfire rifles because of their strength and beauty! The Conetrol ring is made up of two halves and a tiny cap that mates them at the top. The three components are machined and polished assembled. Thus, once installed the ring appears to be one piece! The Conetrol "Daptor" mount bases will slip onto any grooved receiver, clamped securely by Allen screws. However, if the rifle is drilled and tapped, as are the Model 54 and Remington 541-S, it is better to use the standard Conetrol bases.

All of the Bushnell Banner line come with dual-diameter "Multi-X" reticle and the Bullet-Drop Compensator built-in. Four interchangeable BDC dials accompany each scope. Three are calibrated for standard centerfire cartridges. The fourth is left blank for the shooter to record his own readings. It's a simple matter for you to sight in your .22 rimfire at 50 yards and record the settings for other yardages as far as you can see!

Leupold

During the past 30 years, there has been a tendency on the part of scope makers to increase the size and weight of their products to improve performance, resulting, in some cases, in trombone-sized tubes with enormous objective bells—OK for heavy-barreled varmint rifles or bench rest matches, but unhandy in the field, and certainly counterproductive as far as use on

Either the Bushnell Custom 22 variable (top) or the fixed power 4X (bottom) can be sighted in at 50 yards. Then all ranges beyond are simply dialed in on the elevation knob. You have to try it to believe it!

Bushnell's Banner line of 1-inch tube scopes offers quality at reasonable cost. The Bushnell Banner 4X-12X (top) offers top magnification plus an objective bell adjustable for any range down to 50 feet! It is practical only on *big* rifles, such as the Remington M-541S. The variable 1.5X-4X (bottom) is short and light enough to fit well on nearly any standard-sized rimfire rifle.

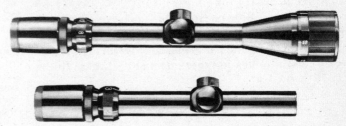

Conetrol Scope Mounts offer owners of high-priced rimfire rifles the ability to match the quality of the gun with a like-quality mount. Conetrol "Daptor" mount bases will fit on grooved receivers, clamped securely by Allen screws. Then any of three optional heights of sleek Conetrol super-smooth projectionless rings can be used.

This diagram (printed courtesy of Leupold), illustrates the reason rimfire shooters encounter parallax problems when using bigbore scopes on .22 rifles. When the target is too close, the scope adjusted parallax-free at 100 to 150 yards exhibits positive parallax. That is the target appears to move the same direction, as the eye is shifted behind the scope. All of the major scope manufacturers polled by the author stated that they would adjust scopes to suit the customer's rimfire needs. Request your scope set for 75 yards.

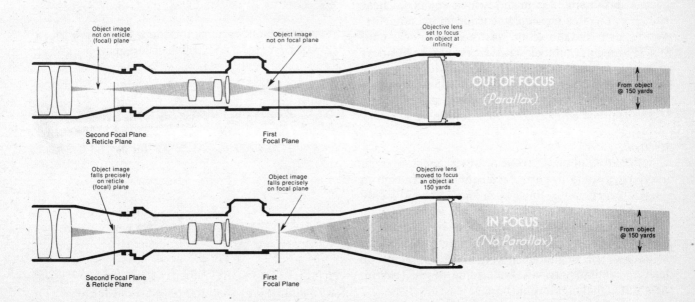

rimfire rifles is concerned! Finally, someone has turned the tables. Leupold is newly out with a duo of miniaturized scopes, the M8-2.5X Compact and the M8-4X Compact that just fill the bill for size and weight where standard-sized rimfires are concerned. The 2.5X Compact even looks right at home on the Ruger 10/22 Carbine! Leupold's newly developed optical/ mechanical designs feature optimum balance between magnification, field and eye relief, compressed into minimum practical dimensions—8½ inches for the 2.5X and 10.3 inches for the 4X. Respective weights are 7.4 and 8.5 ounces. Both boast ample 4-inch eye relief, with fields of 42 and 26.5 feet at 100 yards. But the amazing thing is how Leupold has managed to retain their famed crisp, bright optics in these minimal packages! In the

Leupold's new M8-2.5X Compact scope blends perfectly into the trim lines of this Ruger 10/22 Carbine, with Leupold STD mount base and rings. The light weight and small dimensions of this new scope make it ideally suited for medium-to-small rimfire rifles whose owners nonetheless demand quality optics.

LEUPOLD RETICLES

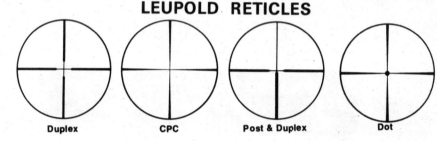

Leupold pioneered the extremely popular dual-diameter crosshairs with their famed "Duplex" reticle in 1962. They also offer the CPC wide-narrow-wide crosshair reticle, Post and Duplex, and CPC with dot.

Duplex   CPC   Post & Duplex   Dot

evening long after my eyes ceased to define detail in a tree across the yard, the Leupold M8-2.5X clearly revealed the pattern of the bark! These two scopes are as solid an investment as pure gold bullion!

Lyman

William Lyman established the Lyman Gun Sight Company in 1878. For many years, it was a family owned and operated company which enjoyed a near monopoly on reloading equipment and telescope sights. The Lyman Alaskan scope was the one to beat until WWII brought a number of new firms into the business with war-developed technical skills. In its centennial year, 1978, Lyman made new wide-appeal scope of variable 2X to 7X power, relatively short at 11⅝ inches, and weighing a conservative 10½ ounces.

Redfield

Redfield Traditional fixed power scopes are relatively reasonable in cost, yet unquestionably high in quality. The 2½X, is 10¼ inches long and weighs only 8½ ounces; the 4X, is 11⅜ inches long, and weighs 9¾ ounces. Exclusive with Redfield is the ¾-inch diameter tube 4X, scaled down from the big four, to 9⅜-inch length and amazing 6-ounce weight. This petite scope has undeniable eye appeal on a medium to small rimfire rifle, such as the Browning auto.

Lyman Gun Sight recently introduced their new 2X-7X variable, for use on larger rimfire rifles.

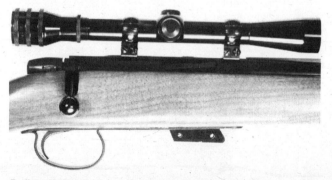

Petite dimensions of the Redfield 4X ¾-inch tube scope for rimfire rifles is apparent on this Remington Model 581. Redfield rings are used on grooved receiver.

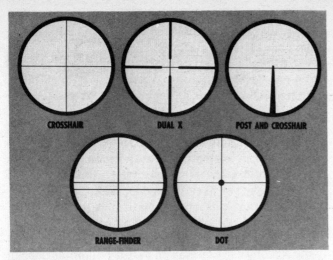

Weaver offers a variety of reticles. The author prefers either the Dual X or the Range-Finder. The latter has two horizontal wires, a heavy wire centered and another measuring just 6 inches lower at 100 yards. If you sight in at 50 yards, that second wire should be just about on at 100 yards using high velocity ammo.

This Weaver K4 fixed power scope (top) is a good example of outstanding quality at a remarkably reasonable cost. (Bottom) Weaver's excellent Model V4.5-W features a wide field, notably smooth power transition, and that firm's new "Micro-Trac."

Cutaway of Weaver Model V9-W illustrates the complexity of the instrument that so many of us take completely for granted.

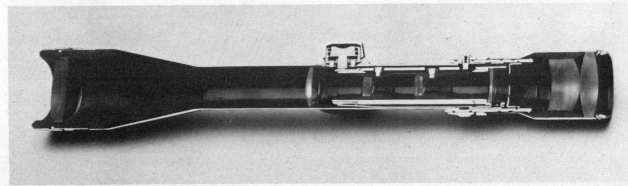

Weaver

William R. Weaver began making scope sights in the early 1930's. It was 12 years after that when I bought a used Savage lever action Model 99 with Weaver 330 scope already mounted. I was pretty impressed with that scope, my first, and *only* for a long time! It was tough as only steel tubing could make it, and between the three of us, we made a pretty good team. Weaver scopes are still made of steel, but by state-of-the-art methods—cold-form swaged from a steel blank that begins the diameter of the objective bell. The molecular structure of the steel is compressed in the process, further toughening the finished tube. Steel strength might not seem all that important to the average rimfire hunter, until sometime on a pack trip when a fractious bronc kicks your rifle and sends it cartwheeling down the trail. You might dent a Weaver scope, but you'd play hell breaking it! The tubes are finished to a high luster on a centerless grinder, and finished to a deep blue-black. The strength of Weaver scopes comes at a price—one that most of us are well willing to pay—they weigh slightly more than comparable scopes with alloy tubes. For example the K4, 11¾ inches long, weighs 12 ounces, 2¼ ounces more than the 4X Redfield International. However, it is slightly less expensive. Weaver's top-of-the-line Model V4.5-W (wide field) is well proportioned for man-sized .22 rifles, at 10⅜ inches long, 15 ounces. This rugged scope exhibits a notably smooth power transition from 1.5X to 4.5X, and features Weaver's new "Micro-Trac" internal windage and elevation adjustments, utilizing carbide ball bearings at all four contact points with the erector tube. This results in consistent, repeatable adjustments, without the irritating "crosswalk," wherein one adjusts, say for elevation and finds the windage shifts unpredictably at the same time.

With an eye to the youngster's pocketbook, Weaver manufactures three rimfire scopes of good quality at reasonable prices—the fixed power D4 and D6 (with "Dual X Reticles"), and the V22 variable 3X to 6X. I recommend the latter for its versatility and superior optics. Also from Weaver is the unique "Qwik-Point," but you'll hear more of that later.

Mounting Your Scope

Installing a tip-off mounted scope on a rimfire rifle consists of tightening two screws—the easiest do-it-yourself job of all time! However, if you purchase your scope from a gun dealer, let him install it—you may save yourself some ammunition. Chances are he'll bore sight it for you with one of the sight collimating devices, such as the Sweany Site-A-Line or Bushnell's Bore Sighter. Then when you repair to the range to sight in, your first shots should be in the black at 50 yards! Don't make the mistake of asking the gunsmith to sight your rifle in for you. No two people hold a gun exactly the same way. What works for him could be inches off when you shoot. For that reason, let your youngsters sight in their own rifles. The process is educational as well, demonstrating to them at the outset just how important it is to have their guns properly sighted, in order to make contact with that ubiquitous tin can or paper bull's-eye.

Lacking an obliging gunsmith, you could acquire one of Bushnell's new TruScope collimators, selling under $25, and be forever independent. The minimal cost is soon amortized in saved ammo during sighting of various rifles and scopes. It works on the same principle as a professional device, comprised of a sturdy dark gray plastic housing about the size of a cigarette pack, containing an optical sight collimator at the top and a steel, expandable arbor at the bottom. It comes with one arbor, only. Be certain to specify .22 caliber! You can purchase the other two arbors, to cover calibers up to .45. In use, the arbor is inserted into the bore of your .22 rifle and secured there by tightening a knurled knob. Then you merely look through your scope and align the cross hairs with those in the collimator. After making minor corrections at the range for final sighting, you return the TruScope to the muzzle of your rifle, again look through the scope, note the position of the scope's cross hairs in relation to those of the collimator, record that data on a small card provided with the TruScope, and insert that card into the plastic cap for the device. Thereafter, you can take the TruScope with you on hunting trips and use it to check your scope from time to time. It comes in especially handy if you should happen to bump your scope, possibly disturbing its zero. A number of blank charts are provided, so that different rifles can be calibrated. If the scope on any one of them is accidently knocked off zero, it can be quickly re-aligned without firing a shot! Bushnell's TruScope will not work on rifles with muzzle-length, tubular, under-barrel magazines.

Sighting In a Scoped .22

Meanwhile, back at the range—the only way to sight in your rifle is from a bench rest with sandbags for support. Trying to sight in on a rock across some windy

(Above and below) Bushnell's professional quality Bore Sighter is used by many gunsmiths to align the customer's sight with the rifle bore. Three expandable arbors fit anything from .22 to .45 caliber.

Sighting in is made easier with the use of Bushnell's Tru-Scope pocket-sized bore sighter. Align the scope's cross hairs with those in the TruScope, and you should be within inches of the bull's-eye at 50 yards.

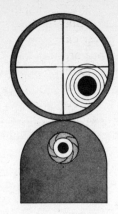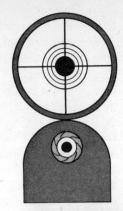

If a bore collimator is not available, you can bore sight your rifle by sighting through the bore at the bull's-eye, then without moving the rifle, correct the position of your scope's cross hairs to quarter the bull.

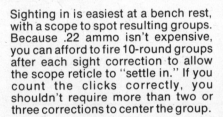

Sighting in is easiest at a bench rest, with a scope to spot resulting groups. Because .22 ammo isn't expensive, you can afford to fire 10-round groups after each sight correction to allow the scope reticle to "settle in." If you count the clicks correctly, you shouldn't require more than two or three corrections to center the group.

wash is eminently unsatisfactory! I know, I've tried it innumerable times! You'll want a spotting scope—unless you need the exercise—and a dime. No, not to phone for help—just to turn the adjusting dials on your new scope. Hopefully, you saved the instruction sheet that came with the scope, therefore you know what the clicks or graduations represent. For example, the clicks on a Weatherby Mark XXII scope represent ¼-minute of angle, or about ¼-inch at 100 yards. The graduations on the friction dial of a Weaver .22 scope stand for 1-inch at 100 yards. Remember to double the number of clicks at 50 yards, and multiply them by four at 25 yards.

It's advisable to fire your first groups at 25 yards. Then, even if your rifle wasn't bore sighted, you should be on the paper. Fire a 10-shot group to allow the reticle of your scope to "settle in." Then take note of the group's position and make appropriate corrections. A word here about targets. Buy some Williams Gun Sight Co.'s "Dial Scoring" targets with radial lines fanning out from the bull's-eye to each point of the clock. You'll be money ahead because of the ammo you'll save! Put one Williams Dial Scoring target on the holder at 25

yards and keep one on the bench beside you. After firing your group, check in the scope to see the center of impact. Mark that on the target at your side. With the help of the radial lines, you will have no trouble getting it in exactly the correct position. Measure the distance in inches to the vertical line of the target for the needed windage correction—ditto the horizontal line for elevation correction. Turn the scope adjustment knobs accordingly and fire another 10-shot group. It should be right on. If not, make the final fine adjustment.

If you're only sighting for a plinking session, that's the end of it. If you plan to go hunting small game, move your target to 50 yards. You can zero in at 50, unless you expect some long-range shooting. In that case, sight in about an inch high at 50 yards, and you will be dead-on at about 70 yards, and require about 5 inches holdover at 100 yards, using high velocity hollow point ammunition. Which brings up another point—always sight in with the same ammo that you plan to hunt with. A change of type or even a change of brands of the same type, could change your point of impact enough to miss a squirrel at 30 yards.

After sighting in, take some time to shoot from various field positions, including offhand, to confirm your group placement. You may find your groups shifting somewhat from the sandbag results. Group position may even be different for the various positions. If the pattern is consistent, record this data and review it before venturing afield, so that you can compensate accordingly. If the groups move around unpredictably, you're not holding your rifle consistently, and you'll have to practice a bit more!

Sighting In Iron and Receiver Sights

Maybe you opted for iron sights instead of a scope. Perhaps you even elected to use the open sights that came with the gun. There was a time when manufacturers would sight in every rifle leaving their plant, but precious few observe that formality these days! So it's likely that you'll have to sight in the open sights yourself. It doesn't improve the appearance of the rear sight to hammer it willy-nilly back and forth in the dovetail slot with a ball peen. Better to interpose something twixt hammer and sight—say a brass drift punch. It requires a certain nicety of judgement to strike the sight just enough to move a group ½-inch at 50 yards. I usually

tap the punch lightly at first, increasing the weight of the blows until something moves and just hope for the best! Make coarse elevation adjustments by pushing back the step elevator wedge, and fine changes by loosening the screw that holds the notch piece in the sight (if it comes so equipped) and move it up or down as required. If your sight lacks the moveable notch piece, and the steps in the wedge are either to low or too high, there's nothing for it but to go to the step that's just a little high, and file it down with a Swiss file to the proper height. Bear in mind, that the group always moves in the *same direction* as the rear sight, and in the *opposite* direction of any movement of the front sight.

If you harkened to my earlier advice and purchased an aperture receiver sight, making the needed adjustments is a breeze, but you may find that you have another problem! Even with the crossbar of the receiver sight almost touching the receiver, the line of sight is likely going to be higher than that of the original open sights, meaning that you're going to need a higher front sight. The best way to determine the proper height for the new sight is to fire some test groups at 100 yards. Then consult the accompanying chart below, published with the courtesy of Lyman, to see what sight height you'll need.

AMOUNT OF ADJUSTMENT NECESSARY TO CORRECT FRONT SIGHT ERROR

DISTANCE BETWEEN FRONT AND REAR SIGHTS		14″	15″	16″	17″	18″	19″	20″	21″	22″	23″	24″	25″	26″	27″	28″	29″	30″	31″	32″	33″	34″
Amount of Error at 100 Yards Given in Inches	1	.0038	.0041	.0044	.0047	.0050	.0053	.0055	.0058	.0061	.0064	.0066	.0069	.0072	.0074	.0077	.0080	.0082	.0085	.0088	.0091	.0093
	2	.0078	.0083	.0089	.0094	.0100	.0105	.0111	.0116	.0122	.0127	.0133	.0138	.0144	.0149	.0155	.0160	.0156	.0171	.0177	.0182	.0188
	3	.0117	.0125	.0133	.0142	.0150	.0159	.0167	.0175	.0184	.0192	.0201	.0209	.0217	.0226	.0234	.0243	.0251	.0259	.0268	.0276	.0285
	4	.0155	.0167	.0178	.0189	.0200	.0211	.0222	.0234	.0244	.0255	.0266	.0278	.0289	.0300	.0311	.0322	.0333	.0344	.0355	.0366	.0377
	5	.0194	.0208	.0222	.0236	.0250	.0264	.0278	.0292	.0306	.0319	.0333	.0347	.0361	.0375	.0389	.0403	.0417	.0431	.0445	.0458	.0472
	6	.0233	.0250	.0267	.0283	.0300	.0317	.0333	.0350	.0367	.0384	.0400	.0417	.0434	.0450	.0467	.0484	.0500	.0517	.0534	.0551	.0567

EXAMPLE: Suppose your rifle has a 27 inch sight radius, and shoots 4 inches high at 100 yards, with the receiver sight adjusted as low as possible. The 27-inch column shows that the correction for a 4-inch error is .0300 inch. This correction is added to the over-all height of the front sight (including dovetail). Use a micrometer or similar accurate device to measure sight height. Thus, if your original sight measured .360 inch, it should be replaced with a sight .390 inch high, such as a J height sight.

The Marlin 39A with Glenfield 400A scope. Here the front ring and the internal adjustment bell positions combine to place the scope too far to the rear for proper eye relief.

Merit Gunsight Co. manufactures this tiny suction cup attachment (far left) with variable iris, for your shooting glasses, to sharpen up those open sights and target! Center is Williams Foolproof receiver sight with Merit variable iris peep disc installed. Last is Merit target disc with variable iris and large rubber eyecup to exclude stray light from the rear.

Scopes for Handguns

Smallbore handgunners will find that most of the foregoing advice fits their situation aptly as well. Thompson/Center Contender owners will be interested in the new Foolproof sight from Williams. It makes an already eye-catching gun that much more impressive and adds the ease and precision of real micrometer adjustment, plus an improved sight picture, with deep square notch. If you habitually hold your Contender close in a two-handed grip, you might like the Foolproof with Twilight aperture. Because recoil is not a factor with .22 caliber T/C barrels, it is practical to position the gun close enough to use a peep rear sight.

The Contender is an ideal handgun for scope use, extremely accurate and lends itself to two-handed holding. Thompson/Center markets its own pair of pistol scopes, the Lobo 1½X and 3X, along with appropriate mounts for their own gun, as well as the Ruger Blackhawk and Smith & Wesson K and N frame revolvers. Both Lobos share the same octagonal extruded ⅞-inch tube with bottom mounting rail. However, the 3X model has an enlarged objective bell to gather in a bit more light. Even so, the relative brightness drops from 127 for the 1½X to 49 for the 3X. The principal advantage offered by a scope on a handgun is a precise sight picture, *not* magnification. Increasing the scope's power narrows the field and limits lateral eye relief, as well as increasing the apparent tremors of the sight. In general, the less power in a handgun scope, the better! Both Lobos are shock proof, a factor of importance with hard-kicking bigbores, but not with a rimfire, and both feature micrometer windage and elevation adjustments.

Leupold seems to have struck a happy medium with their M8-2X long-eye-relief scope. Originally designed to allow mounting ahead of the receiver on the Winchester Model 94 top-ejecting .30-30 lever action rifle, it was quickly adopted by bigbore pistol buffs as the perfect glass for mule-kicking magnums. It works equally well on rimfire pistols, using Leupold's own mount on the Contender, or Maynard P. Buehler's wide range of pistol mounts that fit the Contender, Smith & Wesson K frames and Model 41, Colt's Woodsman, Ruger's Blackhawks and .22 autoloaders, Hi-Standard's Trophy and Citation .22's, and the spectacular Remington XP-100.

As this book goes to press, we received a release stating that the M8-2X now has a brother, the M8-4X, with the same long eye relief to allow use on handguns or mounted ahead of the receiver on any rifle that ejects spent brass straight up instead of off to the side. The new 4X shares the same rugged innards that allows it to withstand severe recoil of bigbore handguns. Although not an important consideration for the smallbore buff, it is reassuring to know that your scope is in effect shockproof! More to the point, the Leupold M8-4X is short, light and bright!

Leupold's new M8-4X mounted on a Smith & Wesson via Leupold's own STD mount. The higher magnification costs something in terms of heavier weight and more bulk, plus a reduction in width of field. However, some shooters happily accept those handicaps to get the greater image size.

Here's the Williams sight with Twilight Aperture and target adjusting knobs on Thompson/Center Contender.

The Leupold M8-2X long eye relief scope mounted on a Ruger .22 autoloader, using a Buehler mount base and rings. The fixed receiver of the Ruger is well adapted to scope mounting.

"Dot-Point" Optics

A relatively new generation of optical sights is beginning to find favor with American shooters. Variously known by such trade names as "Single Point," "Qwik-Point," and "Aimpoint," they provide no magnification of the target, but merely superimpose a colored dot of light over it. They don't require precise positioning of the eye directly behind the tube, as does a scope. If the eye is off somewhat, the dot is still visible, and there is no parallax problem. This fact accounts in large measure for the speed with which the sights can be used. They are so quick to find the target, that they are widely used on shotguns as well as rifles. For plinking aerial targets with a .22 rimfire, they are without peer! Such sights are also excellent for tracking running rabbits. Given a handy autoloader such as the Remington Nylon 66 and one of the "dot" sights, you can pick up a moving target, establish the proper lead, and get off a hit in record time!

The Single Point is an English import, available by mail order from MK-V, P.O. Box 5337, Orange, CA 92667. It consists of a single 1-inch diameter tube, with an expanded portion amidships holding the windage and elevation adjustment dials, and an enlarged objective bell. Forward is a translucent tip of plastic to gather ambient light and compress it into a bright red dot. Any standard 1-inch mount can be used, such as tip-off rings from Bushnell, Redfield, Weaver, etc.

The Aimpoint AB is a Swedish invention, available from Aimpoint USA, 29351 Stonecrest Road, Rancho Palos Verdes, CA 90274. While the price may be a little high, be assured that there is ample value received! The sight is well constructed to withstand bigbore recoil, and exhibits obvious quality fabrication. It consists of twin tubes of lightweight alloy, joined in a horizontal figure 8, with an integral dovetail that mates with any of the standard Weaver style scope mount bases. The over-the-bore mounted tube is for looking through at the target. The second tube offset to the right side, provides the battery chamber and electronic magic that projects the diode-lighted red dot into the sighting tube. The sighting tube is provided fore and aft with removable polaroid filters to cope with excessive brightness of existing light. Rotating the rear polaroid filter varies the effect. Under low light conditions, the filters are removed entirely. At the rear of the right-hand tube is a dial that turns the light on and off, and varies the intensity of the light to suit existing ambient lighting conditions. At night, for example, the light could be kept very dim, while a brightly sunlit day might call for maximum brightness in the dot also. The dot subtends approximately 3 minutes of angle (3 inches at 100 yards). Battery life is hardly a worry, with a projected 500 to 1000 hours on tap. Windage and elevation adjustments are provided within the mount.

The Qwik-Point, from W.R. Weaver Co., is made up

One of the new generation of optical rifle sights, the Single Point, is mounted here upon a Remington Nylon 66 using Bushnell 1-inch rings. The sight mates well with an autoloader, being designed for quick off-hand firing at moving targets.

of two tubes stacked vertically over the bore. The bottom see-through tube projects a blaze-orange dot out to the image plane of your target, without regard to distance, parallax, etc. The top tube has a lucite light-gathering knob up front, plus internal windage and elevation adjustments like those found on Weaver scopes. The sight incorporates an integral tip-off mount to fit any standard rimfire dovetail.

The author tested all three sights and, as might be expected, discovered good and bad points in each. The Single Point is the most compact, with but one tube, which contains the bright red dot. Because the front end is closed, you can't see through it. Both eyes must therefore be open. An optical illusion places the dot over the image of the target, as viewed by the left eye (if right-handed shooter). Because my shooting eye (right eye) is my master eye, and the other is a little weak, I found this a disadvantage. However, several other people who used the sight at the same time, found it no problem at all. Even I was able to use it for quick shots on a variety of targets at different ranges. But if I attempted to hold on a bull's-eye, I found the dot tended to wander a bit.

The Aimpoint is a beautiful piece of equipment, about on a par with a quality Swiss watch. I would have liked to see the open tube slightly larger in diameter. It seemed to intrude into my mind, when I should have been thinking only of the target. Likely that feeling would disappear with a little practice. The importance of stock fit cannot be ignored with any of these sights.

The Swedish Aimpoint AB mounted upon a Marlin 39A, using the integral Weaver-styled mount. With its battery-powered diode-lit aiming spot, the Aimpoint is the only one that is practical for use at night, or under very low light levels.

This is Weaver's Qwik-Point mounted on a bolt action rimfire rifle. Not too great a combination. Better to mount it on an autoloader, lever action or pump! Note the Qwik-Point has its own integral tip-off mount.

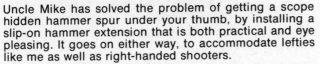

Uncle Mike has solved the problem of getting a scope hidden hammer spur under your thumb, by installing a slip-on hammer extension that is both practical and eye pleasing. It goes on either way, to accommodate lefties like me as well as right-handed shooters.

As with a shotgun, the gun should shoulder and be on-target without conscious aiming. Then the dot would simply *be there* when you needed it. The Aimpoint is the only one of the three that could be used in the near absence of ambient light. Where night hunting is legal, it would be a true blessing!

Obviously most inviting in terms of price is the Weaver Qwik-Point. It was also handiest to use. The see-through tube is large and easy to find. The dot remained brightly visible even as light waned late in the evening. As with the Aimpoint, it can be used with both eyes open or with only one, as desired. I don't know why every shotgun owner doesn't have one of these on his field guns! And as mentioned above, they are certainly the ticket for picking off running game at moderate ranges. In target testing, the Qwik-Point and Aimpoint both fired groups that were better than those made with normal open sights, and often nearly as good as those resulting from the use of a scope, although they were certainly not designed for punching paper.

Hammer Extensions for Scope-Sighted Lever Guns

Various rimfire rifles and handguns with visible hammers sometimes present problems with low-lying scopes blocking access to the hammer spurs. Michaels of Oregon, better known as "Uncle Mike's," has come up with a practical and attractive solution in the form of a round knurled knob that slips on the hammer from either side, locking with a small Allen-head screw. They are available for the Winchester 9422, Thompson/Center Contender, the Marlin Model 39, and Browning BL-22

Summary

The preceding information should help you in making your decision where rimfire rifle or handgun sights are concerned. The .22 is often taken too casually by sportsmen who feel the little rimfire is merely a fun gun. Granted, it's indeed a "fun gun" but it is certainly deserving of a good sighting system. A good .22 rifle is capable of delivering 1-inch groups at 100 yards providing the shooter does his part and the gun is equipped with *quality* sights. When and if you decide to buy a scope for your favorite rimfire be sure that scope is a good one—one that will enhance the usability and accuracy of the rifle it's mounted on.

If you are satisfied with the iron sights that came on your .22, then by all means use them, making sure they're properly adjusted. The ultimate choice of sights is, of course, left up to you; just be sure *your* sights are firmly mounted, properly adjusted and regulated for the rimfire fodder you'll be shooting.

CHAPTER 4

Practical Plinking

THE WORD "PLINKING" is defined by the *Shooter's Bible Small Arms Lexicon and Concise Encyclopedia* as, "the sport of shooting novelty targets at random distances with rifle or pistol." That leaves a lot of room for imagination—and that's all to the good! For your information, I would like to include a wider range of shooting pastimes within the parameters of plinking. In addition to the usual "novelty targets" (tin cans, Necco wafers, animal silhouettes, etc.), I will encompass an entertaining encounter with instinctive aiming at aerial and stationary targets, some tales of trick shooters past and present, some sidelights on the art of fast draw, past and present, and some practical practice preparatory to the big game hunt.

The age old art of plinking dates back to the days of Dan'l Boone, when the target consisted of a fire-charred board with an "X" scratched down to the stark white beneath to provide an aiming point. Whoever put his round ball closest to the intersection of the "X" was winner of such practical prizes as a live pig or a demi-john of white lightnin', and was, of course, hero for the day! Another form of an early-day plinking party was the "turkey shoot," with real live turkeys. The birds were crated so they could stick their heads out through the slats. The crate was placed behind a log at some considerable distance so that the only aiming point was the turkey's ducking, bobbing head—that is, when it chose to stick its neck out!

Youngsters of bygone years could enjoy the carefree pursuit of plinking a short bike ride away from a rural community, in wide open countryside, with little concern for ricochets or stray bullets. Today those wide open spaces are much harder to find. The local rifle range may be the only choice for most young plinkers.

There still exist small islands of semi-undeveloped land, where the lucky plinker can while away a few hours with his .22 rifle.

Present-day plinkers have no such delightful contests to attend, but they can still enjoy some of the camaraderie of like-thinking friends and companions, seeking nothing but a day of shooting entertainment with no more at stake than a round of beers for the boys at a nearby pub, courtesy of the least talented, or *least lucky* marksman of the day.

Youngsters of prior years enjoyed the carefree pursuits of plinking. They could repair to the local hardware store or gunshop and come away with an afternoon's fun, packaged 50 to the box. A short bike ride away was ample open country where rabbits abounded, and lacking live targets, tin cans served as well. Now, a young man or lady requires a parent in tow to purchase a box of .22 ammo, and the once wide open spaces are literally seas of shake shingle roofs, stretching as far as the eye can see in every direction. At what price do we embrace this ogre called "civilization?"

I was fortunate enough to grow up at a time when the

great Owens Valley in California still consisted mostly of just space, with only the battered shack of an occasional desert rat breaking the cactus-studded horizon line. My link from Los Angeles to this plinker's heaven-on-earth was a battered Model A Ford coupe that overheated at the drop of a radiator hose. Somehow it transported five jubilant boys and their .22 rifles to the Littlerock City Dump, in the Lancaster/Palmdale area, where a wealth of tin cans challenged our marksmanship. Abandoned car bodies defied the penetration of our mighty rimfires, and myriad bottles stood ready to disintegrate in sunlit showers of dazzling diamonds! The surrounding clumps of sage and prickly pear served up a steady supply of energetic four-legged legal targets that more often than not escaped unscathed from our misdirected barrages.

For many years, city dumps have been happy hunting grounds for youthful aspiring nimrods. My Alaskan guide of several years back admitted without apology that he began his hunting career in the city dump of Chicago, picking off disease-bearing rats with his .22. No more such innocent pleasures! Presently, plinking is confined to the increasingly rare islands of bare land, isolated by concrete ribbons of interstate highways jammed with bumper-to-bumper traffic. Should you discover such an island in the sea of urban sprawl, guard it as jealously as you would a favored fishing hole!

Plinking—The Safe Way

An excellent place to search for those bits of forgotten territory is along the meandering country roads that have been all but abandoned after they were by-passed by the high-rise interstates. All you really need is an isolated piece of ground with a soft dirt bank behind it to soak up your bullets after they pass through the targets of your choice, and an area far enough removed from human habitation so that the innocent "pop" of your .22 won't bring down a brace of state troopers upon your head. Unfortunately, plinking cannot be quite as carefree as of old, when you could pick random targets in a 360-degree circle, firing without regard to the final destination of the bullet. These days it's pretty difficult to get *that* far away from the works of man!

Always be assured of a safe backstop! Dry riverbeds with high embankments on both sides offer ideal plinking territory. Given a sharp turn in the river on both ends, you can hazard shots in just about any direction save straight up, without fear of tagging some unwanted target in the distance. However, take care in shooting across any large body of water. A .22 bullet can skip along the surface, sometimes taking off into the air again, high enough to clear the opposite bank, destination *unknown!* Avoid rocky backstops that might ricochet bullets or flecks of rock off into space.

Once my wife and I were standing side-by-side as I and a friend plinked at tin cans set up among a clump of rocks. Suddenly my wife let out an "Ouch!" and

A row of empty .22 cartridge cases and some Necco wafers offer dual levels of challenge to suit the abilities of the various marksmen and their guns. Youngsters like to see something explode or disappear when hit!

Animal crackers are "big game" to small-fry with big imaginations! The targets explode in a satisfying manner, are inexpensive and are biodegradeable.

reached down to a spot of blood on her leg. Incredibly, a piece of rock had been driven back from a distance of about 30 yards, with sufficient force to penetrate her skin! She was understandably gun shy for some time after that!

There is a great temptation, especially in what appears to be unspoiled wilderness, to plink at a pine cone dangling high in a tree, or a rabbit tantalizingly silhouetted against the skyline. However, this type of target presents harrowing hazards to the unaware. Either shot could result in a clean miss, or the bullet could completely penetrate, with ample energy left to speed off into space—and a totally unpredictable destination. The long familiar admonition, "Dangerous within one mile," has been updated by most makers to extend that red zone out to a 1½-mile radius. How many places do you know where you can reach out in any direction the length of 26 football fields without encountering livestock or people, or a building of some kind, even if it's only an outhouse.

I've encountered those venerable structures with a half-moon cut into the door, literally riddled with bullet holes! Can you imagine the occupant's reaction? The shooting fraternity can ill afford such irresponsible displays. Equally inexcusable is the practice of shooting up old buildings in the few remaining ghost towns that

form a romantic reminder of our early-day heritage.

Only a dearth of imagination limits target selection. There are the ubiquitous tin cans, milk cartons, dirt clods, etc., but *please,* NO BOTTLES! Shards of non-biodegradable glass cluttering the landscape do nothing to improve the public image of shooters. Crush and bury or carry away bullet-riddled tin cans, as well. Leave the land cleaner than you found it!

Games Plinkers Play

Plinking at random targets can be a delightful means of whiling away the time, but somehow it palls rather quickly if totally lacking in direction. Adding an element of competition to your plinking, even to the point of making a harmless wager, will add spice to an already entertaining pastime.

A case of clay pigeons offers infinite possibilities. You could line them up on a dirt bank in threes, for each contestant, and whoever breaks all of his birds first is the winner. If you make it a rule to reduce the round discs to powder, each shooter will be obliged to shoot at the remaining segments of his birds as they become increasingly smaller and more difficult to hit. If there are more than three in your party, you'd better appoint one of them as judge, alternating the position with each game. Some rather spirited controversies can spring up when the contestants finish in a close heat! You may have to work out some sort of handicapping system when you find an autoloader shooter pitted against someone with a bolt action, etc.

A couple of really redoubtable marksmen might line up a row of empty .22 cartridge cases and see who can pick off the most in a given time limit. If the tiny targets are "too easy" standing upright, try shooting at them with just the bases pointed your way! Kids are fasci-

The ubiquitous tin can, usually a former beer container, is head and shoulders above all other targets for the plinker. Carry them away with you, or burn, crush and bury them!

nated by animal crackers, especially if the crackers represent big game animals—lions, tigers, elephants, etc. Along the same line, animal silhouettes, full-sized or reduced, are interesting and informative targets, especially for the embryonic nimrod in your family. If you set them up along a predetermined route, at unexpected intervals, at varied ranges, and partially hidden by brush, you can duplicate most of the excitement and thrills of a real hunt while instilling some sugar-coated training at the same time.

How about lighting kitchen matches, or blowing out candles? Both are visually impressive demonstrations of unerring aim! Any exploding target, from eggs and oranges to small tin cans of water, will elicit squeals of pure delight from the small-fry. When you have conquered all of the above targets and begin to feel pretty smug about the whole thing, that's time to try cutting

crossed strings, a stunt indulged in widely back in the days of the slender, graceful Pennsylvania rifle. Let me warn you, this can be a humbling experience! Those two threads can be mighty elusive.

Necco candy wafers are about the cheapest "bustable" targets available, and they're small enough to be challenging. You can tape them to a board, or just stick them into cracks in an old plank. Any good hit will disintegrate them into a satisfying cloud of white chips, that dissolve with the first rain and won't clutter up the landscape.

Doubtless the all-time champion Necco wafer plinker was the late Rodd Redwing, who powdered untold thousands of the tiny white discs with his two .22 rimfire Colt Peacemakers, specially altered by Colt with skeletonized bushings to retain as nearly as possible the weight and balance of the original. Using a

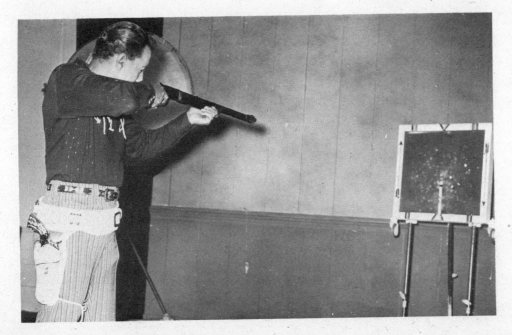

Exhibition shooter Rodd Redwing of Hollywood, California, was the all-time champion Necco wafer buster, exploding literally thousands of the tiny candy discs during his extraordinary exhibitions of shooting prowess. Rodd used a steel backstop designed and built for him by the Los Angeles Police Department. One of his stunts was to shoot through the tiny hole in a Lifesaver mint and hit and shatter a Necco wafer. You can see the wafer here, exploding at the backstop.

57

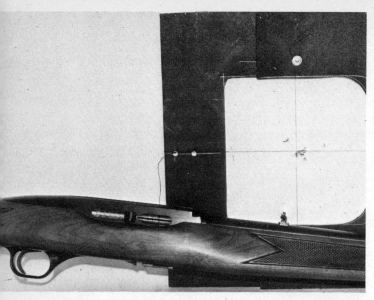

Whenever you think that you're really getting good, try cutting the crossed strings, a stunt that originated with the pioneers and their muzzle loading rifles. Note how close you can come, as indicated by the holes in the paper, and still not cut the strings.

Rodd used a method called, "instinct shooting." The shooter bypasses sights and merely points the rifle or pistol the same way you would a shotgun. The instinct stance is not unlike that of a Skeet shooter, as displayed here by many times Skeet and trap champion, Alex Kerr.

2-foot-square steel backstop and bullet catcher, Rodd performed exhibitions in which he shot two Necco wafers from about 20 feet, fast-drawing the pair of SA Colts, firing them simultaneously from the hip. He performed another spectacular stunt, breaking *two* wafers with *a single bullet* from his Marlin lever action Model 39M. He fired at a knife blade held in a fixture in front of the backstop, splitting the bullet in two—each half shattering one of the wafers. To make the shot more interesting, he used a transparent pendulum with a 2-inch hole in the center. The wafer was always covered by a portion of the elongated swinging pendulum except when the small hole passed in front. Thus no one could accuse Rodd of shooting after the pendulum had swung to one side or the other. Rodd also shot *through* an ordinary Lifesaver mint, to break a Necco wafer positioned directly behind it. No less than the late Ed McGivern, noted six-gun fast-draw shooter, saw fit to challenge that shot, saying that a .22 bullet couldn't pass through a Lifesaver without breaking it. However, I saw Rodd do it, not once, but many times!

Instinct Shooting

Rodd Redwing was also expert at popping *aerial targets* with nary a bobble, making the entire exercise look ridiculously simple. However, 'tain't so! Even a quart can spinning end for end through the air can look like a pin head across your rifle or pistol sights! In addition Rodd fired these astounding stunts without ever using sights on his rifles or handguns—a method commonly called "instinct shooting." During World War II, even Army brass recognized the value of the idea of hitting without sights, and used sightless BB guns to teach recruits the rudiments of leading moving targets. For a time, Daisy had an entire instinct shooting system, complete with sightless BB guns and a trap for throwing reusable plastic pigeons.

Instinct shooting was revived by the Army during the close quarters combat of the Viet Nam conflict. Renamed, "Quick Kill," it was taught to wholesale lots of recruits at Fort Benning, Georgia, using almost 4,000 Daisy BB guns in the process. The practiced instinct shooter does everything "wrong," according to all of the tenets of shooting that you've likely ever heard. For starters, he keeps his head erect with his cheek (or more properly chin) contacting the rifle stock *high* rather than snuggled down low, as my Skeet coach had always urged. To become an instinct shooter, just forget all that you've ever learned about shooting, and start anew! Adhere religiously to the following commandments for best results:

Commandment 1: Look ye *not* down the barrel! Look only at the *top of the target* as it wingeth skyward. (Usually hand-thrown by some long-suffering friend.)

Commandment 2: Be your gun a .22 rimfire, removeth or cover all sighting equipment before commencement.

Walk-and-draw contests hit the "big time" in Las Vegas, during the national championship competitions. Here a contestant cuts loose with a five-in-one blank.

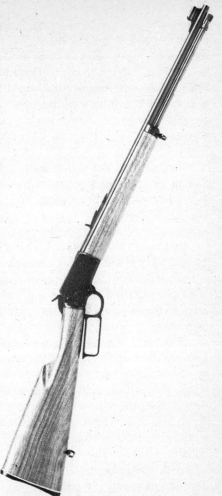

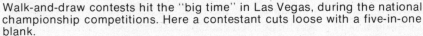
Instinctive shooting at aerial targets is safer when using BB Caps or CB Caps. The new CCI Long CB Caps will function in any rifle that will handle ordinary Long cartridges, such as the Marlin Model 39M (shown here), or its stable-mate the 39A.

Commandment 3: Firmly grabbeth pistol grip and forend, with no digits distractingly sticking forth.

Commandment 4: Keepeth both eyes open! (Suitably protected by shooting glasses!)

Commandment 5: Be ye not disappointed if at first ye succeed not!

Watching the stunts that Rodd performed without benefit of sights just had to make anyone a believer! Despite that, I was hard to convince, being by nature highly skeptical. My biggest difficulty was an innate predilection toward mechanical performance. I even tried to "aim" a shotgun, therefore had never become more than a passable Skeet or trap shooter. And I'm a backslider by nature also, meaning that even after I learned from Rodd, I had a tendency to return to my old mechanical, *missing,* ways. I have to learn all over again every time!

Hopefully, you'll be smarter than that! In essence, instinct shooting consists very simply of letting nature take its course. Don't fight your inner self, just flow with it, and help it along by doing a few mechanical things as directed, and *most* important, *the same every time!*

Rodd's stance was much the same as that of any good Skeet-trap shooter, left foot forward, toe pointed straight ahead, legs well spread for stability, with knees slightly bent and weight slightly forward, leaning into the shot. He held his gun in the prescribed Skeet ready position, with the stock visible below the forearm. He shouldered the gun smoothly, but without undue haste, and always kept his head high! That is where conventional and instinct shooters part company! The former insisting upon a tightly cheeked gun, the latter maintaining only enough contact to establish a reference point for the mind.

BB guns make superlative training tools for instinct shooters for one reason. It's possible to watch the BB in flight as it strikes, or misses the targets. The latter situation is more important because it allows you to see whether you're shooting high or low. Seldom will you shoot to either side. And *almost never* will you overshoot! Therefore you have but one place left to miss, and that's under the target! In theory at least, a line drawn from your eyes (both open, remember?) to the target should be almost parallel to the boreline of your rifle. However, you want the lines to intersect at the point where the target is positioned when your trigger finger gets the message from your subconscious to cut loose. Note that the signal to fire is never a conscious command from the upper levels of the brain. And that's a *hard one to remember!* You *must* let go with your conscious mind and relinquish control to the subconscious, or you may as well bolt the sights back on and forget the whole thing! Fact is, those lines never really intersect. That's why you must look *over the top* of the target, high enough to compensate for the distance between your eyes and the boreline of the rifle. If you miss a shot under, just look a little higher over the target. If necessary invent a companion target in your mind that travels along with the real one, only just a little bit higher.

You can start out shooting at 2-inch diameter cork fishing floats, and systematically shrink these down half-size as your skill picks up. How small a target can you hit without sights, anyway? Would you believe aspirin tablets? Would you believe that you can hit a BB (hand-thrown) with another BB? It's incredible, but it's all true! Try it and see for yourself.

In order to get the most out of your instinct training, your thrower must direct the target as nearly as possible through the same arc every time. He should be standing far enough behind you so that your peripheral vision won't detect his hand movement, causing you to try to anticipate the appearance of the target. Targets should be thrown at a high angle, say 60 to 70 degrees from horizontal, and straight out in front of you. You should be watching the spot where the target will appear, not down low in an effort to see it sooner—much as you would never watch a trap house when waiting for a clay pigeon. You shoulder the gun and fire after you see the target climbing. In one flowing motion, without hesitation or spasmodic movements.

You can start your instinct training with the usual BB gun, or you can start right out with a .22 rimfire, preferably shooting BB Caps. Lacking BB Caps, you can start with CB Caps. Remember the importance of shooting in an area where you can be assured that your bullets will land in isolated country. Incidentally, you can see .22 bullets in flight, given a little practice. If possible, shoot with the sun behind you, and the bullet's flight will be apparent as a silver or golden streak in the air. The image will linger in your mind for a moment, allowing you to call your misses, in much the same way as you could with a BB gun.

Though one of its leading exponents, Rodd Redwing wasn't the only practitioner of instinct shooting. Another name that comes to mind is Dee Woolem, often referred to as the "Father of Modern Fast Draw." Dee's shooting career began when he fired blanks as one of the "train robbers" at Knott's Berry Farm during the early '50's. He had a lot of spare time between train robberies, which he used to good advantage in the mail car by practicing fast draw with Single Action Colts, from traditional Western-styled holsters. With all of that practice, Dee understandably became *damn quick!*

Some instinct shooting hints that Dee passed on to me: Grasp the pistol grip of your rifle with the tang centered in the "V" formed between your thumb and forefinger, with your hand held open, palm-down; Place your left hand well forward on the forend; Hold the gun firmly and lock your wrist and elbows; To change your point of impact, twist or bend at the waist—don't move your arms up or down or side to side; Don't allow yourself to be conscious of the gun—concentrate upon the target; The gun should be lined up centered between your eyes. There you have it from the expert. Now it's up to you to practice until you get the knack.

The obvious hazard of firing at aerial targets can be reduced by using a minimum power ammo, namely BB Caps or CB Caps. Despite their limited power and range, either has sufficient velocity to let daylight right through an airborne tin can. Progenitor of all twenty-two-dom is the "Bulleted Breech Cap," invented by M. Flobert about 1845, by the simple expedient of necking down a common musket cap and inserting a tiny round lead ball. Flobert rifles imported from France, and copies thereof, were popular in the United States for a time. Around the turn of the century, long after the rifles themselves were outdated, the ammo remained popular among the small-fry because BB Caps could be had for about half of the cost of Shorts. American ammo makers abandoned "Caps" with the approach of World War II, but they are still available from foreign firms such as Eley, Alcan, and RWS.

"Conical Bullet Caps" surfaced about 1900, combining the BB Cap case and the 29-grain Short bullet. World War II sounded the death knell of these low-profile rounds as well, but they were recently revived by the "Good Ol' Boys" of CCI, with the improvement of a full-length case that feeds through any rifle that handles ordinary Longs, but with a 29-grain slug that travels a mere 650 fps. Low velocity or no, treat "Caps" with the respect due any cartridge!

Any rifle that will handle ordinary .22 Longs will feed CCI Long CB Mini Caps also. Among the lever action rifles, that includes the Browning BL-22, plus Marlin's 39A and 39M. Although billed as a Long Rifle gun only, the Winchester 9422 feeds CCI Long CB Caps like a champ! Not so with the Ithaca Model 72, which just *will not* feed anything *but* Long Rifles. Remington's pump action Model 572-A and 572-BDL, and the Rossi pump will all feed Long Caps.

A little experimenting revealed that the Ruger 10/22 and Remington Nylon 66 will both fire Long CB Caps—however not as autoloaders. You must operate the cocking handles manually for each shot, but that's no big deal. The amazingly versatile and tractable Weatherby Mark XXII also feeds and fires Long CB Caps, in the autoloading mode, with manual operation of the bolt handle. Few guns lend themselves to ready removal of the sights, but the Nylon 66 front sight is attached with easy-to-remove screws that are just as easy to replace when desired. Cover the rear sight with electrician's tape. The Ruger rear sight flips down out

Instinct shooting with a handgun actually predated its use with rifles. "Hip shooting" is really a form of instinct shooting. The basic requirement is merely to keep the gun in the same position at all times, relative to the body. Aiming is done by bending or pivoting at the waist.

Both the Ruger 10/22 (left) and Remington Nylon 66 (right) will handle Long CB Caps, providing that you operate the action manually.

(Top) Remington's pump action Model 572 handles Long CB Caps to perfection and provides a quick second shot — which shouldn't be needed!

(Above) The use of BB Caps is pretty well restricted to single loaders, such as the Savage/Stevens Model 71 or 72.

Most autoloading pistols fire .22 Long Rifle ammo only, making them somewhat hazardous for use in aerial shooting. A revolver, however, such as this Iver Johnson Cattleman can handle the full spectrum of .22 rimfire ammo, from BB Cap to .22 WMR.

of the way, and you can learn to ignore the front sight for instinct shooting.

If you choose to use BB Caps, you are somewhat restricted in your choice of guns by the fact that the tiny Caps are too short to feed through any known mechanism, thus must be single-loaded. Any single shot rifle will do the trick and falling block actions, such as the Ithaca Model 49, Stevens Model 89, and Savage/Stevens Model 72 Crackshot, are ideal because of easy access to the chamber for loading. Virtually none of the autoloaders will work with any facility, because of the small ejection ports that don't allow your fingers to reach the chamber.

Can you transpose the instinct shooting system to the use of a handgun? Certainly! The basic premise of instinct shooting is that the gun remain in a fixed position in reference to the eyes and body. Thus the mind becomes accustomed to where the gun will point when the body assumes a given position. It relates closely to the manner in which a skilled tennis player knows where his ball will land in the opposite court, or how a golfer can drive a small ball over a distance of 300 yards or so, and have it land within 12 feet of the pin.

Using the proper stance, with a two-hand hold on the handgun, you should be able to do almost everything with a pistol that you can with a rifle. To assume the correct stance you place the left foot forward, pointing it toward the target. The right foot is back, toed outward. Calf and thigh muscles are tense, knees slightly flexed, torso erect, weight carried mostly on the left leg. You hold the pistol in the right hand, with the left wrapped over it. The only difference in instinct shooting is that the pistol is not raised to eye level. Instead, the gun is held lower, sort of half-mast. You can experiment to discover what works best for you.

Before you attempt instinct shooting with a handgun, make certain that you master the basics with a rifle first! Otherwise you may well end up a classic case of frantic frustration.

Virtually any .22 rimfire handgun can be used for instinctive shooting, autoloader or revolver, double action or single. Note that most autoloading pistols will function only with Long Rifle ammo, although most can be single-loaded with Caps. Revolvers handle BB Caps and CB Caps equally as well as Long Rifles. You needn't remove or cover the sights of a handgun, just keep it low enough so that the sights don't distract your eyes.

Most writers advise that you fire a double action revolver *double action*. That sounds sensible enough. But my own experience leads me to say that *if you have time*, shoot *single action* for best accuracy. It takes many hours of practice to develop the skill required to fire double action without deflecting the gun muzzle from the target. If you use the thumb of the left hand instead of the right to cock the gun for repeat shots, you won't have to disturb your basic grip, and flicking the

hammer back doesn't take that long! For the initial shot, you can cock the hammer with the right hand as the revolver moves from holster to horizontal. However, for safety observe the old fast draw dictum, *never put your trigger finger inside of the guard until the gun is almost level!*

Instinct shooting isn't limited to firing upon aerial targets or even moving targets, although the quicker aiming ability is best demonstrated when the target is in motion. Note that Rodd Redwing used it in firing upon stationary targets, and you can do the same. However, if the *target* is not moving, then you will find instinctive shooting works best if the *gun* is moving. That is, start your rifle from a lowered position. Shoulder it smoothly and fire as soon as it comes to bear on the target. With a handgun, start it from the leather, and again, fire as soon as it comes to bear. If you pause before firing, you blow the whole deal! It ceases to be instinctive shooting, and you begin ''aiming.''

Maybe instinct shooting just isn't for you! You don't believe in yoga or fairies dancing on the head of a pin. You want some way of directing that bullet *with absolute certainty* at its designated target, *but with all due haste* as well! *Have I got a sight for you!* It doesn't make the target look larger, smaller, closer or farther. It doesn't do anything except tell you *where the target is* relative to your gun, or vice versa, by means of a luminous dot ''floating'' in the air just above your rifle barrel.

Several such sights are presently available from various sources, including the English import Single Point, the Swedish-made Aimpoint, and all-Yankee-made Weaver Qwik-Point. Judged on cost alone, the Weaver version wins hands down. But it has solid merit on its side as well as economy. The Qwik-Point is lightweight, solidly mounted, and it allows you to use just one eye, if that is your pleasure! However, you do realize the greatest benefit from ''point'' sights if you shoot with both eyes open. Point sights allow you to track a moving target with *almost* as much speed as if you weren't using sights at all. During target tests, I found the Qwik-Point and Aimpoint were capable of delivering near the precision of a scope, in terms of group size, but ever so much faster in use. (For more details, see Chapter 3.)

America's Professional Plinkers

Adolf and ''Plinky'' Topperwein

How would you like to earn a comfortable living by proudly proving your plinking prowess before admiring throngs? ''Plinky'' Topperwein and her husband ''Ad'' (Adolph) did just that for the better part of a lifetime. Plinky acquired her nickname because she would load up her .22 and say to Ad, ''Throw up a tin can and I'll plink it!'' Elizabeth Servaty met Ad in 1902, when she was but 18 years old. Ad was employed as an exhibition shooter by Winchester Repeating Arms Company with a whole year's tenure behind him. The young couple

Often referred to as the "Father of exhibition shooting," Ad Topperwein set an incredible record of shooting in 1907, during a 10-day marathon of plinking at 2½-inch wooden cubes with a Winchester Model '03 autoloading rifle. He broke 72,491 cubes, far outstripping all previous endurance and marksmanship records.

were soon wed. Pretty Elizabeth had never handled a gun up to that day, but within a month, she was plinking pieces of chalk from between her husband's fingers! Before long, she became forever, "Plinky!"

Ad met his first love, a .22 rifle given to him by his father, at age 8. Before he was 10, Ad was shaming most of the men in the region with his uncanny marksmanship. However, many years were to pass before this shooting prodigy gained national acclaim. Ad worked for a time as a cartoonist for the San Antonio Express, a job that augured one of his later innovations—bullet-hole cartoons.

Ad was almost 20 when he had his first opportunity to exhibit his shooting prowess before an audience, when he won a local talent show. The show manager, George Walker, financed a trip to New York for Ad in hopes that the young marksman could land a job with one of the vaudeville shows. However, Ad was turned away, until he gained notoriety by putting every shooting gallery on Coney Island temporarily out of business with his unerring aim. Soon he was traveling the big-time circuit with star billing!

Ad Topperwein originated the "bullet cartoon" firing 300 .22 rimfire bullets through a sheet metal plate in three minutes, to picture an American Indian with full head dress. Ad finally retired from his professional shooting career in 1952 at age 82, having bridged the period from the Wild West shows before the turn of the

century to the less bizarre exhibitions of today. On March 4, 1962, Ad passed on to a happier hunting ground where aerial targets hang in space until your bullet connects.

Often referred to as the "father" of exhibition shooting, Ad was an all-around marksman with rifle, pistol and shotgun, but he will be forever remembered for his most impressive feat of plinking with a .22 rimfire Winchester Model '03 autoloading rifle. In 1907, in a 10-day marathon at the San Antonio Fair Grounds, Ad broke 72,491 wooden blocks, 2½-inches square, hand-thrown into the air. Out of the first 50,000, Ad missed just four, with several runs of 10,000 straight hits, and one that ran on for 14,450 without a miss.

Tom Frye

That record remained invincible until October of 1959, when a field representative and exhibition shooter for Remington, Tom Frye, set himself the grueling task of shooting an even 100,000 2½-inch-square wooden blocks! Tom was inspired to his block-busting feat by the Topperwein record. When Ad made his mark, it silenced a gaggle of self-declared "World's Champions." Tom wanted the mantle of top rifleman of the world and knew that if he could top Topperwein, he had it made! Long-time friend, Newt Crumley, owner of the luxurious Holiday Hotel in Reno, and a man with a keen eye for a unique publicity stunt, offered to stake Tom to the tune of over $5,000—$3,600 for the cubed pine, $1,600 for ammo. Newt also provided the location

It remained for Tom Frye, modern-day exhibition shooter, formerly with Remington Arms, to top Topperwein! Frye set out to shoot an even 100,000 2½-inch pine cubes, near Reno, Nevada. When the dust settled 14 days later, Tom had fired on 100,020 cubes, with only six misses!

of the event, his Holiday Game Farm on the outskirts of Reno. The open fields could be kept free of people in order that bullets launched off into space could come down onto deserted ground. Spectators were held to a limited area, and kept quiet to avoid disturbing Tom's concentration. Overall, the audience was as hushed as that of a golf match.

Despite constant interruptions from autograph hounds, well-wishers, newspapermen, and TV crews, Tom managed an initial uninterrupted run of 32,860 cubes without a miss! He had better than doubled Topperwein's best run of 14,540. Tom racked up other no-miss runs of 14,322, and 13,017. Of the total of 100,020 cubes that Tom fired at, he missed only an incredible six times!

Tom himself had nothing to do with the scoring. Crumley recruited four stalwart residents of Reno to act as Tom's seconds, keeping score, throwing targets and loading the 14-shot tubular magazine Nylon 66 rifles. One was score keeper, using trap score cards with 300 entries per card. At the end of 300 shots, the four men rotated jobs, the thrower became scorekeeper, and the one who had been handing him the 2½-inch squares of soft pine stepped up to do the throwing. The fourth became the reloader, filling the 14-shot stock-enclosed tubular magazine of the Nylon 66 rifle, and handing it to Tom as another became empty.

The thrower tossed each cube about 25 feet into the air, in a more or less constant direction, but Tom could never know for certain just where the fleeting pale brown target would appear against the open sky. Often it would take off at a tangent as the thrower's arm tired from the strain.

With this production-line setup behind him, Tom often fired on 1,000 targets per hour. Some days, he totaled up 10,000 or more shots before the light waned. Early on the twelfth day, Tom had burst 72,501 pine blocks, breaking Ad Topperwein's record that had stood invincible for over 52 years! Up to that point, Tom had missed only an unbelievable *three targets!* Topperwein had missed nine. Without even pausing to open a bottle of champagne, Tom kept up the monotonous cadence of track-target-and-fire, slowing only momentarily to exchange an empty rifle for a loaded one.

The monotony of firing shot after shot for 10 to 12 hours was agonizing. To ease the mental tension, Tom turned aside from his inanimate targets for something more challenging. Five pigeons that swooped by at various times during the shoot to see what the fuss was about, joined the pile of "dead" wooden blocks. At one point, a bird came hedge-hopping along about 5 feet off of the ground, about 150 feet away over a plowed field. Tom said to his companions, "Watch this!" Then tracked the bird in flight for a moment, established his lead and squeezed the trigger. The bird bounced hard and settled in a cloud of dust, amidst cries of, "I see it, but I don't believe it!" from his incredulous audience.

Track those hares-on-the-lam from an offhand position, and it will steady your swing when the target looms large. And more important, choose a rifle that matches your bigbore, as this Ruger 10/22 matches the Ruger .44 Magnum Carbine. Note Ruger backup revolver as well!

Temperatures ranged in the 90's all during the shoot, and that was in the shade. *There was no shade,* save for a circus tent erected to afford the audience some protection from the unrelenting sunshine. The Nylon 66 rifles were lying on a card table under the full force of the sun. The sun, coupled with the heat from shooting, made the guns too hot to touch. "Every time I picked up a gun," says Tom, "I'd hear the hissing sound of burning flesh. I had Band-Aids all over my fingers. My trigger finger had two Band-Aids running lengthwise and two across. After awhile, they would split. I had to change them several times every day. Sometimes I handed the guns back to the loader covered with blood."

Tom set out to perform this stunt with a trio of untried guns. He had three Nylon 66 rifles, designed by Remington just the year before. They had been tested to be sure, but certainly not in the unrelenting way that Tom was about to! Assuming that the guns were used about equally, each had well over 33,000 Long Rifles fired through it in 2 weeks of constant use. They were cleaned five separate times during the shoot. Other than that, they received no attention or maintenance.

Because the Nylon 66 is an autoloader chambered for .22 Long Rifles only, Tom was obliged to forego the use of Shorts, which he prefers for aerial shooting because of their more limited range and lesser recoil. Note that a

4-pound rifle exhibits appreciable recoil with a Long Rifle, even the standard velocity used by Tom. With as many as 10,000 impacts upon the shoulder every day without let-up, even light recoil becomes a factor to be reckoned with! Also, lifting a 4-pound rifle 10,000 times in one day is tantamount to lifting a total of 40,000 pounds in one day. By the end of the third day, Tom collapsed in bed at night with his shoulder muscles twitching. By the fifth day, the muscles across his shoulders and back had hardened into a knot as hard as a board. They have never quite relaxed again.

Happily, Tom Frye is still very much with us, and continues to make frequent exhibitions, despite his "retired" status. But who's to step into his high-heeled boots when the Lord plays taps on this last greatest of all the world's shooters? No one!

Scoring rings on the animal silhouette targets show vital zones and reward the shooter with points for hitting them correctly.

Sharpening Big Game Skills

Any plinking could be termed, "practical" in that it makes you a more relaxed, happy individual. Plinking can have all of the benefits of the psychiatrist's couch without the excessive cost. However, practical plinking can also be directed toward more practical goals, such as improving your marksmanship come next big game season. To this end, spend most of your plinking hours firing from the offhand position, because most of the trophies encountered in the tall timber will be on the run, or about to run, affording but little time for assuming a more steady shooting position. For those rare opportunities that do offer some spare seconds, *position plinking* will make you more nimble at assuming the kneeling, sitting, and prone positions. Practice dropping into position, getting on target, and firing double time. Never mind the misses, concentrate on smoothness and speed. The hits will come later. Pass up those tin cans at two car lengths, and try 1-gallon paint cans at 100 to 125 yards. You'll learn more about windage and drop in one afternoon with your .22 rimfire than in a lifetime of big game hunting.

Sharpen your stalking skills by substituting live targets. To maximize the benefits of your rimfire nimrodding, seek out terrain that most nearly duplicates the trails you will follow come fall and winter. If you plan a hunt after woods-running whitetails, load up with hollow points and boot some bunnies out along the nettled eastern fence rows, or among western cactus patches and sage. Take them on the gallop—*offhand!* Master that art form, and a bounding buck will loom as large as a garage door on rails.

If you're planning to purchase a rimfire rifle, choose a .22 twin for your favorite bigbore. Many makers offer such choices, for example, the Winchester lever action 9422 lookalike for the timeless Model 94 .30-30. You might choose a bolt action rimfire rifle to match your bigbore, so you won't have to mentally shift gears and learn a new system come big game season. Also, such rifles as the superb Remington Model 541-S offer incomparable accuracy for long-range shooting, and adapt readily to scope sights so that you can avail yourself of that accuracy potential!

If your big game rifle sports a glass sight, install a matching scope on your rimfire, of the same power and reticle. However, if you prowl the winter woods with a buckhorn-sighted lever action carbine, stick with notch and bead on your rimfire. At average plinking ranges, open sights are more than adequate for tin can accuracy.

Regardless of whatever direction you aim your plinking pursuits, don't let them degenerate into work sessions. Number one priority is just to keep them FUN! Whether routed along practical lines or not, you can't help but learn much of value that will carry over to your big game hunting without conscious thought.

CHAPTER 5

Trail Guns and Trail Leather

"TRAILING" NEEDN'T BE confined to the exercise of Shank's Mare. Trailing can involve horseback hunting or adventuring, as well as four-wheel-drive journeys into the outback. Any and all of these events call for the practical utilization of a rimfire rifle or handgun.

Wilderness campers, whether they arrive on two legs or four, or are transported in rubber-tired elegance, could use a .22 rimfire to augment their limited larder and prevent pack rats, porcupines, et al, from raiding the rest. Rabbits, squirrels, partridges, even the above-mentioned porcupine are all "pot-able" fare, and all are readily bagged with .22 Long Rifle high velocity hollow points, Winchester-Western Dyna-points, or Federal Semi-Hollow Points—CCI Stingers or W-W Xpediters leave too little for the pot!

Any .22 trail companion can deliver up one of the greatest joys of the wilderness adventure—simple plinking! There is more pure entertainment per square inch packed into that tiny 50-round box of .22's than you'll find in any other product. You can casually cancel tin cans, pine cones, dirt clods, etc., that you encounter trailside, or enter into friendly competition with companions, to see who washes the camp dishes that evening.

Then there's the survival aspect of .22 trail companions that will be discussed at length in the next chapter. The principal requirement of a survival gun is simply that it *be there* when needed! If you develop such an affinity for a particular .22 rimfire rifle or handgun that you can't bear to enter the field without it, you have won two-thirds of the battle right there. That a .22 rimfire can serve ably as a survival gun goes without saying. The major use will be to supply food animals for the survivor. You are far more likely to encounter small game than big game. Small game animals are well handled by the rimfire. Not so with a bigbore center fire, which destroys more meat than it delivers. The late Townsend Whelen, one of the true all-time greats of

shooting once worked out some reduced small game loads for his .30-06 that would print in about the same spot as standard big game ammo at near to medium ranges. That system is at best a stop-gap measure, hardly comparable to having a precisely sighted-in rimfire rifle or pistol. Poachers (curse 'em) proved long ago that a .22 Long Rifle will take deer with a well-placed head shot. However, a deer is the *last* thing you want to shoot. It involves processing a huge amount of meat, pinning you down in one spot perhaps for a week or more, while you dry and smoke the flesh to preserve it.

Obviously a .22 rimfire doesn't provide the same degree of protection against marauding wild animals that a .30-06 rifle or .44 Magnum revolver would. However, a .30-06 or a .44 Magnum can't provide the degree of protection that a machine gun could. A machine gun isn't as powerful as a howitzer, etc. You have to draw a line somewhere. I draw it in front of the muzzle of a .22! Besides, your chances of being struck by lightning are greater than the likelihood that you'll encounter a raging beast in the woods of North America!

Choosing Your Trail Gun

Prejudice plays no small role in your choice of a rimfire trail mate. Given my "druthers," I'd sooner select my .22 rimfire carryin' guns from the quartet of lever action rifles, plus a single action revolver. More specifically, I have to vote for the Marlin 39A with full-length 24-inch barrel, and either the Ruger stainless steel Super Single Six with dual cylinders, or the Iver Johnson Cattleman, also with twin .22 Long Rifle/.22 Magnum cylinders. Both revolvers are classic designs that have never been bested for all-around dependability and versatility.

If you wonder at my choice of the long-barreled Marlin lever gun rather than its 20-inch barreled sibling, I have another surprise for you—I like the bolt action

Whether the hunter arrives on foot or in rubber-tired elegance, he will find ample use for a rimfire trail buddy. Even shotgun or bigbore big game hunters find a .22 rimfire a welcome backup.

On the trail, a .22 rimfire rifle or handgun can augment a limited larder with small game, discourage camp pests, offer the pleasure of plinking, or provide the measure twixt life and death in a survival situation.

Remington Model 541-S as a trail rifle! However, I would add a sling and scope sight—probably the Bushnell variable 3X to 7X Custom .22, with BDC (Bullet Drop Compensator)—plus a couple of 10-shot clips. At 5½ pounds, the 541-S isn't really all that heavy, and its 42⅝-inch overall length is not exactly outsized for carrying. What's more important, the Remington 541-S puts 'em *where you point* out to the *maximum* effective range of a CCI Stinger!

If you see your .22 rimfire trail companion as merely snake medicine, it doesn't have to be super-accurate, merely *quick!* Chances are, you'll be nose-to-nose with a rattler before you even know it's about.

Everyone has his own ideas about the role a trail rifle or pistol should play. I see it as a hunting/protection/plinking arm; and, I want the best I can get, even if that means carrying a somewhat heavier arm. It all boils down to how much you want to sacrifice in terms of quality and performance in order to lighten your burden. If you insist upon the lightest, smallest gun available, you might well end up with a derringer in your hip pocket. Better carry a salt shaker in the other pocket, because you'll have to sprinkle salt on a bird's tail before you can bag it with that tiny tool!

This is not to say that there aren't viable compromises available. One of the truly pleasant surprises, resulting from testing a wide array of rifles and handguns in connection with this book, came in the form of much better than expected accuracy from several of the lighter weight rifles—notably the Remington Nylon 66! The Nylon 66 is an outstanding example of modern technology at work, trimming 1½ pounds and more than 4 inches in overall length from the 541-S. Reliability suffers little if any, and the 19⅜-inch barrel of the 66 delivers about all of the velocity one can expect from a .22 Long Rifle.

It would be easy to condemn this unique rifle out of hand, because of its "plastic" look. My friend and

Given his "druthers," the author would opt for a Marlin Model 39A with 24-inch barrel, with scope and sling as a trail rifle.

If you see your .22 trail companion as strictly snake medicine, it doesn't need to be super accurate, merely quick! You'll likely be nose-to-nose with a rattler before you know that it's there!

cohort, Jim Beck, a superb marksman, was openly hostile to the 66, referring to it as, "Mattell's wonder." However, he had to respect the fact that it printed some exceptional groups for a rifle that weighs a mere 4 pounds. The best 25-yard 10-shot bench rest group measured ½-inch center-to-center, fired with Winchester Super-X Dynapoint .22 Long Rifles. Federal Semi-Hollow Points printed nine shots in ⅜-inch, with a flier out at 12:00 o'clock opening the group to ⅝-inch. Stingers registered a slightly oblong ⅝-inch string. In practical terms, this indicates that the Remington Nylon 66 could be used for hunting game as small as tree squirrels out to about 75 yards—not bad for so light a rifle!

Although it's 1½ inches shorter, the Ruger 10/22 weighs a pound more than the Nylon 66. That's still pretty light for a trail companion, certainly no unbearable burden! And the 10/22 Deluxe Sporter comes equipped with *sling swivels!* The test Ruger was a little more picky about which ammo it preferred, but it fired a pleasing ⁹/₁₆-inch group with Stingers and a ½-inch pattern with Remington Rifle Match ammo.

Ithaca's Model 72 Saddlegun boasts a silky-smooth lever action and extra accurate 18½-inch barrel that grouped nine Stingers into a nice round ⅜-inch (center-to-center) group. Number 10, outside of the group at 1:00 o'clock, opened it to a still respectable ½-inch. With one exception, the other makes of ammo tested remained inside of ⅝-inch. With the addition of sling swivels, the Ithaca Saddlegun in either .22 Long Rifle or .22 Magnum, would make a stalwart trail buddy!

Bear in mind that all of the groups mentioned were for

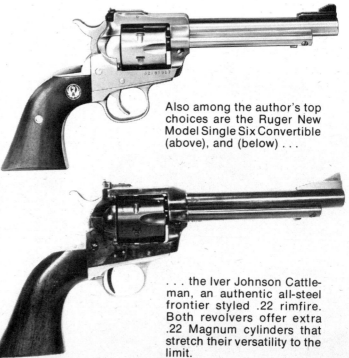

Also among the author's top choices are the Ruger New Model Single Six Convertible (above), and (below) . . .

. . . the Iver Johnson Cattleman, an authentic all-steel frontier styled .22 rimfire. Both revolvers offer extra .22 Magnum cylinders that stretch their versatility to the limit.

Perhaps the ultimate backpacker's rifle is the Charter Arms autoloading AR-7, which can be taken down and stowed in its plastic stock inside of your pack sack. Once assembled, the rifle is capable of handling all of the chores normally assigned to a .22 trail partner.

10 shots. Many believe that five-shot groups are a better reflection of field accuracy, inasmuch as a hunter seldom has time to get off more than a couple of rounds before the game has flown. Firing five only, the same group size could be maintained at double the distance!

The Browning BL-22 with 20-inch barrel weighs but 5 pounds and packs some impressive pluses into that light weight, including a short-throw lever action and a trigger that travels with the lever. Again, with the addition of sling swivels, it makes a fine trail carbine.

Winchester's 6¼-pound Model 9422 in either standard or magnum rimfire, is hardly in the featherweight class, but plenty of lads swear by it as a trail rifle, especially those that cut their teeth on the ever-constant "thutty-thutty" deer and range rifle. Shucks! Who cares what it weighs when it rides most of the time in a saddle sheath, anyway.

A duo of autoloading carbines worthy of more than honorable mention, are the Marlin Model 99M1 and Model 989M2. Both styled after the famed military M1 Carbine, complete with handguard, they differ only in magazine style; nine-shot under-barrel tubular for the former, seven-shot clip for the latter. Both (bless 'em) have sling swivels, and weigh but 5 pounds, with 18-inch barrels.

The ultimate backpacker's rifle is the Charter Arms

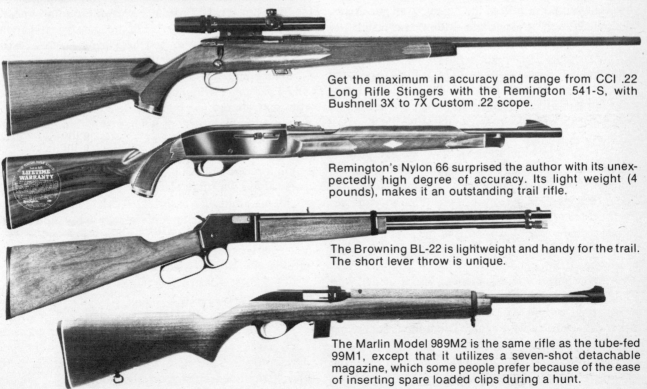

Get the maximum in accuracy and range from CCI .22 Long Rifle Stingers with the Remington 541-S, with Bushnell 3X to 7X Custom .22 scope.

Remington's Nylon 66 surprised the author with its unexpectedly high degree of accuracy. Its light weight (4 pounds), makes it an outstanding trail rifle.

The Browning BL-22 is lightweight and handy for the trail. The short lever throw is unique.

The Marlin Model 989M2 is the same rifle as the tube-fed 99M1, except that it utilizes a seven-shot detachable magazine, which some people prefer because of the ease of inserting spare loaded clips during a hunt.

The single shot top-break Thompson/Center Contender pistol is one of the few that looks and handles well with a scope aboard. Most handguns are anything but handy with scopes mounted.

Another fine kit-sized revolver is the Charter Arms Pathfinder, a six-shot swing-out cylinder all-steel, revolver with adjustable sights. It is highly reliable and accurate, and smoothly streamlined.

For years, author has carried this Smith & Wesson .22-32 Kit Gun in a Bianchi holster. The backsweep makes it easy to grasp.

Hi-Standard's Sentinel with nine-shot swing-out cylinder and compact, yet hand-filling grips.

autoloading AR-7, featuring a tough Cycolac plastic stock, hollowed out to accept the barrel, receiver, and seven-shot clip, under a water-tight plastic butt cap. Weighing only 2½ pounds, the unit will float, whether assembled or stowed within the stock.

Whenever the subject of the "ideal" trail gun arises, there resumes the great debate—rifle versus pistol. Obvious advantages of the rifle are greater velocity resulting from a longer barrel, greater accuracy, and a longer sighting radius if iron sights are used, leading to reduced sighting error. If both firearms, long and short, are scope sighted, the longer sighting radius is academic. However, a scope is more acceptable on a rifle than on a handgun. A scoped handgun becomes somewhat unhandy both to tote and to shoot. The one exception is Thompson/Center's top-break single shot Contender, which is more of a short rifle with its 10-inch barrel than a long handgun. It performs like a rifle, as well, delivering tight groups and top velocities without any loss from a cylinder/barrel gap, or from the operation of an automatic action. Also, the Contender can be switched in seconds from standard .22 to .22 WMR by merely exchanging barrels. The Contender can be scoped with Thompson/Center's own 1½X Lobo with T/C mount, or with the Leupold M8 2X long-eye-relief scope, using either T/C or Leupold mounts. The Lobo is somewhat more compact than the Leupold M8, but the latter contains superior optics. Bushnell offers their Phantom Handgun Scopes, in either 1.3X or 2.5X, along with

integral dovetail mounts that cinch down on a pair of inverted cone-shaped studs that can be mounted upon virtually any handgun with a solid top strap.

Balanced against the higher velocity and greater accuracy of the rifle, is the ease of carrying a handgun in a suitable holster. It's instantly available in time of need, yet never in the way, leaving both hands free to handle traps, camping gear or just help hang on to a steep precipice. The pistol is also handy for big game and varmint hunters. It augments their bigbore rifles, taking small pot game without driving every trophy buck into the next county, or perhaps delivering the *coup de grace,* without destroying a mountable skin. Bird hunters, armed with smoothbores, can also find great use for the .22 rimfire handgun, on the trail and in camp.

On a recent Alaskan hunt, I was the only man in a party of five who didn't have a .44 Magnum belted on! I prefer my Smith & Wesson .22/32 Kit Gun in a compact hip holster, tip tucked out of the way in my hip pocket. A box of ammo travels unnoticed in a side pocket. Did you ever try to ignore 50 rounds of .44 Magnum ammo strung around your waist or bulging in your pockets?

Other kit-sized revolvers that could fill the bill on the trail are the swing-out cylinder Hi-Standard Sentinel and Charter Arms Pathfinder (in either .22 Long Rifle or .22 WMR), or the standard .22 Harrington & Richardson top-break Model 926 with nine-shot cylinder. Both the Sentinel and the Pathfinder are smooth and streamlined enough to slip into a parka pocket without snagging, despite fully adjustable target-styled sights.

Holster-sized but still considered a lightweight at 30 ounces is the Harrington & Richardson top-break Model 999, with nine-shot automatic-ejection cylinder, ventilated full-length rib and adjustable sights.

The Hi-Standard "Camp Gun" is just the Sentinel with the barrel stretched to 6 inches in length; and, would you believe the Smith & Wesson K-22 Masterpiece with an 8⅜-inch barrel? This is a righteous fact! So too is the S&W Model 18 .22 Combat Masterpiece with Baughman-style forward-slanting front sight atop a 4-inch barrel. The standard 6-inch barrel is, of course, still available on both of these S&W rimfires. Given proper holsters, all three lengths (with the possible exception of the 8⅜-inch K-22) are practical on the trail; although, the shorter tubes are likely to be less tiresome. All of the S&W offerings are also available in the .22 WMR chambered version, as well.

Since 1936, the woodsman's basic side arm has been the Smith & Wesson .22/32 Kit Gun. Recently, the identical design became available as the Model 63, constructed of stainless steel, highly resistant to all forms of corrosion that are the constant enemy of any gun in the moisture-laden out-of-doors. In addition to the compactness and lightness of the original Kit Gun, the M63 boasts a ⅛-inch wide front sight with red insert that remains brilliantly visible even against dark backgrounds. The front sight is backed by a black stainless micrometer adjustable rear sight.

A pair of Western-styled double action revolvers that fit into the trail gun category are the Hi-Standard Double Nine, with nine-shot swing-out cylinder, and the six-shot Harrington & Richardson Model 676, both with interchangeable .22 LR/.22 WMR cylinders.

To reassure you autoloading pistol buffs that I'm not 100 percent wheel-gun oriented, let me say that for years, I carried a Hi-Standard Model HD with 4-inch bull barrel in the field. A present-day equivalent—minus the HD's exposed hammer—would be the Hi-Standard Sharpshooter, a gun of target quality, but at a bargain basement price. The Ruger Mark 1 with bull barrel is an impressive piece of hardware and is as formidable in the field as on the target range! Both of the above self-shuckers are target-sight equipped, a positive plus in their favor. A sharply defined sight picture is an absolute necessity if you're going to score on small game targets possibly in poor light and obscured by brush. Micrometer adjustments allow you to precisely sight for the ammo you're using. Having said this, I must add that the Ruger Standard Model, which offers only windage adjustment of the dovetailed rear sight, via the old hammer and brass-punch trick, is still a damn fine trail pistol—once you get it sighted in! All of the above pistols are somewhat on the heavy side for constant carrying, thus they will require better than average holster/belt combinations to ride in relative comfort.

The H&R Model 999 Sportsman is one of the author's favorites with its short action and crisp single action trigger pull.

The K-22 with a 4-inch barrel and Baughman-styled front sight, makes a relatively small package, but retains precision and accuracy.

Although the author prefers target adjustable sights, he acknowledges that the Ruger Standard Model is excellent on the trail, once the shooter gets it properly sighted in for the ammo he will be using.

The ever popular Smith & Wesson .22-32 Kit Gun is now available as the stainless steel Model 63. Even the rear sight is stainless!

Trail Leather

The basic trail holster of old seems to be an all but forgotten breed among modern makers, with the exception of the George Lawrence Company of Portland, Oregon. The first "store-bought" holster and belt I ever owned was the Lawrence #18 cartridge belt in .45 Long Colt, with a #120 holster to fit a 5½-inch barreled Peacemaker. The #120 is a high-ride pouch, with a standard safety strap, designed by the renowned Elmer Keith. As a teenager, I devoured every word written by Keith. I thought any holster that he had a hand in designing would have to be functional and free of gimcracks. I wasn't disappointed! Lawrence still makes the Keith design, and it's just as viable today as it was over 30 years ago when I first met up with it. Other Lawrence holsters that trail well are the #100 with quarter-flap and quick release thumb strap, the new "Columbia Hunter Holster and Belt Set," and the #52 for autoloaders, with spare clip pouch. George Lawrence puts out a commodious cartridge caddy for .22 rimfire ammo, holding up to 100 rounds conveniently at the belt in a snap-top pouch.

I met John Bianchi when he was making holsters in his garage after hours as a patrolman in Monrovia, California. He began by hand-fabricating superior rigs for fellow cops and branched out into sportsmen's designs, some of which endure to this day. John made his first full flap holster for me. I still use the rig regularly, and John still makes it as the Model 16L, with the added features of a rear sight recess, eliminating sight/leather contact, plus silicone suede lining. Bianchi's Model 1L is a conventional high-ride pouch for single action revolvers, with butt pitched forward, cut off cylinder-high for quick access, with no-frills safety strap—hard to beat in the outback! For .22 rimfire autoloaders, Bianchi offers the Model 89L, with steel-reinforced molded sight channel to protect both high, undercut front sights, *and leather*. Angle and cut resemble that of the Model 1. Both make fine trail partners. John has always fancied the traditional western cut rig, as does yours truly. His Model 1898 "Texan" drop-loop cartridge belt and skirted holster offer the beauty and utility of the original, combined with the finest of modern improved tanning and strong, long-wearing nylon thread. Bianchi also offers a wide array of rifle carrying straps, most featuring the cobra design.

One of my favorite trail companions is a holster custom-made for me by Bianchi during the days when he was still a one-man factory. It carries my S&W .22/32 Kit Gun and has exaggerated backsweep and protector flaps to keep the hammer from catching on coat or shirt. I carry it with the muzzle tucked out of the way in my hip pocket. Someone has to remind me that it's there!

Safariland holsters are instantly identifiable by their 360-degree perimeter seams, surrounding the sheath on

Bianchi offers a wide array of rifle carrying straps, many in the Cobra configuration. These are straps, and not *slings* in the strict sense of the word. They are of no assistance to marksmanship.

Safariland holsters are instantly recognizable by the seams running full circle, back, bottom, and front. The front seam holds the patented Safariland Sight Track, an extruded tough plastic trough that cradles the sight, protecting both it and the holster from damage.

Modern holsters are better designed and made than ever before, using modern-tanned top grain cowhide. Only the choice portions of the hides are used.

Today's holsters are double seamed using nylon thread that won't rot away as even the finest linen cord used to do in the old days.

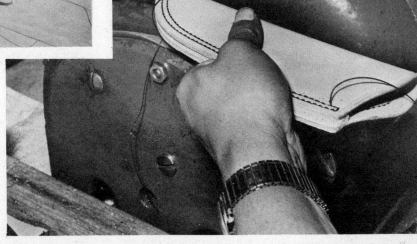

all sides. Back and bottom bear the usual thick leather welting, but the front seam retains the patented "Safariland Sight Track," an extruded vinyl strip with a channel up the inside that allows the front sight, however high or sharp, to slip smoothly out without grabbing or shaving leather. This feature is especially appreciated by those who like to tote their target .22 autoloading pistols, high sights and all, to the field! Many Safariland holsters thoughtfully provide a protecting lip for the rear sight as well. Holsters that are cut out halfway down the top strap of the revolver frame or the slide of an autoloader (in an attempt to release the barrel a little sooner) are OK for fast draw, but a poor investment for the field, where that opening inevitably scoops up twigs, dirt and assorted debris, plus exposing the rear sight to bumps and scrapes.

For large frame revolvers such as the Smith & Wesson K-22, you could hardly do better than the Safariland Model 25 Sportsman Holster. It's a high-rider, back-swept, with Sight Track and rear sight protector and available with either conventional safety strap or quick-release thumb break.

The traditional safety strap has become supplanted in large measure by the far faster "thumb break" method of securing a pistol in a holster. A thumb break strap loops over the gun and back down the other side, where it snaps to a stiff upthrust tab. In drawing, the thumb flicks the steel-stiffened tab aside separating the snap, and the gun simply shoves the leather loop aside as it is drawn. The conventional safety strap can be tucked behind the belt and only utilized when some strenuous action is anticipated, or while riding horseback—when you can be pitched on your tail at any moment without warning!

If you would like to afford some protection for the works of your revolver without sacrificing reasonable speed of access, you could opt for the Safariland Model 58-B Quarter Flap Holster, also with Sight Track. In the Western motif is Safariland's Model 43 "Outfitter Holster," a perfect pouch for the likes of a Ruger Super Single Six or Iver Johnson Cattleman single action! Pure cowboy is the Safariland Model 50 "Virginian" drop-loop holster/belt rig, lacking the Sight Track, but with metal reinforcing around the cylinder section of the suede-lined holster—available in top-grain leather or rough-out. Most Safariland holsters are available (at slight added cost) with optional elk suede lining that serves to protect the finish of your finest pistols against holster wear. Also, lining the belt helps hold the rig in place without shifting.

Holster Style—The Choice is Yours

The style of holster that carries your trail pistol depends in large degree upon your type of gun, your mode of travel and your purpose afield. Of late, shoulder holsters have become rather popular for carrying large-frame revolvers such as the K-22. However, if you're hiking, a shoulder holster will most certainly get in the way of your pack straps. If riding horseback, the weight jouncing against the shoulder harness all day long could become highly irritating. The best rig for horseback travel is still the traditional hip holster, proven over a century of satisfactory use—it's usually accompanied by a belt of waist-girdling cartridge loops. On the other hand, the Jeep cowboy will be ill-served by a corset of cartridges that gouges his back and erodes the upholstery in the bargain. Practical hip holsters ride up near the belt line, not Hollywood-style down around the knees. A low holster is continually in the way, digging in the dirt, catching in brush, exposing the gun to rock damage. High holsters benefit from a rearward rake of the muzzle to accelerate the draw and bring the butt forward for easy reach.

A small revolver such as the Charter Arms Pathfinder carries secure and comfortable in a crossdraw rig, riding high and handy on horseback or in a Jeep. Where temperatures rise, holsters tend to descend. A shoulder harness can sweat you like a sauna in the sun; but snow, wind and rain elevate revolvers up under the armpit, where they carry snugly under outer wear, warm and dry—even if they are a little slow to reach.

The state of the art shoulder sheath is Bianchi's new open-front, suede-lined "Phantom," with fully adjustable shoulder yoke, internal cylinder recess, sight guard, and belt strap dividing the load between shoulder and waist. The Phantom is available to fit medium and large frame revolvers and large frame autos.

Modern holsters are better designed, better made, of better materials than ever before. Prime, top-grain cowhide is tanned for a lifetime of trouble-free service. It's treated with silicone and oils to preserve it as never before and is molded to exactly fit the revolver or pistol, eliminating the jiggle and jounce that used to wear away blue and even the metal itself. Many of these holsters are lined for further protection, and just about all quality leather is double-seam stitched with nylon thread that won't rot away with age or exposure. Such makers as Bianchi, Safariland, George Lawrence, Ranger Leather, etc., can be relied upon to deliver more than your money's worth.

An interesting, innovative, field design comes from Ranger Leather Products, Camden, Arkansas, in their wrap-around, straight-drop holsters for revolvers and autoloaders. It sports a unique reverse quarter flap that wraps over the works of the pistol from the *outside,* and comes with a thumb break style snap that's placed next to the body, well protected from snags by brush and tree limbs. This unusual holster is centrally looped to the belt, placing the gun butt much higher than normal. In addition to black and tan, Ranger rigs are available in unique camouflage finish.

Saddle Scabbards

Horses and lever action .22 rimfire rifles go together

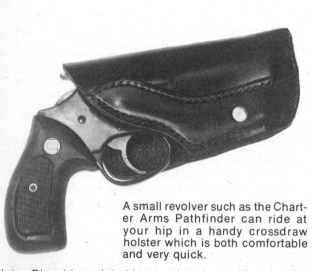

A small revolver such as the Charter Arms Pathfinder can ride at your hip in a handy crossdraw holster which is both comfortable and very quick.

John Bianchi models his own latest shoulder rig, the open-front suede-lined "Phantom," with adjustable shoulder yoke, cylinder recess and sight guard. Strap at the bottom distributes load between shoulder and waist belt.

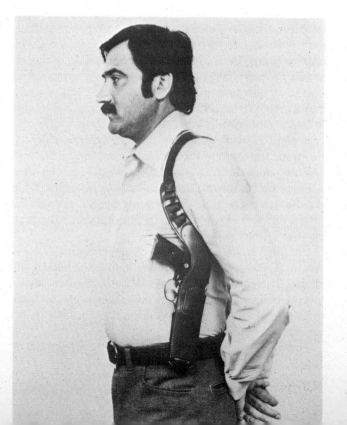

74

Rig used by the author combines the Safariland high-ride Model 43 holster plus ammo pouch, on a classic 2-inch tapered Model 49 "Vaquero" belt without loops. This is the kind of rig you can live with all day long without fatigue, and wear on foot, horseback, or in a Jeep with complete comfort!

like bacon and eggs frying in a cast iron skillet over a fire of sage and manzanita. "Saddle carbine" is an apt title for such guns as the Ithaca Saddlegun, Marlin Model 39M, Browning BL-22 and Winchester's 9422! However, a saddle *carbine* needs a saddle *scabbard*. Some of the best come from Lawrence, S.D. Myres, Hunter Co., and Triple-K Leather, of San Diego, California. Triple-K cranks out four different styles of scabbards for rifles and carbines with and without scope sights. Their Style 117 is glove leather lined, with a fold-over snap-flap for security and protection. Every horseback hunter has his own method of tying on his carbine.

You'll see them hung vertically below the saddle horn on the left, angled butt-up toward the rear on the right side, so that the rider can pluck the rifle out with his right hand as he dismounts, or even riding horizontally on the right, butt rearward. I never could understand this particular carry. Seems the first hill that that Cayuse lunged up, the carbine would go cartwheeling downslope; plus, the rider has to walk around the horse to get at his gun. Some scabbards come with a hood—great to protect the gun from rain, snow, etc., but a bloody nuisance when you need the gun in a hurry! I missed a good chance at an elk once because I had my

Every cowboy has his own way of tying on a saddle scabbard. Here you see the rifle riding horizontal on the pony in a position to slide out backwards when he climbs a steep hill. Note Colt Woodsman at the hip.

rifle securely stowed under a leather cap instead of instantly available.

Perhaps the widest array of saddle scabbards comes from the Hunter Company, Westminster, Colorado; large and small, from simple to ornate, with and without hoods.

Rifle Slings

In choosing your ideal trail .22, you must balance off the weight and bulk of the gun against its ability to perform its assigned tasks. A pistol hangs handy at the hip. Where does the rifle reside? Well, if it's an as-issued Remington Model 541-S, Winchester 9422, or Browning BAR, etc., it is occupying one or both hands. The above guns, delivered across your dealer's counter come without sling swivels. Of course, virtually any

(Left) In a blizzard, the rider is apt to start looking for ways to protect his precious rifle from snow and wet.

(Below) Author (right) found a way, by covering his rifle with a cap on the scabbard. However it cost him a shot at a fine elk during an Idaho hunt.

Carrying rifles on the trail without slings merely means that one or both of your hands will be eternally occupied with the task of caring for the gun.

Ken Warren demonstrates how to use a sling, *note I said sling not carrying strap,* to aid marksmanship. (L to R) First the "hasty sling" for offhand use. Second, the sling encircles upper arms to hold rifle steady in sitting position. Third the hasty sling in a modified kneeling position. Bottom photo demonstrates proper use in prone position, with sling tightly encircling upper arm.

rifle can be equipped with sling swivels at modest cost in dollars and effort. (For details, see Chapter 14.)

Happily, the excellent .22 Magnum Marlin Model 782 clip loading or tubular magazine Marlin Model 783 both come with swivels and sling, factory-furnished! The autoloading Weatherby Mark XXII comes equipped with fixed sling swivels; and, Marlin's Model 39M and 39A lever actions both come with fixed sling swivels attached. Ruger's autoloading 10/22 Deluxe Sporter also comes with fixed swivels. *Kudos to all of the above!* I wish all makers realized the importance of installing swivels on their smallbore rimfire rifles. (To be completely fair, I should mention that Remington offers the option of factory-installed sling and swivels on their Model 541-S, 552 Speedmaster autoloader and 572 pump action, and their autoloading Nylon 66, at nominal additional cost. By all means, order your Remington with swivels attached, especially the Nylon 66, which is particularly unhandy for installing after-market swivels.)

Sling King of the world is Michaels of Oregon, P.O. Box 13010, Portland, Oregon, 97213, makers of an infinite variety of sling swivels to fit every rifle, bigbore or small. Affectionately known in the gun trade as, "Uncle Mike's," they even offer easy-to-install fixed or QD swivels to fit the front of tubular magazine, lever action and pump action rifles that always presented a particular problem to gunsmiths and do-it-yourself firearms fixers. Uncle Mike's front swivel consists of a streamlined band that encircles the magazine tube just ahead of the stock. Only the butt stock need be drilled to accept the traditional wood screw swivel base.

Uncle Mike's also supplies some of the finest slings to be found. These include the popular cobra-style "Chief Joseph" with decorative stitching, and the basket-stamped "Three Fingered Jack," both lined with shearling lamb wool for maximum comfort; the "Eagle Cap" with basket-stamped sheepskin-lined sliding shoulder pad, and the "Mt. Hood" with sheep-lined plain pad. All of the above are made from specially tanned latigo leather, valued for its deep mahogany coloring. Other slings from Uncle Mike's are the suede-lined "Cobra Strap" and "Military Sling." The last is the most capable of infinite adjustment, and can be used in "position" shooting.

What value is a sling anyway? Is it just a strap to carry the gun around? Hardly! Properly used, a sling can immensely improve your marksmanship. Just follow the example of Oregon big game guide Ken Warren, pictured here courtesy of Uncle Mike's, as he demon-

Four-wheel-drive hunters often tote their rifles in racks that are as much for display as for carrying. The author has had unfortunate experiences with these, indicating that they are in fact invitations to steal. Better to have your guns locked out of sight in a bolt-in vault such as those made by Treadlok.

strates the "hasty" sling for steadying the rifle in off-hand and kneeling positions, and the military/target style sling for sitting and prone positions. For the latter two, you must make a tight loop from the forend around your upper arm and pull the sling keeper down snug against your biceps. Properly adjusted, the sling will hold the rifle tightly to your shoulder without support from the right hand.

Entirely unique is the "Latigo" sling from Brownells, Inc., Montezuma, Iowa, 50171. The Latigo is composed of a single strap of 1-inch wide leather, 84 inches long. It loops through the swivels at both ends, and has a square eye amidships, equipped with a roller to reduce friction. Only super soft pit-tanned Swiss or German leather is used, for a suppleness seldom seen in a sling! The one-of-a-kind concept results in a sling that, once adjusted to the proper loop for your bicep/forend fit, will never change. The Latigo can be stretched taut between the swivels simply by pulling downward on the inner strand of the endless loop, resulting in three plys of leather snugged together. The sling can be brought into action in an instant by yanking downward on the two outer strands, expanding it for carrying on the

shoulder or assuming a sling-assisted sitting or prone position. Brownells sells the Latigo for about the same price as an ordinary sling. This marvelous device defies adequate description. I can only urge you to try it for yourself! The Latigo is entirely free from metal hooks, buckles or snaps. There's nothing to click or clink against the rifle and tip off game to your presence.

Vehicle Gun Storage

If you do your trailing in a Bronco that was foaled by Ford rather than a quarter horse mare, you likely have a hooked affair bolted over one window to hold your rifles proudly displayed for all to see. That's all very *macho;* but, it's also an engraved invitation to steal! And it doesn't take long! A friend and I were enroute to a deer hunt one year, when we stopped at a market in St. George, Utah, to augment our provisions with a few steaks and some cold milk. We couldn't have been gone more than 15 minutes, but we returned to find the gun cupboard bare! Someone had pried open a windwing, opened the door and ripped off three rifles and a .44 Magnum Smith & Wesson. Nobody saw anything! If they did, they weren't about to admit it and become

The Porta-D-Tect is an electronic device that sets off the vehicle horn if anyone attempts to enter your vehicle without an invitation! It contains ultrasonic sensors in a solid state circuit.

involved in a criminal case that might require them to appear in court.

A friend of mine keeps a trio of rifles concealed behind the fold-forward seat of his pickup; and in his Jeep Commando he built in a lockable floor compartment with a rifle rack. He had to sacrifice the rear passenger seat to do it, but I consider that a good trade.

On the wider rigs, such as the Chevrolet Blazer, Plymouth Trail Duster, Dodge Ramcharger and the new Ford Bronco, you can build in a covered rifle rack running the width of the vehicle behind the rear passenger seats, and fit in any normal-length rifle, big-bore or small. You can also improvise a lockable compartment yourself out of ¾-inch marine-quality plywood, to hold your rifles, cameras, binoculars, etc. Or you can opt for a "Treadlok Rumble Seat Security Chest" (from Tread Corporation, P.O. Box 5497, Roanoke, Virginia, 24012), which stretches the width of your rig inside of the fender wells, providing lockable steel storage and integral seat as well. Tread uses thick 13-gauge sheet steel, with welded seams and heavy-duty continuous piano hinges. Two compartments are provided, one behind the lazyback, and one under the seat. Cushions are of high density 3-inch thick polyurethane foam and the rifles are firmly held in Plastisol-coated spring steel racks, to prevent scratching. Tread also offers security chests that span the width of a pickup truck bed behind the cab, offering weatherproof, theft-proof protection for your rifles, tools, etc. Treadlok chests feature counter-balance shocks at each end of the heavy lids to make them respond to finger-tip pressure. The lids will remain in the upright position until deliberately lowered.

A superb burglary detection device is the "Porta-D-Tect Mobile 1" from Interarms, 10 Prince St., Alexandria, Virginia, 22313. This device is mounted inside of the vehicle and wired into the electrical system. The Porta-D-Tect Mobile 1 is a solid state electronic device that employs advanced ultrasonic technology to sense any unauthorized entry of your rig, and set the horn blowing an alarm. It blows until you disarm the device. Sure, it might run down your battery if you're out of earshot for a length of time, but it'll also run off would-be burglars!

Choosing and transporting a .22 trail companion may sound complicated, but be reassured—with all of the many excellent options available, it's pretty hard to go wrong with any one of them.

CHAPTER 6

Smallbore Survival Potential

THE REALIZATION OF being "lost" can come with stunning suddenness. A friendly forest can unexpectedly become a sea of white as a blizzard descends without warning. Even after the clouds depart, a blanket of snow remains to blot out the trail and mask familiar landmarks. Or, you heedlessly take a wrong turn in the trail, and by-and-by find yourself in an unfamiliar area brimming with breathtaking scenery—and little else! Such a seemingly innocuous error could suddenly plunge you into a situation of primordial self-reliance, with your life hinging upon the items in your pocket or pack, and your knowledge of how to use them.

At a time like this, you could use a little help from your friends! What better friend could you have than a .22 rimfire rifle securely slung across your shoulder, or a rimfire pistol tugging comfortingly at your belt? If you are out hunting small game, you already have your "survival gun" in hand, but suppose you're merely fishing or hiking, will your gun be with you or back in camp? Perhaps only a few miles distant as the crow flies, that camp might as well be on the other side of the moon! The answer is to choose a survival gun that you can live with as a constant companion, then keep it forever at your side during wilderness jaunts!

What should you expect of a wilderness survival gun? First, it must provide moral support. Therefore you must have confidence in its reliability and its capacity to perform whatever task you put it to. Second, it should provide sustenance by bringing to bag whatever wildlife the area has to offer. Third, it should afford a reasonable degree of protection from wild animals.

It is on the last count that the .22 rimfire has been subjected to the most abuse from detractors of its role as a survival gun. "You couldn't stop a charging grizzly bear with a .22!" goes the usual comment. I'll concede that point! But just how often do you expect to encounter a charging grizzly, unless you're ambling about

in Alaska. Even there, grizzly bears are few and far between. As one who hunted them in Alaska for 2 years running, without ever setting eyes upon one of the beasts, I speak from experience! Even if you should find yourself sharing the same woods with a grizzly, it is likely to split the instant that it catches your scent. If you somehow manage a face-to-face encounter with a grizzly, again the chances are better than even that it just wants to be left alone. If you quietly retire from the scene, it won't pursue you. However, if you anticipate getting lost in the hinterlands of Alaska and foresee a battle to the death with an irate grizzly, I'd advise you to take along a .340 Weatherby Magnum rifle, and just in case, back that up with a .44 Magnum side arm.

Seriously, a far greater threat to the hunter or hiker is the danger of attack by a pack of feral dogs—they are domestic dogs, lost or abandoned by their owners, that have turned wild and hunt in the same organized manner as a wolf or coyote pack. These animals do not share the same aversion to man that true wild creatures display. Like trained lions or tigers, when feral dogs turn upon man, they are malevolently vicious! In the unlikely event that you should be subject to such an attack, careful, sustained fire from a .22 should readily discourage the animals. It's usually not necessary to kill each and every one of the critters to save your own skin. Normally, the moment you present an offensive/ defensive posture to these dogs, they'll clear out in record time. Wild predators, like predatory humans, are for the most part bullies, with little intestinal fortitude to back up their bravado. If you wound or kill a couple of the animals, the entire bunch will turn tail.

A recent survey revealed that most big game hunters using centerfire rifles enter the field with no more than 24 rounds of ammunition, of which four are in the magazine of the rifle. Setting aside for the moment the fact that your best bet for obtaining food lies with small game, which abounds in most forested areas that are oth-

Oftentimes searchers in light planes pass directly overhead and fail to see the lost person. A small pocket flare rises 400 feet into the air to alert aircraft of your location. It is bright enough to be clearly visible even in daylight.

Sometimes scanning the surrounding country from a high point with binoculars will help you to find familiar landmarks and point the way home.

Once convinced that you are truly lost, inventory your pack to see if you have the items needed to keep body and soul together.

(Left) The realization of "being lost" usually overtakes one late in the day. In most cases the best move is to make yourself comfortable for the night. At a time like this you can use a little help from your "friends" — like this Charter Arms AR-7 survival rifle, which assembles in seconds, beginning with joining the receiver and tough, lightweight cycolac stock.

(Top) A threaded collar holds the barrel in place. Add a loaded eight-shot magazine in the bottom of the receiver, and you're loaded for bear — almost!

erwise sparsely inhabited with big game animals, how long will 24 rounds last? You can't escape the feeling of being a pauper as far as ammo is concerned—unless, you have a rifle or rimfire handgun and say two small boxes of ammo stashed on your person or in your pack. Then, you're rich! You have 24 rounds that can be reserved for hunting the larger game animals that you might run across, and over four times that number for taking the far more numerous small animals that will more than likely form the backbone of your bill-of-fare during your unscheduled stay in Mother Nature's open-air motel. You should also consider this: 24 rounds of rimfire ammo, and two spare boxes of the same fodder (100 or more rounds) weighs ounces. The same amount of centerfire ammo *weighs pounds*. In a survival situation extra weight can be a liability.

This brings us to another basic point concerning your choice of a survival gun. Should you carry a rifle or a handgun? The answer depends primarily upon your degree of skill with a pistol. If you have trouble connecting with the 10 ring at 25 yards when you're calm and relaxed and shooting under ideal lighting conditions, what luck do you think you'll have hitting the head of a squirrel playing hide-and-seek high among the thickly bunched needles of a tall spruce when you're tense and

out of breath and balancing on one leg atop a none-too-steady deadfall? Being scared doesn't magically endow you with flawless marksmanship. The effect is likely to be just the opposite! The more desperate you become, the more the sights wiggle and wave. Techniques to promote better field accuracy described in the upcoming chapter about hunting will, of course, help immensely. On the other side of the coin, lies the troubling question: If you settle upon a rifle, will it be with you when you need it, or back in the Jeep? You are the best judge of your own willingness to be forever burdened with a rifle. A handgun on the hip is worth a whole rack of rifles back in the den!

Takedown and Combination Survival Rifles

Any of the guns mentioned in the previous chapter as suitable trail companions will also serve as viable survival tools. However, let's consider some .22 rimfire guns specifically designed for maximum service and minimum weight and bulk. Indisputably, the purest of breed among survival guns is Charter Arms' AR-7 Explorer. At first blush, you might mistake it for only part of a plastic stock for some kind of an air rifle. However, you have but to remove the flexible plastic butt cap, and

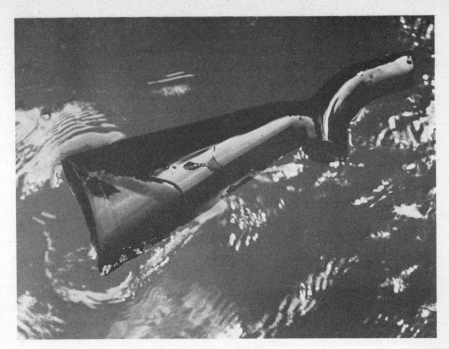

One of the "survival" benefits of the AR-7 is that it floats like a cork. It even floats assembled. The flexible plastic butt plate effectively seals out water from the hollowed-out portion of the stock.

neatly nested within are the makin's of an autoloading firearm! Slide out the flat-sided anodized aluminum alloy receiver and drop it into the waiting slot at the front of the stock. Secure it with a wing-head bolt, thread the knurled collar of the barrel into the front, slide the eight-shot clip in the bottom, pull out the bolt knob, crank 'er back, and you're loaded for bear! Well—almost. The Explorer chambers .22 Long Rifles only. Average assembly time is 45 seconds. Even the barrel is made of lightweight alloy, sleeved with a rifled steel tube. The skin of the stock is made of nearly indestructable cycolac, with foam interior for stiffness, hollowed appropriately to accept the AR-7's three major metal components in snug cavities. When stowed, the entire assembly measures only 16½ inches in length. Total weight is just 2½ pounds. You can shove this one in your day pack and never notice it. To

discourage rust, the steel bolt and knob are hard-chrome plated. Believe it or not, the AR-7 *floats,* stowed or assembled. Accuracy with the peep-and-post sights is adequate enough to nail down small game out to about 50 yards.

Another takedown style survival arm is the compact Camper's Companion from Savage. Cataloged as the Model 24-C, this gun isn't exactly self-contained, but it comes with a soft plastic case that accepts the stock/receiver assembly in one half, and the barrel/forearm in the other. The two halves are then folded over and tied into a bundle just 22 × 6 × 4 inches. When you assemble the gun, you're in for a surprise—it's actually two guns in one, a top-break over/under .22/20-gauge rifle/shotgun with 20-inch barrels, with a total weight of only 5¾ pounds. The butt stock is drilled out to accept two shotshells and 10 rounds of .22 Long Rifle, closed by a

The Savage Model 24-C Camper's Companion (top) compares favorably with the AR-7 for size, although it is somewhat heavier. This over/under .22/20 gauge packs some heavy firepower in that bottom barrel, launching a ⅝-ounce rifled slug at 1600 fps. The Camper's Companion takes down into a 20-inch long package that stows in a plastic case provided with the gun. A trap in the butt holds 10 Long Rifles and two shotshells.

swinging hatch. Using 2¾-inch #6 shells, a Camper's Companion (with cylinder choke) laid down some well centered, dense shot patterns for the author at 20 yards. That lower barrel can also be used to launch a ⅝-ounce rifled slug at 1600 fps. Perhaps that's the answer to that grizzly bear we're always hearing about! Would you believe ¾-inch 10-shot groups at 25 yards with high velocity .22 Long Rifles? This despite a trigger pull that almost requires a windlass to crank it all the way back in order to release the visible hammer with its integral barrel selector. The rebounding hammer must be cocked manually for each shot, but that is in effect the safety. The notch-and-post sights are more hinderance than help, but the barrel top is grooved to receive a scope. The only problem is the possibility that you might find yourself wearing the scope tube in your eye socket (when firing the shotgun barrel). Perhaps a better answer would be a Williams 5D receiver sight.

If a combination gun appeals to you, but you'd like to upgrade that upper barrel to .22 Magnum, your choice should be the Savage 24-D, with 24-inch barrels (but

nut and will not warp, crack, fade, chip or peel. It includes such niceties as white-lined black forend tip, pistol grip cap and butt plate, plus hand-gripping sharp-diamond checkering. The Nylon 66 holds 14 Long Rifle cartridges in a tubular magazine within the butt stock. Adjustable open sights are backed by a grooved receiver that's ready for mounting your choice of scope. Remington also offers two black-stocked models, one with blued barrel and receiver, the other with rather gaudy but highly rust-resistant chromed, steel parts. Coupled with its absolute dependability, the extreme lightweight nature of this 4-pound rifle makes it a near ideal choice for a smallbore survival gun. Sling and swivels are available as an option—a good investment in convenience!

Also noted for absolute reliability is the Ruger 10/22, a rimfire carbine that looks like a training rifle for its older brother, the .44 Magnum Ruger Carbine. The original Plain Jane version is still available, but I heartily recommend the fancier 10/22 Deluxe Sporter with checkered American walnut stock, sling swivels, plus a

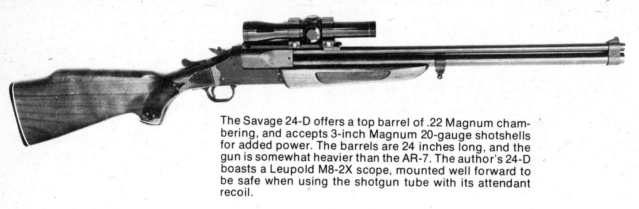

The Savage 24-D offers a top barrel of .22 Magnum chambering, and accepts 3-inch Magnum 20-gauge shotshells for added power. The barrels are 24 inches long, and the gun is somewhat heavier than the AR-7. The author's 24-D boasts a Leupold M8-2X scope, mounted well forward to be safe when using the shotgun tube with its attendant recoil.

with no carrying case). As a power bonus, you'll find the bottom barrel chambered for 3-inch 20-gauge Magnum shells instead of just the 2¾-inch variety.

In my opinion, the 24-D has a couple of drawbacks: It measures 24 inches taken down, weighs a substantial 7½ pounds and is somewhat unhandy in a backpack. You can't afford to have your hands taken up with carrying a gun (either the 24-C or 24-D) all the time, so the only answer is a sling—preferably one of quality and wide enough so it doesn't cut into your shoulder after hours of walking.

Measured in terms of ruggedness, reliability and light weight, it would be hard to beat the Remington autoloading Nylon 66 rifle. Nearly the entire rifle is made of molded Du Pont structural nylon, save for the 19⅜-inch barrel, action parts (bolt, trigger, springs, etc.) and the stamped steel action cover. And "cover" is all that it is. The action parts all move in contact with nylon, not steel, therefore require no lubrication—a distinct advantage in sub-zero climates. The stock of the Mohawk brown model realistically simulates well-grained wal-

higher comb and shotgun-type butt plate. Ruger's unique rotary box magazine affords a full 10-round capacity without protruding from the bottom of the rifle. I recommend carrying a couple of spare, loaded magazines for the Ruger or any other clip-loading rifle, not only as backup (quick) reloads, but to avoid having your rifle become a rather inefficient single-loader should you lose the clip! Highly functional and rugged bead-and-folding leaf sights top the 18½-inch barrel. The Ruger 10/22's short and streamlined receiver, along with the sensible barrel length, make this autoloader a very compact and relatively light (5 pounds) rifle—ideal for survival use. Adding a scope to the dovetail mount-base supplied with the rifle detracts from the handiness somewhat, but it certainly provides for some superior aiming equipment. Williams markets a receiver sight designed specifically for the 10/22. This streamlined sight helps the 10/22 retain its smooth lines and provides a better sight picture.

The 3-second takedown and assembly time of the Browning Automatic .22 makes it an excellent knap-

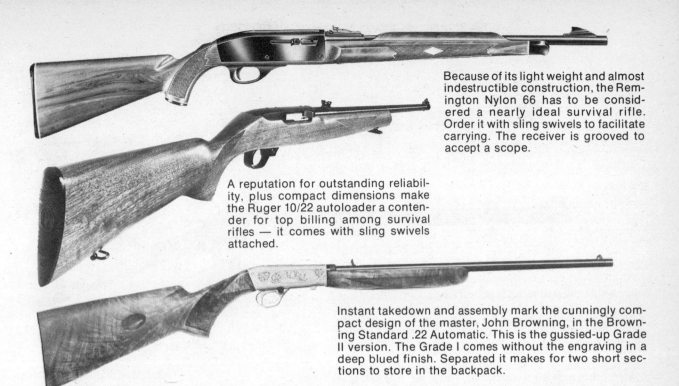

Because of its light weight and almost indestructible construction, the Remington Nylon 66 has to be considered a nearly ideal survival rifle. Order it with sling swivels to facilitate carrying. The receiver is grooved to accept a scope.

A reputation for outstanding reliability, plus compact dimensions make the Ruger 10/22 autoloader a contender for top billing among survival rifles — it comes with sling swivels attached.

Instant takedown and assembly mark the cunningly compact design of the master, John Browning, in the Browning Standard .22 Automatic. This is the gussied-up Grade II version. The Grade I comes without the engraving in a deep blued finish. Separated it makes for two short sections to store in the backpack.

sack rifle. With the butt/receiver and barrel/forearm units separated, it reduces to a mere 19 inches in length. Assembled, it retains the small proportions and slender lines that make it one of fastest-handling rifles available. The amazingly simple breakdown requires only that you press a small latch on the bottom of the slim receiver and rotate the barrel one-quarter turn to release the interrupted thread joint—a takeup adjustment in the breech end of the barrel assures continued firm fit. An 11-shot tubular magazine loads through a port in the right side of the selected walnut stock, and a set of high grade bead-and-folding leaf sights grace the top of the Browning's 19-inch barrel. Although a scope mount is available, the Browning Automatic is at its best with the low-profile open sights or a receiver sight. Weighing less than 5 pounds, it constitutes a nearly ideal survival rifle.

Any of the larger autoloading rifles, such as the new Browning BAR or the Weatherby Mark XXII could serve as survival guns, but the very assets that make them outstanding hunting rifles, i.e., their man-sized proportions and bigbore rifle weight, make them high risk candidates for residing in the rifle rack or back at camp when they are most needed!

By now, you may be questioning my preoccupation with autoloading rifles for survival use. Aren't they infamous for jamming at critical moments? Don't they promote wasteful expenditure of ammunition? What worse contraindicators could there possible be? In the first instance, all of the rifles mentioned have more than proved themselves through extensive field tests to be totally without feeding problems. Some low-priced autoloaders and some now-abandoned action designs

have given these guns a bad name over the years. Just remember to buy *quality* and you'll have no action-feeding problems! Regarding the waste of ammunition: The solution to that problem, if there be one, lies within your own mind. If you fire every round as if it were your last (and in a survival situation, you *must* think that way), you won't waste ammo. Should the situation ever arise where you would be called upon to protect yourself from marauding predators, the auto offers the best chance of effective sustained fire. Listed in order of desirability I would choose the autoloader first, then lever action or pump, thirdly the traditional bolt action, and lastly the single shot.

Your choice of a survival rifle might well hinge upon (in the final analysis) what style of magazine the gun possesses. In general, the larger the magazine capacity, the better. However, any magazine will sooner or later run out. Then speed of reloading could become a critical factor, especially in those instances where game might be escaping or you were under attack. Tubular magazines are noted for holding the most ammo, usually 11 to 14 Long Rifles, but the somewhat small keyhole loading slot might be hard to find with frigid, fumbling fingers. (The Browning Automatic with its funnel-shaped stock opening is perhaps the only exception where tube-fed autos are concerned.) Given a couple of spare 10-shot clips, the rifle with detachable magazine looks pretty good both from the aspect of capacity and speed of reloading, making it an attractive option!

Among lever action rifles, the 20-inch barreled Browning BL-22, Marlin 39M and Winchester 9422, and the 18-inch barreled Ithaca Saddlegun, fill the bill

Among lever action rifles, the Marlin 39M (top) and Winchester 9422 (bottom) both have 20-inch barrels, making them short enough to be practical as survival rifles. Both will take down with the removal of a single screw, for stowing in your pack. Note that the Marlin's shorter receiver results in a shorter overall length, despite the same barrel length. The Marlin comes with those essential sling swivels that are lacking on the Winchester. The stock and receiver of the Ithaca Model 72 Saddlegun (center) are as long as those of the Winchester. However, the barrel is only 18-inches long, resulting in reduced overall length.

The author regards these double action revolvers as practical survival handguns because of their light weight and relatively small size. Top to bottom they are: H&R Model 999 Sportsman with 6-inch tip-up barrel; S&W .22/32 Kit Gun with six-shot cylinder; Hi-Standard Sentinel with 3-inch barrel and nine-shot cylinder; and the diminutive Charter Arms Pathfinder. Note the S&W has Pachmayr Presentation Campac SJ grips, and Pathfinder has Bulldog grips.

admirably! All have under-barrel tubular magazines of ample capacity. All can be equipped with scopes, if desired. These carbines are fast-handling and compact, and utterly reliable!

Survival Handguns

If you opt for a handgun, remember, the principal reasons for choosing it over a rifle—its light weight and small dimensions. Don't saddle yourself with a long-barreled heavyweight that you'll soon abandon. Adjustable sights and a good sight picture are desirable for accurate bullet placement, but a primarily target-intended pistol will usually have sights that are entirely too tall for convenient holster carrying. Best bets among autoloaders are the Hi-Standard Sport King with 4½-inch barrel and the Ruger Standard Model with 4¾-inch barrel. Most of the small precision-made foreign autoloaders are priced entirely too high for practical consideration.

One long-time favorite with backpackers is the Smith & Wesson Model 34 22/32 Kit Gun which has recently become available in stainless steel, making it all but rustproof. With 4-inch barrel, it still weighs only 22½ ounces, and sports fine adjustable sights. Considering

The Ruger New Model Single Six Convertible now comes in stainless steel for almost total resistance to corrosion. A survival gun is subject to more abuse than one used under normal circumstances with frequent drenching or dunking not at all unlikely!

its weight and now-rustproof qualities, the Model 34 would make a good choice for the survival-minded hunter.

Charter Arms' kit-sized Pathfinder double action, six-shot, swing-out cylinder revolver with 3-inch barrel has all of the assets of light weight (22½ ounces), plus it has micro-adjustable sights and comes in either standard or magnum chambering

A notch above the kit gun in size (it has a 6-inch ventilated rib barrel) is the Harrington & Richardson Model 999 top-break, .22 Long Rifle, nine-shot, double action revolver. It is a fine choice for a survival handgun, because of its excellent balance and feel and for the fact that it is highly accurate and reliable. The 999's longer sighting radius is also a decided advantage when it comes to accurate shooting.

Single action revolvers are slow to load, slow to empty, and slow to fire, however, I sometimes wonder if they don't offer some other assets that outweigh these apparent debilities. *Reliable* they most certainly *are!* Plus, they seem to find the target as if with built-in radar. No other handgun is so easy pointing. Once

If your preference runs to autoloading handguns, Hi-Standard's nickel-plated Sport King (top) with 4½-inch barrel offers high resistance to corrosion—an important consideration—plus rapid aimed fire, large magazine capacity and quick reloading. The Standard Model Ruger (right) with a 4¾-inch barrel is among the best values on the market, and it's one of the most reliable autoloaders. Autoloaders generally run heavier than revolvers, but make a flatter fit on the hip. They are, on the whole, highly accurate.

Despite slow loading and slow firing, the single action revolver remains tops in popularity among a wide segment of shooters. Some assets include: high degree of reliability despite bad weather and dirty environment; and ability to switch cylinders to shoot either standard .22 Long Rifles or .22 Magnum ammo. The Ruger Super Single Six also includes readily adjustable sights.

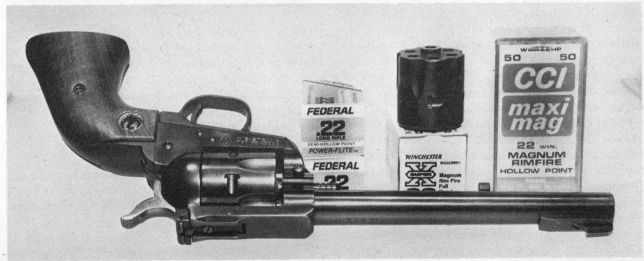

accustomed to the reloading procedures, most shooters accept this as merely the pause that refreshes. And if you happened to grow up with a Single Action Colt, as I did, no other gun can ever quite take its place. Modern rimfire single actions offer yet another plus—they are available with instantly interchangeable cylinders, allowing the shooter to boost his killing power from .22 Long Rifle to .22 Magnum in a twinkling. Two outstanding examples are the Iver Johnson Cattleman Trailblazer and the Ruger New Model Super Single-Six Convertible. Both sport excellent adjustable sights and come with dual cylinders. For these, I recommend getting 6½-inch barrels. For some mysterious reason that must be the result of any single action's anatomically fitted grips, the longer barrel lengths don't slow the shooter down, and the longer sighting radius improves accuracy and provides more muzzle velocity.

For purposes of protection in a survival situation, there's no disputing that a .22 Winchester Magnum Rim Fire wins hands down! For taking larger game animals, say bobcat size and up, the .22 Magnum excels, but when it comes to bagging small animals such as tree squirrels for the pot, better stick to .22 Long Rifle ammo, or use solids in the .22 Magnum. Otherwise, you will have precious little left of the animal to eat! CCI's new Stingers are also too destructive for pot hunting. A good compromise is the Federal Semi-Hollow Point or Winchester's new Dynapoint .22. Both of these have abbreviated, hollow-pointed bullets that expand sufficiently for good killing power on small game without tearing it to shreds. CCI shot cartridges are useful only at *very* close range for driving off small camp pests such as pack rats. Don't seriously expect these shot rounds to stop any larger animal. Also, forget about carrying .22 Shorts, CB Caps, etc. They just complicate your logistics at a time when you don't need extra problems!

Optics

Should you equip your survival .22 with a scope? If it's a rifle that you plan to hunt with as well as carry for survival insurance, it definitely should be scope sighted. Admittedly, some degree of handiness is sacrificed when you burden a rifle with a scope. If you prefer to keep your equipment as light and compact as possible, consider the option of a receiver sight such as the Williams Foolproof or Lyman 66. However, there's no disputing the fact that a scope makes any man a better shot, especially under conditions of poor visibility or bad lighting. Even such specialized survival guns as the Charter Arms AR-7 and the Savage Camper's Companion can be fitted with scopes. The latter is already grooved, and the former can be equipped with a B-Square dovetail mount that attaches to the alloy receiver via an existing screw located amidships on the left side. Thenceforth, any scope with a dovetail tip-off mount, including B-Square's, can be quickly installed. You can sight the scope mount combo in, and carry it

separately when the rifle is stowed in the stock. I haven't had the opportunity to test this unit, but it looks as if it should return to the original zero.

When it comes to buying a scope for a potential survival rifle, be sure to choose a lightweight, compact scope with the best optics you can afford. Among these scopes you should consider are the Weatherby Mark XXII, with its razor-sharp definition and bright image, or the new Leupold M8-2.5X—it's short, lightweight, bright and features a wide field of view. Also, Bushnell's 3X to 7X Custom .22 scope, and Weaver's V-22 (3X to 6X) offer the ability to dial in low power to afford the most light-gathering ability possible for those late evening and early morning dimly-lighted shots when small game is most active. These two scopes also possess the wide field of view needed to take rabbits on the run. When light is good, the higher powers can be used to help pick up small targets hiding in the brush at longer distances. Order your scope with a dual-diameter-type reticle which offers fine center cross hairs that won't blot out small game, plus broad lines away from the center that are readily seen in poor light.

A scope on a handgun destroys its major virtues of quick handling and easy portability and pointability, adding so much bulk and weight that the average hiker sooner or later tires of the burden and leaves it behind. Furthermore, it's difficult to find a comfortable holster to fit a scoped pistol.

Survival Cleaning Supplies

Under survival conditions, you won't be able to pamper your gun. It will be exposed to the elements as never before. It behooves you to provide some protection! The handiest item I have yet discovered for the purpose is Birchwood Casey's Sheath Take-Along Anti-Rust Gun Cloth, a 5½ × 8-inch wipe, impregnated with Sheath Polarized Rust Preventive sealed in a 2½ × 3-inch foil envelope. You can use it to wipe off the gun, and it will displace moisture on the metal without harm to the stock finish; it can also be used to wipe out the bore if you happen to have a cleaning rod handy. Another well-known rust preventive, WD-40, is available in a pocket-sized 2.75-ounce spray can—hard to beat for easy use under difficult conditions. As much as some people disdain nickel-plated guns, they do resist rust far better than those that are merely blued. Of course, the ideal solution is stainless steel! Note that the Ruger Super Single Six and S&W Model 34, .22/32 are available in stainless.

Wilderness Survival and the .22

A new generation of "survival" lore has recently surfaced, pointing up methods of outliving a total collapse of our national order, complete with insurrection, riots, and rampant anarchy, even including invasion by a foreign power! The "system" as put forth in these writings, presupposes that you have already abandoned

(Right) Adding a scope to your survival rifle costs something in terms of compactness, but adds a lot to your accuracy potential! Even such a gun as the Charter Arms AR-7 can be scope-equipped thanks to a side mount from B-Square Company, combined with their 1-inch ring dovetail mounts. The scope must be removed to stow the receiver in the butt stock.

(Left) A scope for your survival rifle should be lightweight and not too bulky. This quartet offers the best of both worlds. Top to bottom: Leupold's new M8-2.5X Compact with exceptionally bright optics in a short-short tube; Bushnell's 3X-7X Custom .22 provides the unique assistance of an elevation knob that dials range distance to do away with holdover; Weatherby's Mark XXII 4X scope is doubtless the best scope designed primarily for rimfire use with a wide bright field; and Weaver's V-22 3X-6X with good optics at a reasonable price.

the concrete jungle in favor of a backwoods hideaway, complete with truck garden and pure-water well. That idea is certainly not without merit, to which any city dweller plagued by smog and confiscatory taxes will readily attest!

If we accept the basic premise for the moment, and assume such a sanctuary exists, certainly the .22 rimfire rifle and pistol should play a major role. You could hunt small game with a .22 without alarming other animals and driving wildlife from the area. Moreover, the dim "pop" muffled by the woods shouldn't alert "hostile" forces that might be lurking nearby. Rimfire guns and ammunition are relatively cheap. A number of guns could be stashed along with supplies of ammo and food in various strategically located caches, to be dug up in time of need. Rimfire guns could be used for all non-critical uses, saving centerfire ammo that might well be in short supply.

Whether your survival problems are occasioned by national disaster or merely a wrong turn in the trail, your basic need will be for food. Those snares so alluringly depicted in survival manuals are, in truth, a snare of delusion. Long before you could learn to use them effectively, you would be down to skin and bones! You don't have time to take an on-the-job, do-it-yourself course in trapping. The same goes for the oft-heard advice about sneaking up on unsuspecting game and clubbing it to death. You couldn't wield a club long enough to reach most wary wild animals! However, a .22 rifle or pistol can stretch your reach from 25 to 100 yards, much closer to the average stalking ability.

It pays to know your game. Often a squirrel when caught in the open will freeze and remain that way until you are almost within arm's reach. If you find that you can approach an animal or bird without its instant flight, you may have it pinned down for the moment because it fears to move and reveal its position. Then it pays to stalk as close as possible without driving the animal away. Don't feel guilty about taking "easy" shots. Make them as easy and positive as possible! Don't be above "ground-sluicing" a Franklin's grouse or "fool's hen" if the opportunity affords. Where your very life is at stake, you should consider the game laws temporarily under a state of suspension. If a game warden should stroll by, ticketbook in hand, I suspect you would welcome him with open arms, even if you had a deer down out of season. If the incident ever came to light, I would hope that local judges could understand your predicament! One thing that can never be suspended are the laws of nature. If you make a mistake, you can expect to pay for it with your life! Nature knows birth and death daily, and it makes no distinction between men and animals.

Incidentally, you may have heard the one about how easy it is to shoot fish in a rain barrel. It should be just as easy in a small pool or stream, right? Not so! For starters, your own eyes play tricks on you. That fish which looks so near the surface in one place may really be a lot deeper than you think and actually in a different place. We all know that glass and water bend light rays. Sight through the edge of a water glass at some object and move the glass. The object moves with it. So lesson

Traditional Boy Scout knife from Case provides for essential tools of survival, sturdy stainless steel Kershaw Stockman with three sharp cutting edges, Kershaw Model 1034 with 5-inch blade, are all good tools in the outback. The machette-like Woodsman's Pal provides the services of an axe, hammer, shovel, etc. The pruning hook on the end is handy for reaching up to cut a high limb.

one: A fish may not be where he appears to be. Next, take into consideration the fact that a bullet striking the water at an angle will be deflected to a greater or lesser degree away from the target, and you can see that shooting fish could well be an exercise in futility!

Better to take a few fish hooks along, plus line, sinkers, and a small bobber. In an emergency, you can make a passable sinker out of a .22 bullet. Work the bullet loose by bending it one way and then the next until the brass case releases its grip. Don't throw away the powder. It makes priceless tinder to start a fire under difficult conditions of wet or snow. Save the Long Rifle case as well. It makes a fine whistle to signal for help. Just blow briskly across the top.

To make the sinker, split the bullet about halfway down with your knife. Insert the line and squeeze the bullet together to grip it. You may have to use your teeth if you lack a pair of pliers. If you can't get a good grip, lay it on a rock and tap with the butt of your knife or a small rock to close the gap more tightly. Improvise a pole from a small springy sapling.

Gut even small fish before cooking. Lacking utensils, you can cook fish and birds in a thick coating of clay, immersed in the hot coals of your fire for about an hour, more or less, depending upon size. Breaking away the clay removes the skin, leaving the meat sweet and juicy. Eating local vegetation can be a risky business unless you know what you're doing. Recently a young camper near Santa Cruz, California, died from eating poisonous water hemlock, which he mistook for watercress. You can eat frogs, snakes, lizards, turtles, even wood grubs and grasshoppers if you get desperate, but better steer clear of toads. Try to shoot turtles in shallow water, because they sink when killed. Various rodents

and marmots, such as prairie dogs and woodchucks, as well as coyotes and bobcats all can assuage that gnawing in the pit of your stomach.

Burnham Brothers' "Squeeker" game call is worth its weight in gold. No great skill is required to blow coaxing sounds from it, attracting all manner of critters from foxes to coyotes, sometimes even deer. If you down an animal, don't lose yourself again in your zeal to find it! Play it cool, and first mark the spot from which you fired that shot with a streamer of blaze orange ribbon, a strip torn from your red handkerchief, etc., then move quickly to the spot where the animal was last seen. If you don't find it immediately, don't despair. I have searched for the better part of an hour to find an animal that dropped within yards of the spot where it was hit.

Always work methodically. Mark the location where the animal went down. Then circle the marker in ever widening loops, looking for the animal or signs of its passing. Keep an eye out for spots of blood, fresh ruts torn in the earth by hurried hoofs, bent or broken branches or grass. When you cut sign, follow with studied haste always watching well ahead. The animal might be down close by and try to take flight as you approach. Be ready to make a follow-up shot if the animal gets up within range. If not, watch it carefully through your binoculars. Even if it disappears into a wash or over a ridge, you may catch sight of it again if you patiently maintain your vigil. I recall a wounded antelope that escaped under cover of a fierce wind-driven snow. I watched it through occasional lapses in the wind until it was several miles distant, before it finally settled down. I followed it up and bagged the animal with a *coup-de-grace*.

A wounded animal will seek the easiest path of escape, usually one that offers sufficient cover. Thus you should expect to find it downhill, probably in dense brush. It may well freeze under a bush and let you walk right by it if you're not alert enough to spot it. Keep watching the spoor! Time is on your side so don't rush it. If you allow the animal to bleed and stiffen up, it may not be able to rise when you approach.

Because you can't overpower your quarry with a .22 rimfire at long distances, you must compensate through good woodsmanship, stalking and accurate bullet placement in vital areas. A lung shot is not satisfactory bullet placement with a deer-sized animal. It will likely escape to die later to no avail. With a gun of limited power, as the .22 rimfire certainly is, you cannot in good conscience try shots at running deer. Accept only a standing shot (preferably from the side) so that you can aim for the base of the ear, and channel through to the brain, or aim about a third of the way from the top of the neck to sever the spine. You would do well to confine your survival hunting to small game at the outset. It would be criminally wasteful to down a deer, only to leave most of the carcass to rot!

Only in a situation of long-term isolation in the wilderness is the taking of a big game animal justified. If the climate is cold enough, you can hang the animal, and its flesh will be fit for eating for many weeks. I recall a time in Alaska when I and four others were isolated by a sudden spate of weather that prevented our pickup plane from coming after us. We had two caribou in camp. It was so cold at night that a cup of hot coffee would crust over with a thin skin of ice within minutes. We lived off of the caribou for about a week after our provisions ran out.

If you down a big game animal such as a deer in mild weather, plan to spend about a week jerking or smoking meat. To jerk deer meat, cut strips 8 to 10 inches long, 1½-inches wide, and about 1-inch thick from the neck and back. Cut a couple of forked sticks to support a long slender pole, across which you drape the strips above your camp fire, high enough to dry out in the smoke without actually cooking. A hot sun will also dry meat, given enough time. A generous coating of salt and pepper will help cure it and ward off flies. To eat, cut the meat into short lengths and cook on a spit.

With a large food supply assured, you may be planning to hole up for awhile, perhaps until rescued. Often that can be the best course to pursue. Time after time, would-be rescuers find former encampments of a lost person, only to discover that he has moved on, leaving no clue as to when or what direction he may have taken. Then it becomes a game of hide-and-seek, with everyone the loser! Also, when at rest, the human body consumes only about 150 to 200 calories daily. Heavy activity such as mountain climbing can elevate that to 500 or more. The more you do, the more you must eat.

Concentrate upon making yourself as comfortable as possible. Try to locate your "camp" on the lee side of a mountain, low enough to escape winds that sweep down from the ridge, high enough to stay above streams or swampy areas where insects swarm. You can dig in under a windfall that offers natural protection, and enhance it by making a tent of loose bark peeled from nearby trees. Lacking that, stack pine boughs (needles pointing downward) along both sides. Insulate yourself from the cold ground with a bed of springy evergreen boughs, cutting only the young sprigs with flexible stems. Don't locate in a low spot that will collect and hold water in the event of a rain. Also, avoid a position near old dead snags that might topple over in storm or under aging trees that could pelt you with broken limbs.

During the day, gather fuel to last the night. If possible, store enough wood for several days. A sudden snow could cover downed timber or a rain render it too soggy to burn. Stack your wood at the base of a tree or under a rock overhang to keep it dry. Build your fire against a reflecting rock to conserve heat and shield it from the wind. Keep it small to avoid flying embers that could touch off a forest fire. Towering flames could even leap into the lower branches of surrounding trees, turning them into torches that could incinerate you in the bargain. Never build a fire upon a bed of peat. Always dig down to mineral earth, lest the peat smolders until it sets the forest ablaze, perhaps days after you have left the scene.

It's wise to follow a pattern of eating early in the afternoon, and hitting the sack at sunset. In high country, the air becomes chilled the moment the sun sinks behind the mountain. A drop in air temperature of 30 degrees is commonplace. Admittedly it's not very exciting to remain in the sack for the long hours from sunset to sunrise, but it's far better to retain body warmth than to try belatedly to regain it! If you wake up cold at night, don't jump up and do an Indian war dance. You'll just waste energy. Instead, squirm around and use the isometric system of straining one muscle against another to increase metabolism and circulation. Avoid drinking too much water just before bedtime. Getting up to relieve yourself in the middle of the night can be a chilling experience.

When you read in the newspaper about someone dying of "exposure," the actual killer was hypothermia, an abnormal lowering of the body's core temperature. A drop of as little as 3 degrees can lead to uncontrollable shivering, clumsiness and loss of judgement. If the body's core temperature drops as low as 88 degrees, death is almost a certainty. Long before that point is reached, the victim will be suffering from frostbite of the extremities, such as the ears, nose, fingers and toes, as well as areas where the skin is stretched over bony structures such as cheek bones, etc.

Your own best hope for escaping a similar fate lies in proper preparation before you find yourself in this predicament. For starters, you should be wearing wool

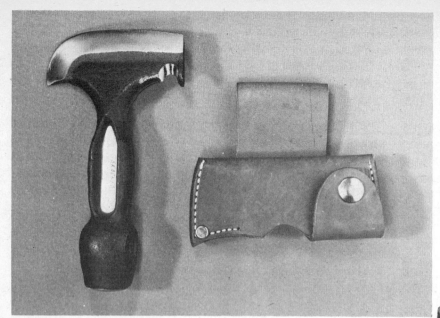

One style of the excellent Wilkie Compass, the Model 111L, is available from Precise Imports, and is somewhat large for the average camper/hiker/hunter, but it comes with a leather belt pouch for easy carrying.

The Skachet from Charter Arms is one of the best survival tools. It has a threaded eye, into which a limb can be screwed to make a handle. Then the tool becomes an axe or hammer. The knife edge is backed with a gut hook for swiftly unzipping the abdomen of big game animals.

clothing which protects you even when damp, unlike cotton which acts as a clammy conductor of body warmth to the outside air. A down-filled undershirt from Eddie Bauer is in fact a lightweight jacket that can be stuffed into an unbelievably small space and pulled out when needed. Covered by a water-windproof parka with built-in hood, it will keep you warm even in sub-zero temperatures. A Sherpa-styled Balaclava cap, also from Bauer, can be pulled down around the neck to prevent all of your body heat from escaping out the chimney! You'll also need gloves or mittens to keep fingers functional.

It doesn't necessarily require sub-zero temperatures to kill. Many cases are on record of people suffering hypothermia when the air temperature was well above freezing. The villains were wind, rain and cold, linked in an awesome conspiracy against man. Wind chill charts link temperature and wind velocity in an equation indicating the severity of the threat. For example, with ambient air temperature at 35 degrees Fahrenheit and a wind velocity of 40 miles per hour, your body loses heat at the same rate as if the temperature were 3 degrees in calm air. And that's assuming that your clothes are dry!

Under stress, a person tends to perspire more readily than normal. If you're wearing a zipper-closing impermeable outer covering, heavy exertion will saturate your clothing as much as drenching rain without protection. A poncho is excellent under these circumstances because it allows ready evaporation of sweat, while still protecting you from the elements.

Perspiration is to be avoided whenever possible. It results in the loss of valuable water and salt from your system, leading to possible dehydration. By the way, dehydration can occur in an ice and snow environment as well as the sandy desert. Salt is required to transfer fluids into the cells where it can be utilized by the body. Lack of salt can make you literally die of thirst, even though you pour gallons of water through your body.

Water is in fact more important to your survival than food. A man in good physical condition can live up to a month without food, but seldom over a week without water! Food without water is of little value. Body chemistry requires liquids. If you eat without water, you may end up with a monumental belly ache! If you were smart, you took a canteen with you. If you're lucky, there's a stream or pond nearby. If you're like the rest of us, you start lookin'. Follow flights of birds at dusk or game trails downhill. Both often lead to water. Eating snow is a poor substitute for water. Better to melt it over the fire than to have it reduce your body temperature even more. It takes a lot of snow to make a little water. Better to melt ice, if available. Contaminated water could give you dysentery, typhoid, worms, etc. If in doubt, boil water briskly for 5 minutes at sea level plus 1 minute for every 1,000 feet of elevation. Or add one 8-milligram iodine tablet per quart. Tea, cocoa and boullion cubes are easily stored in cramped spaces, provide instant energy, and make brackish water more palatable.

If you have established a base camp with a fairly elaborate shelter and must make a foray for food with your faithful .22 rimfire, take care that you don't lose the shelter! Before venturing out of sight of camp, make a wide circle of the area, noting any prominent landmarks. Place a marker high above your shelter. Pull over a tall sapling and tie your handkerchief to it. When it springs back up, the marker should be high enough to be visible from every quarter. Outbound on your foraging trip, "blaze" a trail by cutting a noticeable notch in the bark of a tree or tying a strip of blaze-orange ribbon to a limb on the side facing your return path, as often as necessary to keep these guides constantly in sight, looking back over your shoulder.

If you can't reasonably expect a search party to find you and decide to walk out, travel the ridges, which run to more or less straight lines, where sparse growth makes movement easier and improved visibility aids in spotting smoke by day and lights by night that could mark human habitation. Following a stream downhill has its hazards. Streams tend to meander and are often bordered by swamps or tangled thickets that impede

power on slippery rocks as Vibram lugged boots. You can hedge your bet by removing your socks and wearing just the boots across. Then dry the boots as well as you can, put the still-dry socks back on, then the boots. Given good weather, you will probably walk the boots dry by afternoon.

Perhaps even more important to your survival than your .22 rimfire rifle or pistol is a good knife. Better yet, take two! Carry a heavy-duty folding knife for fine cutting, and a sheath knife for chopping wood and splitting the brisket of any deer you might bag. As a lad, I carried a Boy Scout knife with me wherever I went. I still take one along on camp-outs and find ample use for its screwdriver, awl, can and bottle opener, plus stout, spear-point cutting blade. Another favorite two-knife combo is my Kershaw Stockman folder—with three working blades of stout stainless steel—backed by a Kershaw Model 1034 sheath knife with versatile 5-inch

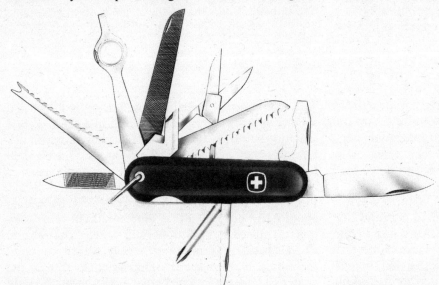

Traditionally, the Swiss Army Knife has represented the tool kit you carry in your pocket. A number of brands are available, check your local sporting goods store.

travel. Often the stream must be forded time after time, or sheer rock walls may suddenly rise from the sides, forcing you to backtrack or ride a log down the rapids. Never travel by night! In the dark, you could break a leg or tumble over an unseen cliff.

Even a sprained ankle could prove disastrous. When "shank's mare" is your only means of transportation, treat your legs and feet as if they were made of fine china! Hopefully you're wearing good boots with heavy wool socks. Oxfords and stretch socks don't go far in the woods. If your boots get wet, stop and make camp early. Heat some small stones in the fire and drop them into the boots to dry them out before it becomes cold. Dry your socks by the fire, but *not too close*. I recall one night when I tried to warm my feet *sans* boots before the fire. The soles burned out of my wool socks before I even felt the heat! If you find yourself obliged to ford a stream in the afternoon—don't! Make camp and wait for morning. Another "No, no!" is crossing in your bare feet. There's too much of a risk of cutting your feet on rocks. Also, your feet don't have as much gripping

blade. The Woodsman's Pal, looking much like a machete with the end broken off square, can be used to hammer, hack, dig and cut. It comes with its own belt sheath, but is easily carried in a rucksack or pack. Charter Arms offers another unique cutting tool called the "Skachet," a combination knife/hatchet. You can use its razor-sharp edge to cut a green limb for a handle, which can be screwed into the threaded eye of the Skachet for hammering or chopping.

Billed as the "Survival system you carry in your wallet," the Walle-Hawk from Allison Forge Corp., Belmont, Mass., offers "40 ways to stay alive," in the small pamphlet that accompanies this firm's thin, rectangular, razor-grade stainless steel tool. This amazing utility is derived from a plethora of cutting edges, irregular-shaped cutouts, holes and notches; plus, an area on one side that's serrated for filing. In addition, you can suspend the Walle-Hawk by a string and it will point out north for you! Also included in the flat plastic pocket pouch that holds the Walle-Hawk is a .020-inch plastic Fresnel burning lens with which to start a fire.

Sheer panic is probably the most dangerous enemy faced by the temporarily misplaced person. A .22 rimfire goes a long way toward dispelling fear, but a survival kit can be even more helpful. At the end of this chapter you will find lists of items that I have compiled in three escalating degrees of preparedness, which can be used to meet varying danger levels: 1. The "Micro Pack" is small enough to drop into your shirt pocket and forget. Make up several of these and put them into the pockets of your hunting jacket, ski parka, etc. There's no excuse for not having one handy every time you go afield as the Micro Pack provides you with firemaking and limited food procuring ability; 2. The somewhat larger "Pocket Pack" includes such luxuries as tea bags and boullion cubes, plus arrow heads that can be used to make spears if need be, and a survival manual!; 3. The "Total-Protection Pack" requires you to shoulder an Eddie Bauer Teardrop Rucksack. I've worn one on many a hunt without ever finding it a hindrance. Ample room remains for packing your lunch, camera, lenses, etc. Contents of any of these kits can be varied to suit personal tastes or types of terrain.

For those of you who haven't time to round up all of the items listed (normally available at backpacking shops), Eddie Bauer again comes to the rescue with his Parka Survival Kit, containing an 8-foot tube tent for shelter, candle, waterproof match box, aluminum cup, signal mirror, whistle, plus assorted food items. Also from Bauer is an emergency Signal Kit with 400-foot altitude flares and a smoke pot.

Users of prescription glasses should carry a spare pair in case of breakage, plus a pair of good quality sunglasses. Personal medicines, such as insulin for diabetics and nitroglycerine tablets for heart sufferers, should also be a part of the pack. Fire is vital to your survival. Inasmuch as few of us can create flames by rubbing two sticks together, it behooves us to carry one of those throw-away butane lighters. Another good motto is, "A fire stick in every pocket." The "fire stick" is unaffected by wet or cold, and works every time!

Any injuries or cuts, however, minor, suffered under a survival situation should be tended to immediately, to prevent them from becoming aggravated or infected. A first aid kit designed for trail use is marketed by Cutter Laboratories, Inc., Berkley, CA. Housed in a 4 × 8 × 2-inch fold-over plastic "Camp Pack," it contains a snake bite kit, ammonia ampules, scissors, bandages, first aid book, etc., over 50 items in all.

The wonders of freeze-dried dehydrated foods have made it possible to cram a remarkable amount of nourishment into the nitches and corners of your pack. If local stores can't supply you with the essentials of survival, you can purchase by mail order from either *Back Country,* 8272 Orangethorpe Ave., Buena Park, CA 90620, or *Sports and Trails,* 1491 W. Whittier Blvd., La Habra, CA 90631.

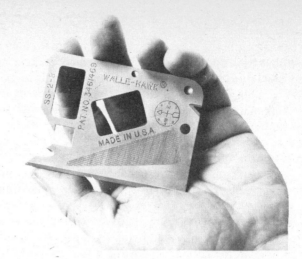

"Unique" seems like a pale word to describe the incredible "Walle-Hawk," the survival tool that you carry in your wallet. Numerous sharp cutting edges, a variety of holes and openings, plus the ability to point north when suspended on a string, make this one tool capable of doing a multitude of wilderness chores.

If your quest for fresh air runs more toward sage and sand than pines and rippling brooks, include a "desert still" in your pack. It may well be the only way you will have to obtain moisture in the arid areas. One survival book advises having several stills operating at one time, because of the painfully slow way that they work. Briefly, a "desert still" is created by digging a hole about 2 feet deep by 3 feet wide. A cup or other container is placed at the bottom in the center. Then a large sheet of plastic is spread over the hole, weighted around the edges, and a rock or other weight placed in the center to form an inverted cone of the plastic directly over the cup. Moisture from the surrounding sand condenses on the under side of the plastic, and drips into the cup. To survive in the desert, "shade-up" during the heat of the day, and travel only evenings and mornings. *Keep your shirt on,* even if you feel better without it.

If you don't crave the adventure of being lost, you can purchase a topographical map of the area in which you plan to hunt/hike, from the U.S. Geological Survey, Washington, DC 20242. A scale of 1/24,000 offers fine detail, but covers only a limited area. Maps of 1-inch to 1-mile scale are normally sufficient for the average needs and cover a much wider area. Your map is only as reliable as the compass you use to orient it. The finest of compasses, the Wilkie Universal Prismatic Compass Model M-110-P, can be obtained from Olsen Knife Co., Howard City, MI 49329. It features night-visible radium dial, total damping action, and direct-reading prism/sight. The popular "Sportsman's and "Silva" compasses are available from Eddie Bauer.

"MICRO PACK" Survival Kit

Container is plastic box measuring 4½″ x 2¾″ x ⅝″.
1 "Metal Match"
5 .22 Long Rifle cartridges
1 12 x 12-inch sheet aluminum foil, tightly rolled.
2 #8 snelled fish hooks
1 GI can opener
3 standard and 1 large Band-Aid(s)
30 feet Orlon cord

5-inch hemp rope for tinder
1 magnifying glass
½ hacksaw blade
1 medium and 5 small safety pins
1 single edged razor blade
1 pocket sewing kit
12 strike-anywhere matches
6 feet heavy waxed twine

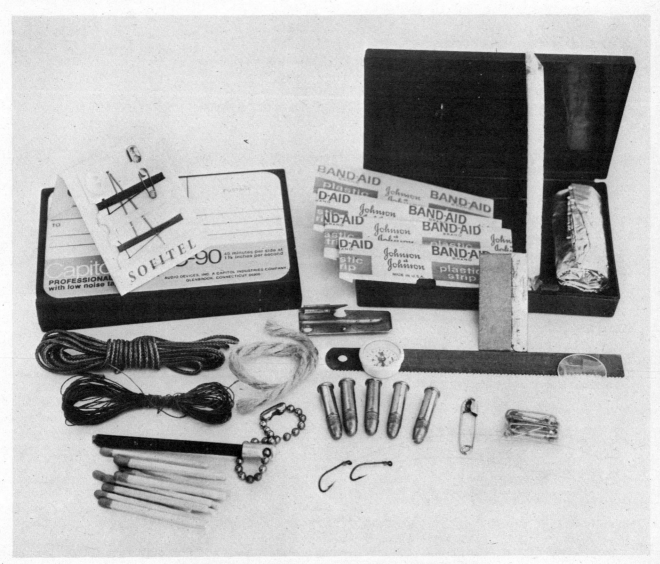

This is the "Micro Pack" which the author recommends be carried at all times. Fish hooks and line provide ability to obtain food when near water. The GI can opener can be used as a lure. A single-edged razor blade and half of a hacksaw blade offer some cutting capability. Firestick, birthday cake candle, and tinder make for a fast fire. Tiny sewing kit, (upper/left corner) keeps clothing together. Tight roll of aluminum foil can serve as cooking utensil. Even magnifying glass and tiny compass are included.

"POCKET PACK" Survival Kit

"Pocket Pack" container measures 5½" x 4½" x 1½". (Alternative containers could be a plastic tackle box, metal tobacco can, etc.)

- 1 copy *Survival in the Wilderness*
- 1 "Metal Match"
- 1 "Elinox" stainless steel folding knife with 2 blades
- 1 small compass
- 1 small magnifying glass
- 1 GI can opener
- 1 "Bod-Kin" arrow point (for making spear)
- 1 "Fish Arrow Point" (for spearing fish)
- 1 14" x 30" sheet aluminum foil, folded
- 20 feet of 27 lb. nylon fishing line & 4 snelled hooks
- 15 feet of 100 lb. test nylon line
- 10 feet of .225" copper wire
- 2 #12 gang hooks with leader
- 1 fresh water spoon with gang hook
- 6 #3/0 split shot for sinkers
- 1 sewing kit (same as Micro Pack)

- 1 whistle
- 5 bouillon cubes
- 2 tea bags
- 5 salt packs
- 2 sugar packs
- 1 dozen salt tablets
- 1 "Wet-Nap"
- 12 Anacin
- 8 antacid tables
- 2 insect repellant towelettes
- 2 cold tablets
- 25 halazone or iodine tablets (preferably in cellophane strip packs)
- 3 safety pins (large)
- 1 4" candle
- 12 waterproof matches
- 1 "Chap Stick"
- 6 Band-Aids
- 2 dimes (for telephone when you finally reach it!)

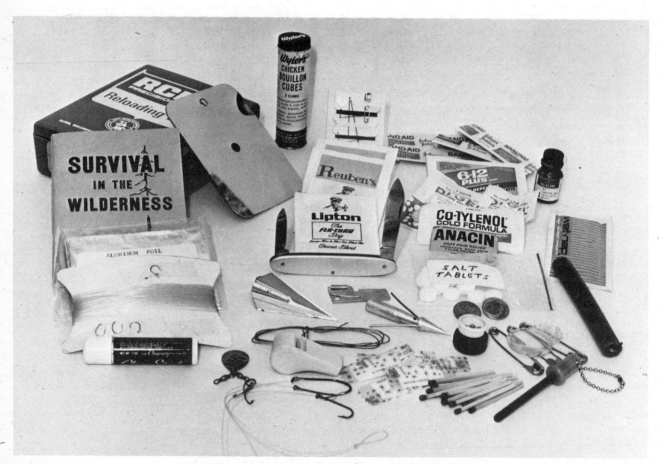

The "Pocket Pack" using an RCBS reloading die box of sturdy plastic with locking lid, the author compressed all of these life-saving devices into a space that easily fits a jacket pocket. Note steel arrowhead for making a spear, and barbed spear point for spearing fish in shallow water. It's actually easier than fishing with a hook!

"TOTAL PROTECTION" Survival Pack

"Total Protection Pack" container is Eddie Bauer's "Teardrop Rucksack," or similar light backpack.

- 3 booklets, *Survival in the Wilderness, Food in the Wilderness,* and *Medical Aid in the Wilderness.* (available from Back Country)
- 1 pocket compass
- 1 emergency space blanket
- 1 wire snare
- 1 wire saw
- 50 feet of 750 lb. braided nylon cord
- 1 heavy-duty plastic tube tent
- 1 signal mirror
- 1 pad & pencil
- 1 plastic poncho
- 10 feet of surgical tubing (for tourniquets, slingshots, etc.)
- 1 "Cutter Camp Pack" first aid kit (including scissors, tweezers, etc.)
- 1 B-D Snake Bite Kit
- 1 desert water still
- 100 halazone or iodine tablets (strip packed in cellophane preferred)
- 1 ½-gallon collapsible plastic jug, with handle
- 1 pint GI pocket water flask (surplus store)
- 1 bar hand soap
- 2 boxes waterproof matches
- 1 6" candle
- 12 fire starter tablets
- 1 disposable butane lighter
- 1 Medalist Universal Sierra Stove & 1 can propane fuel (optional — from Sports & Trails)
- 1 backpacker's cup
- 1 knife/fork/spoon set
- 4 cans HM concentrated foods
- 1 box raisins
- 2 hot cocoa mix
- 1 iced tea mix
- 1 bacon bar
- 1 meat bar
- 1 Everfresh trail mix
- 2 Granola Crunch bars
- 2 Hershey's Tropical Bar
- 2 Mountain House freeze dried foods of your choice
- 1 Johnson "Off" inset repellant
- 1 Desitin skin care (sample size)
- 4 Suprex-T high potency vitamin B complex tablets
- 24 Amitone antacid tablets
- 1 pack Kleenex
- 1 comb
- 4 #4 snelled fish hooks with leaders
- 4 #1/0 snelled hooks with leaders
- 2 dry flies
- 2 #14 treble hooks with leaders
- 50 yards 27-lb test nylon squidding
- 10 #3/0 split shot for sinkers
- 1 Mallory compact flashlight
- 10 feet ¾" duct tape
- 1 pair sunglasses
- 1 spare corrective eyeglasses
- 1 pair of warm gloves

The author's "Total Protection Pack" provides enough food to easily last the average person a week, plus a first aid kit, stove, tube tent, etc., to afford maximum comfort during your stay in Mother Nature's outdoor motel. Included is a small pocket flashlight, which is a good weight/space investment at any time on the trail!

CHAPTER 7

Fair Game

CENTERFIRE FANATICS regard the .22 rimfire as fit only for potting bilge rats and gophers. In point of fact, the .22 rimfire is used successfully for hunting a wide range of small game, from the above-mentioned rats, to such large predators as bobcats and coyotes.

Another misconception concerns practical maximum effective range of the .22. Many modern rimfire nimrods hesitate to fire at animals beyond 60 to 75 yards, believing the cartridge to be either ineffective or too inaccurate for shots at those longer ranges. Check out the 1-inch X-ring of a standard smallbore target fired at 100 yards, and consider that it often takes 10 "X's" to win a match! True these scores are fired with finely tuned rifles and match ammo, but you can come close with many of today's field rifles and highly refined high velocity hollow point ammunition. In his book, *Hunting With The Twenty-Two,* C.S. Landis tells of dropping a woodchuck at 175 yards! His longest shot on tree squirrels was a paced 145 yards.

Admittedly, Landis was a marvelous marksman, but he used guns and ammo of the early 1940's. Think of his delight had he lived to see the introduction of Federal's Semi-Hollow Points, Winchester-Western's Dynapoints and hollow point Xpediters, and CCI's Penta-Point Stingers. These new .22 rimfire cartridges represent dramatic breakthroughs, bringing a new dimension of effectiveness to the .22 Long Rifle cartridge. They literally hand magnum potential to the millions now owning standard .22 rimfire rifles and pistols, without the necessity of investing in the more expensive .22 Winchester Magnum Rim Fire cartridge/gun combo.

.22 Ammo for Hunting

Not every .22 rimfire nimrod can emulate Landis' greatest feats. Most of us do well to stretch the effective range of a .22 Long Rifle to its accepted maximum of 100 yards. To determine your own maximum range

potential on any given small game animal, you must realistically assess the accuracy ability of your particular gun/sight/ammo combination—your "GSA" for short. An essential part of the equation is the size of the animal you hunt and the dimensions of its vital areas. Life-sized animal silhouettes are ideal for determining your GSA maximum range. Printed rimfire targets usually have a circled area that roughly approximates the vital areas of small game—they offer a definite measure of your ability.

Targets of such game animals as chucks, rabbits, raccoons, foxes etc., are printed by Epsen Lithographing Company and are distributed by Saunders Archery Company. They should be available at your local archery dealer. Unfortunately, Stoeger has discontinued selling their animal targets. If necessary, you can trace your own rough patterns with a felt-tipped pen, inking-in the vitals to provide a well-defined aiming point.

Space your targets at 50, 75 and 100 yards. Fire 10 shots at each target from a bench rest, with good light and no wind. Under these ideal conditions, you should be able to score a minimum of seven hits in the vitals of any animal down to chuck-size all the way out to the 100-yard line.

Squirrels possess a vital zone barely 1½ by 2 inches square and this may well limit accurate shooting to about 75 yards. Now you will know the capability of your rifle/scope/ammo, but what of yourself? You won't find any bench rests provided by Mother Nature in the field. At worst, you may have to fire from the relatively unsteady platform of your own two legs! At best, you will be resting across a limb or deadfall. So we proceed to test number two, position shooting: offhand, kneeling, sitting and prone. Seldom do you have an opportunity to shoot prone, but a grassy hillock overlooking some prime woodchuck meadow might afford that chance. Sitting is a likely position if you have taken a stand at the fringe of the forest, keeping a lookout in

Centerfire fanatics regard the .22 rimfire as fit for potting only rats and gophers. This rugged rimfire nimrod looks like he could give them a convincing argument. Armed with Weaver-scoped Marlin Model 783 .22 WMR, backed by Ruger Super Single Six with .22 Magnum cylinder, he's ready for anything up to bobcats and coyotes.

the tall timber for twitching fuzzy-tails. Kneeling is handy whenever the brush is less than waist high.

Fire 10 shots in each of the above positions at each target—50, 75 and 100 yards—and check and paste the targets after each string. If you find less than seven hits in a vital area you have exceeded your GSA maximum on that particular animal. There are ways of stretching that maximum range. The obvious method is to improve your marksmanship. But it's also possible to reduce the dispersion of your rifle with careful tuning. For details, see Chapter 12.

Factor five in the GSA equation is trajectory and your ability to cope with it. Nominally, the centerline of a scope is approximately 1½ inches above the bore line. The barrel is tilted upward slightly to bring the bullet's flight upward to cross the centerline of the scope relatively near the muzzle, then arch downward to intercept the cross hairs once more at the desired zero range.

Trajectory tables are helpful in gauging the arc described by a .22 bullet in flight, but charts are sometimes deceiving. I fired several 5-shot bench rest groups with a Weatherby Mark XXII rifle/scope combination using Remington high velocity hollow points in an effort to accurately chart that ammo's point of impact from 5- to 100-yards. At 5 yards, the bullet was ⅝-inch below the point of aim, ½-inch low at 10 yards, minus ¼-inch at 15 yards. At 20 yards, the bullet centered the cross hairs for the first time, rising to plus ⅛-inch at 25, plus ⅜-inch at 50 yards, and finally striking dead center at 60 yards. The 80-yard line grouped 2 inches low. At 100 yards, a 1¼-inch group was centered 5¾ inches low. Beyond that, .22 drop became rather precipitous, dipping 11 inches below the point of aim at 125 yards.

With the 60-yard zero, you can hold "dead-on" a target as small as a tree squirrel out to about 70 yards, elevating the cross hairs to the top of the spine for an 80-yard hit. You can quarter the shoulder of a cottontail

A lineup of rimfire ammo such as this, encompassing the state of the art today, would have been a pure delight to such early rimfire experts as C.S. Landis, who was obliged to settle for the best available in the early 1940s.

Animal targets can be used to discover the maximum range at which your gun/sight/ammo combination can reliably deliver hits in a vital area. Life-sized woodchuck target was fired on with Winchester 9422-M at 50, 75, and 100 yards (50-yard aiming point was head). No problem keeping all hits in a 1-inch circle all day long, although only 5-shot groups were fired here. Same shoulder aiming point was used at 75 and 100 yards. Again, no difficulty in keeping all shots well within vital zone.

with your cross hairs out to about 80 yards, elevating to the top of the back for a 100-yard hit. Standing on his haunches a foot-tall chuck offers a tempting target all the way out to the 125-yard line, but a hit below the belt will only result in a slow death. Sudden, humane kills, result only from positive hits in the head or chest cavity (preferably the head).

The recent revolution in .22 Long Rifle ammo development has changed the rules to a degree, extending both the effective killing range and predator potential of the potent little cartridge. Some years back, I carried out a series of experiments to determine the comparative disruptive effect of solids and hollow points at various ranges from 25 to 100 yards. I was startled to find that cavities caused in large blocks of pug clay were far greater with the solids than anyone had ever supposed, indicating that the wounding capability of solids was also far underestimated up to that time. Springing from that realization, Winchester-Western introduced their dimpled Dynapoint ammo with full-weight 40-grain slugs bearing just a hint of a cavity in the nose.

Federal followed by releasing their Semi-Hollow Point, bearing a $1/16$-inch diameter by $1/32$-inch deep indentation centered in a normal-ogive 40-grain Long Rifle bullet. Both bullets are copper washed to avoid leading and are launched at high velocity. The added disruptive effect of the "almost-hollow" pointed bullets, added to the 3-grain gain in bullet weight over previous hollow points, makes for some highly effective ammo on larger small game animals, such as the hard-to-stop antelope jacks of the western plains and deserts.

Another route to the same destination was taken by CCI in their Stinger ammo, powering a lighter 32-grain bullet to 1685 fps, a heretofore unheard of velocity for a .22 rimfire Long Rifle cartridge. An added explosive effect results from the five-sided Penta-Point nose opening in the copper-colored bullet. Stingers also flatten out the normal high velocity .22 Long Rifle trajectory curve, deducting about 3 inches from normal drop at 100 yards. With Stingers, it becomes practical to sight in at 75 yards, and more or less ignore holdover out to 100 yards or so. Even with a 50-yard zero, Stingers drop an almost negligible 2.8 inches at 100 yards.

If you were pondering the purchase of a .22 Magnum for greater power in the field, bear in mind that its advantage over the standard .22 Long Rifle, as represented by CCI Stingers, has been roughly cut in half! You might decide to stay with the standard .22 to retain its greater economy and wider versatility. Time was,

Across sand bags on a bench rest, you can discover the maximum GSA (gun/sight/ammo) range, firing at life-sized animal targets. Fire 10 shots at ranges of 50, 75, and 100 yards. You can try 125 yards if your 100-yard groups look promising.

There are no bench rests in the wilderness, and you may find the only practical shooting position is from the rather unsteady platform of your own two legs!

the .22 Magnum clocked almost 50 percent more muzzle velocity and racked up 137 percent more muzzle energy than the standard .22 Long Rifle; however, introduction of CCI's Stinger hot-loaded .22 Long Rifle Penta-Points whittled those numbers to 18 percent on the one hand, and 88 percent on the other. Sort of takes some of the wind out of the .22 Magnum's sales! The Stinger bumps performance figures of the .22 Long Rifle up to the point where you no longer have to envy the .22 Magnum owner all that much.

You can enjoy the economy of shooting standard .22's for plinking and even some hunting and reach for the Stingers when you need more power. During accuracy testing of a wide range of .22 rifles in connection with this book, I was amazed and highly gratified with the groups registered by Stingers. In many rifles, they grouped as well or better than two different brands of match ammo tested. Two outstanding instances came when testing the Weatherby Mark XXII and the Browning BAR. Autoloading rifles are superior hunting guns, for many reasons that we will enumerate later, and here we have two of the finest, shooting like target rifles with ammo designed for maximum performance. Normally, we expect high performance ammo to be a little short in the accuracy department. As Ferris Pin-

dle, a bench rest shooter of note, so aptly explained it to me, "The less disturbance you have going on in the gun, the better it shoots."

The Mark XXII fired 10-shot groups (using Stingers) at 25 yards measuring ⅜-inch, center to center of the widest spread, actually better than both Remington Rifle Match and Western Mark III Super-Match. Widest spread for the BAR was ⁷/₁₆-inch. It would have been better except for one errant slug that printed just outside of the main cluster. The Ruger 10/22, another autoloader of merit, registered ⁹/₁₆-inch—not bad for a relatively light rifle! The Ithaca Saddlegun lever action displayed a definite preference for Stingers, with a ½-inch group, ¹/₁₆-inch tighter than the group turned in by Remington Rifle Match ammo.

In practical terms, what does this mean to the average rimfire nimrod? It signifies that when shooting Stingers in an accurate rifle, you can stretch rimfire range with a standard .22 Long Rifle chamber by at least 25 yards and hazard larger prey as well.

Just what is *fair game* for a .22 Long Rifle? Any answer must perforce be subjective rather than objective, based upon an individual's own personal experiences with his own gun and with the cartridges he may use on a variety of animals. In my opinion, squirrels, burrowing or arboreal, are more than adequately gunned with a .22 Long Rifle. Certainly there's no lack of stopping power there! Note that our concern is with *stopping power,* and not *killing power.*

A .22 rimfire has been known to kill just about anything that walks, short of a mastodon, but our goal is to achieve quick, humane death, not to inflict pain. Thus it behooves us not to exceed the logical level of stopping power afforded by our favored rimfire round. Various vermin or pests, such as prairie dogs, gophers, crows, magpies, etc., fall within the sure-stop range of the .22 Long Rifle, as do brush rabbits and cottontails, assuming the hits are ahead of the diaphragm. Gut-shot rabbits nearly always escape. The long-eared "jackass" rabbits of the West exhibit a tenacity for life that must be seen to be believed! You have to hit them *hard* and *in the right spot* to nail them down with assurance. I suggest you stoke your iron with Stingers when ranging the sage and sand in search of jacks. Turtles and bullfrogs are no match for a well-placed Long Rifle.

Long before the centerfire smallbores made the scene, woodchucks were hunted in large numbers by dedicated rimfire buffs of another era. They learned the limitations of their tools and became consummate experts at judging range and doping wind, with the result that they often picked off rotund marmots at ranges of 125 yards and beyond! Introduction of the .22 Hornet in 1930 ended the rimfire monopoly, but the diminutive round remains popular with many chuck hunters because of its added challenge and low report, which is more readily tolerated in populated areas than the throaty bark of a .22-250 Remington or .224 Weatherby Magnum.

Such critters as raccoons, opossums and badgers will fall to a well-placed .22 Long Rifle, especially if the new dimpled hollow points are used. Toughest of the lot is the badger, which makes its living by digging out the burrows of, and devouring, ground squirrels and prairie dogs. A badger has chest muscles that would be the envy of Charles Atlas in his best days, and which serve to stop a .22 bullet aimed from the front. On those frontal shots, shoot for the snout of the squat low-brow.

Foxes and bobcats represent the upper limits of .22 Long Rifle capability, even in its Stinger configuration. The .22 should only be used at a relatively close range, say out to about 50 yards, and only when shots can be placed with certainty in the heart or head. Coyotes, in my opinion, are just too large and too tough a target to tackle with .22 Long Rifles.

North of the 49th parallel, Canadians use the .22 Long Rifle without qualms on a wide range of furred denizens, from the ubiquitous rabbit to such exotics as

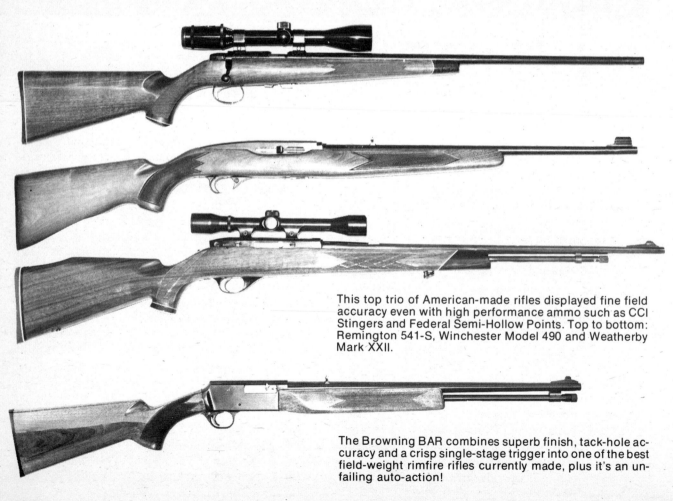

This top trio of American-made rifles displayed fine field accuracy even with high performance ammo such as CCI Stingers and Federal Semi-Hollow Points. Top to bottom: Remington 541-S, Winchester Model 490 and Weatherby Mark XXII.

The Browning BAR combines superb finish, tack-hole accuracy and a crisp single-stage trigger into one of the best field-weight rimfire rifles currently made, plus it's an unfailing auto-action!

Small Game Effectiveness Guide

Unless otherwise specified, effective killing range extends as far as vital hits can be made

	small pests prairie dogs ground squirrels crows/magpies	tree squirrels	cottontails & brush rabbits	jack-rabbits	woodchucks rockchucks	foxes opossums raccoons beavers	bobcats badgers turkeys	coyotes wolverines
.22 Short HV HP	Max. 25 yds.	Max. 25 yds.	**	**	**	**	**	**
.22 Long Rifle SV SP	Max. 40 yds.	Max. 40 yds.	**	**	**	**	**	**
.22 Long Rifle HV SP	Max. 50 yds.	Max. 50 yds.	**	**	**	**	**	**
.22 Long Rifle HV HP	Quick kill	Head or chest to preserve meat	Quick kill in head/chest	Head or chest only	Head or chest only	Max. 75 yds.	Max. 50 yds.	**
.22 Long Rifle W-W Dynapoint Federal Semi-Hollow	Quick kill	Less destructive of meat	Less destructive of meat	Head or chest only	Head or chest only	Max. 75 yds.	Max. 50 yds.	**
.22 Long Rifle Stinger/Xpediter	Quick kill	Highly destructive	Quick kill	Quick kill	Quick kill	Max. 100 yds.	Max. 75 yds.	**
.22 Winchester Magnum Rim Fire & CCI Maxi-Mag SP	Quick kill	Use to have meat left	Not a reliable stopper	**	**	**	**	**
.22 Magnum HP	Quick kill	Too destructive of meat	Quick kill	Quick kill	Quick kill	Good stopper in vital zone	Max. 150 yds	Max. 100 yds.

**NOT RECOMMENDED
HP = HOLLOW POINT
HV = HIGH VELOCITY

SP = SOLID POINT
SV = STANDARD VELOCITY

mink, marten, muskrats, lynx and wolverines, as well as beavers. Virtually every trapper in the cold North Country carries his trusty, and often rusty, "twennytoo" on Skiddoo trips along the meandering rivers and streams as he checks traps.

My moose hunting guide of a few years back, Paul Bowman, carried a .22 Magnum Winchester Model 255 (now discontinued) that came in handy for dispatching any trapped-but-still-live animals without ruining valuable pelts. The battered lever action also accounted for numerous beavers and otters who ventured too near the bank when Paul was around. A swimming beaver or otter must be shot (when legal) in the head, and retrieved immediately before it sinks out of sight into the icy waters. Confident of his marksmanship, Paul uses solids exclusively in his .22 Magnum and shoots game only in the head in order to preserve the pelts. Paul's partner, Wayne Sharpe, also a winter trapper, carries a .22 Long Rifle-chambered bolt action Cooey, one of the few rimfire rifles made in Canada.

Whenever the two got together in camp, cutting wood, cooking or just cleaning up (between arguing politics), they debated the relative merits of the .22 Long Rifle versus the .22 Magnum. Both made some good points in the running battle. Wayne contended that it was cheaper to shoot the standard .22 Long Rifle, and what's more, he could shoot Longs, Shorts, or even BB and CB Caps, if he chose, to clear out camp pests such as pack rats. Wayne hunted beavers, etc. with solid-pointed 40-grain high velocity C.I.L. ammo,

Canadians use .22 rimfire rifles for a wide variety of furred game. Here Canadian guide Paul Bowman shows the author his lever action Winchester Model 255 .22 WMR. The author holds his Ithaca Saddlegun lever action standard .22 rimfire. In an emergency, Paul once killed a young grizzly bear with his .22 Magnum, emptying the magazine into the advancing animal.

Hunting companion Don Egger holds bobcat taken by author with the Savage/Anschutz Model 141-M (discontinued) that he holds. The .22 WMR is entirely adequate for bobcats, given accurate bullet placement in vital area.

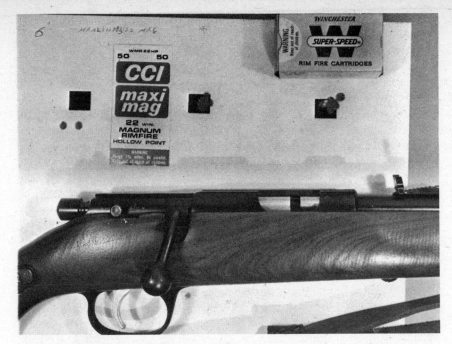

Ten-shot groups fired from a bench rest at 25 yards with a Marlin Model 783 .22 WMR measured barely ⅜- and ½-inch, indicating that both rifle and ammo (namely CCI Maxi-Mags and Winchester Super-X .22 Magnum Rim Fires), are highly accurate. Same ammo from a Mossberg 640 KD Chuckster delivered two groups of 5/16-inch, neatly rounded with no fliers!

manufactured in Canada by C.I.L. Sporting Arms and Ammunition Company of Montreal, Quebec. He confined his shots to the head, therefore didn't feel the need for hollow points, or for the added punch of a .22 Magnum. Paul countered that he had in fact killed a fair-sized grizzly bear (please, don't try it) with his .22 Magnum, a feat far beyond the capabilities of the standard .22. "Besides," he added, "when I shoot an 80 pound beaver, I want to be damn sure that he's dead, so he can't paddle off to his den and leave me empty-handed!"

Beyond doubt, the Winchester .22 Magnum Rim Fire represents a step upward in stopping power on small game animals. Hollow pointed, jacketed .22 Magnum bullets elevate into the sure-kill zone all of those animals considered marginal for the standard .22 Long Rifle, such as badgers, foxes and bobcats, and pushes the marginal area up to include coyotes. I have taken a number of bobcats and coyotes with my bolt action Savage/Anschutz Model 141-M and my Winchester Model 9422-M, both of which are handy field-weight rifles and accurate as well.

The accuracy of .22 Magnum ammo has been questioned in print so often that it has become like the reputation of a good woman, besmirched by unwarranted and unfounded gossip. During accuracy tests I conducted, 10-shot groups fired at 25 yards with .22 Magnum ammo from both Winchester-Western, and CCI scored as well or better than standard .22 Long Rifle ammo. A Marlin Model 783 turned in groups of ⅜-inch with CCI Maxi-Mag Hollow Points, and ½-inch with Winchester Super-X-22 Magnum Rim Fire ammo. The Mossberg 640 KD Chuckster lived up to its name by drilling 10 rounds into 5/16-inch groups with both brands, despite a rather scruffy trigger pull.

Over the years, I have received a number of letters from readers praising the accuracy of the .22 Magnum. One notable example came from a gentleman in Virginia, detailing his adventures with the .22 WMR. His Savage over/under .22 Magnum/20 gauge reliably delivered 5-shot groups of an inch and under at 75 yards, *using iron sights!* Remarkable to be sure, but even more so when you consider that the man firing them was 70 years of age at the time!

Further pointing up the accuracy potential of the .22 Magnum was a letter from Henry H. Durr, a consulting engineer from Waukegan, Illinois. Henry attained 5-shot, 100-yard groups measuring a startling ½-inch! The two groups shown below measure exactly ½-inch

Two top groups of five shots each, were fired with Sears J.C. Higgins Model 42DLM .22 WMR, in hands of consulting engineer, Henry H. Durr, at 100 yards. Crow targets were fired by 70-year-old man, from a bench rest at 65 yards with Savage/Anschutz Model 164 .22 Long Rifle.

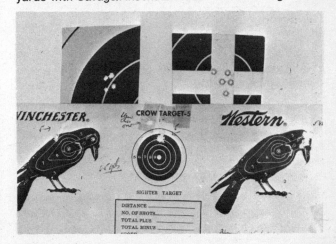

for the one that looks like four rounds (it really is five), and ¾-inch for the one centered on the white cross. Henry uses (now get this!) a Sears J.C. Higgins Model 42DLM for which he paid a whole $30 some 12-plus years ago! He says that it bears a startling resemblance to the Marlin 980 (now discontinued). Henry uses an F.I. Luminar 2.75X scope with 1-inch tube, cross hairs subtending exactly .75-inch at 100 yards. He pastes a cross over the bull with ¾-inch adhesive tape, covers the white lines with the cross-hairs, and squeezes what he describes as " . . . an atrocious trigger!" However, the results speak for themselves and help lay to rest the fable about .22 WMR inaccuracy!

Where to sight in a .22 Magnum? CCI's ballistics chart shows a zero of 50 yards for the .22 Long Rifle and .22 Magnum alike, with 100-yard drop figures of 6 inches for high velocity Long Rifles, 2.8 inches for the Stinger, and 2.5 inches for the .22 Maxi-Mag. Winchester-Western's ballistics table shows a 1.6-inch mid-range trajectory for the .22 WMR sighted in at 100 yards. However, my own Winchester 9422-M sighted dead-center at 100, delivers groups centered just 1-inch high at 50 yards! Field facts don't always jibe with calculated ballistics. If you want to be certain of your own ground, range-fire at various measured distances with the same sight setting, and record the data for future reference.

Calculated, *not tested,* trajectory figures on the .22 WMR indicate a drop at 150 yards of less than 6 inches with the 100-yard zero. At 200 yards', the 40-grain jacketed slug dips 1½ feet, plummeting to about 3 feet below point of aim at 250 yards. The .22 Magnum passes the 150-yard marker traveling about as fast as standard velocity .22 Long Rifle ammo starts out at, dropping below 1000 fps at 200 and to approximately 900 fps at 250 yards.

To me, this means that a .22 WMR can take such game as ground squirrels, rabbits, chucks, raccoons, 'possums, etc. with sure kills out to as far as you can hit a vital zone. Bobcats, badgers and foxes should be "crow bait" for sure out to 100-yards-plus. However, the coyote might best be given a free pass unless you can lure him inside of 50 to 75 yards at the outside. You'll learn *how* by-'n-by!

.22 Varminting

"Varmints," as defined by Noah Webster is a colloquial term for "vermin," meaning any noxious, mischievous or disgusting animal. Lumped together under this single, all-inclusive term are such unlikely bedfellows as ground squirrels and prairie dogs on the one hand and coyotes on the other. That coyotes bear a strong affection for "grounies" there can be no doubt. The canny canines love to *eat* their smaller fellow varmints. That the affection is returned must be open to question! Others included in the varmint category are woodchucks, rockchucks, foxes, bobcats, etc.

Woodchucks

First and foremost among varmint targets is that chubby clown, the woodchuck. With Chaplinesque gait, he waddles from den to dinner, feasting with the finesse of Henry the VIII on the farmer's hard-won crop of corn, wheat, alfalfa, beans, peas, barley, et al. Next to eating, *Marmota monax* is best at digging holes hither and yon in loamy hillsides, under tree stumps, at the base of rockpiles, in fact anyplace that offers concealment and protection from the elements, plus a good view of the surrounding country. Not content with a single den, the woodchuck digs and digs, establishing underground vacation cottages at every hand, which he soon abandons, to be sublet by apartment-hunting rabbits.

The portly pig's prodigious appetite is enough to make him *personna non grata* with his unwilling host, the farmer. Add to that the constant prospect of a broken leg for any cow or horse unlucky enough to stumble into an underground labyrinth of holes and tunnels, and you have the makin's of a mutual non-admiration society! Farmers have little time for the niceties of marksmanship, usually attacking with chemicals, but they welcome allies with soft-spoken rimfire rifles, who can offer assurance of directing their fire away from stock, buildings and water tanks. When applying for permission to hunt on a farmer's land, leave the guns in the car. Assure him that you will respect his property. Check out at the end of the hunt and let him know that you have rid him of some of those pesky pigs. Don't leave the area littered with rotting carcasses though. Bury them in nearby burrows. On your next trip drop off a fifth of Jack Daniels, and you'll be assured of a continuing welcome!

A mature woodchuck boar is known to stand as tall as 12 to 14 inches, when propped up on his haunches warily surveying his surroundings. From March through May, he amorously pursues the sow, resulting in four to six pups. The "dog days" of late summer and early autumn find these pasture pigs holed up in their coolest dens for a summer siesta, fooling unknowing hunters into the belief that early hibernation has begun. Not so! Mr. Chuck is up and around again in the balmy Indian Summer, storing up fat for the 4-month fast to follow.

Woodchucks are to be found in all types of terrain, from manicured meadows to tangled thickets. An estimated 500 million chucks inhabit the nation, from the Atlantic to the Plains states, from Alabama and Arkansas north, with fingers of habitat reaching through lower Canada up into Alaska. Good hunting can be located by cruising back roads and sweeping the area with binoculars in search of the patchwork of brown mounds that mark den entrances.

Don't ever judge the stocky hedgehog as short of brains! He has dodges you haven't even thought of yet.

Foremost among varmint targets is the always hungry woodchuck. Next to eating, the chubby chuck delights in digging holes which, added to his appetite for corn, wheat, beans, peas, etc., makes him unwelcome down on the farm!

Here we have a lineup of chuck rifles used by the author. Left to right: Weatherby Mark XXII rifle/scope, Savage/Anschutz Model 54 with Redfield 4X, Winchester Model 52 with Redfield 3200 scope, and Remington Model 541-S with Bushnell 3X to 9X Scopechief variable.

One favored subterranean subterfuge consists of ducking into his front entrance which is ostentatiously encircled with a high, hard brown mound, only to emerge at one of the many emergency exits dug from underneath which lacks the tell-tale earthen ring and is concealed among brush and tall grass—from there he can watch you in comfortable concealment until you tire of the waiting game.

Unable to pick off pigs from field artillery range, the rimfire rifleman is called upon to exhibit a particular kind of stalking ability, sometimes wriggling into rimfire range on his belly, rifle cradled across his arms commando style. Good clothing for this kind of exercise is a soft cotton camouflage one-piece jump suit that helps to conceal, won't scoop up debris with the waistband, and doesn't rasp noisily against abrasive brush. The Woodsman Hunting Coverall from Utica Duxbak Corporation is just the ticket. The two-piece Woods Camouflage Trail Suit of cotton/nylon blend is another winner.

Shoot from the lowest, and *steadiest* position you can attain. But move into position slowly so as not to reveal your presence to those beady eyes, set in a cone-shaped head that swivels with radar-like precision, constantly on the alert for intruders. Chuck hunters of yore and some modern-day ones, arm themselves with medium-weight target rifles, topped by target optics of 12 to 20 power, thus insuring a minute-of-angle cone of fire, eliminating limitations imposed by inadequate equipment. The 11-pound Winchester Model 52D, scoped with a Redfield 3200 20X, would be a prime example. Then the contest becomes one of pitting the hunter against distance and wind.

Wind is an even greater factor when you shift the scene from an eastern farm lot to the "Big Sky" country of the Great Plains, where rocky pinnacles harbor the

Chuck hunter equipped with binoculars and spotting scope, plus big-X scope on his heavy-barreled rimfire rifle, has given himself the best possible odds of connecting with long-range targets. Prone position is most accurate and least revealing to prey.

woodchuck's western cousin, the rockchuck. Inhabiting the cracks and crevices fashioned by eons of erosion, *Marmota flaviventris* dwells among the huge boulders, left in the wake of the massive glacier that scraped smooth the flatlands of Wyoming, Colorado, and Utah. Rockchuck families inhabit the self-same rockpiles for countless generations, seldom venturing more than

¼-mile from their rocky fortress. When they do hazard out, it is only to raid neighboring farm crops or to feast on nature's bounty in lush green Alpine meadows.

Hunting yellow-bellied marmots requires as much skill and dedication as a safari out after mountain goats or bears. As a matter of fact, once you master the means of approaching within rimfire range of rockchucks, even armed with a .22 WMR, you should find the quest for goats and bears merely light exercise! You can scout some of the rock piles with binoculars from a four/wheel drive rig. But eventually you'll be obliged to desert the Jeep to clamber up rock-strewn talus slopes, trying not to rattle or crunch or stand out like a BIGFOOT.

Rockchucks love to sun themselves atop their granite castles with the wind ruffling their dark brown grizzle-tipped fur. But even dozing in the sun, these hawk-harassed, coyote-coveted varmints are on the alert for the slightest movement, even a shadow drifting lazily by! After you spot your quarry, make every effort to approach unobserved, using either rock piles or the limited vegetation to cover your stalk.

Best not handle a defunct chuck, lest you inherit its colony of ticks which may possibly be infected with the deadly Rocky Mountain fever! It's a good idea also to treat trousers and boots with insect repellant to dissuade the casual "hitchhikers" that cling on the blades of tall, coarse prairie grass.

A couple of rockchuck hunters show justifiable pride in the accomplishment of bagging three of the wary critters. A .22 Magnum is none too much gun to reach these spooky varmints; they're hard to approach at ranges under 100 yards.

Prairie Dogs

Living like serfs on the flatlands surrounding the rockchuck's craggy castles are the playful, plentiful prairie dogs. Their endless tunneling under the grassy meadows, dots the rolling plains with millions of holes—the better to booby trap cattle and horses. As if that weren't enough, whatever grass the prairie dog doesn't cover with high hard mounds of inner earth, it *eats,* leaving hungry cattle and angry ranchers to wonder if they didn't inherit only the holes in the donuts. When the Indians ruled the plains, they shared the land with prairie dog towns that stretched for hundreds of miles, in the happy knowledge that the tiny rodents provided an endless and toothsome food supply. Today chemical warfare by cattlemen and ranchers has whittled the old towns down to sparse settlements here and there.

With all that, prairie poodles are in no way threatened with extinction. Enough remain to provide some challenging shooting, especially for the rimfire nimrod, who must "Indian" up within the limited range of his chosen cartridge. At the first sign of company, sod poodles dive for their holes. Then you will see a head pop up here and there, as they scold you in a falsetto bark that earned them their name. Sometimes you can simply sit down near a dog town and wait. Eventually the curiosity-driven rodents will begin to peek to see what happened. If you don't stick out like a flagpole in a town square, they will soon venture out again as if nothing had happened. Your first shot will likely drive them to ground again, but again a short wait will see them up and about, unless they have been previously educated by other hunters. Pickup trucks, rattling across the prairie on fence-mending errands or delivering hay to livestock, are a common sight on the plains. Prairie dogs pay scant attention to one more that idles up to them—with you or a cohort behind the wheel, while the other handles the iron.

Plodding the prairies or clambering up and over massive rock citadels is tiring work. Best carry a rifle of suitable field weight, equipped with a sling for those times when both hands are required just to hang on. Your gun must be capable of holding near minute-of-angle groups with high velocity hollow point ammo and must be scoped with the best you can afford. Clear optics and good definition are a *must,* high X's (6X and up) an asset.

Ground Squirrels

"Ground squirrel" is just another name for a similar species of rodent residing in another part of the country. "Grounies" love it hot—in the depths of Death Valley—and like it cold,—ranging into the northernmost reaches of Alaska and Canada! Unlike the woodchuck which seeks out the coolness deep in their dens, the ground squirrel is most active in the heat of the day.

Living like serfs on the flatlands surrounding the rockchuck's craggy castles, plentiful prairie dogs offer challenging shooting, especially to the rimfire rifleman with his limited range.

For every minute spent down on all fours browsing, the ground squirrel puts in three standing upright picket-pin style, in contemplative munching, sharp eyes searching the horizon for signs of predatory coyotes or cats. Even in its picket-pin stance, the tiny rat-like rodent presents a target hardly half-a-foot tall and barely 2 inches across, calling for a rifle capable of near minute-of-angle accuracy to connect inside the length of a football field. A scope of 9X to 12X is needed to clearly define the buff target against its blending background. A high-powered scope also aids in doping the drifting mirage, a clear clue to wind direction and velocity. Inasmuch as long shots are the rule with ground squirrels and prairie dogs, best sight in at 75 yards with flat-shooting Stingers or Xpediters. Then you can quarter the tiny bullet-shaped heads with your cross hairs, and be assured of a solid hit out to about 125 yards.

109

.22 Small Game Hunting

Gray and Fox Squirrels

Arboreal cousin to the prairie dog and ground squirrel is the toothsome tree squirrel, favored food of the Colonial settlers and the Indians before them, and still the subject of culinary cravings coast to coast! The most memorable hunts of the Daniel Boones of early America included hand-to-hand encounters with "bars" and "painters." The forested frontiers of early America offered a wealth of game—deer, turkeys, grouse, bears and even huge black panthers, as well as opossums and bandit-masked raccoons from which the early pioneers made their distinctive bushy-tailed hats. Despite that, the Colonists named the graceful Pennsylvania flintlock a "squirrel rifle," in honor of the abundant, prolific critters that were of greatest importance to them, both as a staple of frontier diet and their favored sport.

Although the squirrel rarely receives "good press" these days, it continues to attract multitudes of young and old into the hardwood forests of the East and the pine-studded peaks of the West, ranking behind only the cottontail rabbit as the all-time favorite game animal. To a youthful neophyte nimrod, the squirrel looms as large in the scope of his .22 rimfire rifle as a grizzly bear. And where else could he find such a puree of hunting knowledge distilled into short pleasure-filled hours. The skills of woodsmanship, stalking, silence, personal discipline and ultimate marksmanship are soon learned under the tutorship of the astute squirrel. Seasoned hunters never lose the thrill of spring or autumn in the hardwood forests.

Whether dappled by sun sprinkling through deep green leaves to a mossy forest floor, or damp with misty winter dew, drifting darkly over blazing orange and red, the hickory and hardwood forests draw the smallbore squirrel hunter with an irresistible appeal.

Squirrels receive seasonal protection, as befits the prince of sporting targets, but seasons are long and bag limits generous. In the towering Ozarks hunters in years past carried their squirrels in a tin bucket and stayed afield until it was full to overflowing. This seedbed of squirrel hunting remains one of the most productive, with annual harvests estimated in the area of 3 million. The Missouri season extends through 5 long months, from the first of August through the end of December. Squirrel hunters of the "show me" state take their hunting seriously.

For the most part, early September, once the most popular hunting period, finds the woods closed to squirrel hunting in many states. Game departments consider the tiny bushy-tails too vulnerable during nut-cutting time, when the hickory nuts are ripe for the picking and squirrels are to be found clinging to the ends of the branches to reach the fruit. Seasons vary somewhat state to state, but for the most part, they range from mid-September through November or December, with a few states offering split seasons ending as late as February. Some states offer spring squirrel seasons when the forests are in full bloom, splendidly adorned in deep dense greens, making it all but impossible to pick out tiny bushy-tails among the fully-leafed branches. Away out west in California, the squirrel season begins in August and ranges through January. Alaska offers year-around shooting of their red squirrel.

Top target for squirrel buffs is the bushy-tailed gray, *Sciurus carolinensis,* marked by the grizzled salt-and-pepper fur coat that won it the name, along with white or yellowish underfur. Grays inhabit the high hardwood forests as well as the lush lowlands of the eastern half of the United States, from the Gulf into Canada. A patch of grays occupy pine and oak wooded portions of Arizona, and a wide belt of grays stretches from Baja California up into Washington State.

Western squirrels take to the pines out of necessity rather than preference. (Pine cones offer sustenance, but not to the squirrel's taste.) It will choose stands of oak, maple and beech, even poplar and birch, when they are present.

Squirrel populations ebb and flow with the presence or absence of an adequate food supply. A drought or blight resulting in a poor nut crop will drive the squirrels to another range in search of food, or they may die in droves during a lean winter. Knowing when and where the food is best, is half the battle in squirrel hunting.

Gray squirrels dine on every breed of nut to be found in the forest, including hickory, butternut, walnuts, beechnuts, hazelnuts, pecans, etc.; as well as acorns, blossoms, buds, berries and fruit. They are also known to raid bird nests to devour the young or eggs. Southerners know the gray as the "cat" squirrel.

The highly adaptable gray can be as wild and wary as a hare in the far reaches of the forest, or it can nibble nuts from your hand at a park bench in the local town square. It averages 18 to 20 inches in length, of which about half is devoted to his fluffy tail. Gray squirrels weigh from 1 to about 1½ pounds and share the metabolism of the hummingbird. Frenzied, and hyperactive, they are most often encountered as "blurs" of brown streaking across the forest floor in a flurry of dry leaves, or zipping up a tree trunk to vanish into arboreal heights. You might swear they were in fact birds, as they leap through leafy crowns, seeming to fly across the treetops. They bark nervously when an intruder approaches, warning others of their kind. Gray squirrels favor denning in hollow trees, but lacking that, they will build leaf nests which offer scant protection from marauding raccoons, owls and hawks.

The fox squirrel, *Sciurus niger,* is named for its rust-red coloration similar to that of a fox. It ranges generally throughout the eastern half of the nation from Canada to the Gulf, save for the New England area. Roughly double the size of the gray squirrel, it is less

ing red and orange, count the colors. The more varied the shades, the more likely it is to harbor an abundance of squirrels.

To score on squirrels with a .22 rimfire, you must become a consummate marksman and develop the woods skills that made it possible for buckskin-clad frontiersmen to blend into a tree trunk and escape detection by hostile Indians. You must learn to pick your way through the woodlands without breaking twigs and crunching over brittle leaves. You must develop ears to hear the soft crackling made by buck-toothed squirrels gnawing nuts. Your eyes must catch the twitch of a tail, a furtive twist of a tiny head, wind ruffling fur, or a branch that bends when there is no wind. A pair of high quality binoculars will aid in determining if yonder bump-on-a-log is actually a startled squirrel, frozen in nature's age old attempt at camouflaged concealment.

Although squirrels use their keen noses to ferret out nuts buried deep in unmarked caches, they don't seem to react to human scent. They are intensely alert to motion. If you and a squirrel spot each other simultaneously, freeze in your tracks, and he may come to regard you as part of the scenery, and resume his previous occupation which was most likely eating. Then, after its attention is directed away from you, you might find it possible to get your gun up to take a shot.

Pause long and often, listening and looking. Hold to the shadows, skirting the sun spotlighted patches. Hunt the damp forests with leaves still dripping with rain. It is then that the famished denizens of the tree tops are out in force to stoke empty bellys, and the wet leaves underfoot muffle your foot steps. If a bushy-tail somehow manages to keep a tree trunk between it and you as you circle, throw a rock into the brush on the opposite side, or hang your jacket on a bush and circle. The S-1 Squirrel Call from the Burnham Brothers, a small rubber squeeze bulb, imitates the bark of an agitated squirrel. Try some off-season practice with the call to get the hang of squirrel language. You'll soon come to recognize the difference between a call of alarm and an angry challenge that can lure an old boar out of hiding.

As the season wanes and the squirrels become more wary, try hunting from a stand. Enter the mist-shrouded woods before dawn and wait until the first light filters through the barren branches, bringing Mr. Squirrel out in search of breakfast. Wait until your target is clearly defined before firing. No shot at all is better than a miss or cripple! Confine your aiming points to the head and front shoulders. The latter presents a slightly larger target, with the likelihood of a hit in the heart if you should underestimate the range, or in the spine if you

lively and slower to flee. More often than not, it will freeze when taken by surprise and attempt to hide by flattening out on a limb. Curiosity sometimes drives it to play "hide-and-peek," offering a hurried head shot. Unlike the gray squirrel which hews to deep forests whenever possible, the fox squirrel prefers open woodlots and sparsely wooded ridges. It shares with the gray a penchant for a diet of acorns, nuts and field corn, often driving farmers to distraction with its depredations. Fox squirrels den in hollow trees or leaf nests much as the smaller gray. Mounds of nut husks and stripped corn cobs mark its favored eating places. Squirrel droppings consist of small, dark pellets about ½-inch long, offering yet another clue to their whereabouts.

The most squirrel-productive forests are those with a mixed blend of trees, offering a year-around yield of fruits and nuts. When autumn turns the forests to blaz-

hold a mite high. When your squirrel drops, mentally mark the spot and remain motionless. Often you can bag two or three without taking a step.

Scout the area of your stand ahead of time, spotting den trees by their well-worn hollows, gnawed at the edges by the industrious squirrels intent upon improving their penthouse apartments. Mounds of nut hulls at the foot of a tree are a good sign. Find an observation point with a clear view of the limbs above the pile of cuttings. Take a folding camp stool upon which to plant your posterior. The cold ground can be little comfort under a tired bottom, and legs grow cramped after an hour or so.

As always, if you hunt private land, request permission from the owner first. In California the law states that you must have written permission on your person to hunt private land! If your bag is abundant, share a couple of plump, pan-ready squirrels with the farmer or orchard owner, and he will remember you kindly on your next visit.

Good garb for squirrel hunting is cotton camo clothing, washed soft to eliminate scraping noises against brush. Camouflage flannel shirts are available from Burnham Brothers of Marble Falls, Texas, by mail order, as are camouflage face nets and gloves that render the hunter all but invisible and ward off mosquitos as well. Insect repellant sprayed around the boot tops and trouser legs help to discourage chiggers. Spread on hands, ears and neck, repellant helps you avoid the necessity for slapping at buzzing bugs, thereby revealing your position.

Federal Semi-Hollow Points or Winchester Dynapoints are both good squirrel stoppers, and tissue destruction is measurably less than that resulting from the use of ordinary high velocity hollow points. The .22 Magnum is a case of gross overkill. Any squirrel hit will experience the massive hemorrhaging which makes the flesh too bloodshot to eat. Jacketed solids are slightly less destructive but still more so than might be desired. And what becomes of the projectile after it passes *through* the tree-perched squirrel? With no other obstruction in its path, a 40-grain .22 WMR speeding off into space at 2000 fps could pick a spot miles distant to land. Granted, the odds are way against a person occupying that particular spot at that particular point in time, but even a one-in-a-million chance *is one chance too many!* Stingers and Xpediters are contraindicated for the same reasons.

A running battle still rages between shotgunners, who point to full game bags as proof that a scattergun is the only viable tool in the hardwoods, and rimfire riflemen who pit their skill and cunning against that of the elusive gray or furtive fox. Somehow a squirrel riddled with number 6 shot doesn't taste the same as one neatly beheaded by a 40-grain Semi-Hollow Point. Then there's always the risk of breaking your bridgework on a stray pellet! However, granting the shotgunner his obvious advantage on close-in moving targets, he's stymied when the game spooks out at 40 to 50 yards— easy pickin's for the rimfire nimrod. It requires the maximum of marksmanship to connect at long range with a target whose vitals are no larger than the box that holds your ammo. But that's part of the charm and challenge of squirrel hunting with a rimfire. If it were easy, everybody could do it!

Turkeys

Hunting gobblers is something like a cross between squirrel and whitetail deer hunting. Benjamin Franklin wanted the Tom turkey to become the seal of the United States, rather than the eagle. The elusive, strutting Tom turkey certainly epitomized the America that

Tom (near) and hen (behind) have a number of other distinguishing characteristics, such as the horn growing at the base of the beak on the male (lacking in the female), black-tipped breast feathers on the male (dull white on the female) and the brighter coloration of the male's head.

Big antelope jackrabbits are about twice as big and twice as tough as common cottontails. Both can be taken on the run with an accurate handgun like the Smith & Wesson K-22, given a practiced marksman.

was, proud and unafraid! Using money supplied by sportsmen, game management people have established wild turkeys in many areas where they were heretofore unknown. They are now widely found from Pennsylvania to Florida, west to Colorado and Arizona. We even have a 3-week turkey season here in California.

Meleagris gallopavo is split into five subspecies, marked by variations in plumage. Perhaps best known is the Merriam with tail feathers tipped in light brown. Because most hunting seasons are limited to Toms only, it becomes important to recognize the male bird at first glimpse. The most prominent feature of the gobbler is the beard, growing from the center of the breast. However, that isn't a certain sign. Some hens grow beards also. Perhaps easier to spot is the fleshy horn growing from the forehead at the base of the beak. On a mature male it becomes ½-inch to a full inch in length, while the female rarely exhibits more than a mere bump. The male sports a red or pink head, devoid of plumage, while the female is well feathered but plain. The wattle, or fleshy lobes hanging down from the neck and chin are far more prominent on the male. Breast feathers are perhaps the best measure of the male, with distinctive jet-black tipped feathers, while the female's breast feathers are merely off-white. Of course, the the Tom is larger, ranging from 15 to 24 pounds, contrasted to the female's 9 to 13 pounds at maturity.

The fact is, you'll have no more trouble telling a Tom from a hen than you will a buck from a doe, unless you become afflicted with "turkey fever," which is just as virulent as buck fever! The gobbler is a tough old bird—too tough for a .22 Long Rifle. Turkey hunting with a small-caliber rifle (where legal) demands the superior stopping power of a .22 WMR hollow points. A good aiming point is the center of the neck where it joins the body. You can be off a little in any direction and still get a sure kill. Combo rifle/shotguns like the over/under Savage 24-D offer the option of a 20 gauge 3-inch magnum shotshell for birds on the fly, or the .22 Magnum for wary gobblers that refuse to venture within shotgun range. Most turkeys are taken from blinds, using a call to entice the amorous old fool within range. During spring, the cackle of a hen with an urge to nest is a sure-fire lure which can be duplicated with a number of various calls. Among the most popular is the Diaphragm Turkey Caller, which is available through Burnham Brothers. The horseshoe-shaped diaphragm call is held in the mouth with the open end of the "U" facing forward. It requires some practice to master this call, but it is highly productive. The traditional cedar box call, the slate-and-striker, etc., are all good, given some practice. Before you try to fool a gnarled old gobbler, buy a record of turkey calls and learn to imitate them faithfully. A sour note will send a Tom in the other direction.

During the spring mating season, usually during March, April or May, the swaggering, strutting gobbler has a head full of love and lacks his usual suspicious nature. Thus he answers to a call more readily than in the fall.

Confirmed rimfire afficionados might prefer to enter the field with the purity of a .22 Magnum rifle only, such as the highly accurate and reliable bolt action Marlin Model 783, with its 12-shot under-barrel tubular magazine ready to feed backup rounds, which hopefully won't be needed! A good 4X scope is about right for picking an old Tom out of the forest undergrowth. For best results, install a 1-inch tube bigbore quality scope to get the highest possible light gathering capability during the dawn and dusk periods. The latter time is especially important if you plan to stake out a roost and await the nightly return of the flock.

Toms gobble in the early morning to attract hens. A Tom with a harem already in tow isn't going to be interested in your most seductive plaints, so save your breath. A lonely gobbler is a sucker for a practiced caller, however. By mid-morning gobbling has ceased, not to be resumed until later afternoon.

Rabbits

For every bush in these United States, there must be at least one rabbit. And, it seems, there's a hunter for most every rabbit! Some hunters carry shotguns, which sounds like taking unfair advantage. What's more, it limits the hunter's range to under 40 yards. Away out

Perhaps the most popular bunny for the dinner table is the common cottontail, found just about everywhere in the United States where a little brushy cover exists to supply the necessary habitat. The cottontail is the chief target for numerous nimrods, young and old, all with one thing in common — a love of the out-of-doors and .22 rifles!

west in the boulder-strewn sage flats of the Owens Valley where I rabbit hunt, a shotgun would restrict his bag to tiny timid brush rabbits—that have to be kicked out of cover with the toe of your boot—or an occasional cottontail that tarried too long in its mid-day stupor. The mule-eared ''Jackass rabbit,'' as the early pioneers dubbed it, will be off and running well out of shotgun range. It takes the kind of .22 rimfire marksman who can blaze away standing tip-toe on one foot in a bed of prickly pear to snap a shot into one of those blazing bunnies, as it cuts in its after-burners for a jet assist from a pair of hind legs that a wallaby would envy!

Admittedly, the jackrabbit is a big target, measuring up to 2-feet long, and weighing as much as 7 pounds, but it is *tough,* and it is *fast!* You'd better score a vital hit the first shot, with a high velocity hollow pointed Long Rifle or, better yet, a Stinger or Xpediter. The jack certainly is not overgunned with the .22 Magnum!

A startled jackrabbit usually takes off in such haste that it fails to notice what scared it. Before disappearing from sight, it will pause for a moment on the horizon to size up the situation. If you're ready with your rifle at your shoulder, you have a split second to squeeze off a final convincing round.

In my younger years, I hunted jacks as much for meat as for sport. They may not be as toothsome as plump cottontails, but they are nonetheless table fare of a high order. Favored food among rabbit gourmets is the cottontail in any of its 70 species and subspecies that blanket the country. Cottontails are about half as large and half as tough as jackrabbits. While a jackrabbit demands the spicy disguise of a *hasenpfeffer,* the cotton-tail can be rolled in light batter and pan-fried like chicken.

Equally popular in field and kitchen is the snowshoe rabbit, or varying hare, with the chameleon-like ability to shift from summer brown to winter white. Near perfect camouflage makes them hard to spot without the aid of a busy beagle, bugling up a storm in hot pursuit, floppy ears fringed with snow, as it gallops after a herringbone pattern of tracks across frigid fields. Whereas the jackrabbit pauses only briefly on the brink of safety, cottontails and snowshoes are wont to stop and listen now and then. If a cottontail is not pressed *too hard* by the trailing beagle, it will sometimes allow the hunter a momentarily frozen target. Both rabbits may trail out of sight, but they normally circle back to the starting point, *and the waiting hunter.*

Raccoons

The *arukun,* as he was named by the American Indians, is best known for his Lone Ranger mask. The raccoon, as we now know him, has been declared a bandit for his habit of raiding bird's nests and stealing the eggs, but he eats just about anything that comes to hand, animal, vegetable, or fish. Many states have declared them game animals and southerners hunt raccoons behind baying hounds at night, as they do opossums, well knowing that both make savory dinner dishes. Both can be called with a varmint call, primarily at night, since neither ventures forth very often by day. Both of these predatory animals are small enough to be fair game for the .22 Long Rifle high velocity hollow point, or the dimple points.

.22 Predator Hunting

Badgers

Webster defines "predator" as an animal that, "preys, destroys or devours." Many predatory animals, when found in abundance, can easily reduce both rodent and game-animal populations—sometimes drastically. With the above definition and observation in mind, it's not hard to see why so many states allow those animals they classify as "predators" to be hunted on a year-around basis. For the hunter who fancies himself a stalker and astute sign reader, predator hunting can be a real rimfire challenge.

Among the more "nocturnal" varieties of predator is the badger—these little bundles of dynamite spend daytime hours deep in their dens, emerging at night to dig out other denizens of the dirt, such as ground squirrels or prairie dogs, mice etc. Any badger can give any coyote, bobcat, et al, a stiff fight. Therefore, they seldom tangle. A badger will answer a varmint call, but you may wait a lifetime and never see one. If you *can* find one, the .22 will do the trick.

Foxes

Fox hunting originated in 17th century England among aristocratic land owners, riding magnificent mounts behind packs of coursing hounds. The stylized costumes of scarlet coats and caps, over white breeches, survives to this day wherever the chase con-

The badger is just as mean and tough as he looks! He has chest muscles that will stop a standard .22 Long Rifle. Better use a .22 Magnum on this critter.

Alaskan guide, Al Budzynski, shows author one of magnum-sized foxes that he trapped during winter. Alaskan foxes sometimes grow almost as big as stateside coyotes.

tinues, as it does in the southern United States. Both the red fox, *Vulpes fulva,* and the gray fox, *Urocyon cinereoargenteus,* are widely found throughout the lower 48 States and Alaska. The foxes of Alaska grow far larger than their southern cousins which weigh between 5 and 10 pounds. Some Alaskan foxes grow almost as large as State-side coyotes!

Most eastern states accord the fox game animal status, with winter seasons of 2 to 3 months, while western states either have no seasonal protection, or have seasons ranging from 4 to 8 months. An individual hunter without dogs can outwit the sly fox only by using a varmint call.

In the West, veteran varmint callers using high-powered centerfire rifles seldom fire on a fox. They consider the animal too easy prey. Changing over to a rimfire rifle tilts the scales considerably in the other direction, making the fox a far more sporting proposition! A fairly fragile creature compared to both bobcat and coyote, the fox is fair game for the .22 Long Rifle, especially in its Stinger/Xpediter configuration. The .22 WMR loaded with hollow points would be an even more certain stopper. Because the fox is less wary than larger predators, it is easier for the beginning caller to entice within range. Once, near dusk, when I gave up on seeing any deer from my High Sierra stand, I tried calling for a few minutes. About 10 minutes later, a fox came trotting right up to me, although I was no longer concealed. I was sitting atop a large rock, and remained completely motionless. After studying me for several minutes, it reluctantly walked away, turning now and then to peer back at what he must have thought was the biggest rabbit of all time!

Bobcats

Outside of highly infrequent chance encounters, the average hunter never gets within rifle range of a bashful bobcat. The ferocious feline is normally nocturnal, spending little time prowling by day.

Lynx rufus averages from 20 to 25 pounds in weight, although I have bagged bobcats scaling nearer 35 pounds in the depths of the Mojave Desert. Desert cats develop broad muscular shoulders, full chests and deep lungs—this is a result of coursing long-legged jackrabbits through stands of Joshua, yucca and gnarled mesquite. They eat heartier than their mountain cousins, which have to rely largely upon a rodent diet.

Bobcats have the disposition of a runaway buzz saw, the patience of the Sphinx, and the wraith-like qualities of a puff of smoke! About the only way to arrange a nose-to-nose confrontation with a stubby-tail is run it to ground with a pack of hounds—*OR* invite it to dinner with a varmint call!

With four razor-sharp claws per paw, plus long hook-shaped dewclaws to hold a victim while shredding it with ½-inch fangs, bobcats have been known to bring down full-grown whitetail bucks in the East, when

This bobcat answered a call at night and came within close-up range of the camera and strobe, much to the surprise of both hunter and bobcat!

smaller pickin's get lean. Endowed with better than average "cat-sense," the bobcat prefers to pick on fawns or does, to the tune of about 25 percent of its diet in the New England states. Ground-nesting game birds are also on the bobcat bill-of-fare, including quail, grouse, prairie chickens, doves, pheasants, chukar, etc.

Lynx rufus preys upon domestic livestock, especially sheep and lambs. One recorded attack by a single cat indicated a kill of 30 lambs. In another instance, two cats killed 34 lambs in a 2-day orgy, putting the lie to eco-freak contentions that predators kill only to eat! Poultry raisers are often first to feel the effects of a new bobcat in the area, because chickens and turkeys are easy prey for the furtive felines.

Eastern bobcats den along brushy river bottoms and Southern canebrakes, but Western cats hew to rugged and rocky boulder-strewn mountains, criss-crossed by dry washes and arroyos, with brushy draws of pinion, juniper, sagebrush and manzanita. The Western bobcat dens on rocky outcroppings on the point of a ridge, where it can keep a wary eye on surrounding terrain without lifting its head from its paws.

Coyotes

The American Indians revered the canny coyote, crediting it with such sagacity that they believed it would be the last living being on earth. Could be! In the face of man's determined efforts to control coyote population by means of poisons, and despite rapidly shrinking habitat, the coyote has extended its range

The American Indians revered the canny coyote, predicting that it would be the last living thing upon the earth. Who can say otherwise? Coyotes are among nature's most favored animals — wiley, fecund, adaptable.

The coyote represents the upper limits of killing and stopping power for the .22 WMR; and, bullets must be precisely placed in the head or heart to assure humane kills.

from the days when it was largely confined to the Western United States, until it now covers the country coast to coast and border to border!

During a sojourn in Wyoming, I discussed the coyote problem with the governor and game control officials. It became apparent that a high coyote population equalled a low antelope population. Even elk were adversely affected because of coyote depredations on their breeding grounds.

The coyote is indisputably prolific. Given average litters of eight pups per year over an average life span of 8 years, a domestic couple could contribute 64 new coyote citizens. Their progeny would contribute another 2000-plus coyotes, etc., and theirs in excess of 64,000, on into infinity. Coyotes have no natural enemies. The only limiting factor would be food supplies. And the sheep/poultry/cattle raisers just don't fancy being in business totally for the benefit of coyotes. It is estimated that just to keep coyote populations at present levels would require a constant attrition rate of approximately 25 percent. However, when hard pressed to survive, nature magically endows the coyote with two breeding cycles per year, throwing all arithmetic right out the window. Sounds as if the Indians were right.

Coyotes sometimes breed with domestic dogs, resulting in cross-breeds called, "coy-dogs," usually larger and more intelligent than either of the parents. Coyotes

are often depicted as scrawny critters, as they sometimes are, especially in the absence of adequate food supplies. However, when rabbits are rife, coyotes grow large and plump, weighing as much as 40 or more pounds. With winter fur, they look as luxuriant as wolves!

Greed is the coyote's only undoing. It will answer a predator call in the apparent hope of stealing another predator's meal. The main pet peeve for the coyote is its sometimes escort of ravens (a dead giveaway to its location), circling lazily overhead in hopes of trailing the four-footed predator to an over-ripe carcass.

The bitterest enemy of the coyote is not the varmint hunter who in fact respects his quarry as only a man who matches wits with it face to face truly can, but the sheep raiser. I accompanied a U.S. Fish and Wildlife Service agent on his rounds of the sheep owners in Wyoming one year on a fact-finding expedition. A helicopter was used to search out coyote dens, and make a head count. To a man, the sheep raisers were in favor of total eradication of coyote populations. One sheep rancher remarked to me bitterly, "I don't know why God created the coyote anyway. He's no damn good to anyone!" Sheep ranchers were the most widespread users of the controversial "1080" poison, which was banned by the Environmental Protection Agency in 1972. It became abundantly apparent that the poison which was injected into dead sheep in hopes that coyotes would eat them and die, was getting into the mainstream of countless other animals and birds, including the endangered bald eagle. A number of western states, including Wyoming, Montana, South Dakota, and Colorado, have asked for permission to resume use of 1080, at least on a limited basis, but the matter is currently tied up in litigation.

I've often wondered if it wouldn't be more beneficial to encourage varmint hunting as a means of predator control, rather than return to wholesale poisoning, with its already recognized dangers of adverse effects upon the entire wildlife spectrum in and around the affected community.

In order to make the suggested solution feasible, varmint hunters would have to mind their manners when entering another man's property. Granted, much of the grazing country is Bureau of Land Management (public) land, leased to the sheep and cattle raisers, but the ranchers erect the fences and facilities that you will encounter.

One of those facilities which will be encountered is a water supply. Water is the life-blood of any ranch or farm. It seems incredible that so-called "hunters" could repay the hospitality of a landowner by riddling his water tank with bullet holes! These offenders do not represent the majority of hunters; however, they do immeasurable mischief against *all* hunters. If you should ever witness such conduct, do all in your power to identify the culprit to the authorities! Only through this approach can we hope to maintain our welcome on private land!

Varmint Calling

Varmint calling is a sport that is infinitely more fun and far more productive if carried out under the "Buddy" system. Two men working together see *not twice* as much game, but rather *four times* as much. The spirit of camaraderie generated by working closely in tandem is seldom matched in any other sport. Two callers learn to sense the needs of each other. A gesture or expression is enough to convey a complicated communication, largely because varmint hunters dare not speak while they hunt. The human voice is anathema to critters, sending them into instant flight. Therefore silence is not only golden, but absolutely essential! Adding a third member to the team seldom works well, because that bond of close communication is broken.

Mouth-blown predator calls consist of wooden or plastic tubes containing reeds. Properly manipulated, they give out with the agonized cry of a dying rabbit, or so the story goes. I have heard dying rabbits, and they don't sound like the calls. Whatever the lure, however, calls do bring varmints of every size and color, from housecats to owls. I've even had eagles answer the call, not to mention wolves in Alaska, bears in Wyoming and deer in Utah. To get some idea of the effect upon an animal, try blowing your call around some simple

domestic cats or dogs. I did that once for fun after returning from a varmint hunt. The neighbor's dog made several excited circles of the yard, and ended up urinating all over my sleeping bag!

It takes a certain amount of persistence and courage to learn to use a mouth call, what with all the howling from the neighborhood dogs and complaints from the wife, but cassette and 8-track tape recorded calls sold by the Burnham Brothers, Johnny Stewart, etc., are relatively simple to master. Usually a remote speaker is set up 30 feet or so in front of the caller, directing the critter's attention away from the hunter instead of at him. Often critters will walk right up to the speaker, which they don't recognize as an enemy, presenting the hunter with an easy shot.

There is greater challenge in using a mouth-blown call. It becomes more of a personal duel of wits and skills between hunter and *hunter,* because the predator is in truth hunting you! Of course, it is your fond hope that he'll find you! I once called up a brace of wolves with an ordinary mouth-blown call while in Alaska under highly unfavorable conditions—including a guide that thought I'd lost my marbles—I bagged one of the wily predators, and it gave me a greater feeling of pride than if I'd scored on the grizzly bear that actually was the subject of my hunt.

Most predators are called in and shot from a "stand," which could be defined as a time and place chosen to call predators. Choosing the *right* time and place can be crucial to your success.

Novitiate varmint callers ponder long the problem of where to call. It matters not how skillful you become at wielding a varmint call if there are no varmints there to lend an ear to your virtuosity. Nothing beats pug marks in the soft sand or "dog tracks" around a muddy pothole as signs of bobcat and coyote population thereabouts. Cat tracks resemble those of a domestic tomcat, lacking claw marks because the claws are sheathed save in combat. Bobcat pugs are about 2 inches wide and spaced about a foot apart (leading an untrained observer to visualize an animal much larger than it actually is). Coyotes leave a track similar to a dog, with four toes and claw marks showing. You'll find dirt kicked up behind the tracks, because coyotes are always in a hurry, usually loping along at 5 to 10 miles per hour. On a dead run, coyotes have been clocked at 40 miles per hour.

At night, coyotes course the open flats stretched between ranges of rolling hills and mountains, rooting out and running down rabbits. Come morning, you'll discover the jubilant ki-dogs romping gaily back toward their hillside dens. If you can spot yourself on a rocky outcropping with your back to a cliff, commanding a wide area, high above the critter's line of sight, you stand a good chance of seeing some action come first light. A trick not widely known is to use a spotlight to pick up the critter's eyes before full light floods the

Mouth-blown calls take a certain amount of skill to use successfully. Here is a lineup of good ones: Burnham Brothers Long Range Fox Call and S-2 Close Range "squeeker;" P.S. Olt CP-21 Close Range Predator Call and E-1 Crow Call; Weems Wildcall; and, Circe Call of the Wild.

valley floor. Heads will turn the moment you blow your call, but you won't be able to see them in the dimness of dawn. However, if you use a spotlight, the critter's eyes will continue to reflect the highway markers.

Tolling bobcats presents some special problems that confound even veteran callers. For every cat called and seen, I'd guess that two or three came in unobserved and quietly left after discovering the hoax. Often I've discovered tracks around my stand after I gave up ever calling anything in. I've seen other callers with cats literally at their feet, yet hidden from their positions. Often a bobcat will work up right under a caller's nose, studying the situation for minutes at a time, before pussy-footing away, still unseen. The caller must be that much more alert to every spot of tan or orange showing through surrounding cover. Sometimes a tuft of fur or a shiny tin can hung by a string from a bush in sight of the caller, will draw the curious tabby out into the open. Or, a freshly-killed rabbit in an open spot, staked down so that it can't be dragged off into the brush, will sucker the bobcat into exposing itself. If you spy a bobcat sitting on his haunches, intently studying you from afar, be assured he's not coming any closer! He's already suspicious. Any movement on your part, and he'll vanish!

Time your bobcat stands with a watch because the minutes seem to stretch interminably. Remain for a minimum of half an hour. Bobcats are notorious for their cautious approach, skulking from bush to bush, sometimes taking 10 minutes to cover 100 yards.

The bobcat relies most upon its eyes and ears, but its nose knows man-smell wafted its way! Bottled scent, catnip, or even Ben Gay burn ointment smeared around the stand serves to confuse if not attract. Shooting range for bobcats seldom exceeds 50 yards in a desert clearing or on a rocky hillside. However, the bobcat is all sinew and guts! Even a .22 Magnum is barely adequate to bag a bobcat. Don't attempt it with a .22 Long Rifle! If you can be confident of your marksmanship, aim for the head. A low chest shot is second choice, because the heart is hard to find with assurance.

In choosing a blind, keep the basics well in hand. You are there *to call predators,* then bag them. Predators are smart and wary. The call invites them in, but they come in their own good time, and from the direction that offers them the best chance of sighting and scenting you. To outsmart the predator, you must select a location that offers a good view of at least half a circle, for sufficient distance to at least equal the maximum range of your rifle. Then if a coyote, bobcat, or fox comes skulking around your blind in an attempt to get downwind and test your scent, you can pick him off in the process. If possible, always enter the area of your blind with the sun at your back and the wind in your face! Thus you put the critters at a disadvantage in both seeing and smelling. Once you start calling, you attract the most careful scrutiny, so you must not move after you begin to call! You can't begin calling from a cramped position that will eventually drive you to shift your weight or shuffle about seeking a more comfortable position. Kneeling on one knee, sitting on your foot, etc. may seem fine to start with, but soon the position becomes agony. About the time you can't stand it anymore and simply must move, a coyote will have you riveted in his telescopic eyes. You may never see him, but he's become a smarter critter that will be harder to fool the next time!

Prepare your stand by removing all rocks that might imbed your backside or crunch underfoot. Get rid of twigs that go *snap* at the most inopportune moments. Cut away branches from trees or bushes that might impale you or snag your clothing, impeding movement

119

at a critical moment. A veteran caller I met once in Wyoming always carried a small leatherette-covered cushion with him to every stand. Not *macho,* to be sure, but *comfortable he was!*

When you finally decide that a particular calling position is hopeless, steel yourself for some furious action, then stand up *suddenly,* rifle at the ready to catch any critters that may be lurking nearby. Swiftly scan the area, and you might be rewarded with the sight of a high-tailing coyote or bobcat that you can overtake with a bullet.

Camouflage clothing must match your surroundings to be effective. Green camo stands out starkly against brown brush. Likewise, brown camo is little help in lush greenery. A reversible green/brown suit is handy to meet both requirements. The face and hands can be disguised with camo creams or grease sticks available from Burnham Brothers and others. Or wear camouflage headnet and gloves. Then you can sit *in front* of a bush to disguise your outline. If you position yourself *behind* a bush, you will be forever peeking and ducking your head like a nervous turkey gobbler. Any movement will send a predator packing, no matter how enticing your call. The trick in choosing a good location for a stand lies in placing yourself so that you can see a wide area without denying approaching varmints at least the promise of cover. Both bobcats and coyotes are loathe to cross a clearing by daylight. They will pick their way from one bush to another, taking advantage of every twig for concealment. You have to let them think they're hiding without blinding yourself. Don't call near a dry wash that varmints can use to circle downwind unseen. Unless you have scent on your stand, you'll lose any critters that wind you. If you must call near a wash, position yourself at its edge, so that you can observe traffic in both directions. It could get pretty busy after you start calling!

Park your vehicle out of sight and well away from your stand. Unless you're afraid of theft, best leave the doors just slightly ajar. Even closing them softly results in more noise than you can afford! Enter the area of your stand quickly *without conversation.* Pick your footing to make as little racket as possible. Chamber a round before entering the area of the stand, and if your safety is noisy, leave it off! Keep your finger *away* from the trigger and the muzzle safely pointed.

Where legal, night hunting predators is a thrill that must be experienced to be appreciated. It's a whole different world out there at night! "Spooky" would be a mild term for the feeling you'll experience the first time you witness a pair of predator eyes bouncing in to answer your call. Your skin will crawl, and the hair will stand up, but you'll love it! This sport must be confined to truly remote areas. Or areas with which you are so familiar that there cannot be the remotest possibility of your bullet being directed toward a ranch house or domestic stock. You must also be certain not to fire on deer. In some areas mere nighttime possession of a light and a gun are *prima facie* evidence of jack lighting deer.

That's the bad news. The good news is that you'll remember your nights in the field with nostalgic warmth for the rest of your life! But your hunt can't be any better than your lights. I've lost count of the number of night hunts crippled for me by a succession of lights that couldn't stand up to the beating—batteries that died at midnight, switches that broke, etc. Q-Beam Corporation of Dallas, Texas, makes a "Varmint Special" light that pours on 200,000 candlepower. Patterned after the home-made versions used by veteran night callers, the Q-Beam Varmint Special has a handy pistol grip and a hood to prevent sidelighting the hunter or blinding him with glare. Most varmints will soon be gone if you "burn" them with that much light—slip in a detachable red lens, and the critters don't seem to be aware of the light at all. A 15-foot cord allows freedom of movement, whether plugged into the Jeep cigarette lighter or a portable battery.

The most versatile light that I've yet encountered is the "Cobra Three-In-One," put out by Cobra, P.O. Box 167, Brady, Texas 76825. The 50,000 candlepower Cobra functions as a hand-held light, either plugged into the cigarette lighter or attached to its independent 12-volt sportsman's battery with shoulder strap. But where the Cobra *really shines* is when you attach it to the barrel of your rifle, to punch a hole through the darkness, right down the bullet's path! A quiet switch is within easy reach of the shooter's forefinger. Locate your varmint, bring your rifle to bear, and flick on this powerhouse to pinpoint your target. The Cobra comes in either the 50,000 candlepower Model 450B or the 110,000 candlepower Model 450A. For the latter, Cobra offers an optional rechargeable 12-volt cell with shoulder strap.

All Cobra components feature heavy-duty industrial quality. The sealed-beam bulb nests snugly in a strong steel housing. The rugged gun-mounting bracket is steel, polysol-coated to protect the gun barrel. Two stainless-steel low profile polysol-coated clamps hold the light rigidly on the barrel. Though rugged and powerful, the Cobra is compact, just 4½ × 7 × 3 inches—small enough to fit in a glove compartment. And it weighs only 20 ounces.

For night hunting, stick to a .22 Magnum rifle/revolver battery, loaded with hollow points. You may call up some lesser predators that would readily succumb to a Stinger, but the most likely guests to answer your dinner call are bobcats and coyotes, both of which take some convincing! Why a backup revolver? Some wag once said, "If you can't kill it with a rifle, forget it!" However, that fella never went to fetch a "dead" bobcat in a jumble of house-high boulders, only to find it flown, and have to follow up a blood trail unarmed because he didn't bring a handgun, and the rifle was back at the stand. Many centerfire varmint hunters carry .22 Magnum rimfire side arms to administer the *coup de grace.*

As you might suspect, my own battery of .22 rimfire rifles is rather extensive. One of my favorites for all small game hunting is a semi-auto .22. The autoloader has an intrinsic advantage of taking over the chores of reloading after every shot, thereby eliminating the necessity for tell-tale movements that might reveal the hunter's position. Game can spot even the almost imperceptible pull-push motion of a pump action rifle. A lever action causes quite a flurry of motion—it's easily picked up by alert eyes. If you're shooting a turning bolt action rifle, you're obliged to go through a series of gesticulations calculated to run off every critter in sight. The muted "pop" of a .22 rimfire followed by dead silence does not normally alarm game; however, the "clink-clank" of an action reloading quickly drives all game within hearing to the depths of their dens.

Attached to Mossberg Model 640K Chuckster, the Cobra Three-in-One light can punch a hole through the darkness, right down the bullet's path, spotlighting varmints out about as far as you can hit them.

The Harris Bipod is a bench rest that you can carry with you into the field. Two sturdy legs rotate down from a position parallel to the barrel. They can be used as shown for prone position, or extended to almost 2 feet in length, for the sitting position.

The autos I favor are the discontinued Winchester 490, the currently-made Browning BAR and the interesting new Mossberg Plinkster. The BAR boasts a trigger that allows you to forget the squeeze, and concentrate upon your target! The Plinkster brings the unique comfort of a thumb hole stock within reach of the modest budget.

For those long shots where you wish you had a bench rest handy, try attaching a Harris Bipod, available from Harris Engineering Inc., Box 305, Fraser, Michigan 48026. This device should be far more popular than it is. Once you try it, you'll never again be without it! The Harris Bipod attaches to the quick detachable sling swivel base on the forend of your rifle. (If you don't have Q-D swivels, they're easy to install.) The Harris Bipod features rubber rails that protect the stock finish, and a new base is provided for the swivel. Two hard anodized alloy legs (they are adjustable) are carried parallel to the barrel. A firm tug lowers them to the vertical position. The basic 13-inch length of the Model 1A is ideal for prone shooting. The legs telescope to 23 inches for sitting, perhaps the most useful position. Weighing only 11 ounces, the Harris Bipod adds little to the overall burden of the rifle, but when you need it, the bipod will be worth every ounce in pure gold!

Hunting, be it for varmints, small game or predators, is a highly enjoyable experience for the man with a .22 rimfire. Every year, across the United States alone, *millions* of rounds of .22 rimfire ammo are expended in the pursuit of game. The .22 is not just for "plinkers."

If you've had a yen to try out your favorite beer-can buster on something more animate, try hunting—the rewards are there, and the cost (with a rimfire) is minimal.

CHAPTER 8

Get the Range/Outwit the Wind

IT MAY COME AS a surprise to present-day rimfire fans that between the Great Wars, the .22 rimfire was considered a viable long-range competition cartridge and was regularly fired at 200 yards. Considering the rainbow trajectory of the .22 Long Rifle standard velocity ammo of that period (chronographing from 1050 to 1100 fps), target shooters had to be pretty sharp just to get on the paper at 200 yards. Add to that the problems of wind deflection, and you can recognize the extent of their skill.

The introduction of the Remington Kleanbore ammo, loaded into brass cases that would withstand higher pressures than the old copper ones, with the resultant increase in velocity to 1300 fps, was greeted by target fans as a real breakthrough in terms of both trajectory and reduced wind drift. You can imagine the disappointment when they were informed that the higher velocity ammo actually resulted in *more,* not *less* drift. This news didn't come all at once. Initial reports claimed less wind drift. After the truth was definitely proven, there were red faces amongst some of the most highly regarded shooting experts of the day.

Captain Edward C. Crossman, in his book, *Military and Sporting Rifle Shooting,* told of initial experiments with the new ammo, and the mysterious need to dial in added windage over the old standard velocity ammo that they had been using. Crossman found his explanation in an article by Dr. F. H. Kelly, a well-known British ballistician, writing in the September, 1930, issue of *The NRA Journal,* a publication of the English NRA. Dr. Kelly explained, " . . . wind deflection of a

rifle bullet is proportional to its *retardation* (lag time) by the resistance of the air. The matter is complicated by the fact that the resistance of the air cannot be related regularly to the velocity at all speeds by means of a simple formula which would produce a regular curve of resistance. In practice, it is found that this resistance curve has a sharp upward kink or 'S' bend in the neighborhood of the velocity of sound, this kink extending

Winning or losing a target match, especially at 100 yards, often hinges upon the shooter's skill at doping wind drift. Target shooters make the best use of mirage as an indicator of wind direction and velocity by focusing a high magnification spotting scope just short of the target, and watching the angle of mirage drift.

approximately from 1000 fps to 1400 fps. The result is that a bullet whose commencing velocity is within or slightly above this disturbed region encounters much greater air resistance than one whose flight takes place just below this velocity." He went on to define "lag time" as the difference between the actual time that a bullet required to cover a given range, and the theoretical time of flight in a vacuum, that is if the velocity remained constant over the entire flight of the bullet. Using three different theoretical tables, and averaging the results, Dr. Kelly predicted that the new high velocity ammo was going to require increased wind correction of 71 percent at 50 yards, 53 percent at 100 yards, 30 percent at 150 yards, and 28 percent at 200 yards. The lessening of required correction increase over standard velocity ammo as the range became longer could be attributed to the fact that after 100 yards, the high velocity bullet dropped below the speed of sound, therefore encountered reduced resistance.

Luckily for us, Winchester-Western published a wind deflection chart for high velocity Super-Speed and Super-X ammo, reprinted here with their kind permission. However, wind data on standard velocity ammo

stantially affecting air resistance. Also, the standard velocity ammo of Dr. Kelly's day had a muzzle velocity approximately 100 fps slower than that quoted in the Federal table.

Mirage has been recognized as an eternal enemy of marksman around the world, since the dawn of riflery. Many of us fail to realize that air is like a sea that envelops the earth. Like water, it has tides and waves. It is constantly in a state of agitation, even when apparently calm. When the sea of air around us becomes really excited, it can drive a whisp of straw through a plank! It can lift a home and shatter it to kindling, or deposit it gently on another lot hundreds of yards distant.

Like water, air has the facility of bending light rays. Mirage makes full use of that talent by maliciously moving your target up, down, or sideways, as whimsically as the breeze that drives it. Withal that, mirage can become an unwitting ally, a spy that tells us what we want to know about velocity and direction of the wind, providing we know *how* to extract that information. Unaided, the human eye cannot see clearly the movement of mirage, but with the assistance of a high-

TABLE OF WIND ALLOWANCES
22 L.R. Super-Speed and Super-X . . . Deflection of Bullet in Inches and Minutes

Distance	Wind Velocity (Miles Per Hour)	1, 5, 7, 11 o'Clock Winds		2, 4, 8, 10 o'Clock Winds		3 and 9 o'Clock Winds	
		Inches	Min.	Inches	Min.	Inches	Min.
50 Yards	5	0.33	0.66	0.57	1.14	0.66	1.32
	10	0.67	1.33	1.15	2.31	1.33	2.66
	15	1.00	1.98	1.72	3.45	1.99	3.98
	20	1.34	2.66	2.30	4.61	2.66	5.32
100 Yards	5	1.25	1.25	2.17	2.17	2.50	2.50
	10	2.50	2.50	4.33	4.33	5.00	5.00
	15	3.75	3.75	6.50	6.50	7.50	7.50
	20	5.00	5.00	8.67	8.67	10.00	10.00
200 Yards	5	4.28	2.14	7.42	3.71	8.56	4.28
	10	8.56	4.28	14.84	7.42	17.12	8.56
	15	12.84	6.42	22.26	11.13	25.68	12.84
	20	17.12	8.56	29.69	14.84	34.24	17.12

ranges from sparce to nonexistent. I turned up one number for comparison. Federal's rather extensive ballistics chart includes deflection for a 10mph crosswind for all cartridges at 100 yards. The figure for a 40-grain solid starting out at 1150 fps is given as 4.4 inches. For the same wind velocity at the same range, Federal high velocity ammo deflection reads as 5.5 inches. Harking back to Dr. Kelly, we find that his prediction of a 53 percent increase from standard to high velocity ammo was more than a little pessimistic. However, we have to consider the innumerable variables involved. Bullet shape is the most influential, sub-

powered telescope, we can see the waves of air as they radiate upward from the ground, weaving like cobras in a basket as the wind calls the tune.

With a 20X spotting scope, *focused short of the target,* you can watch the "cobras" dance. If they boil straight up, you can give thanks for a windless day. If they bend to the right or left, you have established wind direction. The angle of that bend can tell much of wind velocity, but unfortunately I can't give you a formula for determining velocity by observing mirage. Learning to "dope" mirage is more an art than a science! It must be learned by personal observation of cause and effect,

Target shooters (and smart hunters) use streamers and pith balls on the end of a string as indications of wind direction and velocity. When using Kentucky windage, it's easier to compensate for a steady wind than it is for a puffy, on-again, off-again breeze. The targets above were fired at 100 yards, on a day with a fairly steady wind from 9:00 o'clock. On the left-hand bull, the first group, displaced to the right of the bull, was fired without compensation. The second group, which almost centers the bull, was fired by holding off into the wind. The right bull's-eye was fired the same way, but on a day when wind was unsteady and puffy. Note that both groups strung out horizontally. The high/left shot was made with compensation, just as the wind suddenly died.

If you can get a buddy to spot misses for you through a pair of binoculars, you can compensate accordingly, for both windage and elevation errors. If in doubt, pick a spot of bare ground about the same distance as your intended target, and fire at the center. Your spotter can then tell you how much to hold off.

in a given place and time, under the particular lighting conditions that then exist. The almost infinite number of variables render accurate description literally impossible. You must learn by doing.

Estimating wind velocity is difficult at best, but it is generally conceded that a side-wind of 15mph or more will carry the mirage away before it can register on your eyeballs. The late Townsend Whelen in his book, *Small Arms Design and Ballistics, Volume II* offered the following guidelines:

2 to 4mph wind, a very light breeze.
6 to 8mph wind, a gentle pleasant breeze.
10 to 12mph wind, a rather strong breeze.
14 to 18mph wind, quite strong wind.
20 to 25mph wind, a very hard, strong wind. We pull our hats on tighter and lean against it.
30mph or over, a strong gale, too strong for any successful rifle shooting.

Wind effect varies directly with velocity. That is, a side-wind of 20mph has twice the effect of a 10mph wind, a 5mph wind has half the effect of a 10mph wind, etc. Wind *displacement* of a bullet varies by the *square of the distance* to the target. Thus the bullet will be deflected by a given wind velocity four times as much at

100 yards as at 50 yards, assuming that wind velocity is consistent all of the way downrange. And that is doubtful, to say the least. Often the firing line feels like a calm sea, while the target area is a storm center! How to tell? Veteran target shooters put out sticks with streamers or pithballs on string, at various distances downrange, say at 50, 75 and 100 yards. If the ribbons are strung out horizontally, then prepare for the worst. A little flutter now and then just lets them know that things are about normal. Breezes ebb and flow, usually reaching a peak every 6 to 8 minutes. When time allows, knowing competitors will wait out the worst winds. You can't dial in a windage correction on your target scope or receiver sight and forget it for all time! In seconds, the wind could rise or drop off to nothing, leaving you with a "6" printed on the target, instead of that "10" you were counting on.

So far, we've only discussed cross winds blowing from 3:00 or 9:00 o'clock. If the wind chooses to enter from an oblique angle, the effect upon your bullets will vary, becoming less as the angle increases. The effect of a wind from 45 degrees is roughly half that of the same wind cutting directly across the bullet's path.

Some target shooters resort to "Kentucky windage," rather than be forever tinkering with the windage dials of their sights. It's not difficult to hold off the proper number of inches, especially with a scope. Rimfire hunters in the field *dare not* risk tampering with a well sighted-in rifle, unless they are super-systematic and can keep track of the number of clicks added on and subtracted.

In the field, you won't find concentric circles neatly spaced an inch apart on the sides of a hoary marmot or ground squirrel. However, if you know the approximate size of the animal involved, you can do some educated guessing, which is what Kentucky windage is really all about. Given a ground squirrel propped up on its haunches at 100 yards in the familiar ten-pin pose, you can figure about 3 inches through the shoulders. Supposin' a 10mph crosswind, you just hold the vertical cross hair of your scope to the windward side a mite over 1½ squirrel-widths, and you should center the varmint!

Out where Mother Nature rules the roost, you won't find any pennants flying or pithballs bouncing. Unless you carry an anemometer around in your hip pocket, you'll have to learn to observe natural wind gauges, such as swaying prairie grass, leaves and branches of trees, or the fur of the varmint you seek. Even if you seem to be standing in an island of calm air, don't count on it all of the way out to the target. Especially if there is a deep canyon intervening between you and your target, you can expect some pretty fierce air movement along the bullet's path. Use a pair of high-X binoculars to observe trees, brush, and grass near your target for clues to wind direction and force. One side benefit of shooting a rimfire is the relative absence of recoil. You can observe the effect of your shot through the scope sight, whereas the bigbore shooter momentarily loses sight of his target as the gun rears back. A buddy with binoculars can be immensely helpful in any case, in the capacity of a spotter. Sometimes it's easier for another to spot misses and gauge the needed corrections.

Rimfire nimrods should take note of the fact that winds tend to rise steadily from an early morning calm to an afternoon crescendo, beginning to taper off at about 3:00 o'clock to near nil at dusk, barring a storm in the offing. You can time your long-range shooting to avoid the windy midday, when most of the critters are taking a siesta in any event.

Long-range rifle shooters have proved beyond the shadow of a doubt that a headwind results in a lowered point of impact, and a tailwind will raise the point of impact. Whether this will have a measurable effect at only 100 yards is open to question.

A more or less vertical mirage has the effect of displacing the target upward in relatively calm air, causing the sights to be raised, resulting in a high hit on the actual target, which really hasn't gone anywhere at all, despite what you *think* you saw!

The instant a .22 bullet leaves the bore of a rifle, it becomes subject to two forces, air resistance and gravity. Air resistance takes those beautiful numbers representing muzzle velocity and compresses them as irresistably as an anvil crushes an egg! At the same time, gravity pulls the bullet toward the center of the earth, with equal implacability. Because a bullet isn't rocket-propelled it has only its remaining momentum to carry it forward.

The shape of most .22 rimfire bullets leaves much to be desired in terms of exterior ballistics. Other considerations take precedence over good ballistic efficiency. If the soft lead bullet were given a suitable point, it would dulled by contact with the front of the detachable magazine, other cartridges etc. Thus the nose is rounded off in a compromise configuration.

If we seem a little top heavy with trajectory and ballistics charts, that's because over the years this information has proved to be the most elusive to the author. I determined once and for all, to make ballistics information as available for rimfire buffs as it has been for centerfire shooters. Puzzle not that these charts, or others you may see, don't offer identical numbers for every value. Some may be a little optimistic, and others grimly realistic. *If they did agree, that would be a source of wonder!* Scott Heter of CCI once told me that every lot of ammo varies to some degree from those before. A new lot of powder can result in slightly differing velocities, but they all fall within the limits of variables allowed under the guide lines of the Sporting Arms and Ammunition Manufacturer's Institute Inc., which sets standards for the industry. Perhaps CCI has been the least overawed by these standards and has been seeking all the while to exceed the performance figures prescribed in the SAAMI book of *Voluntary Industry Performance Standards For Pressure and Velocity of Rim Fire Sporting Ammunition.* A case in point is certainly CCI's Stinger Ammo, which has opened up a whole new ball game for .22 Long Rifle shooters.

Detailed ballistics charts may seem on the esoteric side to the average rimfire plinker/nimrod, but tables of numbers such as those shown here have highly practical applications, especially to the smallbore hunter, who has to eke out the last vestige of performance from his diminutive .22 cartridge if he's to make humane kills. Drop tables can answer some pressing questions, such as, "At what range do I sight in?" or "How high must I hold over the target at longer ranges?" "Where will my bullet strike at near ranges, if I sight in farther out to get the greatest advantage at long range?"

The size of your target's vital kill zone actually determines how far away your sighting-in or "zero" range should be. For example, a woodchuck propped up on its haunches presents a vital zone approximately 4 inches wide by 8 inches high. With a mark like that, you can afford to be generous with your mid-range trajectory! Suppose that you sight in at 100 yards so that you can take chucks out to the limits of .22 Long Rifle effectiveness, duplicating some of the feats of early-day chuck hunters who thought nothing of picking off chucks out to 200 yards or more! Using a standard high velocity .22 Long Rifle 37-grain hollow point, your mid-range trajectory would be just over 2½ inches. With a target zone 8 inches tall, that presents no hazard of a miss should you encounter a chuck at 50 to 75 yards. At 125 yards, your bullet would be striking less than 6 inches low. Still no problem! Away out at 200 yards your bullet's path would be about 32 inches low. If you had your wind well doped, a holdover of a chuck-and-a-half should be entirely feasible.

That long-range exercise comes under the heading of post-graduate activity! But suppose that same chuck is down on all fours. What then? Your target becomes 8 inches wide, but only half that tall. You have a much broader allowance for windage error, but elevation becomes far more critical. Near targets would come into some jeopardy at 50 to 75 yards, because your mid-range trajectory of 2½-plus inches, added to the probable size of your cone of fire, which might come to 1½ inches, could be enough to cause a high or low hit. In all probability, you would still connect with the chuck, but maybe not in the boiler room (that is ahead of the diaphragm in the vital organs of the chest). To play it safe, you could move your zero range back to 75 yards, resulting in a mid-range trajectory of approximately an inch—far more precise! Your bullet would be about 3 inches low at 100 yards, and about 9 inches low at 125. At 200 yards, your bullet's path would be over a yard below line of sight, a rather improbable holdover. But if you figure the percentages, the likelihood of your connecting beyond 125 yards is poor at best, and it would pay you to place your bets where they do the most good. Hence the 75-yard zero looks like the most practical by far! That same zero should do for most small game animals, from rabbits to wolverines. Only tree squirrels call for more precise aiming than that. For tree squirrels, I would move the zero range back to 50 yards. That would give you virtually no rise at mid-range, and your drop at 75 yards would be less than 2 inches. Lethal hits on tree squirrels beyond 75 yards are pretty "iffy" at best. If you're that good a shot, you don't need any advice from me!

Range estimation between 25 and 100 yards isn't that critical as you can see from the above trajectory figures. It is when you are trying to guess if yon marmot is 115 or 125 yards distant that it begins to get hairy! And that's the critical zone for .22 rimfire shooters. There is one trick that you can use to advantage, if you're really in doubt. Choose a bare spot of earth about the same distance away, and far enough from your intended target so that you won't put it to flight. Aim a round at the center of that spot, and see if you're on. If you have a buddy with binoculars, he can probably tell you just about how many inches high or low your strike is and read the windage for you as well! Make your corrections accordingly and swing over to the real target.

A firm called Ranging Inc., of East Rochester, New York, manufactures precision rangefinders for en-

gineers, surveyors, architects, etc., plus some devices aimed primarily at hunters. The Ranging Model 610 "Rangematic" is computed for ranges between 15 and 200 yards, making it ideal for .22 rimfire hunters. By means of triangulation, it reads out directly in yards, with an accuracy factor of plus-or-minus ½-yard at 100 yards. Closer ranges are even more precise! The pocket-sized instrument weighs only 15 ounces, and is constructed of rugged, shock-resistant cycolac. Ranging Inc. is currently conducting a "first shot probability study," comparing the likelihood of hits based upon individual range estimation, and ranges read from the 610-Rangematic. Unfortunately data is not complete at this time, but judging by a similar study that Ranging conducted on big game hunters, it's safe to say that the fellow using the rangefinder is ahead!

Rimfire nimrods equipped with .22 Winchester Magnum Rim Fire rifles can sight in at 100 yards, smug in the knowledge that their mid-range trajectory is less than 2 inches! Bullet path below the line of sight at 125 yards is about 2 inches, and only about 5 inches at 150 yards. Need we say more?

Stinger/Xpediter fans sighted in at 50 yards, have nil mid-range trajectory to worry about, and a drop at 100 yards under 3 inches. Sighted in at 75 yards, they have mid-range rise of only about an inch, and drop at 100 of approximately 1½ inches. Sighted for 100 yards, the mid-range is barely over 2 inches, and drops at 125 yards less than 3 inches.

All of the above trajectory figures are based upon the supposition of a rifle equipped with a telescopic sight, centered approximately 1½ inches above the bore line. In conjunction with this chapter, you will find a chart of trajectory curves, laid out on a grid so that you can establish mid-range rise and drop beyond the zero range. Each cartridge has two sight markings, the top one 1½ inches above the bore line for scope-sighted rifles, and one ¾-inch above the bore for use with iron sighted rifles.

To use the chart, align the left end of a straight edge with the appropriate sight marker. Swing the right end of the ruler down until you expose the maximum mid-range trajectory that your target size allows. Wherever the ruler intersects the trajectory line, that is your sighting-in range. If you use a transparent ruler, you can read the drop at ranges out to 125 yards.

The chart was calculated by Fred Jennie, formerly vice-president of Weatherby, Inc., using sophisticated computerized equipment. Next to Roy Weatherby himself, Fred played the greatest role in designing the fine Weatherby line of rifles, shotguns, and cartridges.

The accompanying collection of tables and charts is one of the most comprehensive ever assembled. With their help and the skill that you are acquiring, you should be truly formidable afield! You will conquer wind and distance, and wring the last foot pound of power potential from your .22 rimfire.

RIMFIRE TRAJECTORY CURVES

Each small rectangle of space represents 2 inches of height and is broken into 1-inch increments on the left and right margins of the graph. Before using the chart you should remember that each game animal has its own "mid-range trajectory allowance" (in inches). For example: squirrels = 1"; rabbits = 2"; woodchucks = 2"; crows = 1" and bobcats = 2½". (Simply put, these allowances are the "boiler room" measurements of the game to be hunted.)

To use the chart, align the left end of a straight-edge ruler with the appropriate sight marker. Swing the right end of the ruler down until you expose the mid-range allowance of the animal you intend to hunt. (This measurement will be from the top/center of the trajectory arc to the edge of the ruler.) At the point where the ruler intersects the downward swing of the trajectory curve (to the right) lies your sighting-in range.

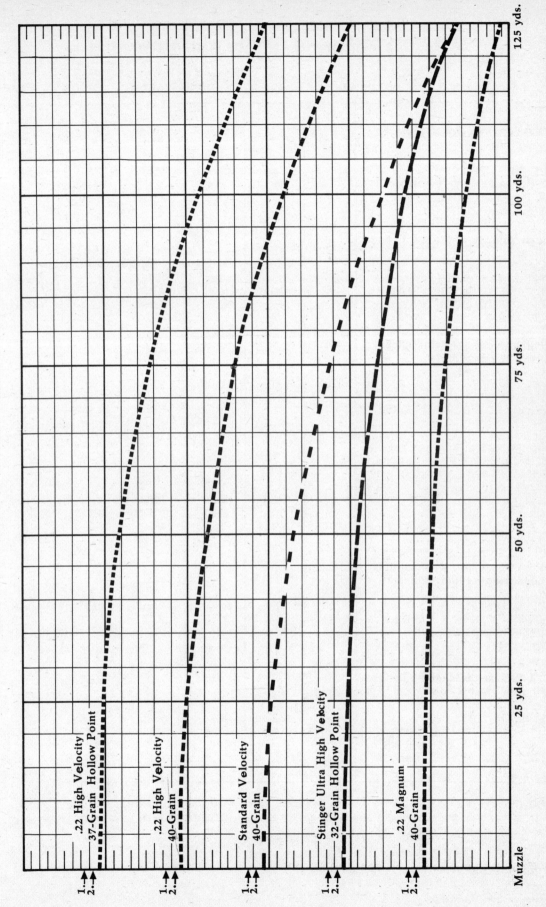

.22 High Velocity
37-Grain Hollow Point

.22 High Velocity
40-Grain

Standard Velocity
40-Grain

Stinger Ultra High Velocity
32-Grain Hollow Point

.22 Magnum
40-Grain

Muzzle   25 yds.   50 yds.   75 yds.   100 yds.   125 yds.

1. Scope Sight 1 1/2 inches above the bore line.   2. Iron Sights 3/4-inch above the bore line.

127

Rimfire Velocity and Drop Chart

	MUZZLE	25 YARDS	50 YARDS	75 YARDS	100 YARDS	125 YARDS	150 YARDS
Standard Velocity 40-grain .22 Long Rifle							
VELOCITY/FPS	1145	1090	1045	1005	975	945	
TIME OF FLIGHT/SECONDS		.0689	.1400	.2170	.2857	.3646	
DROP FROM BORE LINE/INS.		.9	3.6	8.7	14.9	24.0	
*BC=.1381							
High Velocity 40-grain .22 Long Rifle							
VELOCITY/FPS	1285	1190	1120	1070	1025	985	
TIME OF FLIGHT/SECONDS		.0660	.1328	.1951	.2649	.3413	
DROP FROM BORE LINE/INS.		.8	3.25	6.9	12.6	20.6	
*BC=.1238							
High Velocity 37-grain Hollow Point .22 Long Rifle							
VELOCITY/FPS	1315	1210	1130	1070	1020	975	
TIME OF FLIGHT/SECONDS		.0614	.1263	.1924	.2635	.3441	
DROP FROM BORE LINE/INS.		.7	2.9	6.7	12.4	20.7	
*BC=.11197							
CCI STINGER Ultra-High Velocity 32-grain Hollow Point .22 Long Rifle							
VELOCITY/FPS	1687	1530	1385	1260	1158	1080	
TIME OF FLIGHT/SECONDS		.0450	.1000	.1550	.2170	.2900	
DROP FROM BORE LINE/INS.		.4	1.8	4.2	8.0	14.0	
**BC=.0997							
5mm Remington Magnum Rim Fire 38-grain Hollow Point							
VELOCITY/FPS	2100	1965	1840	1720	1605	1500	1400
TIME OF FLIGHT/SECONDS		.0373	.0760	.1177	.1635	2116	.2640
DROP FROM BORE LINE/INS.		.3	1.0	2.5	4.7	7.8	11.8
†BC=.1448							
.22 Winchester Magnum Rim Fire 40-grain Hollow Point							
VELOCITY/FPS	2000	1830	1670	1525	1390	1270	1175
TIME OF FLIGHT/SECONDS		.0388	.0818	.1285	.1808	.2386	.2992
DROP FROM BORE LINE/INS.		.3	1.2	2.9	5.6	9.5	14.6
†BC=.1080							

BC (BALLISTIC COEFFICIENT)—the higher the stated number, the greater the ability for a particular projectile to overcome wind resistance during flight.

*Nominal. Calculated from SAAMI statistics.
**Actual. Calculated from CCI statistics.
†Based upon maker's statistics and Ingall's Tables.

TRAJECTORY DATA
RIMFIRE CARTRIDGES

Cartridge	Bullet Wt.	Bullet Type	Velocity in FPS at 0	Velocity in FPS at 100 yds.	Energy in ft. lbs. 0	Energy in ft. lbs. 100 yds.	Mid-Range Traj. in Inches-100 Yard Range	Barrel Length-Inches
22 B.B. Cap	18	Ball	780	—	24	—	—	24
22 C.B. Cap	29	Ball	705	—	32	—	—	24
22 Short	15	Dis.	1710	—	97	—	—	24
22 Short	29	Dis.	1045	—	70	—	—	24
22 Short S.V.	29	Ball	1045	—	70	—	—	24
22 Short H.V.	27	H.P.	1155	920	80	51	4.2	24
22 Short H.V.	29	Ball	1125	920	81	54	4.3	24
22 Long H.V.	29	Ball	1240	965	99	60	3.8	24
22 L.R.S.V.	40	Ball	1145	975	116	84	4.0	24
22 L.R.H.V.	36	H.P.	1365	1040	149	86	3.3	24
22 L.R.H.V.	40	Ball	1335	1045	158	97	3.3	24
22 Win. Auto.	45	Ball	1055	930	111	86	4.6	20
22 W.R.F. H.V.	45	Ball	1450	1110	210	123	2.7	24
22 W.M.R.F.	40	H.S.P.	2000	1390	355	170	1.6	24
22 Rem. Auto.	45	Ball	920	—	84	—	5.5	22

RIMFIRE MATCH CARTRIDGES

Cartridge	Bullet Wt.	Bullet Type	Velocity in FPS at 0	Velocity in FPS at 100 yds.	Energy in ft. lbs. 0	Energy in ft. lbs. 100 yds.	Mid-Range Traj. in Inches-100 Yard Range	Barrel Length-Inches
22 L.R. (Rifle Match)	40	Ball	1120	950	116	84	4.0	24
22 L.R. (Pistol Match)	40	Ball	1060	—	100	—	—	6¾

Dis. —Disintegrating   H.P. —Hollow Point
S.V. —Standard Velocity   H.S.P. —Hollow Soft Point
H.V. —High Velocity

CHAPTER 9

Serious Shooting Games

NO ONE WOULD DARE dispute the preeminence of the .22 rimfire as *the* plinking caliber, but would you believe that the tiny .22 is also king of competition cartridges, the world around?

Plinking is an entertaining game in a frothy sort of way, especially to the very young. However, its lack of compelling challenge or defined discipline cause it sooner or later to pall. Before you get your back up, consider that even lemon meringue pie can become cloying if eaten to excess! One place that challenge is never lacking is on the firing line at your nearby NRA-affiliated club target range! If you have a budding marksman under your wing, give him an opportunity to try his hand in the Junior smallbore competitive program. The other youngsters will see to it that he doesn't become bored!

Competitive shooting has a proud history in the United States, beginning no doubt at Plymouth Rock! However, no organized records were kept until the formation of the National Rifle Association in 1871. The infant shooting organization was almost immediately challenged to show its mettle. In 1873, the Irish national shooting team, fresh from an exhilarating victory over the best marksmen of England and Scotland at Wimbledon, threw down its gauntlet to the Americans. The NRA hastily set up a series of elimination contests to select the most able shooters in America to represent the young nation.

The Irish offered to put up some rather handsome prize money with the understanding that it was to be matched by the American team. *But there was no American team!* The infant NRA didn't have the funds. Happily, two American arms companies stepped forward with offers of prize money—and just as important, guns to shoot in the competition. E. Remington and Sons, and the Sharps Rifle Company provided excellent target rifles, but both breech loaders, much to the amusement of the Irish, who shot only the traditional, time-proved muzzle loading rifles. They viewed the Americans as merely green upstarts, hardly enough to work up a sweat over! Indeed the Americans were not accustomed to long-range competition in the international style of Wimbledon. *The first long distance range in America* has been built at Creedmoor, Long Island *just 2 years before!*

There the competition commenced on September 26th, with anxious thousands of spectators hoping only that we wouldn't be too badly beaten. Ranges were at 800, 900 and 1000 yards. It was a close match, but the upstart Americans pulled it off with an upset win over the cocky Irish. Americans have been winning ever since!

Shooting in America needs youngsters to swell the ranks of competitive shooters. Your son or daughter can begin with the NRA Light Rifle program, which offers young shooters a taste of competition with ordinary field rifles. No specialized equipment is required, just the desire to have some fun with others in the same general age group.

More formal competition is available for 9- to 13-year-olds in the Sub-Junior category. Actually, there is no bottom age limitation save that imposed by a relatively heavy rifle on immature muscles. Generally, a husky 10-year-old can handle one of the lighter competition rifles. By 12 years, it becomes easy. At 14 years, young shooters enter the Junior category, and begin to see some really stiff competition. They need a lot of encouragement through those first few contests, when their names will be among the low scorers. But the competitive spirit is the greatest motivator known to man or boy! *Then finally to be a winner!* That stimulates a renewed burst of effort!

At 19 years of age, young shooters suddenly find themselves classified as adults by the NRA. Being thrust into competition with older veteran shooters can have a jarring effect upon youngsters. Yet they have the

Youngsters find companionship and challenge in competitive shooting. The prone position is perhaps the most difficult to learn at first. Here the young shooters are using rests during a practice session.

Some shooting programs are set up for use of field-style smallbores to allow competition without the necessity of purchasing expensive equipment.

equipment and the desire to continue competition. One solution is a "Maverick" class such as that set up by the Southern California Junior Rifle League, allowing 19- through 25-year-old shooters an opportunity to compete within their own age group.

Many fraternal organizations, such as Kiwanis, Rotarians, Elks, etc., sponsor promising young shooters, helping to offset some of the expense of obtaining needed equipment. Most young shooters begin with a cloth shooting coat and a modestly-priced rifle such as a Savage/Anschutz Model 64 or Remington Model 540-XR, then graduate into the more exotic guns such as Savage/Anschutz 1407 or 1411, Remington 40-XR, or Winchester Model 52D, as their skill and level of competition increases.

No overwhelming physical strength is required to excel at competitive smallbore shooting. Boys and girls, men and women all compete on an even footing. Distaff members can and do win time and again! Even the physically handicapped compete and win. The NRA is always ready to entertain petitions for rule exceptions to accommodate handicapped contestants. Certificates, trophies, medals, and "point" prizes are offered in such profusion that any halfway interested competitor will have something to point to with pride!

NRA courses of rifle competition are widely varied, ranging from Small-Bore Gallery matches fired at 50 feet from prone, sitting, kneeling and offhand positions, to outdoor competitions fired prone at 100 yards, and from four positions at 50 yards.

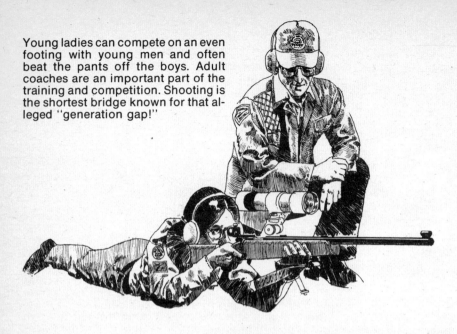

Young ladies can compete on an even footing with young men and often beat the pants off the boys. Adult coaches are an important part of the training and competition. Shooting is the shortest bridge known for that alleged "generation gap!"

(Below) The Remington 540-XR is a starter rifle that any youngster will be a long time outgrowing. It has the deep forend required for position shooting.

(Bottom) The Winchester Model 52 has ancestry dating back to 1919 and represents the first commercial target rifle available in the U.S. It was the first to have a detachable box magazine. Shown is the 52-D for NRA competition.

That 100-yard target has a 2-inch 10-ring, but that's too easy to hit! Perfect scores came with such abundance that a 1-inch X-ring was placed in the center to break ties. To enter this phase of competition, you'll need a scope sight that costs fully half as much as your rifle. Lyman, Redfield and Unertl are most popular. You'll need also a spotting scope of 25X or 30X, with good definition to pick out tiny .22 holes at 100 yards, or a high-quality variable such as the Bushnell Spacemaster. Another essential accessory is a sturdy sling for use in all positions save offhand. Most rifles have sliding stops on the forend to move the sling fore or aft as required to suit each individual position.

The most popular American-made NRA competition rifle is the Winchester Model 52. Introduced in 1919, the 52 was the first commercial target rifle available in the States. The first stock was copied from the Springfield, to win over military rifle shooters and it

The Lyman 25X L.W.B.R. scope features internal adjustments and adjustable parallax. Favored by bench rest shooters and smallbore target shooters alike, it is also available in 20X. These new internally adjustable target scopes represent an improvements in the mounts, which made them relatively fragile and far more bulky.

(Above) One essential accessory for any smallbore competitor is a high quality spotting scope. One of the best is Bushnell's 20X to 45X Zoom Spacemaster, which remains focused as you change from low to high power or vice versa.

It's hard to believe that the Smith & Wesson .22/32 was once considered a "heavy frame" target revolver! Though this most recent version sports a heavier barrel, it still looks like a lightweight.

was first made with a detachable box magazine. The original stock was changed five times before the gun was replaced in 1937 by the new Model 52D, still available.

Target rifles are marked by heavy barrels and massive, straight stocks, with high combs. They are single-shot to stiffen the actions. Target shooters hand-feed the chamber to avoid deforming soft lead bullets. The Remington Model 37 was first with a common sight-line for metallic and scope sights in 1937.

U.S. Competitive Pistol Shooting

Target handgun shooting was added to the National Rifle Association's competitive program in the mid-1920's, with a series of regional contests, leading up to a National Championship at Camp Perry. The first pistol range at Perry consisted of about 50 targets, down at the clubhouse end of the firing line. Since then, booming interest in punching targets with the one-hand gun has forced almost yearly expansions. By 1938, just before World War II brought a moratorium on Perry shoots, it was necessary to divide the shooters into squads, firing in rotation on the 100 targets then available. By 1961, contestants were crowding six 100-target ranges at Perry.

American smallbore pistol shooting has matured over the years. Today it's hard to believe that the Smith & Wesson .22/32 was once considered a "heavy frame" target revolver. The firing lines of the nation were dominated for years by revolvers such as the Smith & Wesson K-22 and the Colt Officers Model. Then the autoloading pistols such as the S&W Model 41 began to creep in, eventually shouldering the wheel guns aside entirely.

The NRA National Match Course consists of slow fire at 50 yards (10 shots in 10 minutes), timed fire at 25 yards (5 shots in 20 seconds, twice), and rapid fire at 25 yards (5 shots in 10 seconds, twice). The entire course is usually repeated three times, to achieve a possible aggregate score of 900 points.

International Competition

There's increasing interest in the United States in international styles of competition, like those used at the Olympic Games. The courses of fire are more difficult and somewhat intimidating to the beginner. The

The Smith & Wesson K-22 Masterpiece (top) was once a formidable contender on the firing lines of America, but it was pushed aside by autoloading pistols such as the Smith & Wesson Model 41 Heavy Barrel (above).

A target-style sling, such as this Mark 12 Target Sling from Savage, is essential to competition shooting. The large collar on the Mark 12 improves comfort with the sling and helps it hold position without slipping.

equipment, from the corset-like shooting jacket to the incredibly accurate rifles is far more expensive than that required for NRA competitions. Regulating Olympic-style competition is the International Shooting Union, with headquarters in Wiesbaden, Germany. The ISU sets standards for firearms permitted, as well as establishing rules of the shoots. In most cases, ISU rules limit maximum overall dimensions of various handguns by stating that they must fit into a "box" of given dimensions.

Free Rifle Shooting

Position Free Rifle shooting has been practiced in Germany and Switzerland since 1898. Under current rules, it consists of firing 40 shots each in prone, kneeling and offhand positions at a target 50 meters distant

Position rifle matches have been practiced in Germany and Switzerland since 1898, and consist of firing on a 10-ring smaller than ½-inch, from 50 meters distant from standing, kneeling and prone positions, using heavyweight free rifles.

International-style rifle shooting requires corset-like shooting jackets to help hold the body immobile. Here are some great ones from 10X Manufacturing Co., featuring a split-cowhide rough-out exterior, and non-slip neoprene pads on shoulders and elbows.

(55 yards) possessing a 10-ring smaller than ½-inch! Imagine if you will, the difficulty of hitting a target smaller than your thumb nail 40 times from a standing position! Some of the tricks employed include wearing heavy, stiff underwear, starchy clothing and a heavyweight leather "straight-jacket," with a row of tension straps marching up the chest, all to immobilize the body to the greatest degree possible. The Russians have gone to great lengths to analyze just what is required for this kind of demanding marksmanship. They determined that it requires 3 to 4 seconds for the heart beat to steady down after shouldering the rifle. If the shot is not fired before a dozen seconds have elapsed, the heart beat will begin to pick up again in response to the load imposed upon the muscles by a rifle weighing over 17 pounds. Even the position of the sling is important. It must be either high up on the biceps or low down near the elbow. In between, it picks up the pulse and moves the rifle.

The rifles used are called, "Free rifles," because just about anything goes as long as they don't go overweight. Thus we find the "shooting machines" with adjustable butt plates, combs, hand rests, sights, and infinitely intricate triggers. The Anschutz Model 5071

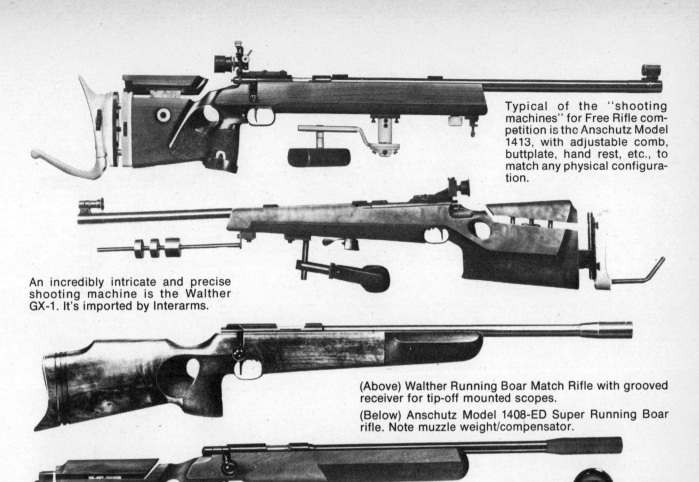

Typical of the "shooting machines" for Free Rifle competition is the Anschutz Model 1413, with adjustable comb, buttplate, hand rest, etc., to match any physical configuration.

An incredibly intricate and precise shooting machine is the Walther GX-1. It's imported by Interarms.

(Above) Walther Running Boar Match Rifle with grooved receiver for tip-off mounted scopes.

(Below) Anschutz Model 1408-ED Super Running Boar rifle. Note muzzle weight/compensator.

Infinitely intricate triggers are an inherent part of any International Free rifle. The Anschutz Model 5071 double-stage trigger adjusts down to less than 2 ounces, and its single stage counterpart, the Model 5075, adjusts from 56 down to just 14 ounces.

double-stage trigger adjusts down to less than 2 ounces! The Anschutz 5075 single stage trigger adjusts from 14 to 56 ounces. Typical of the rifles popular in this demanding competition is the Anschutz Model 1413 Super Match 54, superbly machined and finished, with thumbhole French walnut stock, possessed of adjustable everything! Another incredible Free-style rifle is the Walther Model GX-1, which was designed by a panel of international smallbore shooting experts to provide every conceivable adjustment that might be required. The entire line of Walther competition rifles and handguns is imported into the U.S. by Interarms.

"Running Boar" Match

Walther also manufactures their "Running Boar Match Rifle," specifically designed to meet the requirements of that one event. In the Running Boar match, the shooter is confronted with a moving target 50 meters distant. The boar silhouette runs in both directions, across an opening 10 meters wide, at a "normal run" during which it is visible for 5 seconds, and a "fast run" of 2½ seconds. The shooter must stand with the rifle off of his shoulder, touching his hip until the boar appears. In 2 days, the contestant fires 60

Eley Match ammunition (imported by Savage Arms) has a well-earned reputation for accuracy and sure fire propensities.

135

shots, half at each speed, for a possible score of 600. This is the only international event allowing the use of a telescopic sight.

International Pistol Shooting

The ISU handgun event that most closely resembles the NRA course is the ISU Standard Pistol, fired at a 2-inch 10-ring, at 25 meters, in three stages — slow, timed and rapid fire. The gun is limited to a 6-inch barrel without muzzle brake, and it must be .22 Long Rifle only with open sights. Most top-drawer American rimfire target pistols such as the Hi-Standard Victor, Supermatic Trophy, Supermatic Citation, etc., Smith & Wesson Model 41, and Ruger Target Model qualify for this event, as well as the NRA course. Conversely, such European-made pistols as the Walther GSP Standard, the Hammerli Model 208 and Model 211, handle both shooting events better, but at three to four times the cost!

One of the most demanding .22 pistol matches is the International Rapid Fire Pistol Course, which requires firing one shot into each of five silhouettes at a distance of 25 meters, starting with the gun pointed downward at a 45-degree angle. The turning targets are revealed to the shooter for three time intervals, 8, 6 and 4 seconds per string. Each of the three strings is fired twice, on two successive days, for a total of 60 shots. Competitors fire .22 Shorts, from heavy autoloading pistols, with muzzle brakes to dampen even that negligible recoil. Such refined pistols as the Walther OSP with trigger adjustable down to 7 ounces and the popular Hammerli Model 230 are used.

Perhaps *the most demanding of all* pistol matches is the International Free Pistol Event, which involves firing 60 shots at 50 meters on a target with a 10-ring only about 2 inches across! Here again, restrictions are few. The gun must be a .22 rimfire, no heavier than the contestant can support with one hand. The grip must support only the shooter's hand (no wrist extensions, etc.). No scope sights allowed. The rest is up to you! For years, the Hammerli Model 150, an extremely refined falling block single shot pistol with set trigger and fantastic lock time of just .0016-second, raked in all of the gold medals. Lately, however, a custom-made Free pistol, the Green Electroarm, with an electronic lock, designed and made by American Frank Green, has been garnering laurels! Note in the photo that the pistol grip surrounds the back of championship shooter Don Hamilton's hand. This is a complete innovation. Green is a retired Air Force officer, and himself a Free Pistol champion.

Hammerli makes a budget-priced single shot Free Pistol for beginners, the Model 120, and offers the Model 150 for twice the price of the 120. Unfortunately, most of the exotic European-made competition autoloading pistols are very expensive in these days of inflated dollars. They are guns of infinite precision, in-

Such American-made handguns as this Hi-Standard Victor can compete in the ISU Standard Pistol competition, but fail to qualify for other International handgun competitions.

Hi-Standard's Trophy Model is another outstanding competition handgun, suitable for NRA or ISU Standard matches. Note that slide is independent of the rear sight.

The Green Electroarm single shot with electronic lock, shown here in the hand of Don Hamilton, National Champion in 1965, '66, and '69, has been taking top position in recent years.

volving the kind of machining and craftsmanship that goes into creating fine Swiss watches. The Swiss-made Sig Hammerli begins with a forged steel frame that undergoes 94 milling operations, ending up with one-seventh of its original weight.

International competition may seem esoteric and remote, but who knows — that tyke you're starting out with a single shot Stevens Crackshot may one day be "bringing home the Gold," for the United States! The "how to" of all this could easily fill a couple of books this size. So I'm going to recommend a book called, *Position Rifle Shooting,* by Frank T. Hanenkrat and Bill Pullum. Pullum is described by America's all-time great small-bore shooter, Gary L. Anderson, as "... the best competitive shooting coach in the world." When Gary says someone's the best, you gotta listen!

New Competitive Shooting Games

A newly emerging competitive marksmanship game of *Siluetas Metalicas* has caught the imagination of

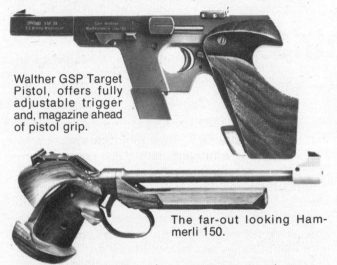

Walther GSP Target Pistol, offers fully adjustable trigger and, magazine ahead of pistol grip.

The far-out looking Hammerli 150.

The newly emerging game of *Siluetas Metalicas* has really caught on in the United States. No pattern has yet emerged on the type of rifles to be used, but it would appear that the heaviest of field rifles would be best suited to the exacting requirements. Although the pure sport demands steel effigies, paper target competitions will no doubt become popular also.

shooters in the U.S. It surfaced in Mexico during the 1950's, and swam the Rio Grande about a decade later. It flourished in random fashion until mid-1978, when the NRA joined forces with the United States Silueta Association and the International Handgun Metallic Silhouette Association to formulate definite rules for the game. The rules included a one-fifth reduced course, using one-fifth scale targets, for a .22 rimfire Smallbore Rifle Silhouette program.

Basically, silhouette shooting, as its name implies, means shooting at silhouettes, of four creatures—a chicken, pig, turkey, and sheep—*from an offhand position only!* The silhouettes are cut from steel, with welded steel feet, sitting upon steel platforms. In order to count, a hit must knock the steel effigy completely off of its base! The game is certainly challenging! And it is a great crowd-pleaser! There can be no doubt of a hit or a miss. Either the animal falls or doesn't. The crowd can keep score, and cheer its favorites. This highly interesting, entertaining game could well prove to be a great asset in educating the general public concerning the very real benefits of shooting not only to shooters, but to the nation as a whole!

Prescribed distances for smallbore silhouette shooting are 40 meters for the chicken, 60 meters for the pig, 77 meters for the turkey, and 100 meters for the sheep. For those of you who haven't converted yet, in yards that equals approximately 44, 66, 84, and 109. Based upon the one-fifth scale, the height of the figures will be approximately 2.2 inches, 3 inches, 5 inches, and 5½ inches. Remember, you'll be shooting from your hind legs!

Scopes of any power are allowed. However, in shooting offhand, any magnification higher than 12X might prove to be more a handicap than a help. Among the favorites with bigbore shooters are the Weaver T Models, in 6X, 10X and 16X. The impeccable Leupold M8 fixed power, as well as their Vari-X II and Vari-X III are perfect for the purpose. Other good choices are available from Lyman and Bushnell.

Your local club may already be setting up a Smallbore Rifle Silhouette program. If not, perhaps you could be the catalyst to get one started! An excellent book is available, explaining the game in detail. Written by Walter L. Rickell, the *Silueta Shooter's Handbook,* is available from Reproductions West, P.O. Box 6765, Burbank, CA 91510. They also distribute paper targets of the various animals, scaled for smallbore practice or competition at the standard 100-yard range.

Regardless of the "type" of competitive shooting one chooses to indulge in, the sport itself will prove to be challenging. If it's a challenge you're after, competitive shooting will indeed provide it, time and again. The .22 rimfire cartridge above all others, is the one that usually leads a path to Olympic gold; and, that my friends, is saying a lot!

CHAPTER 10

State of the Art Ammo

THE HISTORY OF THE .22 rimfire family of cartridges is one of constant improvement and escalation of power, beginning with the original "Bulleted Breech Cap," patented in July of 1845 by French inventor M. Flobert. Flobert little realized the chain of events he had set into motion when he necked down a soft copper musket cap and pressed a round .22 caliber lead ball into its mouth. He designed a simple rifle with no breech save for the pressure of the hammer itself, which relied upon the weight of the mainspring to contain the force of the charge. Flobert's "Saloon" rifles (derived from the French "Salon") were intended for indoor target practice which was and is immensely popular in Europe, and for a time in the States as well.

Step one in the stairway of escalation in .22 rimfire power was the development by Daniel B. Wesson of the original .22 Short cartridge in 1857. It looked much like the one we know today, but contained a mere 4 grains of black powder propellant topped with a 29-grain conical bullet. The .22 Long emerged pretty much in its current configuration, about 1870, using the same bullet, but with the case stretched to .613-inch accepting 5 rather than just 4 grains of black powder. The .22 Extra Long was first produced in 1880, with a case elongated again to accommodate 6 grains of black powder. However, the real contribution of the Extra Long was its 40-grain bullet, which was teamed up with the Long case length to form the .22 Long Rifle cartridge about 1887.

Over the years, a variety of efforts were made to top the .22 Long Rifle, but most of them met with little success insofar as public popularity was concerned. Notable among the efforts to magnumize the .22 rimfire was the .22 Winchester Rimfire. The .22 WRF utilized a new larger case, large enough to allow seating the .22 caliber 45-grain inside-lubricated bullet within the case, in the fashion of centerfire cartridges. All previous .22 bullets were "toe-crimped" into the case, over a reduced diameter at the bullet base. After introduction of

the .22 WRF in 1890, there were no earth shaking developments until 1926, when Remington introduced true noncorrosive priming with their "Klean-bore" ammo.

After the development of noncorrosive priming (which soon spread throughout the industry), .22 rimfire development went into a sort of holding pattern, with little save refinement in progress. The outside lubricant used on the bullets was improved to a dry, non-gooey mixture. (If any of you were here during World War II, and had access to any of the GI .22 ammo of that austere time, you know the difference! That stuff stuck to your fingers, your pockets, the chambers of the guns, in short everything that came into contact with the glue-like bullet covering!)

The .22 WMR

Into this settled scene, Winchester dropped a rimfire bombshell in 1959, in the form of their .22 Winchester Magnum Rimfire. Roughly resembling the old .22 WRF, it was just slightly smaller in both case and head diameter, but lengthened by .092-inch to afford space for a 7½-grain charge of Olin ball powder. The round was capped with a *genuine* jacketed 40-grain bullet, hollow-pointed and with a generous amount of lead exposed at the nose to assure good expansion even as the velocity dwindled out at 150 yards or more. The jacket was deliberately kept thin to promote easy expansion. That system worked so well that the new round was soon set aside by meat hunters because it left so little for the stew pot! Winchester responded by adding a fully jacketed solid point bullet, vastly improving the situation!

At the outset, reader mail was top-heavy with queries about the practicality of deepening chambers on the old .22 WRF rifles to accept the new .22 Magnum. However, chamber pressures reportedly in the 30,000 psi/CUP range made it seem the better part of discretion to

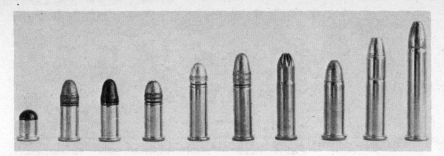

A representative .22 rimfire family portrait begins with (from L to R) the father of them all, the humble BB Cap, followed by a CCI Short and a CCI Mini-Cap (CB Cap), and a Winchester-Western Short, Long and Long Rifle; plus shot cartridge. The short, stubby round is an echo from the past —the .22 Winchester Automatic, followed by the .22 WRF and .22 Winchester Magnum Rim Fire.

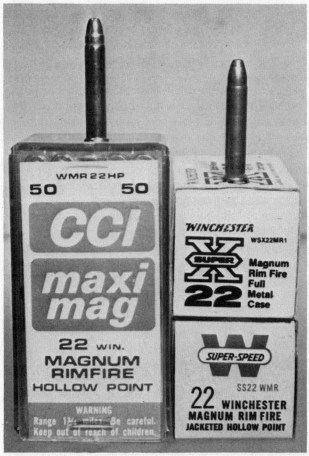

Winchester introduced the .22 Magnum in 1959. The only other firm loading ammo for that caliber is CCI, with their Maxi-Mag cartridges, seen here in their innovative plastic slide-top box.

recommend against such an alteration! Also that slight variation in outside dimensions hovered hauntingly in the background as a further deterrent. The .22 WRF is actually .004-inch larger at the rim with a case O.D. near the head .0035-inch larger than that of the .22 WMR. SAAMI recommended bore and groove dimensions are .220/.226 for the WRF, and .219/.224 for the WMR. Bullet diameters are .2285 and .2245, respectively. These minute variations aren't enough to cause a .22 Magnum chamber to reject a .22 WRF cartridge. Thus, in the interests of economy, the older round found frequent use in the new rifles. It lacks something in terms of accuracy, but at near to medium ranges, say 50 to 100 yards, it does quite well as a game cartridge without the excessive destructiveness of the jacketed hollow point magnum loads.

The .22 Magnum cartridge will not chamber all of the way into a .22 WRF chamber and won't even start in a .22 Long Rifle stoke hole. If ever you're in a quandary as to which you hold in hand, standard or magnum, just peer down the bore from the rear, and look for the same kind of lede that you'll find in any centerfire chamber. If

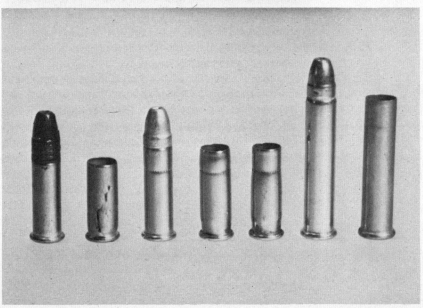

Although it is impossible to chamber a .22 WMR in a standard .22 chamber, the reverse can be readily accomplished! Shown here (from L to R) is a .22 Long Rifle followed by a Long Rifle case fired in a .22 Magnum chamber. Note the split case walls. Next is CCI Stinger cartridge, followed by two Stinger cases fired in .22 Magnum chamber. Note that cases bulged without splitting, and the thicker belt near head refused to expand. Next is .22 Maxi-Mag and fired case. A word to the wise: Don't try it—stick to ammo designed for the gun you are shooting.

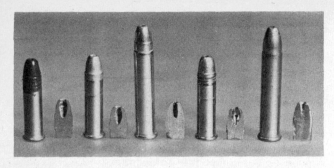

Current contenders for top game-getter honors are the .22 Long Rifle hollow point, CCI Stinger, CCI Maxi-Mag, Winchester Xpediter, and .22 Winchester Magnum Rim Fire.

it's there, you're holding the .22 WMR or a .22 WRF which also has a lede.

Labeled early as, "the poor man's magnum," the .22 WMR did just what it was intended to do — offer an option to the once-in-a-while varmint shooter that wouldn't require him to invest in an expensive varmint rifle, a complete set of reloading tools and innumerable components, or face the other prospect of mortgaging the farm to feed a centerfire varmint rifle with over-the-counter ammo.

The .22 Magnum has proved itself capable of handling all manner of vermin out about as far as you can hit them. Medium-sized predators, such as foxes, bobcats, badgers, et al, are susceptible to the .22 WMR hollow point out to about 150 yards, while the big game of varmintdom, the canny coyote, can be taken by careful marksmen out to about 100 yards. Many turkey hunters regard the .22 WMR as the ideal rifle for tagging a wily old tom. However, toms are tough! It pays to use

CCI invented the Stinger (left) with the same outside dimensions as the standard .22 Long Rifle (next), taking some of the steam out of the rimfire magnums, namely the 5mm Remington and .22 WMR.

the hollow-pointed version rather than solids, as is sometimes recommended.

Not long after Winchester-Western introduced the .22 Magnum cartridge, Omark/CCI came up with their own version, called, CCI "Maxi-Mag" ammo, with hollow point and solid nose 40-grain bullets. CCI added two touches of their own, an internal reinforcing belt of double-thick brass near the case head, and their "Bonded Jacket" bullets, electro-plated with copper alloy rather than jacketed with copper skins. CCI Maxi-Mags were packaged 50 rounds to each slide-top reusable plastic box.

CCI "Stinger" and W-W "Xpeditor"

The .22 Magnum did indeed represent a giant step forward in a .22 rimfire power escalation, but it entailed buying far more expensive ammunition *and another* gun—a gun unable to fire the standard .22 rimfire, with all of its many bullet/velocity options. If they could afford it, owners of standard .22 rifles could buy a .22 Magnum and have both. Or they could sell the standard version and buy a new Magnum model. Or they could just yearn for the bigger hotter cartridge, and try to be content with what they already had.

Then there's the *new* .22 buff who's just considering entering the fold. He's going to look long and hard at the standard .22 Long Rifle guns before he considers a .22 Magnum. Rifles and pistols for standard or magnum rimfire sell for about the same money, but .22 Magnum ammo costs almost three times as much. And what does he lose in the way of versatility? The .22 WMR cannot shoot Caps, Shorts, Longs, or low-cost regular speed Long Rifles. So *the cost* of the greater killing/stopping power of the .22 Magnum will weigh heavily in his decision.

And in the past couple of years, some new numbers have been added to the equation—numbers like 1600-plus fps for a hollow point bullet from the *standard* .22 chamber. A recent revolution in .22 Long Rifle cartridge design has substantially eroded the advantage of the .22 Magnum in the field. Perhaps the most dramatic of these developments could be called the "Stinger Saga." It all began in the Technical Services section of Omark Industries/CCI Operations, where some of the "Good Ol' Boys" of CCI got together and decided to soup up the venerable .22 Long Rifle, which hadn't seen any impressive improvements since Remington introduced noncorrosive priming in their Kleanbore ammo, in 1926.

Whence sprang the original concept has not been publicized. However, according to E.W. "Scot" Heter, in charge of Technical Services and Shooting Promotion, someone at CCI aspired to the lofty aim of pushing a .22 Long Rifle hollow point bullet to 1600 fps. Inasmuch as the then current loading pretty well milked the absolute maximum from the standard .22, obviously *that* was going to take a bit of doing!

There are two methods for increasing velocity: One is to increase the amount of propellant; the other is to decrease bullet weight. CCI endeavored to do both. Mass was removed from the new bullet by shortening it to .396-inch from .4635-inch for the standard 40-grain .22 Long Rifle slug, and ballooning a $^7/_{32}$-inch deep hollow cavity that extended well below the halfway point, bringing the final weight down to 32 grains and contributing to the Stinger's explosive terminal effect. Development Engineer, Kenneth L. Alexander proposed stretching the case by $^1/_{10}$-inch to acquire much needed powder space, enabling a charge of 3.6 grains versus a total of 2 for a standard Long Rifle. Then it became a matter of tailoring the powder burning rate to gain the most from the added capacity.

A popular misconception regarding rimfire propellant in various .22 rimfire cartridges is that it's all alike. Actually, the powder used in .22 Shorts, for example, is in about the same burning range as the canister powder Bullseye. Powder used in standard .22 Long Rifle cartridges burns at about the same pace as Hercules 2400.

Faced with the chore of increasing rimfire velocity within the 1-inch overall length of the Long Rifle, CCI Engineers realized that the only way to speed up a bullet without unduly increasing chamber pressure was to extend the burn time farther up the barrel. The ideal situation would be for the powder to continue burning until the last inch of barrel length was used up, to gain the maximum thrust from the propellant.

Hercules Powder Company produced three experimental lots before the optimum burning rate was achieved. The first lot of Hercules double base powder gave a modest increase in velocity but far from what had been hoped for. However, CCI R&D is nothing if not persistent! They tried another lot of slightly slower powder, and touched 1646 fps—better than they had hoped for! But they felt that there was still room for improvement, so they requested a third test lot, of still a *slower* burning rate and hit an astounding 1684 fps! Extensive testing followed by CCI and various gun makers.

In December 1976, Omark Industries Sporting

This photo provides us with a look at the dissected CCI Stinger. Note the disc-like powder granules, the deep seating of bullet and broad driving band, all of which promote excellent accuracy with this high intensity hunting cartridge.

"The poor man's magnum," was the label that befell the .22 Winchester Magnum Rim Fire, but it does provide the non-reloader with a medium-power varmint cartridge at an affordable cost. Note ball powder and jacketed hollow soft point bullet.

For comparison, here's a dissected Winchester Xpediter. Note ball powder, short bullet with blunt ogive. Bullet has explosive results on game within 100-yard range.

Remington's 5mm Magnum was born of strife and apparently has died without any real struggle. The error was in using a .22 rimfire rifle action for such a high intensity cartridge. Given an action like the Savage Anschutz Model 54, it could have realized its full potential.

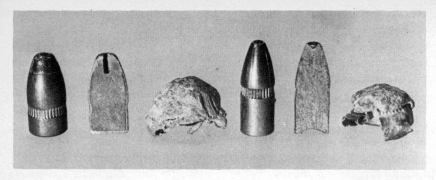

Here we see a .22 Winchester Magnum Rim Fire bullet, plus sectioned and expanded examples, followed by the same from a Remington 5mm. The latter has better exterior ballistics but has died on the vine due to the lack of rifles offered in that caliber.

(Below) Here we have a sectioned Stinger bullet with expanded sample next to a standard .22 Long Rifle hollow point and expanded bullet. The Stinger held together well despite its higher velocity.

Among CCI innovations was the thickened belt of brass near the case head, offering extra strength where it is most needed.

EXCLUSIVE
INTER-BELTED
CASE

Equipment Division of CCI-Speer Operations, mailed a flier to their retailers, informing them that, " . . . CCI-Speer R&D engineers have developed a cartridge that provides significantly greater velocity and flatter trajectory. The new rimfire cartridge—'Stinger'—increases both effective range and killing power of .22 rimfire arms." Stinger ammo was said to provide an average of 1687 fps from a 24-inch barrel, produce more velocity at 50 yards than a .22 Long Rifle high velocity hollow point at the muzzle, deliver higher muzzle velocity from a 6-inch barreled handgun than a high velocity HP from a rifle, and finally effect a reduction in drop at 100 yards of 3½ inches.

Initial suggested retail was slightly more per box of 50 rounds than for high velocity HP ammo. CCI Maxi-Mag (.22 Magnum) hollow points were going for about twice the price. So for a modest 24 percent increase in cost the Stinger cut the ballistic advantage of the .22 Magnum over the .22 Long Rifle by more than half! That's pretty good arithmetic for the consumer, any way you look at it!

After testing, all hands had pronounced Stingers a resounding success. But the final vote was not yet in. How would the public receive it? CCI wasn't long in getting their answer. For the better part of a year, they were back-ordered before they were able to bring production in line with the unexpectedly exuberant response. This was not CCI's first, and probably not their last successful venture into innovation. CCI devised their exclusive belted-head .22 rimfire cases with reinforced inner belts of double-thick brass swaged from the rim forward for almost ⅛-inch.

Another mark of CCI's continuous striving for im-

proved performance is the innumerable bullet ogives that they have experimented with over the years. At one point, CCI conducted some extensive experiments on wadcutter bullet designs to ease the problem of accurately scoring smallbore match targets. The Stinger ogive is quite different than that of the conventional .22 Long Rifle. In fact, the entire bullet shape is new. Its cupped base is designed to expand swiftly and obturate the bore as quickly as possible to avoid gas blow-by around the bullet during the early stages of ignition when the case first opens up from gas pressure and releases the bullet. The Stinger retains the toe-crimp design of the standard .22 rimfire, but with a deeper ⅛-inch bite on the bullet's reduced .2085-inch O.D. heel. Above the heel is a ⁵⁄₆₄-inch wide full-diameter driving band followed by a steep reduction to .200-inch, curving down into a ballistically superior ogive, capped finally by five-sided "Penta-Point" opening into that awesome cavity within.

The eye-catching Stinger with its golden copper-plated bullet and brightly nickeled extra-length case is entirely new inside, but adheres to SAAMI voluntary standards for outside dimensions; thus, will chamber in any .22 rimfire rifle or pistol. Currently, CCI has no plan for any variations upon the theme, such as solid points or shot cartridges.

The Stinger falls smack dab into the middle of that yawning chasm separating standard .22 Long Rifle high velocity ammo and the longer, fatter .22 Magnum, just about halving the comfortable advantage the big .22 once enjoyed. The Stinger is going to make potential .22 Magnum customers think not twice but thrice, before investing in a magnum rifle!

Stingers depart from most handguns faster than standard high velocity hollow points leave a rifle. At 50 yards, a rifle-launched Stinger is still traveling faster than a standard high velocity hollow point starts out. Muzzle energy for the Stinger is 202 foot pounds compared to 142 for a standard high velocity hollow point cartridge, an improvement of 42 percent, and mid-range trajectory with a scoped rifle sighted at 100 yards is less than 2 inches. Stinger bullets spend less time getting to the target, reducing the collective effect of cross winds in the field. The danger of ricochet, always the bane of rimfire shooters, is greatly reduced by the Stinger's high velocity and the Penta-Point's tendency to break up on contact with the ground. Success invites competition. Stingers acquired competition in 1978 when the Olin Corporation, Winchester-Western Division, introduced their Super-X "Xpediter" ultra-high velocity .22 rimfire, with case length extended by .010-inch, but externally sized the same as the Long Rifle. Winchester advertised a muzzle velocity of 1680 fps for a 29-grain Lubaloy copper coated hollow point bullet fired from a 24-inch barrel, generating a muzzle energy of 182 foot pounds. Mid-range trajectory for a 100-yard zero was quoted as 2½ inches. The longer nickel-plated case, plus copper coated bullet, resulted in a cartridge that looked much like the Stinger. Xpediter's hollow cavity is about the same depth, although the bullet itself measures .383, a shade over ⅜-inch in length, and is .013 shorter than the Stinger slug. The case bite on the heel is about ⁵⁄₆₄-inch deep, and the driving band approximately ³⁄₃₂-inch wide.

Stingers and Xpediters add about four-bits to the cost of a box of 50 rounds, but their higher octane performance is certainly worth the difference to pest/vermin hunters; however, both are overpriced for perforating tin cans. The field effectiveness of Stingers and Xpediters is pretty much tit-for-tat, with little to distinguish between them. Both are explosive killers on ground squirrels, brush rabbits, etc., perhaps a little *too* destructive for meat hunters. The high velocity duo are ample for tagging rangy jack rabbits or hoary old marmots that are a little too tough for ordinary .22 Long Rifle hollow points. Raccoons, 'possums, even foxes and bobcats are within the fringe areas of Stingers/ Xpediters, given a deadly marksman who can call varmints into his lap. However, most callers go afield with heavier artillery than a .22 rimfire. If you're considering the possibility of taking predators with a .22 rimfire,

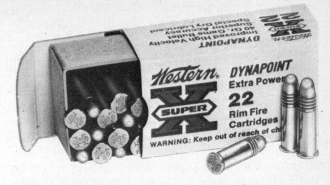

In 1975, Winchester-Western introduced their Dynapoint ammo, with full-weight 40-grain bullets bearing just a hint of a hollow point in the nose. They constituted a fine compromise round for squirrel hunters and other small game hunters who needed more expansion than was offered by a solid, but less destruction than that caused by a standard hollow point.

chances are you're not a seasoned caller; therefore, not qualified to try it. Sounds like a losing proposition!

W-W "Dynapoint" and Federal "Semi-Hollow Point"

While conducting some expansion tests 6 years ago, firing a variety of .22 cartridges into 50-pound blocks of pug clay, I was amazed at the disruptive force displayed by high velocity Long Rifles with 40-grain solid point bullets. It occurred to me then that even a small hollow cavity in the front of a full-weight 40-grain bullet might result in a highly effective stopper for such animals as our big western jack rabbits, which are notoriously hard to put down for keeps.

In May of 1975, Winchester-Western introduced their "Dynapoint" cartridge, with 40-grain Lubaloy bullet, bearing the merest hint of a hollow point! Developed in Australia and tested upon their big and bothersome hares, the new round offered ample expansion with several added grains of bullet weight over the usual hollow point, thereby imparting more foot pounds at the target. It also constituted an ideal compromise for small food animals such as tree squirrels that require more stopping power than usually results with solids but are so small that the excessive destruction of a standard hollow point often destroys a large portion of the edible meat. The slightly heavier bullet also gives Dynapoint a ballistic advantage at long range over standard high velocity hollow points. Starting out at 1255 fps contrasted to 1280 for a 37-grain hollow point, the

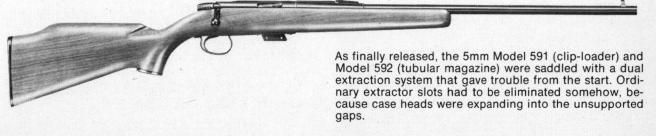

As finally released, the 5mm Model 591 (clip-loader) and Model 592 (tubular magazine) were saddled with a dual extraction system that gave trouble from the start. Ordinary extractor slots had to be eliminated somehow, because case heads were expanding into the unsupported gaps.

Dynapoint is still traveling 1017 at 100 yards, having overtaken the lighter slug which is then clocking only 1015 fps.

Federal Cartridge Corporation began business under its present management on April 27, 1922, under the direction of Mr. Charles L. Horn, then managing partner, today Chairman of the Board. In 1924, Federal began producing a line of .22 rimfire ammunition. Many of the cartridges sold over the years under a variety of "house brands" came from Federal. Also, they produced their own fine ammunition, with a reputation for reliability and accuracy which carries over to their "Power-Flite Semi-Hollow Point" high velocity Long Rifle cartridge. In the nose of this latest *almost-hollow* point is a depression about $1/16$-inch in diameter by $1/32$-inch deep—just a dimple in the ogive. However, the results are most impressive! Federal's dimpled golden bullets take flight at a nominal 1255 fps (actual chronograph velocity from my Remington 541-S was 1303 fps), punch out neat little ½-inch diameter holes for 10 shots at 25 yards, and expand to classic mushrooms in game.

5mm Remington Magnum

Do the above represent all of the "state of the art" rimfire cartridges, or am I overlooking something? How fleeting is fame! We almost forgot a cartridge that was/is perhaps the most spectacular of them all—the 5mm Remington Magnum. Although Remington no longer chambers a rifle for the round, you can still order barrels in 5mm from Thompson/Center for the Contender pistol—reason enough to keep the 5mm alive! Perhaps Remington or someone else will see the light and bring forth an accurate reliable rifle in that caliber.

There seems little doubt that introduction of the .22 WMR inspired Remington to develop the 5mm. The parameters were spelled out in the .22 Magnum. To compete, the 5mm had to demonstrate a clear advantage. Remington engineers took the "Power-Lokt" varmint slug previously so successful in their .25-06 and .222, and scaled it down to .20 caliber, then coupled it to the first modern bottle-necked rimfire case. It resembled an abridged version of Lyle Kilbourne's blown-out wildcat .22 Hornet case. The hollow-pointed bullets were formed in a unique way, by copper electroplating pre-formed lead slugs. The Power-Lokt 5mm bullets demonstrated a greatly improved ballistic coefficient over the .22 Magnum, plus a longer bearing surface in the bore, contributing to better accuracy.

The 5mm cartridge was clearly ballistically superior to any other rimfire round. Why then did it fall by the wayside? The basic problem apparently stemmed from a substantial increase in chamber pressure over that of a standard .22, and even that of the .22 WMR. I was afforded a rare insight into the development problems associated with the 5mm by some correspondence with Michael W. Nagel, one of the engineers who spent 16 months developing the cartridge. Mike designed the tungsten carbide "long nose cutting" die with five triangular-shaped cutting edges that impart the longitudinal serrations on the bullet, from point to crimping groove, to improve expansion characteristics. At the outset expansion was poor and inconsistent. Fired into 20 percent gelatin blocks, bullets from the new dies consistently expanded to a full .40-inch, twice the original bullet diameter.

Accuracy tests which consumed over 25,000 rounds of production ammo, proved the Remington Model 592 (under-barrel tubular magazine) more accurate than the clip-loading M-591. The M-592 was responsible for introducing an accuracy problem to production ammo. Early ammo telescoped in the tubular magazine (the bullet pushing back into the case under recoil). It became necessary to crimp the case deeper, leading to more accuracy problems. Also, the depth of the crimping *cannelure* was critical. If the groove went deeper than specs, accuracy suffered. Despite this, the *worst* 10-shot bench rest group at 100 yards fired during testing was *under* 2 inches, center to center. The *best* group measured just .85-inch. My own testing of two different Model 591 clip-loading 5mm Remington rifles developed 100-yard 10-shot groups under an inch, but also some that measured almost 3 inches.

Mike's ammunition research group felt that a falling block or rolling block replica rifle would have been better for the 5mm than the 580 series rifles which were originally designed for .22 rimfire ammo. Certainly the six-lug artillery-styled bolt lockup was adequate to contain the 33,000 psi chamber pressure of the 5mm, but case heads were expanding into the chamber cuts for the double hook extractors. Initial testing was done with the original .22 rimfire dual-extractor bolt actions. The Rube Goldberg double extraction system was developed in mid-1968 to totally enclose the case head.

Therein lay most of the difficulties that led to the early demise of the 5mm. After initial announcements of the new cartridge were made public in 1968, Remington R&D went back to the drawing boards for another year and a half, allowing the original impact on shooters to ebb away. Eventual release of rifles and ammo became anticlimactic. Even then, all was not well. A letter went out to writers and magazine editors over a May 11, 1970, dateline, requesting that all test rifles be returned for changeover to an improved extractor system. I returned the original rifle that I had received for testing, which had never given me a moment's trouble, and received in return another that appeared identical, but which gave me intermittent extraction problems.

As finally released, the 5mm Model 591 and 592 had the 68-degree turning bolt with phenomenal 1.7 millisecond lock time, and exceptionally crisp single stage trigger of the 580 series rimfire rifles, but the extractor had become a flat spring positioned about 10:00 o'clock on the bolt face (as seen from the front), that rode up a ramp outside of the barrel as the bolt closed. Upon opening the bolt, the extractor slid back down the ramp, contacting the case after initial extraction by a flat spring-loaded hook, riding a slot centered on the opposite side of the receiver, and forming a portion of the tight-fitting case head enclosure. The ⅝-inch O.D. barrel of the 5mm looked too spindly for target accuracy. I talked to Mike Walker, Remington Design Engineer, about adding a heavier barrel to the line. He responded that demand wasn't enough to warrant added production costs.

The .22 Magnum received a considerable boost from the fact that a compromise bore diameter coupled with a dual cylinder made it possible to use both standard .22 rimfire ammo and .22 WMR in the same revolver. There was no such fortuitous circumstance for the 5mm! To date, there have been no handguns made to handle the 5mm with the exception of the T/C Contender. In the Contender, the 5mm realizes most of its velocity potential, plus accuracy, combined with the superb exterior ballistics of the well-designed bullet.

The exterior ballistics of the 5mm were always superior to the .22 Magnum. Starting at a nominal 2100 fps (actual chronographed velocities were faster!), the 38-grain .2045-inch diameter, .525-inch long 5mm bullet was still traveling 1605 fps at 100 yards. The 40-grain .2235-inch diameter, .460-inch long .22 WMR slug starts out at 2000 fps and passes the 100-yard marker at 1390 fps. Despite the slightly lighter bullet, the 5mm started out with a higher muzzle energy, 372 foot pounds, compared with 355 foot pounds for the .22 WMR, and stretched that advantage at 100 yards to 217 over 170.

Finding an objective measure of bullet impact is no easy matter. Regardless of what medium you choose for comparison, someone will challenge it as not representative of living tissue. Mike Nagel insisted that the closest thing to living flesh was the 20 percent gelatin used by Remington for testing. However, gelatin is hard to handle, and results difficult to assess without high speed camera equipment to catch the block at the instant of greatest expansion, before it settles back to its original dimensions. Something anyone can find at his local brickyard is ordinary pug clay. I fired both the 5mm and .22 Magnum into 50-pound blocks at 50 and 100 yards. The 5mm ballooned almost round cavities, while the .22 Magnum gave a little less expansion and more penetration. Dimensions at 50 yards were 5¾ inches in diameter by 5 inches deep for the 5mm, and 5¼ inches by 6 inches for the .22 Magnum. At 100 yards, numbers in the same order were: 5½ by 6 and 4½ by 7, demonstrating that the same bullets at reduced velocities provided less expansion and more penetration. In the field, both the 5mm and .22 WMR vaporize ground squirrels out to 125 yards and would do the same for tree squirrels, making them less than ideal for meat hunters. The .22 Magnum comes with a full metal jacketed slug to reduce meat destruction, but there is no such option with the 5mm. Hollow point bullets from both calibers break up on contact with the ground, reducing ricochets. Both are semi-quiet for shooting in inhabited areas without unduly alarming local resi-

By using multiple-bull targets, one per gun, it was possible to test six types of ammo with each gun, and keep the results straight! Here Jim Beck and the author assess results of some of the early testing.

Some of the rifles tested included, the Ithaca Model 72 Saddlegun, the Ruger 10/22, Winchester Model 490, Marlin's 39A and 39M, Remington Model 541-S, Browning BAR, Weatherby Mark XXII, Marlin Model 783 and Remington Nylon 66.

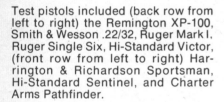

Test pistols included (back row from left to right) the Remington XP-100, Smith & Wesson .22/32, Ruger Mark I, Ruger Single Six, Hi-Standard Victor, (front row from left to right) Harrington & Richardson Sportsman, Hi-Standard Sentinel, and Charter Arms Pathfinder.

dents. Both are lethal on woodchucks out to 150 yards-plus, and deadly on predators at close range. One bobcat taken with a 5mm displayed a wide bloodshot area on the exit side, and the Power-Lokt bullet was found nicely expanded just under the skin, indicating that all of the bullet's energy was transmitted to the predator. One-shot 5mm kills were recorded on red foxes, raccoons, and big Wyoming jackrabbits. The 5mm Remington Rim Fire Magnum had everything going for it except a good rifle.

Understanding Accuracy and Performance

Whenever you read about an "accuracy test" by this or that writer, you should view the entire affair with a certain amount of healthy skepticism—not because the writer is essentially dishonest, but because any such test unavoidably tests many things besides just the ability of a given gun or ammunition. As much as anything else, the writer is testing his own skill or lack thereof in firing the gun. Using a bench rest helps eliminate some of the variables introduced by that willing but imperfect machine—a human being. Even a mechanical machine

rest fails to deliver a perfect performance in terms of extracting the maximum repeatability of which any given gun/ammo combination is capable.

Then there's the matter of "compatibility" between the *individual* gun and ammunition. Note that I'm not talking about a particular *brand or model of rifle* or of a *certain brand of ammunition* being used *at a particular point in time*. Despite the best efforts of firearm manufacturers to make every gun coming off of the production line as much like every other of a given model, inevitable variations creep in. The mere fact that natural wood (God bless it!) is still being used for rifle stocks for the most part, introduces an unavoidable variable. Two barrels off of the same drilling and rifling machines, even given the same lot of steel, will vary infinitesimally in dimensions—enough to affect overall accuracy of the rifle.

Despite near total mechanization of modern production lines, there remain some operations that must be performed by human hands. The individual worker's skill, his state of health, his degree of concentration upon the job at hand when he worked on that certain rifle, whether or not he was distracted by personal problems, or merely tired and inattentive, all can vastly influence the ability of the rifle to perform up to standards. No system of inspection can detect *all* of the poor workmanship, so problems are passed on to the customer. Makers maintain repair stations throughout the country, and are anxious to set any difficulty aright if the customer will but let them know about it.

The ammunition itself also has certain variables—it is made of brass that can vary in hardness or ductility. Drawing dies, that make the cases, wear. Some tolerances must be allowed before replacements are made, otherwise tooling costs would become prohibitive. The lead alloy and lubricant used for the bullets can vary slightly. Most important of all—the propellant will vary somewhat from one lot to another! Ammo producers test each new lot of powder, and adjust charges to compensate, but there are limitations.

The wonder is that ammunition producers do such a fine job of not merely *meeting* industry standards, but *far exceeding* them. Usually when I have chronographed .22 rimfire ammunition, the figures are near the maker's claims, sometimes *higher* than quoted ballistics. This in spite of the fact that published ballistics are derived using pressure/velocity test barrels, with specified dimensions far tighter than those in commercial rifles. Hence they deliver higher pressures and velocities.

We've gotten pretty far afield from our original premise, regarding the efficacy of accuracy tests, but the variations in guns and ammo are certainly part of the

Browning BAR with test target showing results of six different types of ammo. Note tight group with Stingers (lower right).

picture. Bear this in mind as you sprinkle each test liberally with salt!

I claim no magic formula myself. Our tests for this book were probably no better or worse than average even though I did have the assistance of Jim Beck, a superb shot and rangemaster at the I.W.L.A. range in Yorba Linda, California. Most of the testing was performed on a series of warm, sunny days, when the balmy "Santa Ana" was flowing in from the high deserts, thereby stabilizing such variables as temperature and humidity. The breezes that came up the valley at Yorba Linda rose and subsided as each day wore on, creating one unavoidable variable. Ammo was confined to given lots throughout the tests, (except Stinger) to avoid variations from that source. The same sight couldn't be used on all of the rifles, because mounting systems were different. Thus in some instances, we were testing sights as well as rifles and ammunition.

I noticed a peculiar anomaly during accuracy testing at 25 versus 50 yards. (Most of the groups were shot at 25 yards, to reduce the influence of the wind at the Yorba Linda range.) Some of the fliers at 25 yards exhibited definite indications of tipping at the target. Just out of curiosity, I followed up with 50-yard groups, finding fewer fliers and tipping totally absent. Apparently the bullets were stabilizing, or "going to sleep" by the time they reached the 50-yard line. Groups at 50-yards of five shots were about the same size as the 10-shot 25-yard groups.

Groups that exhibited fliers obviously outside of the main cluster show two measurements on the chart—the main group and the overall measure for all 10 shots, including fliers center-to-center. The basic group represents 80 to 90 percent of a rifle's accuracy potential, and that's what you'll be hunting with most of the time. Field rifles might be more aptly judged by three-shot groups, because you'll never get more than three shots at any given animal! If your gun prints nine shots in say ½-inch, and blows one out at ¾-inch, that means that you can hit a crow through the head 9 tries out of 10 at 25 yards. Certainly that is more important than concentrating upon the fact that one shot out of 10 you will miss. It all boils down to the difference between an optimist and a pessimist. The former says a glass is *half full* of wine, whiskey or water (to your taste) and the latter says the glass is *half empty!* Performance of ammo and guns is influenced by a thousand and one variables, some outlined above. So view the test results as an interesting experiment, *not the final word!*

In order of their appearance on the target, the types of ammunition used were: Federal .22 Long Rifle Power-Flite (high velocity); Remington Rifle Match .22 Long Rifle (standard velocity); Western (Winchester-Western) Super-Match Mark III (standard velocity); Winchester Super-X Dynapoint Extra Power .22 Long Rifles (high velocity); Federal .22 Long Rifle Semi-Hollow Point Power-Flite (high velocity); and Omark/

The Ithaca Model 72 Saddlegun was a good grouper with all save the Winchester Mark III.

Like the Marlin 39A, the Winchester 9422 also exhibited vertical dispersion although tight on a horizontal plane.

We found that Marlin's 39A had a tendency to string groups vertically.

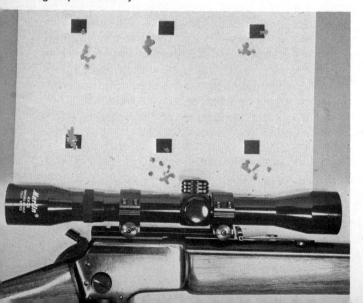

The Marlin 39M gave a spotty performance. Later repeat of the tests failed to elicit any improvement.

CCI Stinger .22 Long Rifles (ultra high velocity). That accounts for the six bull's-eyes on each target. Brought into the program later on a sample basis was the new Winchester-Western Super-X Xpediter .22 (ultra high velocity), and Winchester T-22 Standard Velocity .22 Long Rifle cartridges.

As it worked out, this chapter became a test vehicle not only for various types and brands of ammo, but also for a variety of rifles and pistols. Because we were testing field rifles, we concentrated on high velocity ammo, three with expanding points. Two brands of match ammo were included to give each rifle a chance to do its best. The level of accuracy attained here hardly represents the best that these target rounds can provide. They are designed to be delivered from finely tuned heavyweight target rifles, rather than lightweight field guns.

The accuracy group-size chart and the target show the Browning BAR-22 to be one of the most accurate rifles tested. BAR-22 groups were nicely rounded, with a general absence of wide fliers. Notice the Stinger group! The Ithaca Model 72 Saddlegun also performed in style! The one exception was W-W Mark III, which inexplicably strung out in a vertical pattern. The Marlin 39A showed an inclination to vertical expansion of the groups, but looked good even so. The 39M shot some round groups, and a few that showed vertical dispersion. Could this be a family characteristic of tube-loading lever guns? Jumping ahead to the Winchester 9422, we found that it was very tight in the

ACCURACY CHART
Group Size Chart For Various Guns and Ammo
(10 shots fired from bench rest at 25 yards)

	Charter Arms AR-7 Explorer	Browning BAR-22	Ithaca Model 72 Saddlegun	Marlin Model 39A	Marlin Model 39M	Mossberg Model 377 Plinkster	Remington Model 541-S Custom Sporter	Remington Nylon 66	Ruger 10/22 Sporter	Savage Model 19 NRA Musket	Weatherby Mark XXII	Winchester Model 490	Winchester Model 9422
Federal .22 Long Rifle Power-Flite high vel.	1⅛	⅜-⅝	7/16	⅜-⁹/₁₆	11/16-1¼	½-⅞	7/16	⅝-1	¾-1¼		½-¾	½-13/16	*5/16-13/16
Remington .22 Long Rifle Rifle Match standard vel.	¾-1⅜	½	½	½	½	½	⅝	½	½		5/16-⅝	⅝	*¼-5/16
Winchester .22 Long Rifle Super Match Mark III standard velocity	1⅝	5/16	½-13/16	½	½-13/16	⁹/₁₆	½	½-13/16	11/16		⁹/₁₆	7/16	*5/16-⅜
Winchester .22 Long Rifle Super-X Dynapoint high velocity	1¹/₁₆	½-⁹/₁₆	7/16-⁹/₁₆	½	⅝	¾	5/16-7/16	⅜-11/16	¾-1⅛		5/16-½	7/16	*¼-⅝
Federal .22 Long Rifle Semi-Hollow Point Power-Flite high vel.	¾-1	⅝-¾	⅜	½-13/16	1-1⅛	⁹/₁₆-¾	¼-½	½	1-1⁵/₁₆		7/16-¾	½-13/16	*5/16-¾
CCI .22 Long Rifle Stinger high vel.	1¼	⅜-½	5/16-½	⅝-¾	⅝-15/16	¾-1	⅝	11/16	⅝		⅜	⅜-⅞	*⅜-⅝
Winchester .22 Long Rifle Super-X Xpediter	1⅜-1⅝	1⅜-1⅝					⅝-1⅛			***½- / ****⅝	¾-1⅜	⅞-1¾	⁹/₁₆-1¾

Unless otherwise specified, the first measure represents main body of 10-shot group. The second measure (if any) represents widest spread including any fliers.

*First measure is horizontal, second is vertical.
**5 shots only.
***10 shots.

149

Mossberg's latest offering, the Plinkster, appeared to prefer match grade ammo.

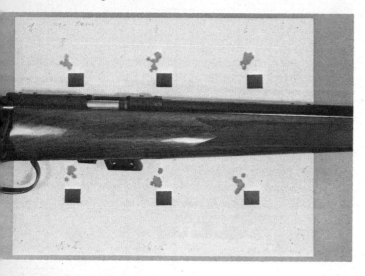

The Remington 541-S was having a bad day when compared to some past performances. Glass bedding improved groups immensely.

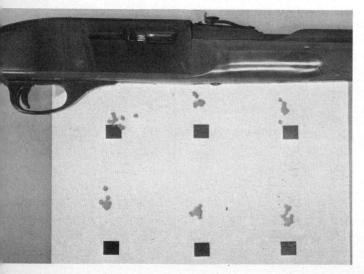

horizontal plane, but displayed some marked up and down movement, to the point where I reported groups in horizontal and vertical measures instead of simply taking the widest holes in the normal manner. The Mossberg Plinkster delivered several nicely rounded groups, plus a few that were strangely scattered. It seemed to like Remington Rifle Match to the exclusion of all others. The Remington 541-S wasn't feeling its best, tending to some vertical group stretching. I think it needs a little tuning in the stock bedding. (A matter I'll tend to in Chapter 14, and report the results to you then.) It has shot much better than this in the past! That's a point to bear in mind whenever you consider accuracy of any given rifle or ammo. They have "good" days and "bad" days, often without apparent reason! If you're easily upset or have a cardiac condition, don't become too interested in accuracy. You can be driven to an early grave by the antics of some rifles. They usually decide to become stubborn at the very moment when you're trying to sight in for an imminent trip to Alaska or some other exotic spot, and you have just enough time left to pack for the plane!

If the Remington 541-S was having golly-wobbles, it seems that the Remington Nylon 66 must have been shooting way over its head! Note the group with those Federal Semi-Hollow Points! Even with the Weaver Qwik-Point sight, the Nylon 66 delivered some fine groups.

The Ruger 10/22 exhibited distinct preference for the target ammo, and the CCI Stingers. It becomes apparent by this time that the Stingers were grouping darn near as well as the target stuff in most of the rifles—pretty remarkable for full-bore hunting ammo. I might

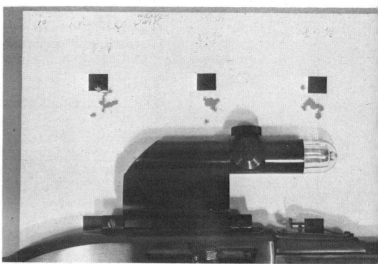

(Above) Remington Nylon 66 groups with Weaver Qwik-Point aboard were also better than expected.

(Left) The Remington Nylon 66 grouped better than expected, certainly adequate for a plinker or medium-range small game rifle.

also mention that three different lots of Stingers were used, just because we weren't able to corral enough from a given lot to get us through the test. All of the Stinger ammo shot like gangbusters!

As always, the Weatherby Mark XXII turned in a sterling performance. No prima donna this one! It shoots anything well! I might add that over the years every Mark XXII I have ever shot was consistently highly accurate.

As of this writing, Winchester's Model 490 autoloaders are fast disappearing from dealer's shelves. When those presently in stock are gone, that's the end of it. The 490 displayed a distinct preference for ammo from its own family, namely the Mark III and Dynapoints, although it didn't shoot too shabbily with the others.

The Marlin Model 783 and Mossberg Model 640K .22 WMR rifles printed exceptional groups with both CCI Maxi-Mags and .22 Winchester Magnum Rim Fire ammo.

A carton of Xpediter ammo arrived from Winchester too late to be included in the original accuracy tests, but it was fired with a few chosen guns which had demonstrated proficiency at driving bullets through the same hole or thereabouts! The Browning BAR-22 which had kept most of the other brands of ammo within ½- to ¾-inch, added a whole inch to that when firing Xpediters, and that was the *good* group! The Weatherby Mark XXII held nine shots in a ragged vertical ¾-inch group, then blew number 10 out to almost double the overall size. By then, doubting both myself and the rifle, I fired 10 T-22's just for record into a neat round ¼-inch. Nothing wrong with *that* gun! Next up was Jim Beck and his chrome-plated Hi-Standard Victor. They

As always, the Weatherby Mark XXII turned in a sterling performance—especially with Stingers!

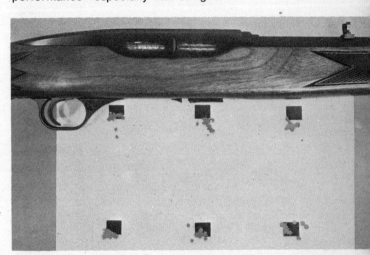

The Winchester 490 much preferred family ammo, note bulls 3 and 4 (Mark III and Dynapoints).

The Ruger 10/22 obviously preferred target ammo and CCI Stingers.

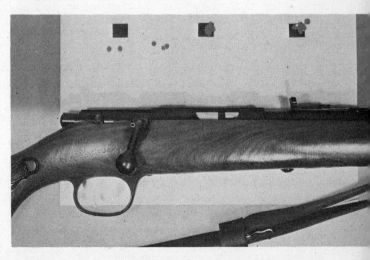

Despite a bargain price tag, the Marlin Model 783 grouped well with both CCI Maxi-Mags and W-W .22 Magnum ammo. Disregard sighters on bull #1.

151

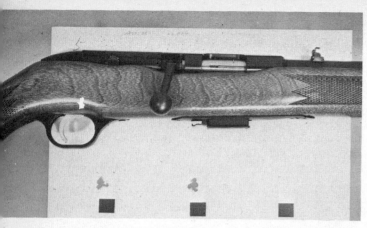

Mossberg 640K grouped slightly tighter than the Marlin. It should be said that some of the best .22 WMR groups seen during testing were fired with Mossberg rifles.

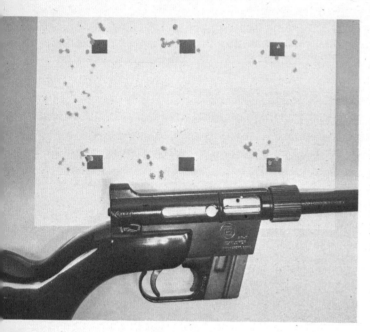

The Charter Arms AR-7 displayed adequate accuracy for near-range small game hunting. Considering its light weight and lack of forend to stiffen the barrel, it shot pretty well.

scattered a string of Xpediters in an ascending pattern angled slightly to the left, measuring 2¼ inches overall, with nine in a 1⅜-inch group. Then for a control, he fired 10 Remington Rifle Match cartridges into ⅞-inch. The Remington 541-S held most of its 10 Xpediters within ⅝-inch, then blew one to open up to 1⅛-inches.

Using Winchester's lever action 9422, I started what looked like a great group, plugging seven rounds into ⁹/₁₆-inch, only to end with three low shots, opening the group to 1¾-inches. That was the best group out of three. The Winchester Model 490 contained nine Xpediters within ⅞-inch, then sailed one out at 1:00 o'clock to open the group to 1¾-inches.

Grasping at straws, I asked Jim to try his Savage Model 19 NRA Musket, a clip-loading bolt action that

hasn't been made since 1933. Manufactured as a competitively-priced target rifle of its day, the Model 19 exhibits workmanship and finish that are simply incredible by today's standards! The aged Savage proceeded to put five Xpediters through a ½-inch hole, followed by a ⅝-inch 10-shot group—way better than any of the modern rifles. Searching for an explanation, we checked the twist on the Model 19 and discovered that it is one turn in 11 inches, rather than the standard one in 16 inches used today. That made no sense at all! A shorter bullet should prefer a slower twist, not a faster one! There must have been some other factor involved, but the fact remains that the Savage Model 19 outshot all others with Xpediters.

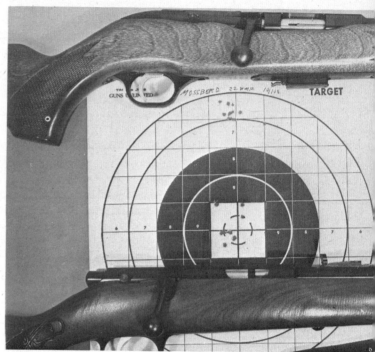

Here we have some 100-yard groups with .22 Winchester Magnum Rim Fire ammo fired with the Mossberg (top) and Marlin (bottom).

Five shots at 100 yards with Winchester Model 9422M. That top hole is actually two bullets.

Ten shots at 100 yards with new lot of T-22 ammo. T-22s represent some of the most accurate budget-priced ammo the author has found to date. You should consider giving it a try—it works!

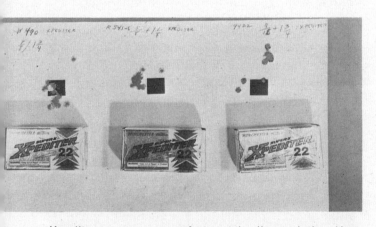

Xpediter groups were, unfortunately, disappointing. Here are groups of 10 shots each at 25 yards, from the Winchester Model 490, Remington 541-S, and Winchester 9422. Best Xpediter groups were fired by Jim Beck with his Savage Model 19 NRA Musket, a collector's item!

Rimfire Ballistics

When CCI Stinger ammo was initially introduced, I ran comprehensive chronograph and accuracy tests with it at the I.W.L.A. range, with the aid of rangemaster, Jim Beck. In the interests of keeping current, many of these tests were repeated with a wider range of guns and ammo represented.

The first sensation upon firing a Stinger in a rifle is an awareness of increased noise and recoil over standard high velocity .22 ammo, enough to be clearly felt. In a handgun, the effect is even more pronounced, perhaps because of the increased muzzle blast resulting from the not inconsiderable amount of Stinger powder that burns outside of the bore. Few people are aware that standard .22 ammo burns out in about 16 inches of barrel. After that, the bullet is pretty much coasting, which accounts for the lack of proportionately progressive velocities as barrel lengths increase beyond 18 inches. The basic premise upon which the Stinger saga hinged was the idea of using a slower burning powder to lengthen burn time out to the end of the average rifle barrel—20 to 24 inches. In handgun barrel lengths, particularly the very short ones, the velocity advantage of Stingers sags somewhat.

During initial testing of Stinger ammo, Jim Beck introduced me to his Heckler & Koch HK-4 autoloading pistol with 3⅜-inch barrel. The little H&K further emphasized the fact that Stingers are really not at their best in short pistol barrels. It's obvious that any ammunition that was deliberately engineered to take advantage of a longer burn in rifle barrels was going to suffer in shorter tubes. In the H&K, the Stinger's velocity advantage shrank to a mere 167 fps, as the short auto turned in 1047 fps with Remington high velocity hollow points, and just 1214 fps with Stingers.

Heckler & Koch HK-4 autoloading pistol failed to function with Stinger ammo. Shown are two Stinger cases from the HK-4, plus two standard .22 Long Rifle cases from the same gun. Note considerable swelling around the head of the Stinger brass—this despite the reinforced belt. Several brands of foreign-made auto pistols don't do well with Stingers. Try before you buy, if possible.

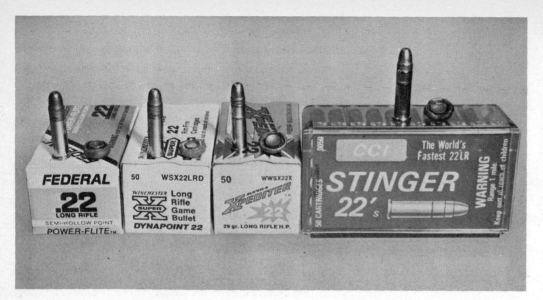

Modern game getters are the Federal Semi-Hollow Points, W-W Dynapoints, Xpediters, and CCI Stingers, shown here with expanded samples.

By contrast, a 5½-inch barreled Hi-Standard Victor clocked 1079 fps with Remington and 1326 fps with Stingers—a more impressive advantage of 247 fps. A Hi-Standard Sharpshooter, also with 5½-inch barrel, registered 1165 fps and 1442 fps, giving Stingers a 277 fps edge. A Hi-Standard Trophy Model, with 7½-inch barrel, delivered 1163 fps and 1510 fps, a Stinger edge of 347. That's actually higher than the difference noted in the Weatherby Mark XXII, which registered the greatest rifle contrast between Stingers and Remington high velocity hollow points, 342 fps. The highest overall reading of 1591 fps, for Stingers was posted by the Remington 541-S rifle, but it gave a high reading for Remington as well, 1302 fps, for a Stinger margin of 289 fps. The 10-inch barreled Thompson/Center Contender pistol recorded 1228 fps and 1522, a Stinger margin of 294 fps.

Stinger ammo boxes are lately labeled with a sticker stating: "Stinger cartridges are intended for use only in firearms with chambers and bores that comply with industry standards for .22 Long Rifle as specified by the American National Standards Institute. Dimensional incompatibility has been found in Spanish-made Llama auto pistols, and may exist in other foreign made firearms, which can result in a hazardous ruptured case condition." The little HK-4 fed Stingers only when hand-assisted, and fired cases revealed a definite swelling near the head. I have heard rumblings about other foreign autos not taking to Stingers. So if your auto pistol speaks with a German or Spanish accent, better try a few rounds before you invest in any quantity of the new ultra high velocity ammo. Likely, the same problems would arise with Winchester-Western Xpediters, although the HK-4 was not available to try them. All of the Yankee-made autoloaders handled Stingers and Xpediters without skipping, with the exception of Charter Arms AR-7, which steadfastly refused to feed the ultra-velocity rounds, and the Hi-Standard Trophy Model, which experienced intermittent failures to feed. One other Trophy Model handled Stingers just fine. It may have been a problem with the particular magazine in that gun, but there wasn't another available at the time to check that theory.

Apparently both Stingers and Xpediters do indeed continue to burn powder out to the end of a 24-inch barrel. In the Marlin 39M with 20-inch barrel, the Stinger scratched out 1456 fps, contrasted to a high of 1591 in the 24-inch barreled Remington 541-S, a difference of 135 fps. Xpediter numbers ran, 1572 fps/1689—difference, 117 fps. From the above numbers, you can see the Xpediters were traveling slightly

Here we have two tin cans that met their fate at the hands of a standard .22 Long Rifle (left), a CCI Stinger (right).

Regular .22LR meets a full can of pop from 100 feet.

Stinger meets a full can of pop from 100 feet.

VELOCITY CHART

Chart of actual chronographed velocities, corrected to the muzzle. Average of 5 or more shots.

(BARREL LENGTHS)	Hi-Standard O/U Derringer Mag./.22 LR 3½-inch	H.S. Sharpshooter 5½-inch	H.S. Trophy 7¼-inch	H.S Victor 5½-inch	H & K-4 3⅜-inch	Marlin Model 39M 20-inch	Mossberg 640KD Chuckster 24-inch	Remington Model 541-S 24-inch	Ruger Super Single Six revolver 6½-inch	Ruger Mark I Auto 4½-inch	Thompson/Center Contender 10-inch	Weatherby Mark XXII 24-inch
Federal .22 Long Rifle Semi-Hollow Point Power-Flite high vel. 40-grain						1219/34		1303/41	1099/26	1109/38	1243/45	1255/80
Winchester .22 Long Rifle Super-X Dynapoint high velocity 40-grain						1163/81		1289/35	1022/44	1011/62	1182/67	1245/31
CCI .22 Long Rifle Stinger high velocity 32-grain hollow point		637/143	1510/54	1326/73	1214/65	1456/133		1591/106	1239/29	1324/48	1522/55	1585/43
Winchester .22 Long Rifle Super-X Xpediter 29-grain						1572/81		1689/73	1259/62	1358/92	1506/123	1634/62
Remington .22 Long Rifle high velocity hollow point 36-grain	678/87	1165/62	1163/90	1079/80	1047/52	1138/64		1302/56	1011/100	1016/86	1228/51	1243/72
Winchester .22 WMR 40-grain hollow point	947/109						1940/36		1328/135		1842/87	
CCI .22 Maxi-Mag 40-grain hollow point	1023/92						1948/69		1387/101		1803/70	
5mm Remington Magnum 38-grain hollow point											1827/63	

In this chart, the first figure represents the averaged muzzle velocity for 5-rounds while the second (smaller) number represents the extreme variance (in feet per second) of the fastest and slowest projectiles fired in a particular 5-shot string.

quicker than the Stingers, but the former sacrifices three precious grains of bullet weight in the process.

Although bullet manufacturers have begun in recent years to list the ballistic coefficients for their various projectiles, makers of .22 ammo fail to do so, probably considering that information redundant. However, if you are using a chronograph which can compensate from instrumental to muzzle velocity, you need to know the ballistic coefficient to program the device. The ballistic coefficient relates bullet shape with its sectional density, which in turn relates the bullet's weight with its diameter. Together, these factors determine how well a bullet will sustain its velocity at extended ranges, also how well it will resist wind drift. Thanks once more to the efforts of ballistics expert Fred Jennie, the ballistic coefficients of various .22 rimfire bullets are published in the chart accompanying Chapter 8, based upon the Ingall's Tables. Note that the coefficients are expressed as decimals. The higher the value, the better.

Rimfire autoloading actions are wholly of the "simple blowback" design, meaning that some of the energy that would normally be used to drive the bullet in a closed-breech rifle or pistol goes into pushing the heavy, spring-loaded breech-block back to extract the empty case and return with a live round. Engineers carefully balance breechblock weight, spring resistance, and frictional forces so that the breech doesn't open until after the normal pressure peak has passed, virtually nullifying any effect upon actual bullet velocity. A half-dozen years or so back, CCI put together an interesting little booklet called, *The .22 Rimfire Fact Book,* which stated that based upon their velocity tests, the loss in an autoloading action was no more than 2 percent. My own chronograph tests at that time pitted a Weatherby Mark XXII against a lever action Marlin 39A, both with 24-inch barrels. With high velocity hollow point ammo, the Mark XXII actually registered a *higher* velocity than the Marlin, 1283 fps for the autoloader as opposed to 1260 fps for the closed breech. Obviously, other factors were involved. A smoother bore or somewhat tighter chamber in the Weatherby could account for its slight velocity advantage over the Marlin, but it appears obvious that there was no substantial velocity loss resulting from the blowback action.

You'll note that in the accompanying velocity chart, the tables are turned. With all types of ammo, the bolt action Remington 541-S (also with 24-inch barrel) registered higher velocities than did the Weatherby Mark XXII. However, this was a different Mark XXII than I used in the original tests several years back. Note that in the current tests the *average* reading for high velocity Long Rifles was 1248, and the old reading was 1283, indicating again that *variations between individual guns* far outweigh any possible loss resulting from an autoloading action.

A rifle-fired Stinger made this cavity in heavy mastic Ballistic Putty. Note that the hollow point section of bullet peeled off and remained behind, while the heavier base portion pushed on to deepen the cavity.

Fired from a pistol, the Stinger made a deeper channel with less ballooning. Note bullet held together.

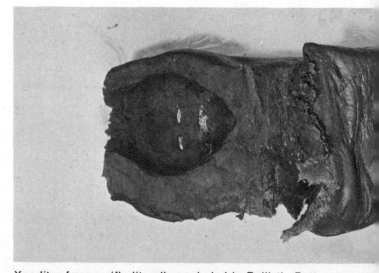

Xpediter from a rifle literally exploded in Ballistic Putty, leaving shards of lead all through the cavity.

Mentioned above were expansion tests that I carried out a number of years back, using blocks of wet clay. More recently I discovered another material, called "Ballistic Putty," sold by Beeman's, Inc., 47 Paul Drive, San Rafael, CA 94903. This highly homogeneous mastic is far denser than clay, therefore channels are shorter and narrower, making it impossible to compare the results in clay against those in the Ballistic Putty. However, both offer a comparative index of bullet penetration and disruption within its own kind. The far greater degree of bullet expansion in Ballistic Putty was a further demonstration of its higher resistance. Even .22 solid point Federal Power-Flite 40-grain bullets expanded to ⅜-inch diameter, equaling the expansion of Federal's Semi-Hollow Point. The latter did, however, peel back more than the solid, and it penetrated almost as far, 3⅝-inches. The width of the channel left by the Semi-Hollow Point was 1¼ inches, compared to only ⅞-inch for the solid point.

Winchester-Western Super-X Dynapoints penetrated 3½ inches leaving a channel 1⅛ inches wide, expanding to $^{13}/_{32}$-inch. Remington 36-grain high velocity hollow points drove 2½ inches deep, with maximum channel width of ⅞-inch, and expanding to $^{7}/_{16}$-inch. CCI Stingers went to a 2¾-inch depth, 2-inch width. It was a shattering experience for the bullet, with the remains too scattered for an accurate measurement. Xpediters achieved 2½-inch depth, 2¼-inch width, and a similar fate befell the bullet.

Federal Semi-Hollow Points made a wider channel and almost as deep, with the obvious moral that the Semi-Hollow Point ammo is better for small game hunting.

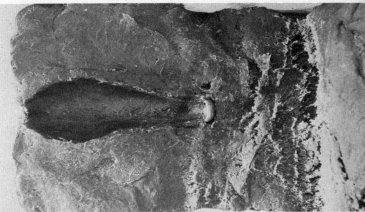

Winchester-Western Super-X Dynapoint ammo rifle-fired, expanded somewhat more than the Federal Semi-Hollow Point, indicating possibly a softer bullet alloy. The channel was slightly narrower and shorter than Federal counterpart.

Even fired from a pistol, the Xpediter bullet shatters, leaving a ring of lead behind while the base continues a short distance.

(Above) Remington high velocity hollow point .22 Long Rifle (from rifle) made this channel, indicating quicker expansion but with less energy transfer by the lighter bullet.

(Left) When it came to sheer penetration, Federal Power-Flite high velocity solids drove deepest into Ballistic Putty, expanding more than expected.

157

CHAPTER 11

Accuracy Versus Cost

MEASURED IN TERMS OF hours of healthful entertainment and pure utility provided per dollar expended, .22 rimfire guns and ammo represent the greatest bargain available today. They're a better investment in physical health than a TV set, and a better investment in mental well being than a series of visits to the "head shrinker."

Some sniff at the idea of using anything but the "best." However, if we all took that view, a lot of us never would enjoy the pleasures of smallbore shooting. I sold newspapers on a street corner, rain or shine, 7 days a week for a long time to possess my first "store-bought" .22 rifle—and it wasn't any deluxe model! There are many accurate, trustworthy rimfire rifles and pistols available that won't break your bankroll, even at today's inflated prices.

RIFLES AND HANDGUNS

Buying a rimfire rifle or pistol on a budget? Marlin offers their Glenfield line of rifles, possessing all of the intrinsic ingredients of their more expensive rimfires, lacking only a few of the refinements. Substituted for genuine walnut in the stocks is highly functional hardwood, stained to a walnut hue, sans only the white-line spacers under the buttplates. The blued finish may not be polished as brightly, but that might be viewed as an asset in that it is less reflective, and not so likely to advertise your presence in the field to every criter within sight. The Marlin/Glenfield line offers ample selection—the Model 60 autoloader with under-barrel tubular magazine, the Model 20 clip-loading bolt action, and the Model 10, a fine single shot bolt action "teacher" rifle for the youngsters.

Or, look at Savage: You can opt for their Rolls Royce of rimfires, the Savage/Anschutz Model 54, or lower your sights a little and settle for the Stevens Model 34. Basically both rifles are the same. Each is a clip-loading bolt action with man-sized Monte Carlo stock. Both can be had as standard or magnum rimfires. Both come with open sights. Sure, the Anschutz is the ultimate, but tell me—do you drive a Rolls Royce or a Ford? Of course it's easier to own an Anschutz than it is a Rolls, and I highly recommend it. But if you have a beer budget, you won't suffer any great deprivation by shooting a sturdy, reliable "beer" rifle! In the case of Savage, there is a middle ground. The Savage/Anschutz Model 64 just about halves the cost of the 54, but it sure as hell is a lot more than half the rifle!

Maybe you aspire to a Savage Model 24 over/under .22/410 or .22 Magnum/20 gauge. If you're willing to forego the genuine walnut stock with impressed checkering, you can choose the Field Grade, and save some bucks. Mechanically, the guns are identical.

Standard line Mossberg rifles have never been accused of being overpriced. Yet the best .22 Magnum groups that I've seen to date come from a Mossberg! Mossberg perhaps delivers more gun per dollar than any other maker, but did you know that they have an "economy" line? The New Haven brand by Mossberg offers essentially the same firearms with less fancy wood, sans checkering, and not as highly finished. The New Haven Model 453T autoloader is really the Mossberg Model 353 without the fancy fold-down forend. The New Haven Model 740T bears a striking resemblance to the clip-loading bolt action Mossberg 640K, with no checkering and plainer sights.

Entertaining dreams of becoming a pistol champ? If money's no object, you can approach the firing line with the square-shouldered, high-ribbed, autoloading Hi-Standard Victor. Or you can settle for their Sharp-shooter, which has delivered Ransom Rest groups just as compact as the best of them, and at half the cost. Hi-Standard's Military Trophy Model has long been accepted as the measure of excellence in rimfire competition handguns. However, they also offer the Citation, alike in every detail, save for having a less

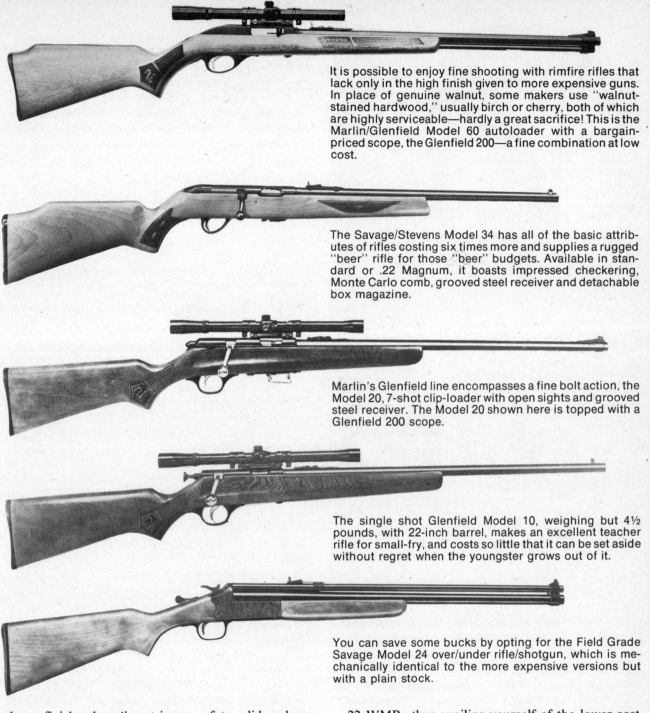

It is possible to enjoy fine shooting with rimfire rifles that lack only in the high finish given to more expensive guns. In place of genuine walnut, some makers use "walnut-stained hardwood," usually birch or cherry, both of which are highly serviceable—hardly a great sacrifice! This is the Marlin/Glenfield Model 60 autoloader with a bargain-priced scope, the Glenfield 200—a fine combination at low cost.

The Savage/Stevens Model 34 has all of the basic attributes of rifles costing six times more and supplies a rugged "beer" rifle for those "beer" budgets. Available in standard or .22 Magnum, it boasts impressed checkering, Monte Carlo comb, grooved steel receiver and detachable box magazine.

Marlin's Glenfield line encompasses a fine bolt action, the Model 20, 7-shot clip-loader with open sights and grooved steel receiver. The Model 20 shown here is topped with a Glenfield 200 scope.

The single shot Glenfield Model 10, weighing but 4½ pounds, with 22-inch barrel, makes an excellent teacher rifle for small-fry, and costs so little that it can be set aside without regret when the youngster grows out of it.

You can save some bucks by opting for the Field Grade Savage Model 24 over/under rifle/shotgun, which is mechanically identical to the more expensive versions but with a plain stock.

glossy finish, plus *silver* trigger, safety, slide release and roll marks, rather than the 24-carat variety found in the more costly pistol.

If your heart's set upon a double action rimfire revolver, instead of insisting upon a K-22 Masterpiece, settle for a Hi-Standard Sentinel or a Harrington & Richardson Sportsman. Both are accurate, reliable, and comfortable in the hand—plus they cost a lot less!

RIMFIRE AMMO

One obvious way to save money and still enjoy rimfire sports is to buy a standard .22 rimfire, as opposed to

a .22 WMR, thus availing yourself of the lower-cost ammo, for target practice or plinking, and use ultra-velocity Stingers or Xpediters when you need more power for small game hunting.

Target competitors routinely shell out roughly twice as much money for ammo to scratch out an extra "X" at 100 yards. Most of us don't require the ultimate in accuracy from our .22 Long Rifles, but even those who do are missing a good bet if they overlook Winchester-Western T22, billed by Winchester as, "... standard velocity ammunition designed for target-type accuracy and all-around performance at a non-

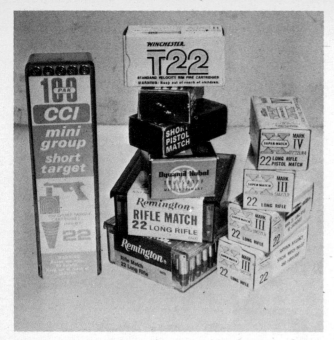

A confirmation run with another ammo of known velocity convinced me that it was no electronic failure at work, but rather impossibly precise ammunition. Normal variations on the chronograph run between 30 and 100 fps. T22 was clocked time after time with no more than a 5 fps variation. Round after round bridged the 10 feet between the electronic screens in exactly the same time reading. T22 quality hasn't suffered in the intervening years. I purchased a case just recently (lot #1LK32X), and found it still punched out one-hole groups with the same regularity as before! Try T22! If your rifle hasn't become so jaded as to insist upon a steady diet of Eley or some other exotic ammo, you

Winchester's bargain-priced T22 ammo tops a stack of far more costly target rounds, symbolizing its accuracy potential and low dollar cost advantages. T22s chronographed more consistently than high-priced target ammo.

If local department or discount stores have sales of name brand .22 ammo as "loss leaders," buy them by the carton. Your savings will be substantial.

premium price." Winchester states that cases are made from custom formulated brass, held to unusually precise tolerances. The familiar "H" headstamp has given way to a highly stylized "W." T22 bullets are contoured for maximum stability and greater wind-bucking ability, and coated with a new nonleading dry lubricant. The bullets exhibit only a slight "waxy" feel, and the lube doesn't wipe off onto hands or clothing. T22 ammo is loaded with clean-burning smokeless ball powder, and a special noncorrosive priming mixture designed to deliver consistent accuracy. You'll find no nickeled brass or golden bullets, just target performance at plinker prices!

When T22 was first introduced, I test-fired it in several guns for accuracy and was startled at the results. Even more surprising was the fact that it registered on the Telepacific chronograph with so little shot-to-shot variation that I thought the machine had broken down.

may find that you never again have to plunk down $3-plus for target ammo!

Often major department stores such as Penneys or Montgomery Ward will have pre-inventory stock-reduction sales to avoid floor taxes. Brand name .22 ammo will be cut along with everything else. Usually ammo sale prices won't be mentioned in newspaper ads, because it represents a small part of the much larger sales of clothing, household appliances, etc. So you must be alert enough to be on the scene at the proper time to benefit.

Watch for sales at local discount stores. Often they will advertise a standard brand .22 ammo at an attractive price as a "loss leader," to get people into their sporting goods departments. That is the time to purchase several cartons, or even a case, if you can afford it. It's better than money in the bank! With our current rate of inflation, ammo prices are going up faster than

If you can afford to invest in a case of .22 rimfire ammo at a time when the price is right, you can realize a great savings, provided that you don't squander it because of a sudden feeling of richness!

For a gallery in the basement, a bullet trap such as this Gunslick bullet trap from Outers Laboratories, Inc. will catch bullets without risk of ricochets. Even so, it is far better to stick to CB Caps or at the most Shorts, for gallery practice.

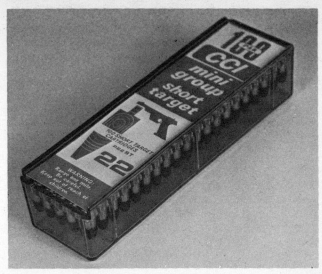

For International style Rapid Fire competition, CCI offers their Mini-Group Short Target cartridges. Their superb accuracy can be enjoyed for indoor gallery competition as well.

the interest rates at any bank could possibly pace. If you find the store is, "out of stock" on the ammo when you arrive, *insist upon a rain check,* so that you can return later after they are restocked and buy the ammo at the sale price. Often the store manager arranges to have a short supply when these ads hit. As long as the customers come in *looking* for the ammo, the ad has served its purpose of creating traffic. The customer can usually be touted onto some other brand, or perhaps sold a bowling ball or a pair of skis while he is handy.

Assuming you come away with a 5,000-round case of .22 ammo that was just a "steal," treat it with respect. Think not of what it cost you, but rather what it *will cost you to replace* at some future date. The normal human reaction is to spend foolishly when supply is abundant. Resist that tendency!

You may not get target accuracy from ammo purchased at a discount. Then again, it may fool you! I still have three boxes from a case of Monark .22 Long Rifle cartridges that I purchased almost 30 years ago. That was an economy brand manufactured by Federal Cartridge Corp., but it groups right alongside a more expensive box of target ammo. I have hoarded those "cheapie" boxes of ammo all of these years, using them when I really wanted to get the best groups from a given rifle. It never disappointed me. I sorrow that it's almost gone!

A case of Remington Hi-Speed Kleanbore .22 Long Rifles, the first I was able to lay hands on after the long drought occasioned by World War II, has dwindled down to the dregs, with only a couple of cartons left. (Note that in those days, an Honest Injun *wood crated case,* numbered 10,000 rounds rather than the 5,000 round cardboard carton of today.) As a measure of retained efficiency for this aged ammo, I chrono-

A lot of potential converts to "Caps" were reluctant to fire the Short-length cartridges in Long Rifle chambers, for fear that they might erode the chamber walls and cause sticky extraction. That fear harks back to the first smokeless powder .22 rimfire rounds, which were highly erosive. That problem no longer exists with modern ammunition. However, CCI solved the problem by introducing CB Caps with cases of Long Rifle length, eliminating forever the fear of chamber erosion! The cartridges are designed for gallery use and are inherently very accurate!

graphed some at random. It registered 1227 fps, I then clocked contemporary ammo—same brand high velocity—and it read 1214 fps, *actually less* than the vintage rounds! The old ammo was then, and remains today, some of the most accurate I have lucked onto. Apparently age alone has no detectable debilitating effect either upon velocity or accuracy.

Under ideal conditions, there is no maximum storage life for ammunition manufactured in the U.S. since World War II. *Age itself* is not a factor. However,

storage *conditions* are extremely important to preservation. Arch enemies of ammo are dampness, excessive humidity, excessive heat, or wide variations in temperatures. Don't store your precious ammo in a corner of the garage under a leaky roof, or in the attic where temperatures undergo extreme variations. Avoid areas near corrosive acids, solvents, oils, or flammables. Also, keep ammo away from furnaces, water heaters, washers, or other machinery. Never store ammo where it will be exposed to direct sunlight! Storage at very high temperatures, say above 120 degrees Fahrenheit, can cause permanent internal deterioration, leading to hangfires, misfires, or loss of accuracy.

The .22 Long has long been the butt of abuse by gun scribes who deride it as defunct, debilitated and otherwise dead as a dodo bird. But maybe there's some excuse for its continued existence. Aside from the fact that a few guns are still around from the old days that are chambered specifically for the Long, the cartridge with full-length case and 29-grain solid point bullet leaving the muzzle at 1240 fps still has some practical reasons for remaining alive. For starters, it's a little cheaper than the run-of-the-mill .22 Long Rifles, thus could be used for economy plinking. It's a good choice for hunting tree squirrels at ranges under 50 yards, because it kills reliably, without excessive destruction of edible portions.

All of the above goes double for Shorts. Remember at one time, *there was no other cartridge*. The .22 Short was the original, and for a number of years, the *only* .22 rimfire cartridge. Many in that unenlightened era took the tiny round in a tiny revolver seriously as a defense weapon.

Today's Short is a far cry from the one used in the Smith & Wesson Model 1. The current cartridge launches a 29-grain bullet at 1095 fps. only 145 fps less than the high velocity Long. The 27-grain hollow-

Owners of the Ruger Mini-14 can enjoy budget-priced plinking with their centerfire .223 rifle, by using Sport Specialties cartridge adapters, for either the .22 Long Rifle (left) or the .22 WMR (right). The adapters look like steel cartridge cases, but are in fact sub-caliber chambers that fit inside of the centerfire chamber.

pointed Short sets out at 1120 fps, far more formidable than many suppose. Some years back, while conducting expansion tests in 50-pound blocks of pug clay, I directed a .22 Short high velocity hollow point at one of those blocks from a distance of 25 yards. The bullet all but disintegrated, opening a balloon-shaped cavity 6 inches deep. That Short-launched hollow point was traveling faster at 25 yards than a Long Rifle hollow point at 100 yards range. Whatever you think you can kill at 100 yards with a .22 Long Rifle high velocity hollow point, you can kill just about as well with a hollow point Short at 25.

Shorts are decidedly cheaper than Long Rifles. Their reduced report and shorter lethal range make them safer for plinking pursuits, and they punch the same caliber holes through a tin can as Long Rifles.

As a matter of fact, so do CB Caps and BB Caps! They cost even less than Shorts—but not much. Caps have other assets, however. They can be used for aerial shooting with far less risk of tagging an unintended target in the far distance. They can be used in a basement or garage target range, without the need of a 2-ton steel bullet trap. Take care that you have *something* to absorb those tiny slugs. I well remember underestimating the power of a rimfire round once in my callow youth. I stacked some magazines, backed by a couple of old boards, against the inside wall of the garage, confident that the situation was well in hand. It wasn't! When I peeled away those magazines, I found a hole through the boards, and *through* the clapboard wall of the old garage. I found the bullet lodged in the neighbor's garage wall!

One highly constructive and instructive way to save money while continuing to enjoy the sport of smallbore shooting, is to impress any small-fry trainees with the importance and *cost* of each and every shot! Remind them that every trigger squeeze spends 3 cents.

When I was a small-fry myself, I used to pick up and save empty .22 cases with the same enthusiasm that some boys picked up girls. During World War II, when neither love nor money could buy bullets for centerfire smallbore rifles, I scratched around and dug out a couple of gallon cans full of .22 brass. With the aid of RCBS dies from friend, Fred Huntington, in Oroville, California, I was able to dehead the cases, then swage them over lead cores into soft-pointed varmint bullets. That same hobby is again gaining popularity. With our new realization that natural resources are not inexhaustible, it behooves us to save brass whenever and wherever we can. The future may find you indescribably grateful, as I was two wars ago!

CARTRIDGE ADAPTERS

If you're a centerfire smallbore buff, you can save some important money with Sport Specialties cartridge adapters, for such calibers as .220 Swift, .22-250, .223, .222, etc. These adapters consist of what appear to be blued steel cartridge cases that fit snugly into the rifle chamber. They are naturals for any bolt action, as well as the Ruger falling block single shot rifle. I have had excellent results with one that not many people have thought of yet, using Sport Specialties .22 Long Rifle and .22 Magnum adapters in my autoloading Ruger .223 Mini 14. I can hit the 200-yard gong at the Yorba Linda range with either one of these adapters. Owners of a Smith & Wesson .22 Jet revolver can cut costs significantly by investing in six adapters to fill the chambers with either .22 Long Rifle or .22 Magnum ammo. Thompson/Center Contender pistol owners can find Sport Specialties adapters for most barrels, from the .22 Hornet on up. I used one to good advantage in my .222 barrel, substituting low-cost standard .22 ammo, from BB Caps to Long Rifles, for the high-priced centerfire fodder. Sport Specialties makes complete insert barrels including chamber, rifled tube and extractor, in rimfire calibers, to slip into bigbore Contender barrels, including .357 and .44 Magnums, .45 ACP, .45 Long Colt, etc.

You don't have to be stingy to enjoy .22 rimfire shooting, but by the same token, you can probably shoot more often and longer if you thoughtfully pace your expenditures to stay within the practical limits of your budget.

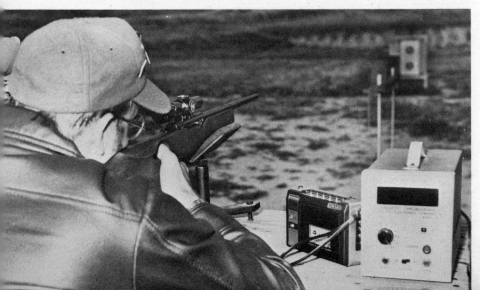

During chronograph testing, the T22 ammo recorded identical readings several times in a row. Thinking that the machine was out of whack, the author tried alternate ammo of known velocity and found it was not computer error but rather some amazingly consistent ammo!

CHAPTER 12

Rimfire Reducers

THE IDEA OF USING .22 rimfire ammo in larger bore handguns and rifles has perennial appeal. A case in point could be illustrated by the Government Model Colt .45 ACP. Firearms genius John M. Browning invented his first self-loading pistol in 1895, a gas-operated unit with a breech locked by a rotating lever. Although unhandy and bulky, it was scheduled for production as a Colt commercial offering, but was set aside when Browning came up with a series of improved designs, culminating in the Model 1911. Browning came up with his basic design for the Model 1911 in 1905, but it was subject to a series of refinements by Colt engineers before it was finally adopted as the United States' official military side arm. Government testing began in 1907, with an endurance test that entailed firing 6,000 rounds of issue ammo, which "Old Ugly" carried off without a single malfunction! There followed a series of torture tests that included rusting the gun and sifting it with fine sand and grit. The slab-sided pistol continued to fire without a bobble, totally astounding Army brass. This was the first time a small arm had completed an official government test with a perfect record!

On March 29, 1911, orders from the Chief of Staff and Secretary of War, made the adoption of the Browning/Colt Model 1911 official. No sooner was the .45 ACP accepted by our armed forces than the Ordnance Command put in a request for a gun of similar design firing a .22 rimfire cartridge for the purposes of training. John Browning set to work to fulfill that need. Browning submitted several designs to the military, but before any steps were taken to make an official selection, the outbreak of World War I caused the project to be set aside.

While drumming up a training substitute for the .45 ACP, Browning tinkered with several design concepts that more suited his own preference for what could almost be described as "dainty" rimfire guns, well typified by his automatic rifle design. In 1914, this resulted in the first of the Colt Woodsman series, a small, slender pistol, that fit the hand like a calfskin glove! The Woodsman survived two World Wars and a depression, but it was mortally wounded by the Colt corporate accounting department, and tragically, was dropped from production a couple of years ago.

The idea of a .22 rimfire-firing Model 1911 was taken up by the armorers at the Springfield Arsenal, birthplace of many military small arms. They tried to entice the .22 Short into operating the 1911 slide, but there wasn't enough energy in the tiny cartridge to energize that huge hunk of steel. Colt picked up the ball, and developed the first Colt .22 Ace Automatic Pistol introduced commercially in 1931. Externally, the gun looked exactly like a commercial .45 ACP, save for a slightly taller ramp-style front sight and a Patridge rear, screw-adjustable for both windage and elevation. Internally, the gun differed in the ejector shape, making it difficult to convert readily to .45 ACP. The original Ace was a simple blowback design, with a delicate balance between cartridge power, slide weight, and spring resistance.

Ten sample guns submitted to Army Ordnance in 1927 failed to result in any orders. One complaint from both civilian and military sources was that the gun in no way recreated the recoil of the .45, making the shift from rimfire to centerfire a rather jarring experience. The military in particular was interested in simulating the recoil aspects of bigbore shooting during recruit training. In 1931 the Standard Ace was released to the shooting public but never had much appeal.

Colt found the answer in a device designed by latter-day genius, David M. "Carbine" Williams of Godwin, North Carolina. Carbine Williams acquired his nickname as a result of his design of the .30 M1 Carbine of World War II fame. This handy-dandy short rifle was the recipient of about as much damning and praise as

No sooner had the Colt Model 1911 .45 ACP been adopted as the official side arm of the United States armed forces, than the Ordnance Command put in a request for a gun of similar design firing a .22 rimfire cartridge for the purpose of training.

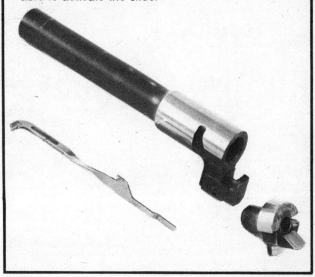

The original Colt Ace, .22 Long Rifle-chambered version of the .45 ACP was subject to frequent stoppages, because of the delicate balance between the inadequate energy supplied by the .22 cartridge and the weight of the large steel slide that it had to activate. The answer came in Carbine Williams' floating chamber, shown here behind (and in line with) the barrel. The chamber afforded added area for the expanding powder gases to work against, increasing the apparent or effective energy available to activate the slide.

Carbine Williams' floating chamber made such a sure-fire .22 pistol of the .45 ACP that Colt felt safe in offering a conversion unit for existing .45 auto pistols, exchangeable in seconds. Here is the .22 Conversion Unit on the gun (bottom) and off (top). The spare clip is shown under the assembled gun. The tiny twist of metal just under the slide is the ejector—a simple solution that actually works!

was Colt's .45 automatic pistol! In the service or out, you never found anyone who was neutral about the .30 M1 Carbine. They either loved it as a God-send or condemned it as God-damned. In the Pacific campaign particularly, the "Dog Faces" were disappointed in the lack of penetration of the straight-case .30 caliber, but it was never designed to punch through 6 feet of palm tree trunks or concrete bunkers. Used in the context for which it was designed, the .30 M1 Carbine *was, and is* an efficient combat weapon!

What made the M1 Carbine go was a tappet piston designed by Williams. In practice, gas was tapped from a hole in the bottom of the barrel and used to impel a piston backward a very short distance, a mere $1/10$-inch. That minimal movement imparted sufficient energy to the operating rod, to rotate and unlock the breechblock and extract the fired case.

The M1 Carbine wasn't Williams' only contribution to U.S. Ordnance. He also came up with a solution to a problem that had stymied Army designers for years, namely a way to operate a .30 caliber Browning heavy machine gun using .22 Long Rifle ammo. They laughed when Williams said he could do it, then gasped at the

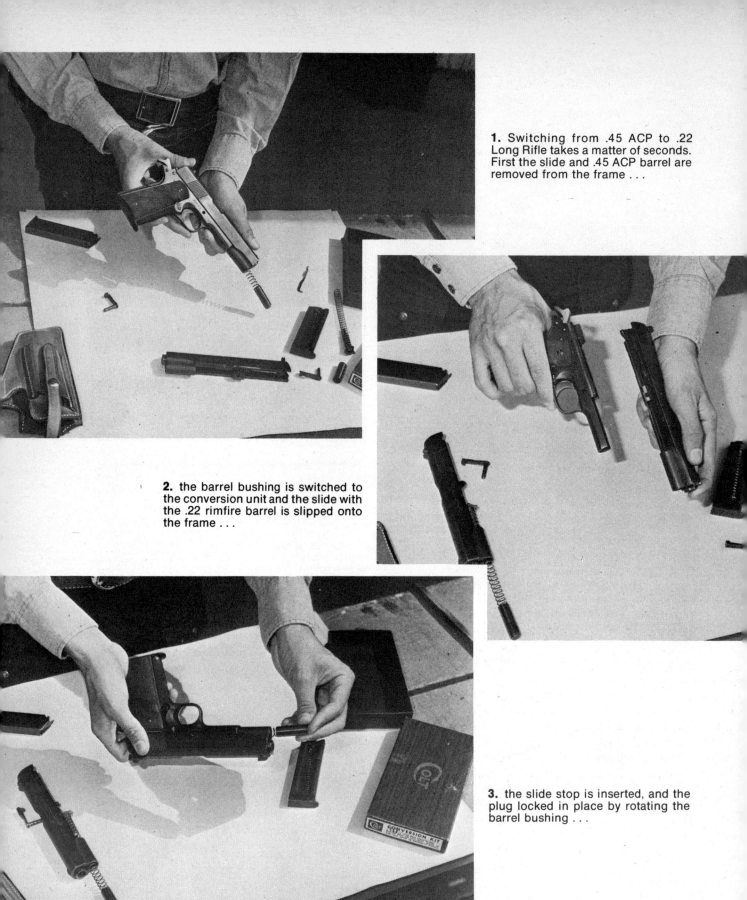

1. Switching from .45 ACP to .22 Long Rifle takes a matter of seconds. First the slide and .45 ACP barrel are removed from the frame . . .

2. the barrel bushing is switched to the conversion unit and the slide with the .22 rimfire barrel is slipped onto the frame . . .

3. the slide stop is inserted, and the plug locked in place by rotating the barrel bushing . . .

4. a loaded magazine is inserted . . .

5. and the slide cranked back to charge the chamber.

A clear concept of the .22 Conversion Unit can be gained from this sectioned view. Note that the barrel in the .22 unit is stationary. Only the floating chamber moves, to impart added initial push on the recoiling slide. Use of the floating chamber also increases the apparent recoil of the .22 chambered auto, making it a better training gun.

Colt discontinued the .22 Long Rifle chambered Colt "Ace" in 1941, but reintroduced it in 1978, with Colt Accro target adjustable rear sight, and ribbed slide. Colt advises that it cannot, as currently offered, be readily converted to fire .45 ACP ammo.

utter simplicity of his solution, and the ease with which existing guns could be altered to the new system, then converted back, in a matter of minutes. Once commissioned to do the job, Williams took just 6 weeks to come up with a .30 caliber recoil operated machine gun that fired .22 rimfire ammo without a stutter. His design utilized a "floating chamber," operating inside of the barrel like a tappet piston. Upon firing, expanding gases were released into the area ahead of the floating chamber. A simple law of physics was thus set into motion. When you can't increase the pressure you have to work with, but need more energy, allow more area for the pressure to work against.

This same unique design was incorporated into the .45 ACP conversion to .22 Long Rifle, commercially released as the Colt Service Model Ace .22 in 1937. Williams received a patent on this design on August 24, 1937. The system functioned with such reliability, that Colt felt safe in offering conversion units to attach to existing .45 ACP frames. Each Colt Conversion Unit included a new slide with target adjustable sights, a .22 caliber barrel complete with floating chamber, a 10-shot magazine, a bushing, a recoil spring, spring plug and spring guide, a substitute slide stop and stamped steel ejector. Switching from .45 to .22 and back took a matter of minutes. Owners of the Service Ace could purchase a Colt kit that converted it to a match grade .45 ACP, complete with ribbed slide, topped by a Stevens target-adjustable rear sight.

Colt officially discontinued production on the .22 Ace in 1941 but apparently continued to assemble pistols from existing parts until 1947. In all, there were about 10,935 Colt Ace and about 13,803 .22 Service Model Ace pistols produced. Production of the Service Model Ace continued after 1941—it was made in both 1942 and 1945, with the last serial number being SM13803.

After a hiatus of 33 years, Colt decided to reintroduce the Colt Ace .22 in 1978. This step seems all the more significant when considered in the light of the fact that Colt had just 2 years earlier axed their entire line of .22 rimfire handguns save for the Diamondback. According to a Colt factory representative, the new Ace .22 Long Rifle pistol, as currently manufactured, is not readily converted to fire .45 ACP ammo. The gun looks for all the world like a standard .45 frame with a factory-installed conversion unit. Logically, it should be convertible back to .45. But apparently not. "That may change at some time in the future," my informed source added with no degree of assurance.

The current .22 Colt Conversion Unit lacks several of the components included in the original. You must use your existing barrel bushing, spring plug and guide. Otherwise, it is about the same. The slide resembles the slide on a Colt Gold Cup, with a broad, low solid rib, topped by the Colt "Accro" rear sight with micro adjustments for windage and elevation. The generously wide rear Patridge notch allows ample bars of light on both sides of the broad 1/8-inch wide undercut front

Gunsmith Jim DeMarco and the author managed to wring out a .22 Conversion Unit alongside a .45 ACP Gold Cup and .38 wadcutter Gold Cup, in an accuracy comparison. The three guns delivered roughly equal groups.

sight. Inside, the slide reveals some milling cuts apparently made to lighten the weight a little. As with the centerfire version, the firing pin is shorter than the distance from rear to front of the slide. Thus, with the hammer down, *the firing pin does not reach the rim* of a round in the chamber. The firing pin depends upon the momentum imparted by the impact of the visible hammer to drive it forward and ignite the rimfire round. As with the .45, a light coil spring holds the firing pin rearward. There have been cases wherein this spring was a little *too* light, allowing the firing pin to fly forward as the slide closed, firing the chambered round. If your pistol should fire "doubles" from time to time, check for that situation. The same style of extractor is utilized, but ejection is accomplished with a twisted stamping that looks odd but nonetheless functions. It hooks into a relief in the left side of the barrel, makes a half-twist and slips into a milled slot in the slide. When the slide recoils, the ejector remains behind to kick out the empty smartly to the right.

The floating chamber is counterbored into the rear of the barrel, and actually constitutes the chamber for the .22 Long Rifle cartridge. Upon firing, it recoils back just .078-inch, confined by a slot in the barrel lug.

The 10-round magazine on the Conversion Unit is a marvel of adaptation. The angle of the grip and the magazine of the .45 ACP were at least partially dictated by the rimless cartridge that it was designed to feed. Rimfire .22 Long Rifles possess a pronounced rim that refuses to stagger neatly into a precise angle. Rather they tend to form part of a circle when laid out one above the other. The Conversion .22 clip allows the rimmed .22 Long Rifles to stack in an orderly manner in a progressively increased angle toward the bottom, yet still present themselves at the head of the line properly

angled to feed into the waiting chamber. The follower rotates as it descends to accommodate the sharper angle. Sometimes the magazine will fail to feed the final round in the stack. If the malfunction occurs often enough to convince you that the clip is the culprit, the easiest solution is a new magazine. A knurled button on the right side of the magazine facilitates loading.

All safeties are functional with the Conversion Unit in place, just as with the .45. The half-cock notch on the exposed hammer is not a safety! It is there only to catch the hammer should it start to follow the slide down—a condition often resulting from tuning the trigger pull too fine!

To install a Conversion Unit, you must remove the .45 barrel and slide in the normal manner and replace them with the parts furnished with the unit. You will have to use the same barrel bushing, spring plug and guide with the unit. Take care not to mix up the springs themselves. The spring furnished with the Conversion Unit is tuned to the lighter recoil of the .22 Long Rifle cartridge, which *is less,* despite the floating chamber.

Switching back and forth between center- and rimfire ammo doesn't require as much shifting of gears as it used to with the old Colt Ace, thanks to Carbine Williams' tiny floating chamber, which multiplies the recoil energy of the .22 Long Rifle about four times. Loaded, pistols in the two calibers weigh about the same, and the recoil is well within hailing distance. What more could you ask?

The idea of practice with low-recoil/noise/cost ammo is well served by the Colt Conversion Unit. However, it falls rather short of match accuracy, so the concept of using the same gun in center- and rimfire competition has never been realized. Most competitors get better results by using a .22 rimfire target handgun, such as

Colt .22 Conversion Unit aboard Government Model frame (right) was test fired in comparison with .38 wadcutter Gold Cup (left) and .45 ACP Gold Cup (center). Groups were roughly equal between the three guns. Later accurizing of the .22 Conversion Unit by the author improved groups from the smallbore substantially.

one of the fine Hi-Standard "Military Grip" models, which duplicate the grip angle of the 1911 .45 ACP.

I decided to try accurizing a conversion unit just to see if the idea was feasible. The usual slide-tightening procedures firmed up the fit with the frame. I utilized a four-fingered MK IV bushing to remove the slop between slide and barrel at the muzzle—.45 fans will be scratching their heads about now. Colt went to a lot of expense devising just the right configuration for the barrel that they pair up with their spring bushing, finally arriving at a cone shape with the large end at the muzzle, so that the bushing comes to a snug fit as the slide rams into battery. The .22 conversion unit is outfitted with a barrel possessed of a reduced diameter of about .573-inch, behind a ⅜-inch wide shoulder at the muzzle that mikes .579-inch in diameter on my unit—not at all what Colt had in mind when they designed the bushing! But it works! And you can't argue with success. The back end was pretty firm as it was. I toyed with the idea of making a slide stop with an oversized pin to take *all* of the play out, but decided to test-fire the gun on the range first. The results indicated that further tampering would be redundant. For side-by-side comparison, I had a Conversion Unit just as it came from the box, to function as my "control," plus the accurized version.

With the .22/45 firmly clamped in a Master Series Ransom Machine Rest, I proceeded to burn up a couple of boxes of Western Mark IV Super-Match pistol ammo, firing 10-shot groups at 50 yards. Control groups ranged from 6 to 7½ inches, about what I had expected. The accurized unit, firing from the same .45 frame, shot clusters that measured from 2½ to 3½ inches, center-to-center. That compares favorably with match-grade ammo from a .45 ACP that has been accurized! With the addition of a set of Pachmayr Signature Model Auto Pistol Grips that offers consummate control of an intractable .45, I feel that I have just about as good a competition .22 auto pistol as I'll ever need, plus a fine tool for keeping in shooting trim and practicing combat techniques at relatively low cost. You can fire a magazine full of .22 Long Rifles almost as cheaply as you can loose a *single* factory-loaded 230-grain .45 slug downrange.

If you have a Colt Conversion Unit on a .45 frame or one of the new Ace pistols, accurized or otherwise, it will pay you to try several brands of ammo in your little jewel, to see which performs most reliably and with greatest accuracy. In general, high velocity ammo is best for reliable feeding. Failures to feed are not entirely unknown to the Colt Conversion Unit, especially with standard velocity ammo. And it does tend to lead up some with ordinary outside lubricated lead bullets. You'll have fewer problems with fouling if you use copper plated bullets. In any case, always clean the gun soon after firing, with particular attention to the outside of the floating chamber, and the inside of the barrel where it is counterbored to accept the chamber. After a

thorough cleaning, I would recommend a new Teflon synthesized lubricant named, "Tri-Flon," that actually penetrates the pores of the metal and reduces the hazard of having the floating chamber freeze up on you.

Over the years, there have been other efforts at devising sub-caliber add-on units for the .45 ACP that met with varying degrees of success. In the 16th edition of the *Shooter's Bible,* in 1931, there was listed a device that replaced the .45 ACP barrel-slide assembly with a single shot tip-up barrel unit, secured to the frame with the slide stop. List price with a leather carrying case was just $16. I wonder what a collector would pay for one of those units today?

R. F. Sedgley marketed a more simple straightforward device, a .22 caliber barrel that slipped inside of the .45 ACP barrel, with a knurled nut at the muzzle to secure it in place. The .22 bore was offset to the right, so that the centrally located firing pin would impinge upon the rim of the .22 cartridge, and the existing extractor would grasp the rimfire case head.

Between the Great Wars, the Government Model .45 was altered by lengthening the spur of the grip safety and by the addition of an arched mainspring housing. A chamfer was milled in the frame at the rear of the trigger guard, and the trigger itself was shortened (which I fail to regard as an improvement!), and the gun redesignated the, "U.S. Pistol, Automatic, Cal. .45 M1911A1."

Even though World War II GIs weren't totally enamored of "issue" .45's, the fault lay primarily with poor training, coupled with some "loose-as-a-goose" pistols that came from a variety of contract makers enlisted to fill the wartime needs for hundreds of thousands of pistols in a hurry! In recent years, the .45 ACP has come to be recognized for what it is—the best damn combat pistol ever to come down the pike! Modern combat competition shoots are largely dominated by old "Slab Sides," and numerous law enforcement agencies have adopted it as duty weapon. Much of its current popularity can be laid to the efforts of Jeff Cooper. Jeff touted the assets of the .45 to me many years ago, before he became a well-known writer. He had already altered his safety to a duckbill configuration for easier functioning. That alteration is S.O.P. these days whenever a .45 is modified for combat. The standard carry is cocked-n'-locked, that is, hammer back and safety on. Looks kind of spooky in a holster, but it seems to be the quickest-into-action carry. Most modern holsters provide safety straps that go *under* the hammer, effectively preventing accidental discharge in the leather.

One of the primary advantages of an autoloader in a combat situation is the ability to reload swiftly under fire. As combat competition shooters perform the operation, the instant the slide remains open, signaling an empty gun, the left hand speeds for a loaded magazine usually carried tandem in a belt pouch. The right

A primary advantage of an autoloading pistol for combat use is the ability to reload quickly, by dropping the empty clip to the ground while a new, fully-loaded replacement is on the way.

presses the clip release dropping the empty magazine as the loaded one is enroute to the gun. The new magazine is inserted into the pistol grip with the left hand, and the right releases the slide. Elapsed time is usually about 3 seconds!

The idea of using low-cost, minimum noise, and zero recoil, ammunition in a bigbore centerfire gun is highly attractive from every angle! It's not a new idea. Nearly every military firearm of modern times has been duplicated or adapted to fire .22 rimfire Long Rifles.

During the reign of the M1903 Springfield, the U.S. Army used a series of .22 rimfire chambered look-alike rifles for training. Civilian rifle clubs also used the guns for training and competition shooting. External dimen-

sions and weight of the smallbore Springfield mimicked the .30-06 version almost exactly. Civilian versions were made available through the DCM with excellent single stage target triggers and fine Lyman target receiver and globe front sights, for only $40!

The German storm troopers of World War II trained with .22 rimfire "Sport Rifles," that resembled in every important aspect their service Mauser rifles. Not many of these rifles were imported into the United States before the war, but a lot of them came back as war souvenirs and they exhibited the usual impeccable German workmanship, finish, and target accuracy. Even the British S.M.L.E. .303 rifle had its .22 counterpart for training.

Rimfire Adapters

Various .22 rimfire adapters for other military pistols have been offered from time to time. Walther once made an adapter for their 9mm P-38. Now they manufacture a complete .22 rimfire pistol on the P-38 frame. Erma and Stoeger both made .22 rimfire adapters for the Luger, also. Parker-Hale even made adapters to change the ungainly British Webley and Scott .455 or .38 revolvers to fire .22 rimfire ammo.

Hunters afield in search of big game or varmints often come face-to-face with a toothsome squirrel or two, or perhaps a rabbit that would make a fine stew, but for one problem—the centerfire rifle would reduce any small animal to shreds. Hamburger on the hoof is anything but appetizing! But hold! Harry Owen, president of Sport Specialties, P.O. Box 5337, Hacienda Heights, CA 91745, offers the solution—a series of rimfire adapters to fit virtually any smallbore rifle, from the never-say-die .220 Swift, to more modern offerings such as the .222, .223, .22-250, .221 Fireball, etc. The adapters resemble steel cartridge cases for each caliber, with internal chambers for either the standard .22 rimfire or the .22 Magnum. Each chamber is situated as far forward as possible without having the bullet protrude beyond the end of the adapter, to avoid an unnecessarily long leap from case to rifled bore. The space behind the rimfire cartridge is taken up with a slip-fit soft alloy steel cylinder, or "Centerfire to Rimfire Converter," with a neoprene "O" ring positioned midway to hold it in position. At the front a chisel-shaped protrusion functions as the firing pin for the rimfire round. The rear of the soft steel cylinder has a small indentation machined into it to cradle the bigbore firing pin, preventing any peening action as the centerfire pin drives the cylinder forward to ignite the rimfire round. In use, the adapter is loaded with a rimfire cartridge, and the steel cylinder is inserted behind to hold the assembly together. Thanks to the "O" ring, even if you carried several adapters in a pocket or pouch, they would not become disassembled. In fact, if you anticipate using Sport Specialties rimfire adapters as survival aids, or merely for potting small game to enrich your wilderness

Rimfire adapters from Sport Specialties fit into a variety of centerfire smallbore rifles and handguns, and chamber standard .22 Long Rifle (as well as Shorts and Longs) or .22 Magnum ammo.

The adapters from Sport Specialties look like steel cartridge cases but inside they are reamed out to chamber either standard or magnum rimfire ammo. Here is the .220 Swift adapter for the .22 Long Rifle. The steel plug at the rear with neoprene ring, transmits the impact of the firing pin to the rim of the .22 cartridge.

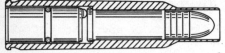

.22 LR/.222 Remington Adapter

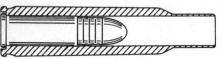

.22 LR/.222 Remington Adapter
Special Thompson Contender Version

Sports Specialties adapters for the highly popular .222 Remington are available in .22 Long Rifle for rifles and for the Thompson/Center Contender with reversible firing pin.

larder, it would pay to buy a minimum of five, and keep them loaded and handy at all times.

Because the adapters lack a bullet at the front, resembling just an empty case even when loaded, they will not feed through most magazines. The best way to handle them is to tilt the muzzle slightly down, with the bolt open, and just drop the loaded adapter into the empty chamber. It will extract in a normal manner. The empty case is removed from the adapter with an ejector rod furnished with each unit.

The Thompson/Center Contender pistol, with its either/or firing pin, that ignites center- or rimfire ammo with equal aplomb, takes a special adapter, without the converter. These are available for any of the .22 caliber Contender barrels, including the .22 Hornet, which is too short to make for a centerfire rifle because it doesn't allow room for the converter. The T/C Contender is ideally suited to the use of Sports Specialties adapters because of its top-break loading system. You can purchase one of the larger centerfire smallbore barrels, such as the .222 Remington, and use it either as a standard .22 or a .22 WMR, with the appropriate adapter.

Accuracy testing with a variety of centerfire smallbore rifles and the T/C Contender indicates that accuracy with the Sports Specialties rimfire adapters is ample for taking small game animals to average ranges of 50 to 60 yards. At those ranges, the bigbore sight settings resulted in a point of impact an inch or two low, but without any significant windage variations. Once the point of impact is established by range firing, you'll

have no difficulty in tagging a ptarmigan on the first try!

Sports Specialties sub-caliber adapters offer an ideal method for introducing a youngster to a centerfire rifle without his having to endure the huge "bang" and recoil right at the outset. Small-fry can get the hang of a big gun years sooner this way and take full bore ammo in stride when they have grown into it.

Rimfire adapters offer the additional advantages of hushed report for use in basement ranges. If you have one of the new Bushnell 4X to 12X variables with the adjustable objective lense, you can focus down to 50 feet. The Leupold Vari-X III with adjustable objective can be focused down to 50 feet with the aid of a low-cost add-on lens adapter from the maker.

If you don't have a close-focusing scope, you will likely have to revert to iron sights for indoor ranges. Most big game scopes are pretty fuzzy up close. If you find that it is possible to focus your scope well enough for basement target practice, be sure to carefully align your eye with the axis of the scope each time, because parallax of a big game scope at near distances is enough to affect your groups.

In addition to his rimfire adapters, Harry Owen manufactures sub-caliber adapters for various .30 caliber rifles, such as the .30-06, .30-30, .308, etc. that fire either the .30 M1 Carbine cartridge or the .32 ACP. The latter is excellent for taking small game in the field without blowing them to pieces. Harry will custom machine a sub-caliber adapter for just about any American-made cartridge. Harry also markets the Colt .22/45 ACP conversion unit by mail, with no FFL (Federal Firearms License) required, at 10 percent under the going list price. Not a bad deal what with today's poor markup on firearms and accessories!

CHAPTER 13

.22 Training for Tots

JUST HOW OLD IS "old enough" to start training your boy or girl in the .22 rimfire basics of shooting? This subject could very well engender some spirited debate with the distaff member of the family! I must admit that I hedged the question to some degree at our house, when my own son, Michael, was a stripling. I started him out at age 8 with a BB gun. By the time I purchased his first .22, he was pretty well indoctrinated with safety procedures as well as the basics of marksmanship. I felt it was high time for Mike to have a rifle, and when I heard that the Winchester Model 69 was discontinued and fast disappearing from dealer's shelves, I hustled out and bought the last 69A, with target sights, that I could find in town. The gift was presented 6 months later on Michael's 12th birthday.

As an average-sized 12-year-old, Michael had some difficulty handling the bolt action clip-loader, and the shooting jacket purchased at the same time, hung rather loosely around his sparse frame. But it wasn't too long before he grew into and then *out of* that jacket. The Model 69 still gets an occasional workout as an all-around able plinking/hunting rifle, though Mike currently favors his Weatherby Mark XXII tube-fed autoloader. Age and the ability to accept responsibility are linked to a high degree, but some youngsters are more adult than others in the same age bracket. So numbers alone are not the determining factor. Nor is physical development all that important. The *American Rifleman*, journal of the National Rifle Association, recently carried an article by a man who started his son out with a .22 rifle at age 3! He had to hold the gun for his son who yet lacked the strength in his little arms to support a rifle. At 6 years of age, the boy was a "veteran" shooter, looking forward to his first hunt.

Certainly most youngsters of 10 to 12 years are ready to learn the serious aspects as well as the joys of .22 rimfire shooting. A good starting point would be an NRA sponsored Basic Small Arms Training Course and Hunter Safety Course, available at any National Rifle Association affiliated rifle club. Many states now require the latter as a prerequisite for obtaining a hunting license. The NRA sponsors an entire program directed toward the development of junior marksmen, including a 15-stage marksmanship qualification course, featuring team and individual rifle matches on both postal (by mail) and shoulder-to-shoulder basis. If that sounds overly complicated on the face of it, let me assure you that the youngsters love it!

Encourage your child to join one of the more than 4,200 NRA affiliated junior rifle clubs across the country. He will enjoy the sportsmanship and competition of kids his own age. He can receive coveted Ranger awards from the NRA, along with brassards and badges, for visible proof of his skill, which command respect and often awe from his chums.

Helpful booklets are available from the National Rifle Association, 1600 Rhode Island Avenue, N.W., Washington, D.C. 20036, and the National Shooting Sports Foundation, 1075 Post Road, Riverside, Connecticut 06878.

If NRA clubs are not available in your area, you'll have to be your own instructor. Teach your child to open the action and check every gun for himself, even if someone assures him that the gun is unloaded. Then have him treat the empty rifle with all the respect due a loaded one. The one most important lesson that you must drum into your youngster's ears is: *WATCH WHERE THE MUZZLE OF THAT RIFLE OR HANDGUN IS POINTED!* The gun muzzle must *always* be pointed in a safe direction, whether *loaded or empty!* The direction of the gun muzzle *must* always be under control, even if the person carrying the gun should stumble or fall. I know of one deer hunter who was shot squarely in the middle of the back with a high-powered rifle when the man walking behind him stumbled and fell. Note that the safety was ON! The

How old is old enough? A sturdy lad of age 10 to 12 can handle the lighter target rifles without undue effort and is generally adult enough to accept the responsibilities involved with shooting. The tenets of safety are the most important consideration. Older boys make excellent instructors because they can still remember their own mistakes.

gun should have been carried *pointed to one side.* Then an accidental discharge would not have harmed anyone. Religiously observing that one rule—*KEEP THE MUZZLE SAFELY POINTED*—would virtually eliminate all gun accidents.

In the field, teach your child to absolutely identify his target before pointing the gun in its direction. I've lost count of the number of times that I have watched *adults* swing a rifle or shotgun toward a movement in the brush, or *even a sound—only to have it turn out to be another hunter!* That kind of behavior is inexcusable! One can only wonder where these people learned their field manners. Another precursor to disaster is to lose track of hunting companions, then swing on a bird or rabbit headed in their direction. A statistical study conducted by the NRA some years back pointed up that one situation as the most likely to result in serious injury or death.

Rabbits and ground squirrels will prove a more than adequate challenge to your young nimrod's budding talents. Your first lessons should stress safety and sportsmanship. Marksmanship and *stalking* are important but secondary considerations. Until he or she learns to instinctively watch the direction in which the gun muzzle is pointed, hunting should be done with the bolt handle up on a single shot and with an empty chamber when using a repeater. Very few shots will be lost during the second required to work the action, and your youngster will learn to value the first shot. Unfortunately, not many .22 rimfire safety mechanisms can be relied upon absolutely.

Father and child should wear blaze orange in the field—you don't want to be taken for a couple of

Encourage your youngster to join one of the more than 4,200 NRA affiliated junior rifle clubs across the country, to enter into competition with others in his general age group for coveted Ranger awards, brassards and badges, as proof of his shooting prowess.

"bucks" on an outing! Train your youngster to recognize the vital areas of game animals, and stress the importance of aiming at these particular spots, rather than the entire animal. Teach your son or daughter *not to shoot* at road signs, telephone poles, high tension wires or insulators, mail boxes, and farm animals. If you think that this goes without saying, let me assure you that I've witnessed all of the above at one time or another.

On plinking forays, always be assured of an adequate backstop. Many years before I acquired a .22 rifle of my own, I went plinking with a neighborhood boy in his backyard. The weed-grown vacant lot behind his house stretched for several blocks. The houses that ringed it looked small and distant. We failed to reckon with the boarding-house reach of an ordinary .22 Long Rifle! My friend opened the festivities by shooting a tin can from atop a fence post. Replacing the can, he handed the rifle to me. Instead of firing from offhand position as my friend had, I sought a steadier hold by kneeling. I little dreamed of the consequences of that simple act! It was only a matter of minutes before I was informed by a justifiably irate householder, whose window I shot out! By kneeling and firing at an upward angle, I had sent that bullet nearly two blocks, to an unintended destination. Such incidents result from lack of training and supervision. It could have turned out tragically. *I was lucky!*

If you start your child out shooting a rimfire at 6 or 7 years of age, likely he won't be able to manage position shooting with any degree of assurance. As a rule, youngsters this small aren't strong or well coordinated enough to manage even the lighter rimfire rifles. My son, Mike, was still a little short when he received his Winchester 69A for his 12th birthday, but I rebelled at trimming that fine little rifle at either end, so he just had to grow into it. He had something of a struggle at first, but time toughened his muscles. Meanwhile I started him shooting from a bench rest.

A bench rest transfers the burden of steel and wood from your boy's aching arms to a pair of sandbags, allowing the neophyte marksman to concentrate upon his trigger squeeze and sight picture, rather than yanking desperately as the sights waver in the vicinity of the bull's-eye. That way, boy and gun can realize the greatest accuracy potential inherent in both. Once he witnesses those tight little clusters on the target, he will never be content with patterns that resemble those from a shotgun, regardless of what position he shoots from!

As your child's strength and abilities grow, you can introduce the sitting position, which is steady and relatively easy to assume. Then teach him kneeling, then offhand, and last of all, prone. The prone position is the most accurate and the most excruciating to endure! Don't force it upon him until he is ready, and then only if he has a properly padded jacket to protect his elbows!

Your budding marksman must assume his share of the responsibilities of shooting. Let him fetch and carry to the limits of his strength. You won't hear any complaints. Boys take to guns like ducks take to water. The heritage of shooting is bred in the bones of Americans and God grant that it will always be thus! Such names as Daniel Boone, David Crockett, Sergeant Alvin York, et al, ring like bells in the ears of Americans. They demand and deserve reverence and respect. Without the rifle, the republic of the United States of America would not exist.

Start small youngsters shooting from a bench rest. It takes the weight off trembling immature muscles and transfers it to sturdy wood. Then the youngster can concentrate upon holding and squeezing. If you have two kids, it's safer to have only one shooting at a time. The other can act as spotter.

Once he becomes accustomed to those tight little clusters that result from shooting from a bench, your youngster will never be satisfied with "shotgun" groups, regardless of what position he shoots from.

(Below) A young recruit to the ranks of shooters may need a little help at first with such basic tasks as filling the rotary magazine of a Ruger 10/22. It's guidance like this that starts the new shooter off on the right foot.

Teaching Firearms Care

Along with the pleasures of shooting must go the work of caring for the gun. Every young shooter should clean his own gun. One day down the road, he will savor the sweet smell of Hoppes #9 with a nostalgic longing for a time that can't be called back, save through watching his own son experience the same wide-eyed thrills of gun ownership and use. Note that a lifetime of shooting will not wear out a .22 rimfire barrel, but one enthusiastic lad with a cleaning rod can convert it to a smoothbore in a few evenings! I suggest having your son clean the gun with every use, although you and I know that it hardly requires such frequent attention. The idea is to instill a habit of cleanliness that will carry over to bigbores at a later date, and teach respect for equipment of all kinds. One swabbing with a solvent-soaked patch, followed by a dry and then an oiled patch is all that's required. No need to wear out the rifling. Remember all cleaning should be done from the breech end, unless the design of the gun precludes this. The action, especially the bolt face, should also be cleaned with solvent and oiled, and the exterior of the gun wiped clean overall. If it is scope sighted, cover the lenses to protect them from contact with oily fingers!

The First "Shooting" Experience

If you take your son or daughter to shoot on a target range, don't forget the ear muffs! True, the .22 rimfire, when fired outdoors, doesn't make enough noise to warrant hearing protectors, but the bench next to you might be occupied by someone sighting in his .375

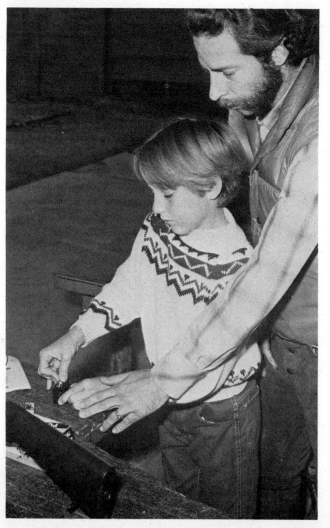

After your son learns the basics of marksmanship at the bench rest, introduce him to the sitting position, which is steady and relatively easy to assume.

H&H Magnum. From time to time, in my wanderings, I've encountered a few uncouth individuals who think it's great fun to hand a youngster a 12-gauge shotgun, or heavy-recoiling rifle, inviting him to shoot it, without advising the boy that said gun *bites at both ends*. The result is a few chuckles for Mr. Uncouth, and perhaps a life-long habit of flinching for the youngster!

Occasionally, it may fall upon you to be rather harsh with your son, if he transgresses a basic edict of safety. However, for the most part, you'll find that he responds far more tractably, and will learn much faster, if you employ frequent words of praise for a job well done, and restrain criticism.

Very young marksmen have an attention span that dissolves as swiftly as an ice cube on a hot grill. When you see little minds wandering, it's a good time to change the subject, liven up the lecture with some shooting demonstrations, or conclude the class for the day.

While it's a fact that young eyes have a rubber reach that seems to focus notched rear, post or bead front sight, and bull's-eye in the same look, you'll give your youngster an edge if you install a peep receiver sight, or better yet, a scope on his rifle. Some might call this "coddling," but it just makes the job that much easier for all hands (especially the instructor!), and iron sights are now in about the same league as a manual transmission, anyway. He can always learn to use them later. Meanwhile, he can concentrate upon breathing, trigger squeeze and holding, without the added hazard of learning open sight alignment.

A quality telescopic sight certainly simplifies the matter of aiming for youngsters. It's very easy to comprehend that the cross hairs must quarter the bull's-eye, and the problem of canting the rifle is more readily explained and corrected. If you use open sights, a drawing showing the relative positions of rear and front sights, and their relationship with the target is worth the proverbial "million words." It's easier for youngsters to understand a center hold than a 6 o'clock sight picture.

At the beginning of every range session or plinking trip into the country, it is well to reiterate all of the rules of safety, or better yet, let your shooting student quote them to you. Then make certain that the words are carried over into actions.

A youngster thrilling to his first experience with

Charts, such as this one from Mossberg, are helpful in illustrating the proper way to assume various shooting positions. Like swimming, once the positions are mastered, they remain for a lifetime, improving performance on the range and in the field alike.

The most useful all-around position in the field is kneeling, because it offers a high degree of steadiness without restricting your field of view too much. Sitting and prone positions usually place the shooter too low to see over surrounding vegetation.

(Below) After watching his father demonstrate proper offhand stance, this young shooter tries it for himself. The Ruger 10/22 is good rifle for small-fry because it is short and relatively light. Observe the obvious safety precautions necessary with an autoloading rifle.

firearms is apt to regard the .22 Long Rifle as a veritable giant killer, capable of bringing to bag anything from a two-headed dragon to a grizzly bear. At the same time, he may well lack an awareness of the actual danger inherent in the tiny cartridge. A field demonstration is in order! Just for effect, load up with Stinger or Xpediter ammo and pulverize an apple, orange, grapefruit, or a small can of tomato juice. The resultant explosion will register on a young mind more graphically than hours of lecturing or dire predictions.

It's a good idea to lock guns away from small children while you're gone from home. The temptation to show off to playmates may be more than his young conscience can resist. Even ammo left available can present a hazard. Given a hammer and a .22 cartridge, a kid just does what comes naturally! Then BANG! Maybe no harm done. Then again, maybe someone will end up with brass shrapnel in his belly, as a neighbor's boy did many years ago. Keep the ammo *safely* stored.

Shooting can be the salvation of a youngster who was slighted when the muscles were handed out. It doesn't require super physical dimensions to compete with a smallbore rifle. Girls can shoot on an equal footing with boys, and often beat the pants off the best of them. Even many physically handicapped youngsters can shoot and win, gaining a source of pride that they would be hard pressed to derive in any other sport.

Older boys make excellent tutors for the younger ones, because they can remember well the difficulties that they themselves encountered along the way, thus are likely to be more understanding and less impatient with imperfect performance.

Choosing the Right Gun

The age and physical size of your son or daughter will likely dictate in large measure your choice of a .22 rimfire rifle. A very small youngster would be well served by the Savage/Stevens Model 72 Crackshot, a

recreation of the easy-loading falling block single shot that so many lucky lads grew up with and learned to love around the turn of the century. With 22-inch octagonal barrel sporting traditional open sights, abbreviated forend, and short stock for short arms, this breath of nostalgia from a wistful era makes a fine teacher rifle even today.

Another single shot Martini-type falling block is the Stevens Model 89, weighing 5 pounds, with 18½-inch barrel, styled after the image of the Old West saddle carbine, with a dummy tubular magazine under the barrel. Like the Crackshot, it has a visible hammer that must be manually cocked for each shot. Both are handy to load even with stubby BB Caps, which make just fine plinking ammo at close range. Neither of these rifles adapt readily to scope mounting.

Rounding out their trio of youngster-oriented rifles is the single shot bolt action Stevens Model 73-Y, with abbreviated 18-inch barrel and stock shortened to a 12½-inch length of pull, for an overall weight of just 4¼ pounds. By contrast, the standard Model 73 has a 20-inch barrel and 14-inch length of pull. The 73-Y represents a fine lightweight bolt action for any boy or girl whose measure from armpits to fingertips is approximately 2 feet. The Model 73 is self-cocking, but has a safety that goes on whenever the bolt is raised.

The slightly older youngster could readily handle the 5-shot clip-loading bolt action Stevens Model 34, weighing 5½ pounds, with 20-inch barrel and 14-inch stock. A clip-loading bolt action rifle can be effectively converted to a single shot by the simple expedient of removing the clip.

Remington took advantage of that idea, and carried it a step further by including a single shot insert with every one of their clip-loading bolt action Model 581 rifles. It is generally conceded that a single shot rifle has the highest safety factor for teaching young shooters. It requires that the action be operated and a new round manually inserted for every shot. It engenders a deep appreciation in the shooter of tender years for the importance of each and every shot! He has time to ponder the success or failure of his last effort while he reloads, making a more thoughtful, therefore more careful marksman. The only trouble with a single shot rifle, is that as soon as a lad or lass learns the basics, and aspires to advanced target competition or perhaps some rabbit hunting, that single shot becomes too slow. The inevitable result is that daddy has to invest in another, *repeating* rifle. Now every buyer of a Model 581 can enjoy the best of both worlds. The single shot adapter is installed by merely removing the stock and inserting it in the opening where the detachable box magazine usually enters. The fact that the stock must be removed to convert the bolt action back to the status of a repeater, discourages casual tampering by ingenious young hands! Then when the student "graduates" to repeater status, dad doesn't have to spring for a new rifle. All he needs is a few minutes with a screwdriver to effect the metamorphosis from single shot caterpillar to beautiful *repeater* butterfly!

Remington's 100 percent single shot Model 580 is still available, weighing 5 pounds, with full 24-inch barrel and man-sized walnut-finished Monte Carlo stock, and utilizing the same rugged action with six artillery-style locking lugs, plus the best trigger action to be found on any medium-priced rimfire rifle. The 580 is available as a "Youth Model," with the stock shortened to 12⁵/₁₆-inch pull. The Model 581 would seem to be a superior investment, and you can trim the stock length yourself, if required. More of that in Chapter 14.

When buying any rifle for a small-fry, keep in mind the arm length and strength. Most sub-teeners have difficulty holding up a rifle that weighs over 5 pounds. Conversely, choosing too light a rifle offers the certainty that he will soon outgrow it. You can buy a cheap interim gun in the knowledge that it will one day have to be abandoned in favor of a larger one, as inevitably as the tricycle must give way to the two-wheeler.

Most modern rimfire rifles are dimensioned to fit adults rather than youngsters. The length of pull—that is the distance from the trigger to the center of the butt plate—is usually from 13½ inches to 14 inches. The normal length of pull of 13½ inches is best fitted to an individual with a distance from arm pit to finger tips of approximately 28 inches. You can tailor one of these "man-sized" rifles to fit your own youngster by shortening the stock to an appropriate length.

The bolt action Marlin 101 is designed specifically for the youngster, with 22-inch barrel and shortened stock. It weighs just 4½ pounds, easily manageable by the youngest marksman or nimrod. This single shot rimfire features an easy-feed loading ramp, and must be *cocked by hand after loading*. To this end, an easy to grasp "T" shaped cocking knob is provided. Open sights are standard, and the receiver is grooved for a scope. The genuine American walnut stock has a Monte Carlo comb and full pistol grip.

Always deeply aware of the utmost importance of gun safety, the Marlin Firearms Co. has initiated a new and novel safety program, hinging upon an utterly simple plastic tab that fits into the trigger guard of almost any rifle and must be removed before the gun can be readily fired. As the tab is removed, your eyes pick up the imperative question in full capital letters of red on a white background, "IS IT LOADED?" Gun dealers have been invited by Marlin to place these patented tabs in *all of their guns being sold*. Marlin also sponsors an annual Hunter Safety Essay Contest for students enrolled in State Hunter Safety Courses, plus an ongoing "Safety Pledged Hunter" program for which thousands of sportsmen sign up every year.

Another excellent single shot bolt action teacher rifle is the Harrington & Richardson Model 750, weighing 5 pounds, with 22-inch barrel and full-sized stock. The 750 features H&R's "Fluid Feed" loading platform to speed the cartridge into the chamber with a minimum of fumbling, plus thumb safety and loading indicator. The walnut-finished American hardwood stock has a scope height Monte Carlo comb, and the receiver is grooved to accept tip-off mounted scopes.

Kids love lever actions, perhaps as much as their dads! A couple of lever action repeaters deserve special mention in connection with kids. The Ithaca Model 72 Saddlegun weighs approximately 5½ pounds, not featherweight perhaps, but not bad for the average teenager. Although quoted in the statistics as 18½ inches long, the barrel measures only 17½ inches for-

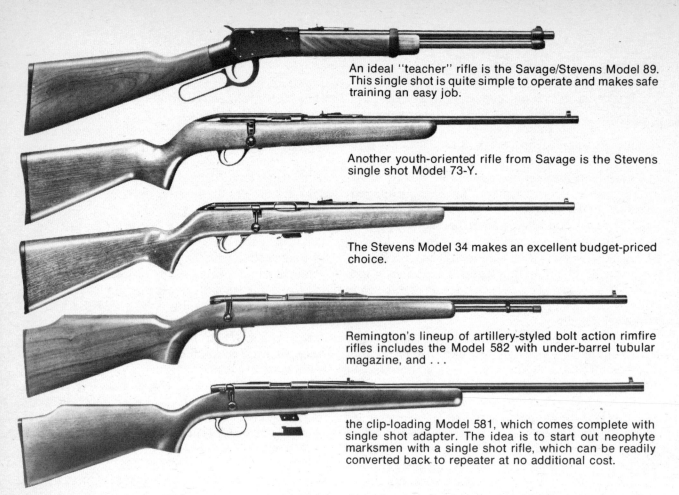

An ideal "teacher" rifle is the Savage/Stevens Model 89. This single shot is quite simple to operate and makes safe training an easy job.

Another youth-oriented rifle from Savage is the Stevens single shot Model 73-Y.

The Stevens Model 34 makes an excellent budget-priced choice.

Remington's lineup of artillery-styled bolt action rimfire rifles includes the Model 582 with under-barrel tubular magazine, and . . .

the clip-loading Model 581, which comes complete with single shot adapter. The idea is to start out neophyte marksmen with a single shot rifle, which can be readily converted back to repeater at no additional cost.

ward from the receiver. Although the length of pull is a standard 14 inches, this highly accurate, reliable carbine is nonetheless readily manageable by most youngsters. And I can guarantee you he won't outgrow this one!

Ithaca Gun Company, Inc. continues to offer their Model 49 lever action single shot with a Martini-style falling block. It has a visible hammer that must be manually cocked after the rifle is loaded. The hammer has an automatic rebounding safety. Under the 18-inch barrel is a dummy magazine tube for that western carbine look. Rifle weight is 5½ pounds. The straight stock with checkered grip area is available shortened to fit small boys.

The Browning BL-22 merits mention also, because it weighs only 5 pounds, with 20-inch barrel and 13½-inch length of pull. The extremely short lever throw is a snap for small hands, and no chance of getting a finger pinched between the lever and the trigger, because the trigger travels with the lever. Both lever guns come with open sights, but both will accept tip-off mounted scopes.

Once widely favored, especially by plinkers and small game hunters, the pump action .22 rimfire rifle is seldom seen these days. One of the few pump guns still available is the Remington Model 572 Fieldmaster, with tubular magazine holding 20 Shorts, 17 Longs or 14

Long Rifles interchangeably, under a 23-inch barrel with open sights, backed by grooved receiver. At 5½ pounds, the Fieldmaster is a good candidate for any young marksman/nimrod.

Several years back, the Brazilian arms maker Amadeo Rossi, revived the old Model 62, quietly interred by Winchester in 1958 after producing almost half-a-million units. Because of its smooth action and ability to continue in action in the face of total neglect, the 62 became the darling of shooting galleries across the country.

The Rossi is a snappy, fast-handling little 5¼-pound rifle, with tubular magazine running almost full-length under the 23-inch tapered barrel. It holds 20 Shorts, 16 Longs, and 14 Long Rifle cartridges. The uncomplicated slide action of the Rossi is as dependable as a Model A Ford and packs just as much nostalgia for anyone who knew and used the gun as a youth.

Because the Rossi is a part-for-part duplication of the old Model 62, it shares that rifle's one failing—it must be used with open sights. The breech block has two locking lugs extending sideways at the front. These drop into two matching slots in the receiver. To disengage, the breech block must rise upward and slide back to extract the empty case and reload. Ejection is out of the top. Neither scope nor receiver sight works well with this arrangement. The current importer of the

A rifle handy enough to fit most teenage shooters is the lever action Ithaca Model 72 Saddlegun.

A quartette of autoloading rifles. Top to bottom: Ruger 10/22, Remington Nylon 66, Mossberg Plinkster, Winchester Model 490. In general, top two are best for short shooters, and bottom pair for older, stronger kids.

Model 62 is Interarms of Alexandria, Virginia.

Accustomed as they are to automatic everything, from dishwashers to automobiles, today's youngsters are predisposed to autoloading rimfire rifles as well. Remington's Model 552 Speedmaster, is a lookalike for their pump action Fieldmaster, except that it reloads without the aid of the shooter. Southpaws will appreciate the empty case deflector bolted just behind the ejection port, to keep flying brass and unburned powder from stinging the shooter's cheek. The Remington Nylon 66 rates a mention if only because it weighs an incredibly light 4 pounds, a feather for the smallest of fry!

There is little doubt that the biggest hit with the smallest shooters is the shortest .22 rimfire autoloader, the Ruger Model 10/22, with remarkable rotary 10-shot clip, weighing just 5 pounds. It has an 18½-inch barrel attached to a drilled and tapped alloy receiver topped off by a one-piece genuine walnut stock. The reasonable price on the standard model carbine makes this an attractive option for a doting dad.

Highest in price, but also tops in precision, is the Weatherby Mark XXII, with man-sized selected walnut stock—a good bet for a strapping teenager—garnished with hand-cut checkering, plus genuine rosewood forend tip and grip cap over white-line spacers, 24-inch tapered barrel with open sights and grooved

receiver. The Mark XXII has an exclusive feature, a thumb lever that converts it to one-shot-at-a-time loading. After every shot (with the lever engaged) the breech block remains open. To close it, the shooter must consciously move the lever forward. The Mark XXII is available as either a clip-loader or with under-barrel tubular magazine.

Other rimfire autos in the "man-sized" category are the Browning BAR-22, with tubular magazine, noted for its accuracy; the Savage Model 80, tubular repeater, with 20-inch barrel and Monte Carlo walnut stock; and the Winchester Model 190, with tubular magazine holding 17 Longs or 15 Long Rifles, and two-piece hardwood stock.

Encourage your son to enter into competitive shooting as soon as his physique allows. A husky 12-year-old can just about handle a 6-pound Mossberg Model 340B, with micrometer receiver sight and ramp-target front. By the time he outgrows that gun, he'll be ready for the big time, and some big bucks from dad, if he's to compete on an even footing with the rest of the gang!

Handguns and Youngsters

If there's anything kids love more than rifles, it's pistols! When is he old enough to start shooting a handgun? As soon as your child learns the basics of good range and field manners and can hold the gun up

If there's anything that youngsters like more than .22 rim-fire rifles, it's .22 pistols or revolvers, such as this Harrington & Richardson Sportsman. Young arms waver under the burden of a pistol at arm's length. Better teach them to shoot two-handed, at least at the outset.

Youngsters love to participate and contribute something of worth. They can be highly helpful in such range chores as recording group sizes cataloging data, keeping track of what ammo was used, etc.

without excessive shaking, he or she is ready to try a rimfire revolver. If you only have an autoloader, load it *one shot at a time,* until you're satisfied that your pupil understands that an autoloading pistol is *always loaded and deadly* with the merest twitch of the trigger! If you have a pistol that has a slide stop which holds the slide open when the magazine becomes empty, just leave the magazine in the gun. Then as each singly-loaded shot is fired, the slide will remain back. It becomes a simple matter to insert a cartridge into the chamber and lower the slide.

Such relatively lightweight revolvers as the Charter Arms Pathfinder, Hi-Standard Sentinel, and Harrington & Richardson Sportsman, are easy for your youngsters to handle and the mechanism is simple to comprehend. Teach your son to cock the gun for each shot. Stubby fingers can't manage accurate double action fire, and there's no purpose to be served by attempting it.

Parting Thoughts

Allowing your son to help with such range chores as sighting in a bigbore hunting rifle will give him insight into the practical application of his smallbore training. Measuring and recording group sizes, cataloging data, can all be handled by any bright youngster of a dozen years or more, and it relieves dad of some time-consuming duties, leaving him free to shoot more!

Around the turn of the century, a couple of generations of lucky boys grew up in a largely rural America, full of optimism, pride, courage, *and a love of hunting,* born of countless hours afield with their trusty .22s. The tousle-haired, freckle-faced boy with a straw in his mouth and a single shot Stevens nestled in the crook of his arm, has faded from a blessed reality into a nostalgic Rockwell poster. Millions of acres of farmland and just plain *country* have given way to concrete jungles and super highways, but the .22 rimfire rifle remains the one best bridge between a boy and his hunting heritage.

You men who were lucky enough to grow up with a .22 owe it to your youngsters to help them share some of the thrills you knew. By all means, teach your son to shoot a .22 rimfire! You never know what may grow out of it! None other than modern-day gun genius, Roy Weatherby, began his illustrious career in firearms with a one-shot-at-a-time Stevens Crackshot rifle, shooting crows and rabbits on a Kansas farm. Neale A. Perkins, head honcho at Safariland Leather Products was somewhat luckier. His doting dad presented him with a Winchester Model 63 autoloading rifle, with the stock shortened to fit his 12-year-old arms. These are but two of many who began shooting with rimfires, and went on to conquer far greater forensic frontiers. Your youngster could well be another John M. Browning in the making—give him a chance!

CHAPTER 14

Simple Self-Smithing Your .22

SOONER OR LATER, every dyed-in-the-wool gun buff is going to reach for a screwdriver and a file, and endeavor to "improve" his rimfire rifle or pistol. The degree and depth of this improvement will vary according to his talent with tools or lack thereof.

I first became a "gunsmith" at about age 10, when I resurrected a rusted relic of what *had been* a bolt action single shot .22 rifle, from the dump, and adapted the stock from a worn out air rifle to the .22 rimfire. I shot it that way for a couple of years, then cut the barrel off to about 7 inches and band-sawed a pistol grip stock for it. I shot that for a time, then sold it for a whole dollar bill—not a small amount to a youngster in that time and place.

I was lucky in that I grew up around an automotive repair shop owned by my father. All manner of tools were readily at hand, and I had free rein to use them, including the deadly band saw, which just about terrified my poor mother!

With the years, I acquired a number of other firearms, including about a dozen Enfield and Springfield military rifles that I customized and sold. During World War II, I made pocket money by purchasing worn Colt single actions and rebuilding them for resale. I had as many as 24 in process at one time.

My first magazine article described a method that I developed for installing a short action on a single action Colt. It appeared in the *American Rifleman* for May 1945, with Admiral "Bull" Halsey on the cover!

Tools for Gunsmithing

If you're going to dabble in gunsmithing, you may as well start out properly equipped, at least insofar as hand tools are concerned. Gunsmiths of frontier America performed perhaps 90 percent of their metal work with a handful of files, which they used with uncommon skill. In this modern day you are somewhat more favored by a diversity of tooling likely limited only by your budget!

Even if you're not planning a serious attack upon the ranks of gunsmiths, you must write to Brownell's, Inc., Route 2, Box 1, Montezuma, Iowa 50171, for their free catalog of gunsmithing goodies that will have you digging deep for funds. Brownell's has been supplying gunsmithing professionals for over 38 years with all conceivable types of tools and equipment. While you're at it, mail a check for $10, for a copy of *Gunsmith Kinks,* a unique manual written by the professionals themselves. You've never seen anything like it!

Another free catalog well worth your time and postage is available from Jensen Tools & Alloys, 1230 S. Priest Drive, Tempe, Arizona 85281. Jensen offers the very finest precision hand tools of every description.

You'll never get off the ground as a gunsmith without a proper set of screwdrivers. Ordinary household screwdrivers are to a professional gunsmith's screwdrivers as a bin of coal is to the British crown jewels! The most efficient and versatile screwdriver set ever devised is the #9600 Kit, from Chapman Manufacturing Company, Route 17, at Saw Mill Road, Durham, Connecticut 06422. The kit includes a standard style screwdriver handle, and extension, 15 separate bits, and a ratchet wrench attachment, all conveniently packaged in a 4½ x 6-inch steel box. Chapman screwdrivers are of hardened chrome nickel molybdenum alloy steel, ground with square sides so that they won't skip out of a screw head and burr it, as do ordinary screwdrivers.

If you're gettin' up a little in years, you'll appreciate the assistance of an Opti-Visor from Brownell's. This device consists of a band around your head, with a swing-down visor containing a pair of magnifying lenses to help see those small gun parts and observe the progress of your work. I recommend the #3 which magnifies 1¾ times, and focuses at 14 inches. If you wear reading glasses, the focusing distance can be shortened by using your glasses in conjunction with the magnifier.

While we're on the subject of eyes, don't forget the

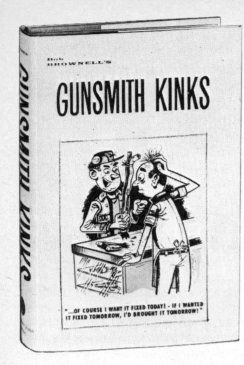

Even if you're not planning a serious attack on the ranks of gunsmiths, you should send for Brownell's *Gunsmith Kinks,* a book written by the pros themselves with a wealth of useful information.

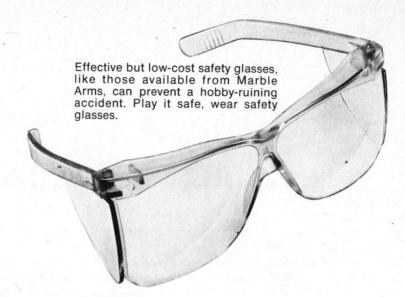

Effective but low-cost safety glasses, like those available from Marble Arms, can prevent a hobby-ruining accident. Play it safe, wear safety glasses.

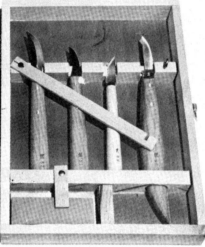

Woodworking will go more smoothly if you have a set of wood chisels. Treat them with respect, and they'll last a lifetime.

need for protective eyeglasses when grinding small parts, etc. Marble Arms markets a rugged yet low-cost set of shooting high-impact plastic glasses with side shields. The amber color actually aids vision under artificial or dull light.

Basic necessities for even minor repair or customizing of your rimfire guns is a set of fine-cut Swiss needle files. Four styles will suffice: equalling (rectangular from the end view), square, three-square (triangle), and half-round. Or you can order Brownell's set of 12 to handle any fine cutting need. You'll be less likely to break your precious Swiss files if you buy the little universal handle sold by Brownell's. You need a few flat mill files of various sizes and cuts for general cutting chores. There are a variety of specialty files, such as one for cutting sight dovetails and one solely for checkering steel. The latter is used by some smiths to checker the front grip strap of a .22/45 auto pistol, for example.

If you have a budget-priced .22 auto pistol, you might wish to emulate that practice.

For smoothing up trigger sears, you'll want several slip stones, a triangular medium India, a "knife blade" hard Arkansas, and a square coarse India. Brownell's also has some unique "flexible Stones," in a variety of cuts that in effect wrap-around the work and get into impossible corners.

An ordinary hacksaw will see constant use in any gun buff's workshop! As will a coping saw, and a set of several sizes and cuts of wood rasps. Add medium and lightweight ball-peen hammers as well, and a center punch or two. If you like unique tools, Brownell's sells an adjustable, spring-loaded, one-hand center punch that banishes forever the old bugaboo of having the punch move ever so slightly and placing the drilled hole off-center.

A low-cost trio of pin punches with replaceable tips

will soon become your best friends if you work much on autoloading rifles. Many have pins that are staked into the trigger groups and must be driven out to work on sears, then restaked when replaced. These pins are hard on drift punches—hence the need for replaceable tips.

It requires a high degree of skill to perform a slide-tightening procedure on a .45 ACP or perhaps in your case a .22/45, without making a mistake and tightening too much! Brownell's markets a set of precision gauges that take the guesswork out of it. These gauges will more than pay for themselves on one job, especially with the high cost of replacement slides these days! Anyone with a standard Ruger auto pistol will greet with pure delight the Brownell Ruger trigger with adjustable backlash setting built in. Brownell's sear blocks with vertical pins place trigger and sear in proper juxtaposition for adjusting sear angles correctly. As an alternative, Brownell's offers trigger adjustment pins that drop into the appropriate holes in the gun itself, again to show correct relationship between sear and hammer.

If you plan to play with stock making or repair, a set of wood carving chisels will prove invaluable, plus barrel channel chisels and files. Useful on wood or metal is the Vibro 88-08 tool that can be used for stippling steel or wood, and engraving steel. With wood-working blades, it can even be used for inletting, carving, and checkering.

Other handy small tools are a hand grinder, trigger scale, feeler gauge, a variety of pliers (especially needle points) and plastic-tipped hammers to use when a modicum of force is required without damage to steel. You'll need an ordinary 1-inch micrometer and a vernier caliper.

You should have a fairly sturdy bench with a precision vise, not the discount store variety, nor yet one of those fine boat-anchors currently being imported from the Far East. Each one weighs about 2 tons and is capable of all of the precision of a sledge hammer! Professional gunsmiths seem to favor the Versa-Vise, which will tilt to just about any angle and will hold small parts without crushing them. I like the Palmgren machinist's vise which can be clamped into any standard drill press to hold items for precision drilling, as well as functioning as a precision bench vise, with optional swivel base.

If you're already a home do-it-yourself gunsmith, you no doubt have a drill press and at least a small lathe in the garage. If not, think seriously about getting them! Hand drills have limited utility around a gun buff's shop, because of the inability to drill holes that are absolutely square with the surface, and exactly placed.

Brownell's markets the unique Unimat 5-in-1 precision lathe/drill/grinder, which can be set up for almost any gun job short of barrel-turning and sells for about the cost of a good drill press alone.

Gunsmithing Schools

By now, you probably think I'm trying to sell you on

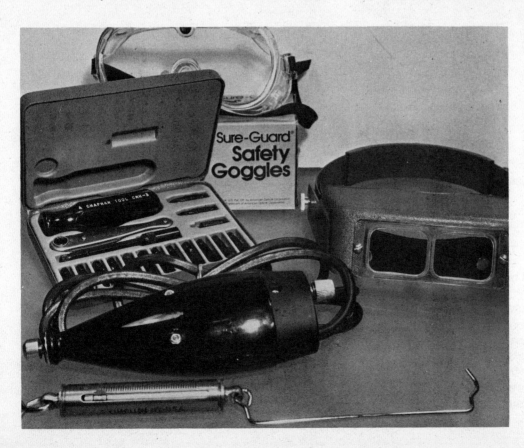

Some of the tools required even by amateur gun craftsmen to do an acceptable job are: a set of Chapman screwdrivers; Opti-Visor; Vibro 88-08 engraving tool; and trigger scale. At the rear are a pair of American Optical Company Sure-Guard Safety Goggles, vital to gunsmithing with safety!

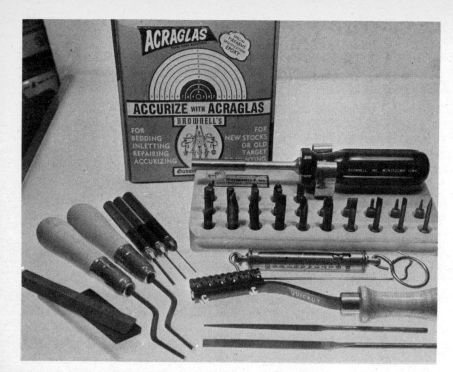

Do-it-yourself gun craftsmen can customize their .22 rimfire guns with a basic set of hand tools. Shown here are some of the best: Brownell's Acraglas bedding kit; a quality screwdriver set; medium and hard Arkansas stones for honing sears; duo of checkering files; trio of replaceable-tip drift punches; trigger scale; Quickut barrel-channel rasp; and a pair of fine-cut Swiss needle files.

Yet another lineup of hand tools includes: vernier caliper for precision measuring; feeler gauge; Handee Grinder; Brownell's screwdriver set; Swiss needle files; medium and hard Arkansas stones; trigger scale; and author's favorite Palmgren precision drill vise.

the idea of becoming a professional gunsmith! Well, you could do worse! Competent gunsmiths are surely in short supply. Those that are around are worked half to death trying to keep up with demand. Gunsmiths are among the few people left in the world who aren't chained to our increasingly urban society. They can choose to reside and work in a rural community, usually adjacent to good hunting, because that's where the action is. Personally, I think I took a wrong turn somewhere in life. That's where I should be today!

Even if you're not interested in making a profession out of gunsmithing, it makes an engrossing, rewarding hobby, and you can make a little pocket change by working on the side for friends—money that you can use to buy more .22 rimfire rifles and pistols, without having to justify the expenditure to the better half! A good many men looking forward to early retirement

have their skills at gunsmithing to fall back upon for added income during retirement. Also, a gunsmith enjoys a unique position in community life. He's looked upon with as much respect and a lot more friendship than the local doctor.

Gunsmithing is one of the few skills that can be self-taught to a large degree, especially if you have had a modicum of machinist training in school, so that you can operate a lathe and drill press with fair facility. Most home gun craftsmen begin by botching up a few tired old guns, then working into better quality arms as their skill increases. There are a number of excellent books currently available.

We're not trying to rush you into anything, but if you're a young man in search of a career in this day of uncertainties, take a hard look at gunsmithing! You can spend 8 years in college preparing to be a physicist, as did my son, and find that no one needs physicists!

Today, the embryonic gunsmith can follow many well-charted routes to his chosen career, attending one of the half-dozen or so resident gunsmithing schools. Such campuses as the Colorado School of Trades, Lakewood, Colorado; Lassen Community College, Susanville, California; Oregon Institute of Technology, Klamath Falls, Oregon; Pennsylvania Gunsmithing School, Pittsburgh, Pennsylvania; and Trinidad State Junior College, Trinidad, Colorado, offer comprehensive classroom instruction in all phases of gunsmithing.

There is a viable alternative to anyone interested in gunsmithing either as a career or an absorbing hobby. He can take a correspondence school course. Certainly measured in terms of knowledge acquired versus dollars expended, a correspondence course clearly cuts the problem down to size—a size that virtually any pocketbook can handle. To examine just one outstanding example, the "Gun Pro" course offered by the North American School of Firearms, 4500 Campus Drive, Newport Beach, California 92663, requires a total expenditure *well under* $600! (And they accept Master Charge!)

What does the student buy for that nominal sum? He gets a million dollars worth of specialized knowledge, packed into 15 comprehensive lessons, or "Units." Immediately upon enrollment he receives the first two Units. Return of the completed examination from Unit I triggers delivery of Unit III, leaving the student working on Unit II during the turn-around time. Thus he is never left without work on hand. Unit III is accompanied by the initial kit of "Basic Gun Pro Tools," including a set of hones for smoothing actions and trigger pulls, a professional gunsmith screwdriver set designed *not* to burr screw heads, a trigger pull scale, a .30-06 No-Go gauge, and an assortment of shimstock. Later mailings include such goodies as throating reamers, length-of-trigger pull and drop gauges, a professional set of checkering tools, a Speer Ballistic Calculator, and finally the Powley PSI Calculator and Powley Computer for Handloaders, devised by one of the ballistic geniuses of our age, Homer S. Powley.

Two large-capacity three-ring binders accompany the lessons, providing a permanent reference, to be consulted by budding gunsmiths should puzzling problems develop later. Feedback from North American School of Firearms graduates who have indeed become gun pros, stresses the timeless reference value of the bound texts.

Each individual lesson from North American is divided into a "Study Unit," detailing theory and background information, coupled with a "Gun Shop Unit," covering in depth and detail subjects as basic as stripping and refinishing a stock, to projects as complex as constructing a muzzle loading rifle, lock, stock, and barrel. Exploded drawings, and step-by-step photos lead the student through a variety of workshop projects, to promote practical practice as well as mental involvement. Employing the latest teaching techniques, North American incorporates self-checking exercises into each Study Unit, allowing the student to gauge his own success, in effect rewarding him for a good performance, and pointing up any weak areas. The material is written in an interesting as well as instructive manner, couched in concise, clear language, without ever talking down to the students. The three-part glossary, "Let's Talk Guns," provides a guide to gun jargon. Special supplements augment the text with such

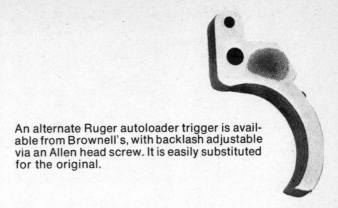

An alternate Ruger autoloader trigger is available from Brownell's, with backlash adjustable via an Allen head screw. It is easily substituted for the original.

titles as "How to Get Your Federal Firearms License," "How to Import Firearms," and "Home Gunsmithing Safety." In addition, students receive a subscription to *Shotgun News,* the newspaper marketplace for gun buffs.

Gunsmithing You Can Do

Adjusting Trigger Pull

The single most useful thing that you can do to improve your .22 rifle or handgun is to hone the trigger sear to result in a smooth, light, crisp trigger pull. In my experience, about one in 10 rimfire rifles comes with an acceptable trigger pull. The balance ranges from lousy to absolutely abominable! Some of the pulls that I've seen on rifles meant for the tiny fingers of small-fry would give King Kong cramps!

Among the easiest to work on are single action revolvers and visible hammer rifles, which share the same style of sear/hammer relationships. In the interests of safety, gun makers usually endow these with deep hammer notches that all but engulf the sear, with the result that the trigger pull is long and creepy! A trained marksman can shoot just about any trigger and achieve a fair level of accuracy, but a duffer will suffer with such a trigger! You can attack this problem from two directions—reduce trigger travel to gain a crisp-feeling pull, and smooth the sear surfaces to get rid of the grind and crunch usually present, plus reducing the weight of the pull. An ideal trigger pull on a field rifle or pistol should be about 2½ to 3½ pounds in weight, and "break" without discernible movement or creep. The third factor involved is "backlash," or trigger movement *after* the sear has released. This is far more important with a handgun than with a rifle, because it is possible to disturb sight alignment of a handgun before the bullet leaves the bore. It's possible with a rifle also, of course, but not nearly so likely because the inertia of the rifle is far greater and resists movement, plus the rifle is better supported at three points instead of just one.

Disassembling a single action revolver is a pretty straightforward affair. Just remove the screws from the

Visible hammer rifles and single action revolvers have similar sear set ups. Shown here is a cutaway of a Single Action Colt, illustrating the relationship between the trigger sear and hammer notches. Note that the angle of both are wrong.

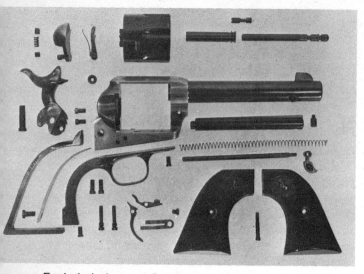

Exploded photo of Colt Peacemaker shows economy of parts in Sam Colt's revolver.

The do-it-yourselfer might find the New Model Ruger Single Six more complicated to work on with the increase in parts.

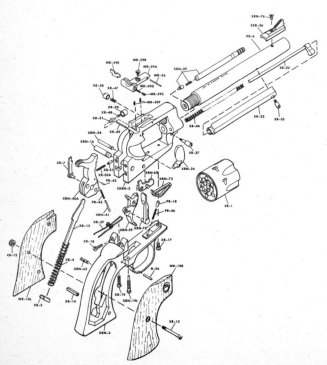

trigger guard and backstrap, which is usually a one-piece molded alloy unit on modern-day rimfires. That is all except for the Iver Johnson Cattleman, which is a true replica of the original, with trigger guard and backstrap separate. You can observe the sear angles from the bottom, but a better idea of just how they mate can be gained from the cutaway photo of an original Colt Frontier. One of the wonders of Sam Colt's original product was the paucity of parts. Note the exploded photo of a genuine Colt to appreciate just how few pieces were involved to work the wonders of the Peacemaker! The Ruger New Model Single Six is shown in exploded drawing. A few additional parts were installed to oblige the government's drop test requirements, but the same basic simplicity prevails, and the sear engagement still functions much as before.

The full-cock hammer notch and trigger sear must be square and parallel in order to have contact over their full width. The angle of these parts should, as observed from the side, be just slightly hooked, so that squeezing the trigger cams the hammer back ever so slightly! As delivered from the factory, the full-cock hammer notch may be hard to distinguish from the safety notch, since it is hooked so much, resulting in those brutal trigger pulls. A line drawn from the notch through the center of the hammer pivot hole represents zero hook. You want just a slightly steeper angle than that. An excellent way to be certain of getting it right, is to place the hammer in a machinist's vise, as shown, leaving only the amount of metal that you want to remove showing above the

If the angle of the sear on a single action revolver is too steep, it can be altered by stoning. A handy way to assure that the resulting angle will be correct and that the sear will be square with sides of the hammer is to place it in a machinist's vise like this, with just the amount exposed that you wish to remove.

jaws. Use a coarse stone to bring the notch down to the level of the vice jaws, then smooth with the fine India, followed by the hard Arkansas. Do the same with the trigger sear, removing no more metal than absolutely necessary to achieve the correct angle. When mated, the trigger and hammer will now have total contact, and the weight of pull will be greatly reduced but still remain safe.

The creep will remain, however! The obvious method for eliminating it would be to just remove metal from the top of the full-cock hammer notch, but that could introduce more problems than it relieves. It's likely, that as the hammer is rotated down after that adjustment, the safety and loading notches would strike the trigger sear. You can effectively reduce the depth of the hammer notch by drilling a hole just below it with a high speed $1/16$-inch bit, about $1/8$-inch deep, angled to miss the hole for the hand pivot. Drive a tight-fitting pin into the hole. File, then stone it down to allow the trigger an adequate bite into the full-cock hammer notch.

This system used for the Colt revolver works equally well with slight adaptation on nearly all visible hammer rifles, and most single action revolvers, and even a few autoloaders, long and short.

Single action revolvers make great "starter guns" for budding gunsmiths. They are easy to understand and simple to repair. With the high cost of new parts today, you can restore the originals by welding up the broken triggers, hammer sears, etc., and filing them back to the

(Right) Visible hammer rifles such as this Marlin 39A resemble the sear/hammer relationship of a single action revolver. The same methods can be used to improve the trigger pull.

original dimensions, using a good part for guidance.

Next to Colts, there are more Ruger single action revolvers around than anything else. The old model Rugers were basically the same as the Colt inside, save for the substitution of coil springs for the flat springs used in the Colts. The New Model Ruger Super Single Six .22 rimfire revolver is a whole new ball game. Introduced in 1973 to conform with Federal regulations stipulating that a revolver had to withstand being dropped directly on the hammer without firing a live round in the chamber, the New Model Ruger incorporated a transfer bar, which is raised by the trigger to carry the hammer impact to the frame-mounted firing pin. With the trigger forward and the transfer bar in a lowered position, the hammer has no contact with the firing pin, hence cannot fire the gun even if you put it in a rock crusher!

The new action entails a somewhat more complicated disassembly procedure: remove grips; cock the hammer and slip a nail into the hole in the mainspring strut;

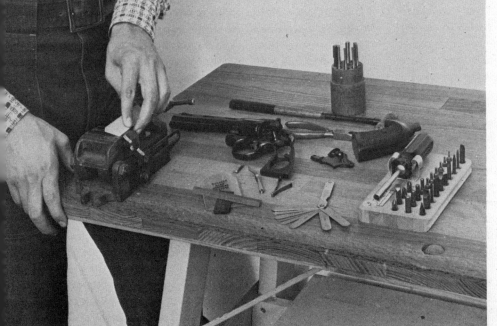

The single most useful thing that you can do to improve your own rimfire rifle or pistol is to hone the sears to improve trigger release.

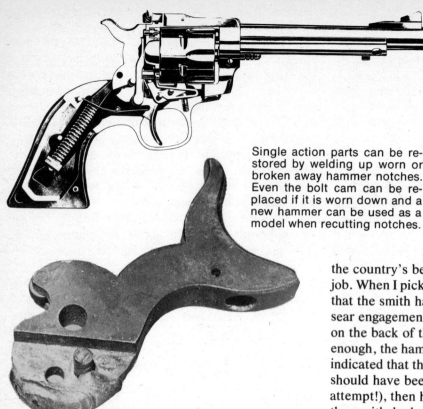

Internally, the Ruger New Model Super Single Six has been altered to use a transfer bar, which "transfers" the impact of the hammer to the frame-mounted firing pin. Note when hammer is down and trigger forward, the hammer has no contact whatsoever with the firing pin. The New Model may be carried with all six chambers loaded, with complete safety.

Single action parts can be restored by welding up worn or broken away hammer notches. Even the bolt cam can be replaced if it is worn down and a new hammer can be used as a model when recutting notches.

lower the hammer and remove strut with spring attached; remove the screws holding the grip assembly to the frame (memorize positions because lengths vary); remove grip assembly, taking care not to lose the hand spring and plunger located in a hole right/rear, and the bolt spring just ahead of the trigger mortice; invert the frame and press down the gate detent spring, releasing the trigger/bolt pin to be pushed out with a drift punch; push out the hammer pin and remove hammer/hand assembly.

A little judicious stoning of the working surfaces will smooth out the Ruger action considerably. Take care in stoning the sears that you merely *polish,* not *reshape* them. Everything is pretty close to right the way it comes from the factory!

Changing pistol or rifle barrels even on .22 rimfires sort of fits into the post-graduate category, but sooner or later, you'll get around to it. You can construct your own barrel vise with a couple of magnum-sized Allen bolts and some steel plates. The barrels can be gripped with wooden blocks or aluminum alloy blocks drilled to near barrel diameter and then sawed in half through the hole. Make the hole just a little on the nigh side, and the soft material will adapt to the barrel's shape and dimensions. Again, rebarreling falls into the "post-grad" category—it's not for the novice.

Tinkering with triggers on double action revolvers calls for some pretty astute study! Even the pros sometimes screw up on these. I remember turning over a prize Gold Seal Smith & Wesson .38 Special to one of the country's best smiths many years ago for a trigger job. When I picked up the gun, I immediately suspected that the smith had made the pull too light. I tested the sear engagement by cocking the gun and pushing hard on the back of the hammer spur with my thumb. Sure enough, the hammer fell! That should never happen! It indicated that the sear angle was reversed from what it should have been. I had to do it over myself (my first attempt!), then have the sears hardened again because the smith had removed so much metal that he had penetrated the casehardening on both the hammer and trigger.

If you can't resist trying to improve the single action trigger pull on a double action revolver, confine your efforts to the use of the hard Arkansas stone. You can't remove enough metal with one of these to get into trouble, and you might smooth it up some. The double action pull can likewise be smoothed up by lightly polishing all contact surfaces with the medium India followed by the hard Arkansas stone.

If you encounter a set of grips on a double action that are tightly wedged onto the straps, resist the temptation to pry them loose with a screwdriver. You may scratch the revolver, and you're almost certain to dent the wood of the grips where they join the straps, leaving an unsightly gap. Instead, loosen the screw holding the grips, leaving it in place with the screwdriver still in the slot. Now tap the handle of the screwdriver with a light hammer, forcing the grip panel on the offside away from the frame.

Take care in removing the sideplate of any double action revolver. Make certain that you have the correct screwdriver for each individual screw by placing the driver blade in the screw slot and looking to see that it bottoms in the slot, and that it is not too wide. If the driver blade is too thick and therefore doesn't reach the bottom of the slot, it will certainly burr the screw! If the driver blade is too wide, it will score the sides of the countersunk hole occupied by the screw head. A few minutes carelessness here can ruin the appearance of a new gun!

If the screws stick, clamp the revolver between padded vise jaws, below the frame, on the grip straps. In using the screwdriver, remember to exert as much pressure *down* on the screw as you do torque to turn it. If the screw refuses to yield to reasonable pressure, douse it with Liquid Wrench or some other penetrating oil, and let it rest awhile. Place the screwdriver back in the slot, rap the handle smartly with a light hammer. Often the impact will loosen the screw. Conversely, if you want to tighten a screw so that it stays put, tighten it as tight as you can, then tap the driver handle with a hammer. You'll find that you can get an extra quarter-turn that way.

After the screws are out, don't try to pry the sideplate free from the frame! Instead, hold the gun in the palm of one hand, sideplate uppermost, and use a plastic tipped hammer to lightly rap on the grip frame jarring the sideplate loose without raising any burrs.

It's a great temptation to cut coils from the rebound slide spring on a Smith & Wesson K-22 or .22/32 Kit Gun, to lighten both double and single action trigger pulls. If you don't get careless, you can get away with this. The spring *is stronger* than absolutely necessary to do its job of returning the trigger to battery after firing. However, go slow! Cut one coil. If that still leaves the spring a little stiff, cut one more—but stop right there! In the interests of safety, it shouldn't be lightened too much!

The flat mainspring on a Smith is generally no more than adequate to its job. Thinning it to reduce the trigger pull weight could well result in misfires. The same goes for the "V" shaped spring of the Colt double action. Smith & Wessons with the flat spring do have a means of adjustment lacking in the Colt—it's a strain screw located at the bottom front of the forestrap, which can be backed off a little without creating a problem. Tool

marks on the inside of the frame and sideplate can be lightly stoned off for added smoothness. Go easy, though. You don't want to introduce excess tolerances between frame and innards. Sometimes you'll find a slight burring around the edges of the frame where the sideplate touched. If you should stone this back level, you'll be left with unsightly white areas. A better cure is to burnish them back down, using a highly polished, rounded piece of steel, held almost level with the sides of the frame.

Before final reassembly of the revolver, clean the frame, sideplate, and all working parts thoroughly with a solvent to remove any grit left by the stones. Wipe dry, and lubricate with Outer's Gunslick graphite

The V-shaped mainspring of the Colt double action does dual duty, driving the hammer and pressing on the rebound lever, which in turn presses upon the hand. Grinding the spring to lighten trigger pull can result in problems. Best leave it alone!

To remove the sideplate on a double action revolver, rap the grip frame smartly with a plastic-tipped hammer, to loosen the plate without burring the sharp edges where it mates with the frame. *Don't* pry it out with a screwdriver.

grease. Only a thin smear is needed to eliminate drag and wear. During reassembly, be sure that you replace all of the parts, *including the hammer block!*

The sideplate on any quality double action revolver should seat fully flat with no more than finger pressure. If it resists, look for the reason. Never resort to a hammer! The worst offense that you can commit against a fine revolver is to cross-thread a screw. Start all screws with the fingers and make sure that they are threading in freely. Sometimes this will involve several false starts before the threads engage properly. Don't be impatient!

To check for proper timing, cock the revolver slowly single action, while holding the cylinder from turning freely with the other hand. If the sears engage before the cylinder turns far enough for the bolt to enter the slot, you have a timing problem. The reason for inhibiting rotation of the cylinder is to prevent it from continuing to rotate by momentum alone after the hand has ceased to turn it. Sometimes the bolt will engage during single action fire, but fail to lock the cylinder during double action. Remember that the hammer doesn't come back as far during double action. This problem is usually masked by the speed of double action giving the cylinder sufficient momentum to lock most of the time. Also, the trigger will continue to the rear after releasing the hammer, turning the cylinder into alignment as the hammer drops. During those random instances when the cylinder fails to align properly, the shooter finds unexplainable flyers on his target, and his nearby neighbors start swatting at imaginary bees, as the flying bits of lead bite them. The shortest route to correcting a timing problem is to replace the hand with a new one. Normally, replacement hands will be slightly long, and require some stoning to fit.

Just about a week ago as I write this, I was at the Yorba Linda I.W.L.A. target range, when a couple of the shooters appeared to be having trouble with a new Smith & Wesson K-22. They vowed that they were going to send it back to the factory as defective. It seems they couldn't close the swing-out cylinder. It flatly refused to go back into the frame. Inasmuch as they had been shooting the gun for over an hour before the problem came to light, I didn't see how it could be a factory defect, so I asked to see it. They were glad enough to have someone else analyze their problem! I pushed the shell extractor back and peered underneath. A few innocent looking granules of unburned powder lurked there—the cause of all of the problems! A few squirts from the snorkel of my spray can of Brichwood Casey Gun Scrubber dislodged the powder grains and the cylinder closed without resistance. This is a recurring problem, but not serious if properly understood.

Parts Hardening

From time to time, you'll encounter sears that are soft. You can test on a corner with a sharp file. If the file

cuts, the metal is too soft. No matter how good a pull you manage to get, it won't last because the metal surface will wear away too swiftly. You can harden small parts like triggers and hammers yourself, using Kasenite. You need a heat source hot enough to bring the parts to cherry red. Those little propane bottles with a blow torch tip won't quite hack it. The Ridgid Propane Shop Torch is one budget-priced unit that can do the job.

Hold the part in a pair of cheap needle nose pliers (you'll ruin a good pair), and play the torch flame over it until the part becomes cherry-red in normal room light. Then plunge it into a can of Kasenite and stir around until it cools. The part will emerge with a thick crust. Return it to the torch and slowly burn away the crust. At this point, the part will be glass hard, and must be drawn back. Polish one flat surface with fine carborundum, and reheat until that surface comes to a straw color. Allow to cool slowly. The trigger, hammer, et al, will be hard enough to resist wear, but not so hard that they will be brittle and easily broken.

Removing Backlash

Backlash, that is trigger movement after the sear's release, is easy to handle on some guns, impossible on others. Late model Smith & Wesson revolvers have an adjustable stop, but the older ones make no provision for removing backlash. Even so, it's a simple matter to insert a small steel or brass rod into the rebound slide spring. The rod must be small enough to move freely but not a sloppy fit. Use a wooden kitchen match to determine the approximate length, by trimming it a little at a time, until the trigger just releases the hammer sear. This fitting is best done with the mainspring and rebound slide spring removed. Cut the steel rod just slightly longer than the match stick, to allow final fitting, with the rebound slide spring in place. In use, the rod will back up against the rebound slide pin in the frame, and the rearward movement of the slide will be limited, in turn stopping the trigger motion. It is advisable to leave a fraction of a millimeter of motion after the sear's release, to avoid excess wear on the sear.

One method that removes backlash on most rifles and pistols, including single actions is to drill the back of the trigger mortice in the guard and insert a pin. File until it

An inexpensive but handy tool for the pro or semi-pro gunsmith is this front sight installer/remover from Williams Gun Sight.

Small parts can be casehardened with Kasenite and a Ridgid Propane Shop Torch (both available from Brownell's). Often sears are soft, and require casehardening to prevent excessive wear.

Autoloading pistols, such as the Ruger Standard Automatic, will further tax the ingenuity of the home gun tinkerer, but they can be coped with, given thought and careful tuning. Exploded view of the Ruger Automatic reveals relative simplicity of the basic mechanism. The hammer/sear relationship is not unlike that of a single action revolver.

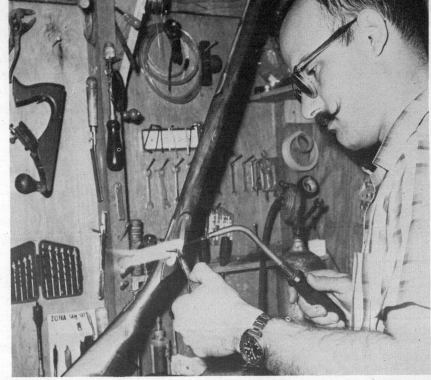

just allows the trigger to release the hammer. Be careful that the safety notch isn't striking the trigger sear! That condition can exist without harm in the absence of a trigger stop, because the trigger gets out of the way before the hammer notches hit it. But with a stop installed, the trigger is locked in position.

Barrel Shortening

The ideal way to shorten a barrel is to remove it from the action, chuck it up in a lathe and cut it squarely, then crown the end. Not too many of us have a large enough lathe for that. The other method is to hacksaw it, with attention to keeping the cut as square as possible, then use an ordinary machinist's square to true it up. All of the old gunsmithing manuals advised using a succession of brass balls with lapping compound to establish the inner curve of the crown. That's a bit much! But it is viable to use a sharp countersink to chamfer the inside of the bore. Hold the barrel vertical in a vise and come down lightly from above with a lightweight ¼-inch variable speed hand drill, turning as slowly as possible, allowing the countersink to center itself. If you have a hand-crank drill, that's better yet, because you have more control over the tendency to chatter.

Stock Refinishing

Stock refinishing is a simple, almost goof-proof job that anyone can enjoy! Modern preparations take most of the elbow grease out of it. In the past, it was always necessary to do a thorough sanding job before any efforts toward refinishing could be made. Today, we have Birchwood Casey Gun Stock Finish Remover, which quickly purges the old finish, *without raising the wood grain!* That leaves only a light finish sanding to do before staining and filling. Another light sanding with fine paper, and you're ready to finish. Either GB Linspeed or Birchwood Casey Tru-Oil will give you that boiled linseed oil finish.

Although both oils are based upon the traditional "boiled linseed oil," they are formulated with quick-drying agents that have taken the drudgery out of attain-

Stock refinishing, if done correctly, can result in a far more attractive rifle. Most rifles are delivered from the factory with perfunctory finishing, and kits such as this from Williams make the job easy by supplying the needed materials in a handy package.

ing a true oil finish. You shouldn't rub these oils. You merely spread them on in thin coats and allow to dry overnight. Sand lightly between coatings with #320 or #400 paper to remove any uneven coverage. After the pores are filled, put on a final coat and don't sand. The finish will glow softly with a look of quality normally found only on custom rifles.

With an oil finish, slight scars picked up in the field can be quickly covered with another light rub of oil. A faster-on but less durable finish can be had with polyurethane spray, available from a number of makers. I prefer the Behr-Manning satin spray because it escapes that bright sheen. However, it seems that most people like brightly shining stocks, so if that's your style, use the bright spray. You can cut some of the gloss with a light rub of wet-or-dry #600 paper. Then wipe it down with Totally Dependable Products' Stock Slik for just the right amount of gloss.

Birchwood Casey makes the chore of stock refinishing super easy by putting everything that you'll need into a trio of packaged kits, each tuned to the degree of effort and time you want to spend.

If the stock that you're refinishing has a dent (not gouge!), you can probably raise it rather than having to sand all of the surrounding area down to the depth of the dent. To raise the dent, heat an ordinary iron and place it over a very damp, not dripping, corner of Turkish toweling. The object is to drive the steam down into the wood, swelling it back up to its former level. Sand off the finish in that area first, so that the steam can penetrate the wood pores. After raising the dent, allow the stock to dry thoroughly before going back to sand away the roughness caused by the steam.

Bluing

Bluing is another area where Birchwood Casey shines (if you'll pardon the pun), with a selection of products that take you from battered to brightly-refinished in short order. B/C goes beyond the usual brush-and-dab cold blues. They offer do-it-yourselfers a cold-dip processing kit, complete with a sturdy yard-long, reusable plastic bluing tank and all the accoutrements required to completely blue your .22 rifle or pistol. There are enough chemicals to refinish as many as 10 guns, with a shelf life up to several months. In use, the Birchwood Casey immersion bluing kit calls for first degreasing the gun, then treating with Blue and Rust Remover. With the stock or grips taken off, the action stripped and the old bluing removed, you polish out any nicks or scratches in the steel surfaces, finishing up with #600 wet-or-dry paper, always working in a lengthwise direction. With the polishing completed, you return the barreled action and other polished steel parts to the Cleaner-Degreaser solution. The gun must be handled with woodel dowels in the ends or with plastic-coated wire from this point forward. You can't risk getting any fingerprints on the surface! Also, the gun must be suspended in the bluing solution, not resting upon the bottom of the tank, in order for the bluing to evenly affect the entire surface. The gun must remain immersed in B/C's Perma Blue for 60 to 90 seconds. Then flush it under running water and hang it to dry. Carefully rub down with steel wool, still avoiding finger contact. It usually requires about three trips to the tank to result in a deep blue-black. The finish is somewhat less durable than that resulting from a hot salts blue job, but the cost is far less, and the process is one that is easily mastered by home craftsmen.

A number of companies market cold bluing solutions or pastes, but few of them are actually designed for a total blue job. Rather, they serve well as touch-up or repair blues, to cover scratches and worn areas.

When using any immersion bluing system, always disassemble trigger groups, bolt assemblies, etc. Springs and, most importantly, alloy parts, should not

This full-spectrum cold bluing kit from Birchwood Casey takes cold bluing out of the "touch-up" department into total coverage, with sturdy plastic tank, capable of accepting any ordinary-length rifle barreled action. All needed solutions are provided in the kit, as well as needed abrasive materials.

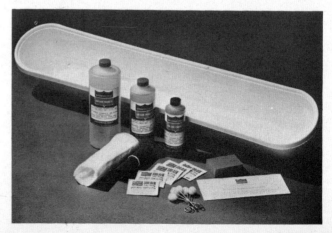

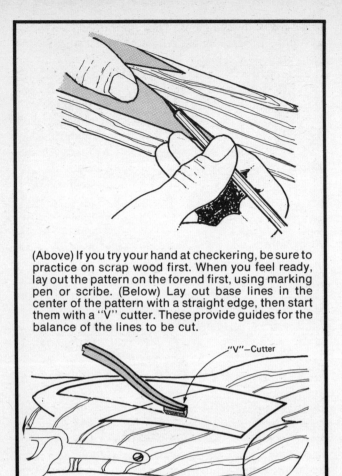

(Above) If you try your hand at checkering, be sure to practice on scrap wood first. When you feel ready, lay out the pattern on the forend first, using marking pen or scribe. (Below) Lay out base lines in the center of the pattern with a straight edge, then start them with a "V" cutter. These provide guides for the balance of the lines to be cut.

"V"—Cutter

be subjected to bluing salts! B/C also offers several products for blacking aluminum, brass, or even soldered joints, that can deface a job with bright silver lines around ramp sights, etc.

Checkering

One customizing job that any halfway handy home smith can tackle with a clear conscience is checkering his own .22 rifle. Dem-Bart markets a "Starter Kit," containing three tools, an 18 lines per inch spacer and two individual cutters. Hardened steel cutting blades are easily replaceable, and extras are included in the kit. A good way to get a feel for the job is to recut the checkering that already exists on one of your rifles. Usually, the checking is impressed by the factory. The look can be greatly improved by going over it and making it a true hand-checkering job.

Before going for broke on a real gun, try your hand at checkering a few chunks of flat close-grained walnut with simple patterns, copied from some gun that you like. Or you can order life-sized patterns from Brownell's to simplify the job. Several simple patterns are available for starters, such as numbers 15, 17 and 18. More complex patterns can be attempted after you master these. The pattern is laid out on the wood with

the assistance of a plastic ruler and a dark marking pencil. Make your first cut a shallow one, all around the borders. At the end of each straight pass, you stop at this line. If you have a tendency to run over the border, try stopping just short, then go back later and carefully finish each line. Note that you want to create diamonds, not squares! Watch the angle at which the lines intersect.

When you feel confident enough to tackle the gun stock, lay out the pattern on the forend first. Go through the entire routine of cutting the pattern there before attempting the pistol grip area. You need the practice! A full pistol grip presents several compound curves that can throw you. Be sure to lay out the base lines in the center of the pattern with a flexible straight edge, so the rows of diamonds won't curve. The angle of the diamonds should run parallel to the forend and in line with the angle of the pistol grip.

Use shallow cuts to lay out the lines for the entire pattern before attempting to deepen them. Then go back and, using a light hand, cut each line a little deeper each time until the diamonds become pointed. Use an old toothbrush to frequently clean out the pattern and the cutter. If the cutter starts to drag, clean it. A dull cutter can tear out the diamonds, ruining the entire job. You'll need patience, especially the first time, but it's fun and a good job is a source of pride!

A great way to get experience at home gunsmithing is to buy a few beat up old .22 rimfire rifles, and refurbish them. After rebluing and refinishing the stocks, if you can bear to part with them, you can sell them at a handsome profit and plow the money back into tooling. Then buy another gun, or two, and do it all over again. In that way, if you make a few mistakes, you don't have to answer to customers, or feel bad about botching up one of your prize guns.

Stock Shortening

Want to be a hero to your sub-teenager? Whether boy or girl, your child "person" will be thrilled to get the gift of his very own .22 rifle. Even the "youth" rifles from most makers are a little more than a 7- through 10-year-old can handle comfortably. One way to hedge the problem is to purchase a standard sized rifle and trim the stock to fit your youngster's arm length. One rule of thumb that works well is to make the length of pull—that is the distance from the front of the trigger to the center of the buttplate—just slightly over half of the distance from your small-fry's armpit to his finger tips. You can make it a point to buy a rifle with a relatively short barrel, or you can trim that to a length that your youngster can handle, but no shorter than 18 inches. Outstanding rifles for the above treatment are the 4½-pound single shot Glenfield Model 10, and the Stevens Model 73, a 4-pound single shot. Both of these rifles are low in cost and light in weight. You can cut the stocks on these and forget them. If you buy a higher-priced rifle, say the 5½-pound Ithaca lever action Saddlegun, give thought to restoring the stock to its original length after your sub-teener starts looking you straight in the eye.

You can be certain of replacing the cutoff section without any distressing offset if you'll remove the plastic butt plate and drill two ¼-inch alignment holes before you cut the stock off. The holes should extend about an inch beyond the anticipated cut, and be at right angles to the cut. Angle the cut to match the original pitch. To assure that the cut is square with the sides of the stock, saw it in a miter box. Lacking that you'll have to eyeball it and pray a lot! Use a fine-toothed saw to avoid chipping, and take it almighty slow when you near the bottom side! True up the end of the stock with some coarse sandpaper on a file, and install a non-slip rubber butt plate such as a Pachmayr #500 White Line. You'll want the "Small" size, which is over 5 inches long—more than enough. With a larger pad, the hole spacing will be too far apart.

After the stock in its shortened configuration becomes too stubby for continued use, you can replace the cutoff section using a couple of ¼-inch dowels for alignment. To compensate for the wood removed by the saw and by truing up, you can use a black, brown, or white ⅛-inch plastic spacer between the two sections. Glue well with epoxy.

Glass Bedding

The greatest friend that accuracy-minded riflemen have acquired in recent years is glass bedding compound. Virtually all of the shooters in the bench rest matches for field-style rifles have stocks that are glass bedded. The term "glass bedding" stems from the small bits of fiberglass floc, mixed into the epoxy resin as a binder and filler.

The owner of just about any rimfire rifle can improve its performance to a high degree by glass bedding the gun. The effect is to gain total contact between the stock and steel, something woefully neglected by factory machine inletting.

For example, I mentioned in Chapter 10 that the Remington 541-S was not performing up to snuff. Removing the stock revealed that wood to metal contact was approximately 15 percent. There was good contact with the receiver in the immediate area of the single screw that held the two units together. The rest of the action was in effect free-floating to the rear, where an area of about ½-inch square was touching. The barrel had zero contact all of the way forward to the plastic forend tip, which was touching principally on the left side. I glass bedded the action and the barrel full length, except for the plastic tip and then relieved the tip of any contact whatsoever. The reason for leaving tip contact until *after* the glass bedding, was to provide support for the barrel until the epoxy set up.

As with most .22 rimfire rifles, the Remington 541-S does *not* have any recoil lug, relying upon the single tie-down screw to prevent the barreled action from

Even the most expensive rimfire rifles are delivered from the factory with machine inletting that displays only token contact with the barreled action. The rimfire gun buff's greatest friend is glass bedding, which can easily correct bedding faults. Be sure to use tape along the sides of the stock to protect the original finish from overflow bedding compound. Use enough in the barrel channel to avoid "holes" or voids in the final bedding.

either rotating or shifting fore and aft in the stock. This rifle would benefit immensely from an added screw to secure the action. There is room for one between the trigger assembly and the magazine. I plan to install one there.

Accuracy with the 541-S—while excellent in "out-of-the-box" configuration—improved dramatically. Group sizes (using all makes and types of ammunition) shrunk to about half of what they had been. I have seen this phenomenon several times in the past, but it never ceases to amaze me. The job is so simple, and the results so good, that I wonder why every .22 rimfire rifle in the world is not glass bedded!

Most of the work goes into proper preparation before you ever start to mix the epoxy. All areas that you plan to glass bed must be relieved by at least ⅛-inch. Try to keep it as even as possible along the barrel channel, without any deep gouges. The handiest device for this and many other bedding chores is the "Quickut," from Brownell's, which stays sharp forever (almost), and cuts so fast you have to watch that you don't get carried away and end up with a hollow shell! Most rimfire receivers are round also, making the same tool useful there as well. Remember that you *must* leave bearing points to support the receiver and barrel while the epoxy hardens. The level of these bearing points determines the depth at which the barreled action will rest in the stock! I try to find a spot immediately ahead or behind the attaching screw, plus one at the rear of the receiver and one at the tip of the forend.

After using the rasp, the entire area of the inletting will have a slightly roughened surface—ideal for good adhesion of the epoxy. Brush the entire area briskly to remove any sawdust that might prevent the epoxy from bonding properly. *Bedding compound eats stock finish!* You can protect the stock from contact with ordinary automotive masking tape. If you don't plan to refinish the stock, better cover it entirely, using the wide tape to ease the chore. It's almost impossible to keep the compound off of your hands, and fingerprints on the stock finish are inevitable.

Modern glass bedding compounds are thermosetting, creating their own heat chemically, rather than relying upon air drying as did the original products. The old air drying compounds used to shrink to the point where it was often necessary to do the job twice to get proper contact. The first bedding products set up so quickly that it often became a race to see whether you could get the barreled action into the stock before the goop got too hard to ooze properly. Nowadays, we have excellent products such as Brownell's "Acraglas," which comes in kit form with all of the necessary supplies to complete the job. The pros use this one! Acraglas patiently awaits your pleasure, but still hardens completely within 48 hours. Usually you can separate the stock and barreled action after a 24-hour period. However, wait an additional day for complete curing before shooting the gun.

Meanwhile, you can trim away excess bedding compound that squeezed into the trigger and magazine mortices, using a sharp knife or chisel, or a hand grinder with wood-cutting burr. When you first lower the steel into the wood, you'll likely get some excess material squeezing out around the sides. This can be wiped away before it hardens, or allowed to remain until the material reaches a rubbery consistency, then trimmed with a dull knife—dull because you don't want to score the steel of the barrel!

When cutting the relief for the bedding compound, avoid cutting up to the top edges of the original inletting. If you remove any wood here, an ugly line of epoxy will show all around the steel.

The barreled action must be liberally coated with release mixture which is included with the Brownell's kit, in order to separate readily. Remove the trigger assembly, any magazine attachments, under-barrel tubular magazine, etc. before bedding. Fill empty holes with modeling clay or putty to prevent them from filling up with epoxy. An alternative is to cover with Scotch tape. Treat the threaded hole for the attaching bolt with release agent, then cover it with a square of Scotch tape, also. After the stock and barreled action are joined, punch through the tape with a drift punch just large enough to enter. This will help align the parts before you install the holding bolt, and push out any compound that has oozed into the hole in the stock. Treat the attaching screw with release agent before placing it in the stock. Cinch it up firmly, but avoid excessive pressure which might crush the supporting bridge left in the wood to position the barreled action in the stock.

Mixing instructions come with the kit. Don't start mixing until the stock and barreled action are completely ready for union. Don't be stingy with the bedding compound, so that there are voids left in the final bedding! At the same time avoid laying it in so heavy that gobs of it are falling on the floor when you tighten the attaching screw. Keep the layer of compound as even as possible end-to-end in the stock.

After the 24-hour initial curing period, the stock and barreled action should part company with only minor reluctance. Sometimes a few raps atop the barrel and action with a wooden or rawhide mallet will get their attention! In no event should you use main strength to pry the pair apart. The likely result is a broken stock. If all else fails, you can set the entire assembly in a freezer for a few hours. The metal shrinks, allowing easy separation.

Scope Mounting

With few exceptions, all modern rimfire rifles have dovetail grooves milled into their receivers to allow mounting any scope with standardized tip-off-style rings. Such rifles as the Marlin 39, Ruger 10/22, etc., that lack the grooves are factory drilled and tapped to accept dovetail mount bases, usually furnished with the rifles. However, there are still some of the older rimfire rifles around that lack both the grooves and the tapped mounting holes.

These able oldsters can be brought up to date by topping them with one of Brownell's 3⅞-inch long dovetailed bases, extruded of aluminum alloy, radiused on the bottom to fit either .840-inch or 1-inch diameter receivers. Three countersunk holes are provided, one at each end and another about one-third of the way back. Normally, the two near holes would go on the receiver ring at the front, and the single hole used to secure the rear. If necessary, another hole can be drilled by the gunsmith (or you) to accommodate an odd-ball receiver.

If the base interferes with the bolt handle, you can notch out a relief or even cut the unit in half and use it as a two-piece mounting base. The black-anodized extrusion is also available in 12-inch lengths without holes and can be cut to the needed length and adapted to almost any rifle.

Brownell's furnishes 8x40 screws with their dovetail bases. You'll need a high speed #28 drill, a drill press,

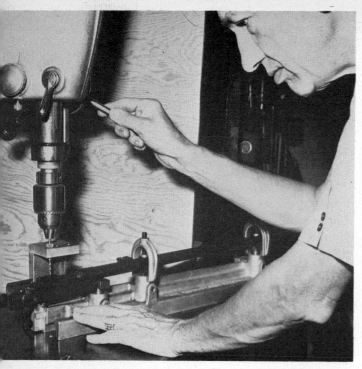

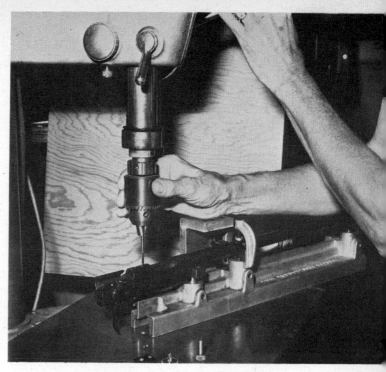

(Above left) Most modern rimfires are either factory drilled and tapped for scope mounting or are grooved for tip-off mounts. However, some older rifles have to be drilled and tapped for scope mounts. A drill jig is certainly handy and places holes with greater certainty, but they can be carefully center-punched and drilled without a jig.

(Above right) Before removing the rifle from the jig or drill vise, change to a tap in the chuck, to assure a square, concentric start. Hand-turn the drill chuck, backing out frequently to clear chips.

(Below) Finally, in attaching the mount bases, clean holes of chips and tapping lubricant, then use a drop of Uncle Mike's Gun Glue to prevent later loosening.

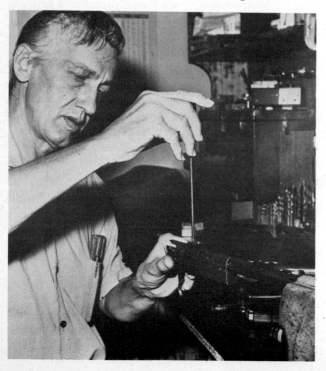

and machinist's vise or set of "V" blocks to hold the barreled action (out of the stock) square and level with the drill table. Scribe a light center-line along the top of the receiver under the spot where the mounting base will be installed. Then you need only mark off the location of the front hole, center punch it and drill. Set the depth of the hole on the drill press limiter stop to avoid drilling through into the chamber. Use a drill-tap lubricant such as Brownell's Flute Juice. Keep it flowing to carry out the drill chips. After drilling the hole and before moving the gun, substitute an 8x40 tap for the drill bit, and start the tap into the hole, turning the chuck by hand. In that way, you can be assured that the tap will be square with the hole. With the tap well started, you can loosen the chuck, and finish tapping with a standard wrench, taking care not to force the tap and break it. It's a good idea to back the tap off every once in a while, and clean out the hole. You need a bottoming tap for any holes that cannot be drilled through. Ideally, you should have a starting tap also, but if you can afford but one, make it the bottoming tap, which has threads almost to the end with only a slight cutting taper on the very tip.

With the first hole drilled and tapped, install the mount and use it to center the other two holes. If the screw is longer than the depth of the hole, you'll know because the mount won't cinch down. Just grind off the end of the screw to the appropriate length.

Solving Malfunction Problems

Rimfire rifles and handguns are heir to a multitude of minor malfunctions, such as failures to feed, failures to

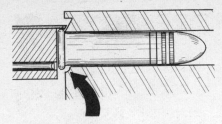

rim recess opposite firing pin worn away, leaving rim unsupported. Certain to cause many misfires.

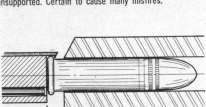

Excessive headspace leaves case rim with insufficient support and may cause misfire or case failure.

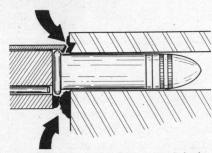

Accumulated residue on bolt face and around chamber prevents bolt from closing fully. Bolt closed by falling striker but blow delivered to the rim too weak to affect ignition.

(Left) These line drawings reprinted from CCI's *.22 Rimfire Fact Booklet,* show some of the common defects that can cause misfires.

(Below) Here we have a variety of firing pin contours, and two common problems that contribute to poor ignition.

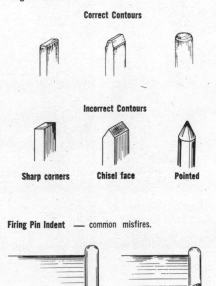

Firing Pin Contours

Correct Contours

Incorrect Contours

Sharp corners   Chisel face   Pointed

Firing Pin Indent — common misfires.

Too shallow   Too far in

Uncle Mike's supplies step drills such as these which cut the holes of correct diameter for sling swivels and make the proper diameter counter-sink at the same time.

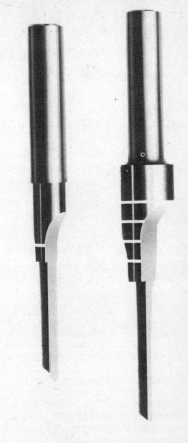

eject, hangfires or misfires. More often than not an energetic cleaning will solve the problem. If that doesn't work, at least you'll be able to see the metal and perform a little detective work. Using either the Opti-Visor, a jeweler's loupe or both, look for jagged edges or surfaces that might indicate either a portion broken off, or perhaps poor finishing at the factory. Replace broken parts, polish any working surfaces that might be causing hangups. Sometimes a part will become peened out of shape, causing a malfunction or misfire. The most common of these is an area hammered into a ridge or cavity at the rear of the chamber by dry firing. Sometimes the metal can be moved back into a semblance of its original condition. Otherwise it will have to be filed and polished. Firing pins often become peened over on the ends, sticking forward in the bolt or breech block. In an autoloader, that may result in an instant machine gun! If misfires persist despite all of the above, replace the firing pin spring!

Installing Sling Swivels, Grip Caps and Butt Pads

The easiest and most productive customizing treatment you can give any rimfire rifle is by installing a set of quick detachable swivels. Michaels of Oregon, P.O.

Michaels of Oregon, better known to gunsmiths as "Uncle Mike's" has solved the problem of installing front swivels on tubular magazine rifles, such as the Winchester 9422 and Marlin Model 39, by using a band that encircles the magazine. They're easy to install at home.

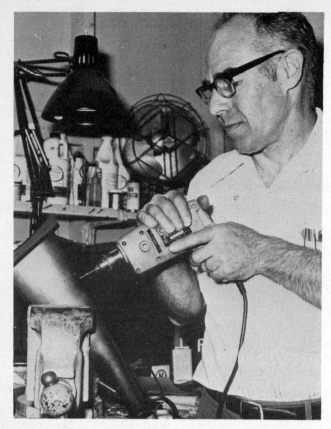

If your .22 rifle lacks sling swivels as it comes from the factory, the greatest favor you can do for yourself is to install them. The installation is not difficult, and, you can save yourself time and money. Drill a hole for the rear swivel about one-third of the way forward of the butt with a 5/32-inch drill, about 3/4- to 1-inch deep. Take care to center the drill and make it square to the bottom line of the stock.

Use a small screwdriver or drift punch to turn the swivel base into place. Never use the QD swivel itself, because it may bend from the strain.

Box 13010, Portland, Oregon 97213 supplies some good ones at reasonable prices. Uncle Mike has solved the problem of attaching front swivels to rimfire rifles with under-barrel tubular magazines, with his slip-on full-band front stud #1341 or clamp-over style #1071, which includes the wood-screw rear stud, you can fit all save the Winchester 9422, with its larger tube diameter, requiring set #1371. Along with the swivels, order a few tubes of Uncle Mike's "Gun-Glu," to lock those screws into place! Wood screw swivels call for drilling a $5/32$-inch hole, $3/4$-inch deep, about one-third of the way from the butt to the pistol grip. Countersink no more than $1/16$-inch with a $23/64$-inch drill. *Take care that your drill is square with the bottom of the stock!* A couple of drops of shellac will prevent the screw from rotating back out. Use a drift punch or small-shank screwdriver to screw the stud in place. Never use the QD swivel itself! The front swivel on a bolt action rifle is normally positioned about 4 inches back from the forend tip. It must be counterbored from inside to accept a threaded nut. Use drills to suit shank and nut diameters. Order 1-inch bows. Slings 1¼-inch wide are too clumsy, and ¾-inch are too stringy. White spacers add a touch of class!

Pachmayr Pistol Grip Caps of gleaming black ebony, with oval centers of gold or silver help to set off any rimfire rifle. A number of sizes and contours are available to fit any need. Pachmayr's RP200 White-Line Rifle Butt pads improve the appearance and stick to the shoulder. If your stock is a little too short for your taste, add a Pachmayr Smooth Side Basket Weave Pad, available in thicknesses of $6/10$-inch, $8/10$-inch, and 1-inch. Pachmayr has a Rube Goldberg device to assure that the pad is flush with the wood, without damaging the finish. You can trim the pad down to size with a little care and patience. But just to be safe, put a wrap of tough plastic electrician's tape around the stock next to the pad before you start!

Gunsmithing your own .22 rimfire rifles and handguns can provide you with endless hours of engrossing relaxation, at nominal cost, with little equipment. You can keep it light, or become as involved as you wish, with no one to answer to except yourself. Your guns will end up functioning with silky smoothness, and glowing with good health—so will you!

(Right) If the stock of your .22 rimfire rifle isn't quite "man-sized" enough for you, lengthen the stock by installing a Pachmayr Smooth Side Basket Weave Pad. Step one is to dress the butt of the stock true and flat. You can use a belt sander, as shown here, or merely a file wrapped with sandpaper.

(Below right) Step two is attaching the pad with two wood screws provided. You must drill pilot holes first. Be sure that they are properly placed, also square with the butt.

(Below) You can trim the pad down by *careful contact* with a disc sander, using a wrap of tape around the stock to protect the finish in the event of a slip. Or you can do it at a more leisurely pace with a file and sandpaper. Take care to retain the *same* angle on the pad as that of the bottom of the stock.

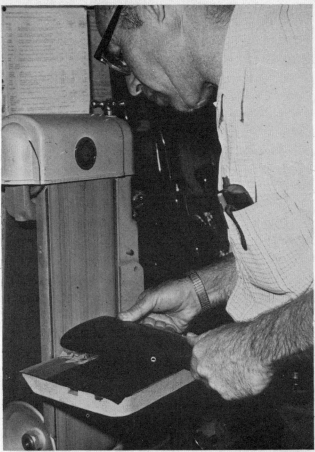

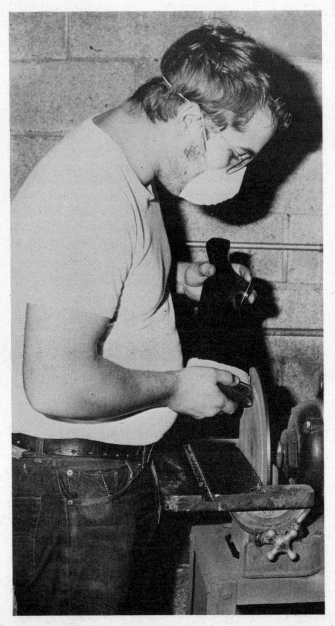

CHAPTER 15

Centerfire Smallbores

THE ORIGINAL non-rimfire smallbore was the .22 Winchester Centerfire, introduced in 1885, chambered into the Winchester single shot rifle because it was too long for most repeating rifles of its day. In its original black powder loading, it developed 1500fps with a 45-grain jacketed slug. The .22 WCF was the springboard for the .22 Hornet.

The Hornet rode in on the coattails of Hercules Powder Company's fast burning, smokeless 2400 powder. Captain Grosvenor L. Wotkyns, Colonel Townsend Whelen, Captain G.A. Woody, and ballistic engineer Al Woodworth experimented with smokeless powder loadings in the .22 WCF at the Springfield Armory in the late 1920's, leading to introduction of the .22 Hornet cartridge in 1930.

Winchester dawdled about chambering a rifle for their own round, thus were scooped by Savage with the Model 23-D in 1932. Winchester finally chambered their Model 54 for the Hornet in 1933. The Hornet was an immediate success with varmint shooters. It leaped the Atlantic to become the 5.6 x 35R, where it was chambered into countless drillings (three barreled rifle/shotgun combos). Where Winchester's claim for 200-yard effectiveness on vermin for the .22 WCF fell rather short of realization, the Hornet pretty well lived up to that boast, actually delivering more energy at 200 yards than the .22 WCF at the muzzle! It was sensationally accurate! In his book, *Twenty-Two Caliber Varmint Rifles,* C.S. Landis shows a 200-yard target with a 10-shot group measuring 1¼ inches center to center!

The original Hornet developed only 2,450 fps with a 45-grain jacketed bullet, but it was soon boosted to 2,650 fps in factory loadings. This tiny yet mighty round inspired a rash of long-distance, precision shooting at both targets and varmints. Where before only a few experimenters indulged in the sport, now anyone with the price of a rifle and scope could participate.

But the experimenters were not to be outdone. The Hornet was merely a beginning! Lysle D. Kilbourn, a gunsmith in upstate New York, turned a magic key to open the door to improved performance when he conceived the idea of "blowing out" the Hornet case, which was sharply tapered in the manner of all centerfire cases of that day. The theory was that the case had to be tapered or it would stick in the chamber. Kilbourn proved them wrong when he reamed out a Hornet chamber to a body taper of only .004-inch on a side and discovered that cases extracted easier than before. He didn't stop there. He started another trend by altering the taper at the shoulder from a lazy 5 degrees-plus to an abrupt 40 degrees. The additional powder space opened up in the Hornet case by Kilbourn's revolutionary inspiration allowed him to boost velocities of his "K-Hornet" into the range from 2,750 to 3,000 fps!

Success of the Hornet inspired a rash of high velocity smallbore cartridges. The .218 Bee, devised by necking down the old .25-20 cartridge, packed a little more sting than the Hornet, when it was introduced in 1938, chambered into the lever action Winchester Model 65, but it never caught on like its older cousin. The .219 Zipper with a much longer case was necked down from the old black powder .25-35 cartridge and bumped velocities above the 3,500 fps mark. But someone at Winchester envisioned it as a big game cartridge, which it wasn't, and chambered it into their Model 64 lever action, instead of a bolt action which would have delivered varmint accuracy. Because they had to feed from under-barrel tubular magazines, both the Bee and the Zipper were factory loaded with blunt bullets that quickly dissipated their velocity advantage. Both died untimely deaths.

Winchester made headlines in 1935 with the .220 Swift — "The fastest factory-loaded cartridge in the world." The semi-rimmed round was based upon the

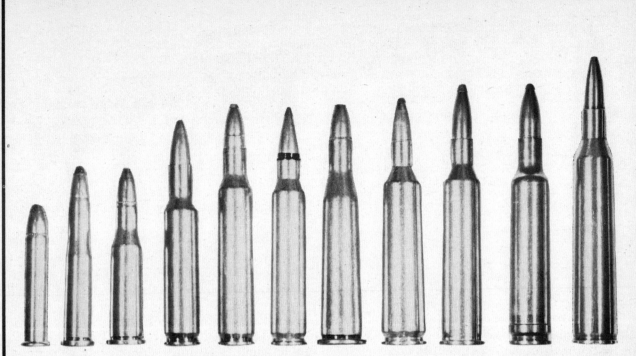

A lineup of timeless .22s, left to right: .22 Winchester Magnum Rim Fire; .22 Hornet; .218 Bee; .222 Remington; .222 Remington Magnum; .223; .219 Zipper; .22-250; .225; 224 Weatherby Magnum; and still standing tall, the .220 Swift—fastest of them all.

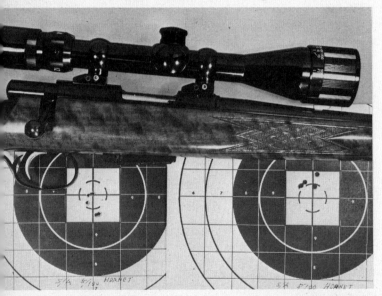

The .22 Hornet was the first giant step to smallbore centerfires with boarding house reach. The diminutive centerfire .22 was highly accurate, even at extended ranges. Here are two five-shot groups fired by the author at 100 yards with a Savage/Anschutz Model 1432, using factory loads (left) and reloads (right). Both groups were under minute-of-angle. Scope is Bushnell Banner variable 4X to 12X, with adjustable focusing along with streamlined Conetrol mounts.

6mm Lee Navy cartridge, necked down. In the factory loading with a 48-grain bullet, it cranked up an impressive 4,110 fps. Winchester sagely chambered this one in their bolt action Model 54. They quietly dropped the round in 1964 for lack of interest.

Winchester had dominated the smallbore field for decades when Remington came up with the .222 Remington in 1950, launching a 50-grain bullet at 3,200 fps Suddenly smallbore became Remington's ball game. The "triple-Deuce" became top choice of bench rest shooters and varmint hunters from Maine to Baja. It was incredibly accurate no matter what bullets or powder were inflicted upon it. However, Remington topped it with the .222 Remington Magnum, adding 5 grains of bullet weight and 100 fps. The .222 Magnum collided head on with the identical ballistics of the .223 developed by Armalite in 1957 in conjunction with their AR-15 assault rifle, which became the M-16 when adopted by the U.S. armed services. It was no contest —the .222 Magnum is dead, the .223 survives.

After selling patent rights for the AR-15 to Colt, Armalite went on to develop another .223 chambered military type rifle, the AR-18, which had many advantages both in ease of production and in field performance. However, it couldn't break into military pro-

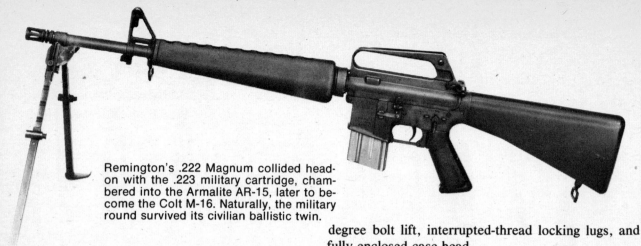

Remington's .222 Magnum collided head-on with the .223 military cartridge, chambered into the Armalite AR-15, later to become the Colt M-16. Naturally, the military round survived its civilian ballistic twin.

curement. At last word, it is still available as a semiautomatic for civilian or police use.

Roy Weatherby's career as the "High Priest of High Velocity" actually began before World War II with his experiments toward improving the .220 Swift, resulting in the .220 Weatherby Rocket. Roy never manufactured ammunition for the Rocket. Instead, he devised an entirely new cartridge, the .224 Weatherby Varmintmaster, in the image of the .300 Weatherby Magnum. Introduced in 1963, the .224 had a belted-head case, with double-radiused shoulder. Along with the .224 Weatherby came the Varmintmaster rifle, with short action scaled down from the bigbore Mark V, to a more suitable size to house the new .22 centerfire. The rifle was a light, 6½ pounds, a short, 43¼ inches, and even with the 24-inch barrel, it swung like a baton! The Varmintmaster retained the Mark V's abbreviated 58-degree bolt lift, interrupted-thread locking lugs, and fully enclosed case head.

In an effort to regain some of its former stature in the smallbore field, Winchester came up with the rimmed, sharp-shouldered .225 in 1964, with a 55-grain bullet at 3,650 fps. It ably fills the gap left when the .220 Swift was abandoned.

Seeing their smallbores ballistically bested, Remington carried off a real coup by legitimatizing the varmint hunter's favorite wildcat for over three decades, the .22-250, which as its name suggests, was merely, the .250 Savage necked down. With about 95 percent of the case capacity of the .220 Swift, the .22-250 topped the competition by 110 fps, not a significant number, but it looks good on the ballistics charts.

Remington made varmint news in 1971 by introducing the .17 Remington, necked down from the .223. Remington shrank their "Power-Lokt" bullet down to .1725-inch diameter and 25-grain weight. It requires 280 of these tiny pellets to make 1-pound. It leaves the muzzle of the 24-inch stainless steel barreled Model 700 BDL short bolt action at 4,020 fps. Sighted in at 200

Straight-line recoil enables the AR-18 to fire full auto without climbing. The rifle is easily controllable in full-automatic as shown here. A semi-auto civilian version is still available.

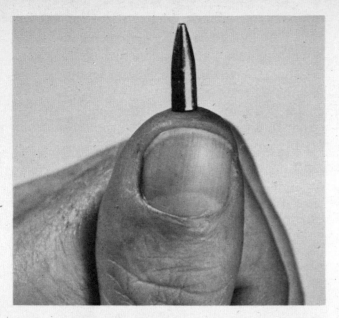

Among varminters, the Hornady 25-grain .17 caliber bullet has proved extremely popular, and it's accurate. It takes 280 of these tiny pellets to equal 1-pound.

In 1971, Remington introduced the .17 Remington. RCBS loading dies are available for the .17, plus swaging dies to convert .223 military brass.

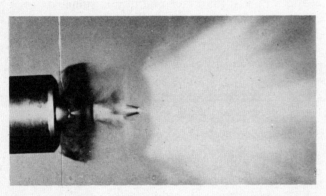

The Remington "Accelerator" cartridge launches a 55-grain .22 caliber, sabot-borne bullet at an astounding 4080fps, from a .30-06 barrel. The plastic sabot peels away within 14 inches of the muzzle.

yards, mid-range trajectory is 1.2 inches. Drop at 300 yards is only 6.3 inches. By then the tiny bullets shed half of their velocity. Vermin still come violently unglued, because of the high rotational velocity imparted by the one turn in 9-inch twist.

Always the pioneers, Remington recently introduced a high velocity .22 cartridge that fires in a .30-06 rifle, launching a 55-grain soft point at an astounding 4,080 fps. This is possible courtesy of a plastic sabot that encases the bullet until it emerges from the muzzle, and peels away within 14 inches, falling harmlessly to the ground. This revolutionary ammo should introduce a lot of shooters to the thrills of varmint hunting.

Although the Hornet remained popular in Europe since its introduction, it fell into a moribund state in the

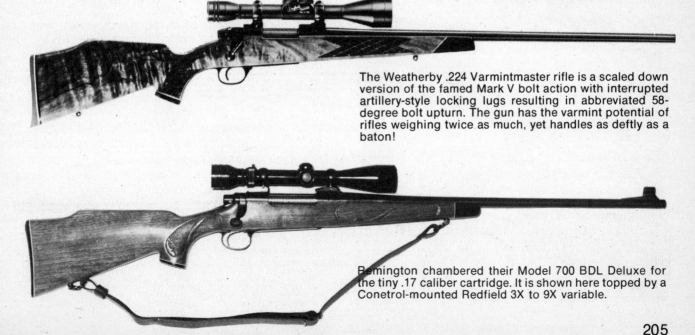

The Weatherby .224 Varmintmaster rifle is a scaled down version of the famed Mark V bolt action with interrupted artillery-style locking lugs resulting in abbreviated 58-degree bolt upturn. The gun has the varmint potential of rifles weighing twice as much, yet handles as deftly as a baton!

Remington chambered their Model 700 BDL Deluxe for the tiny .17 caliber cartridge. It is shown here topped by a Conetrol-mounted Redfield 3X to 9X variable.

U.S. until just recently, when Savage/Anschutz offered it in their bolt action Model 1432. The fit and finish on this rifle is equal to that normally found only in custom rifles! The mirror-smooth milled steel receiver boasts a wall thickness of ¼-inch, for a stiffness that contributes in no small way to its accuracy. The burnished bolt fits as if lapped into place. The trigger on this precision action, lifted from the Anschutz Match 54 rifle which has ruled International competition for years, has zero takeup and backlash, and breaks at 2¼ pounds, with imperceptible movement! The trigger guard is *milled* steel, and the five-shot magazine is also made of the same material—a rarity in today's market place. With gracefully tapered medium-weight 24-inch sporter barrel, the 1432 weighs in at 6¾ pounds, a good compromise between ease of carrying and sufficient heft to deliver sub-minute-of-angle groups out to the limits of Hornet effectiveness. On the target, our test rifle delivered 10-shot groups ranging from ¾-inch to 1-inch, using factory ammo.

The hand-checkered French walnut stock, with rollover cheekpiece, schnabel forend, and deeply curved pistol grip, displayed some of the most beautiful grain I've seen in a factory stock. High quality open

The Remington Model 788 in a centerfire smallbore caliber is a natural for a fine scope such as this Leupold M8-6X on a Leupold STD mount.

sights are backed by a receiver grooved for tip-off mounts, but that would be like placing a carnival cap on the Pieta. A better choice is Conetrol's screw-on mounts for this rifle, topped with a Bushnell 4X to 12X variable with focusing objective lens.

Savage has really taken the varmint hunter's problems to heart, offering their single shot, bolt action Model 112-V (in right or left hand), chambered for either .222, .22-250, or .220 Swift, with varmint-weight 26-inch barrel, high-combed stock of selected walnut,

Solely for the dedicated varmint shooter, Savage produces this heavy-barreled single shot Model 112-V.

Remington's top-of-the-line Model 700 BDL Deluxe is available in many popular centerfire varmint calibers.

Remington also offers a heavy-barreled Varmint Special, in all popular smallbore centerfire calibers.

The Remington Model 788 is the poor man's varmint rifle, chambered for .222, .223, and .22-250.

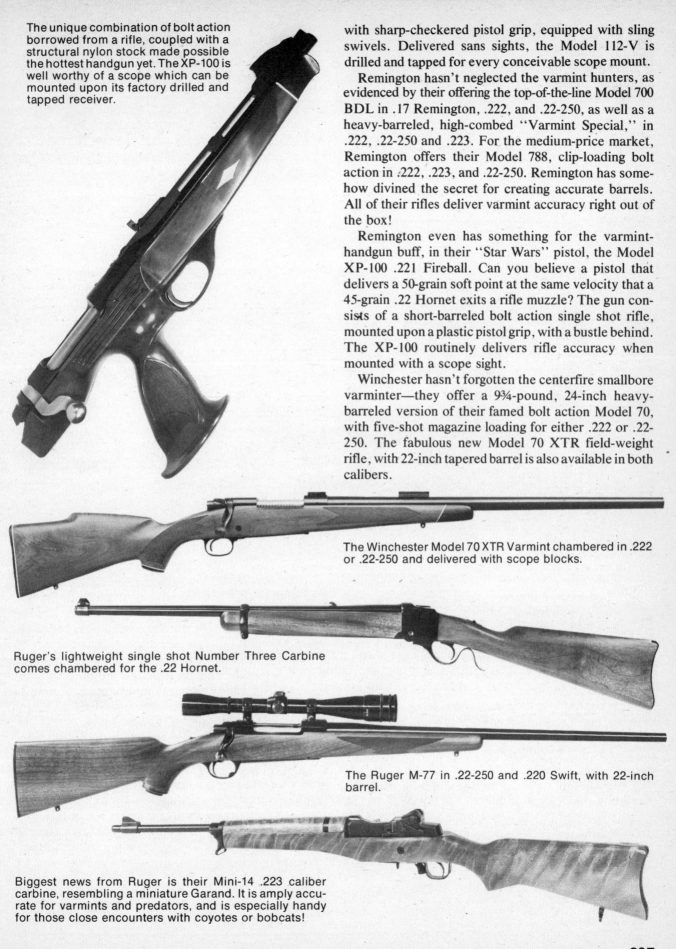

The unique combination of bolt action borrowed from a rifle, coupled with a structural nylon stock made possible the hottest handgun yet. The XP-100 is well worthy of a scope which can be mounted upon its factory drilled and tapped receiver.

with sharp-checkered pistol grip, equipped with sling swivels. Delivered sans sights, the Model 112-V is drilled and tapped for every conceivable scope mount.

Remington hasn't neglected the varmint hunters, as evidenced by their offering the top-of-the-line Model 700 BDL in .17 Remington, .222, and .22-250, as well as a heavy-barreled, high-combed "Varmint Special," in .222, .22-250 and .223. For the medium-price market, Remington offers their Model 788, clip-loading bolt action in .222, .223, and .22-250. Remington has somehow divined the secret for creating accurate barrels. All of their rifles deliver varmint accuracy right out of the box!

Remington even has something for the varmint-handgun buff, in their "Star Wars" pistol, the Model XP-100 .221 Fireball. Can you believe a pistol that delivers a 50-grain soft point at the same velocity that a 45-grain .22 Hornet exits a rifle muzzle? The gun consists of a short-barreled bolt action single shot rifle, mounted upon a plastic pistol grip, with a bustle behind. The XP-100 routinely delivers rifle accuracy when mounted with a scope sight.

Winchester hasn't forgotten the centerfire smallbore varminter—they offer a 9¾-pound, 24-inch heavy-barreled version of their famed bolt action Model 70, with five-shot magazine loading for either .222 or .22-250. The fabulous new Model 70 XTR field-weight rifle, with 22-inch tapered barrel is also available in both calibers.

The Winchester Model 70 XTR Varmint chambered in .222 or .22-250 and delivered with scope blocks.

Ruger's lightweight single shot Number Three Carbine comes chambered for the .22 Hornet.

The Ruger M-77 in .22-250 and .220 Swift, with 22-inch barrel.

Biggest news from Ruger is their Mini-14 .223 caliber carbine, resembling a miniature Garand. It is amply accurate for varmints and predators, and is especially handy for those close encounters with coyotes or bobcats!

Remington hasn't forgotten the pistol/varmint hunters, offering their outer-space looking XP-100, .221 Fire Ball, which delivers a 50-grain bullet at 2,650fps.

Ruger is very much with it, offering its superbly accurate Ruger Number One falling block single shot rifle in .22-250, with a special lightweight Number Three Carbine chambered for the .22 Hornet. Ruger offers an M-77 integral base short stroke bolt action in .22-250 or .220 Swift, with 22-inch barrel, stocked with genuine selected American walnut in a beautifully understated traditional design, with hand-cut sharp-diamond checkering, backed up with a non-slip rubber butt plate. The real news is Ruger's Mini-14 autoloading carbine in .223! With 18½-inch barrel, it weighs a handy, quick-swinging 6.4 pounds, ideal for close-in predator hunting down in the sagebrush of the great Southwest! As delivered by Ruger, the Mini-14 has practical post and peep sights, fully adjustable. However, several companies make practical scope mounts for the fine short rifle. Leupold makes their STD mount to fit the Mini-14 without displacing the rear sight and that same outfit's new Compac scopes are ideal in size for the Ruger .223.

These high intensity centerfire smallbores can do at 300 to 500 yards the same thing that your rimfire can do at 100, only more so! However, in order to hit vermin at that range, a rifle, plus the sight and the shooter, must be capable of holding about ½-minute of angle groups. The rifle usually weighs 8 to 12 pounds, and the scope often resembles a trombone. Equipment and ammo are expensive. The rousing report of many of the centerfire smallbores makes some of those "hot-steppers" unwelcome in most rural areas inhabited by chucks. Out in the wide open spaces of Wyoming, Idaho, and Nevada, however, this kind of outfit shines. If the varmint bug has really bitten you deep, you may one day find yourself wrestling with a bull barreled brute of a rifle with high X scope balanced atop, trying to hit a dot barely visible on the horizon!

CHAPTER 16

Rifle and Pistol Preservation

AFTER THE SLENDER Kentucky rifle slipped grudgingly from an everyday tool into a mere relic, small game hunting with rifles in the United States temporarily died with it. The gaping bores of the later plains rifles and the breech loading buffalo rifles that followed were hardly suited to sniping tree squirrels. That would have been much like using a howitzer to hunt deer.

It wasn't until the late 1890's, when the .22 Long Rifle rimfire cartridge emerged as a viable small game round, that there were once more "squirrel rifles" in the hands of American youngsters and oldsters alike. The earliest .22 Long Rifle cartridges contained 5 grains of finely granulated black powder. It shared the same basic formula as that used by alchemists hundreds of years before, charcoal, sulphur and saltpeter. It left a gummy residue that attracted moisture like a sponge, then combined with the water vapors forming sulphuric acid, to hasten the demise of any rifle thoughtlessly left uncleaned after a day of shooting.

In time, black powder gave way to King's Semi-Smokeless, then clean-burning smokeless powder. But that didn't spell the end of a rimfire shooter's problems. Unless the gun owner was very diligent with his cleaning, he still had to contend with the destructive effects of a hygroscopic residue resulting in severe rust problems. At first, the smokeless powder itself was blamed for the pitted bores until the 1920's, when Dr. Wilbert Huff, of the U.S. Bureau of Mines, published a work called, *Corrosion Under Oil Films.* It pinpointed the villain, the priming component potassium chlorate—similar to ordinary table salt. Previously, black powder fouling had served to dilute the chlorate residue, and shooters were forced to clean with *water,* the only solvent that worked on the black powder and chlorate fouling.

Then came a day in 1924 when James E. Burns, an unemployed chemist dropped in to visit with a couple of friends, W.E. Witsil and Egbert C. Hadley, technicians at Remington Arms. During the course of the conversation, Burns drew a revolver and fired six times at the ceiling. Luckily, the shots were blanks, but they did underscore Burns' request, "Put this gun in a damp place until I return from vacation in Florida." After several weeks, Burns returned and asked to see his revolver. The outside displayed unmistakable signs of rusting, but Burns' interest centered in the bore, which he quickly wiped out with a dry patch on a cleaning rod. The bore was mirror-bright! That was the birth of non-corrosive priming. Burns' formula involved the use of lead styphnate, a product available then only in Europe in small quantities. Remington purchased the patent rights on the Continent and quickly went into production of their revolutionary "Kleanbore" priming.

Beginning in 1926, rimfire buffs were freed for all time from the onerous slavery of cleaning their rifle/pistol bores! Not only was the priming compound noncorrosive, but the bullet lubricant was contrived to leave a protective coating in the rimfire rifled bore, all but ending the need for cleaning .22 firearms.

Well . . . almost! Even .22 rifles and pistols can stand an occasional cleaning to remove accumulated gunk and lead fouling. Every so often someone will bring me a "problem rifle," that has suddenly forgotten the path to the bull's-eye. I always suggest a thorough scrubbing of the bore with a good solvent. It's absolutely amazing how quickly that restores the gun's memory! If a gun is destined to sit on the rack for some weeks, it's a good idea to clean and oil it. If the weeks stretch into months, wipe the bore with a dry patch and inspect it. If all is well, swab the bore with a slightly heavier rust inhibitor such as Gunslick Gun Grease, which won't evaporate the way some of the light oils can do, leaving your bore unprotected.

Any bore with grease or oil in it should be wiped with a dry patch before firing. The least you can expect is a wild first shot. The worst that can happen is a ringed or

The introduction of Remington "Kleanbore" noncorrosive priming, combined with "Kleankote" dry bullet lubricant that was deposited on the bore to protect it from corrosion, finally spelled the end of the cleaning drudgery that once afflicted .22 rimfire shooters.

Tri-Flon, a synthesized multi-purpose lubricant, contains tiny particles of teflon shaped like miniscule marbles, that roll away friction!

Sprayed upon the working surfaces of a firearm, Tri-Flon penetrates the pores of the steel, imparting a boundary film that reduces the need for repeatedly lubricating.

It is important to be certain that any gun is empty before cleaning. In the case of an autoloading pistol, remove the magazine first, then retract the slide to clear the chamber.

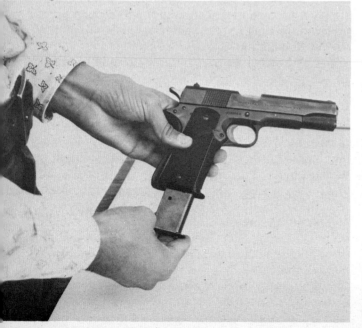

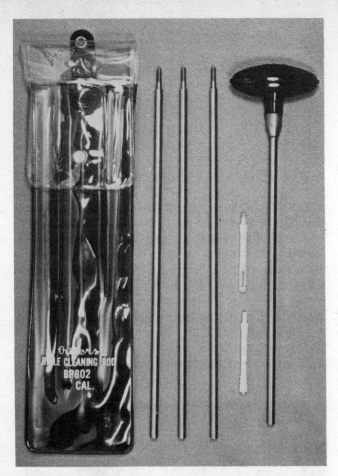

Contrary to common belief, a steel cleaning rod is less damaging to the bore than a "soft" metal such as brass or aluminum. The soft metal tends to pick up abrasive residue and drag it through the bore in a kind of lapping action. Shown is the Outers stainless steel rod — one of the best.

Fe(OH)₂ and ferric oxide Fe₂O₃. Corrosion results from a combining of the metal with oxygen in absorbed water films. Such films are difficult to remove. Covering them over with greases or ordinary petroleum-based oils does little to improve the situation. In fact, many petroleum based oils actually contain impurities that tend to promote rust! That familiar brown paper that you find packed in with your new .22 rifle is treated with VPI (Vapor Phase Inhibitor), a solid which transfers to the metal surface by sublimation, converting the water film to an alkaline base, thereby preventing oxidation.

Cleaning—The Safe Way

The ABC's of gun cleaning must include the dictum: "Be sure the gun is empty before cleaning!" How many times have you read in the newspaper that some unfortunate "accidentally shot himself while cleaning his gun?" Often the gun is described as a rifle or shotgun. How in Heaven's name do you accidentally shoot yourself with a rifle or shotgun while cleaning it? Obviously, the newspaper reporter's knowledge of firearms was somewhat lacking! Autoloading pistols could offer some hazard to the uninformed or inattentive. The sequence of unloading requires that you *remove the magazine* FIRST! Then retract the slide to remove the round in the chamber. If you retract the slide first, you'll be rewarded with a cartridge ejected—but after you then remove the magazine, a round remains in the chamber. If that sounds too basic to bear repeating, I know of an Army officer who made that mistake once with deadly results.

Tubular magazines have been known to harbor a loaded round after normal efforts were made to empty the gun, usually by working the lever until no more live rounds were ejected. The danger here lies in the possibility of a cartridge becoming hung up because of gunk in the magazine tube, or because of a slight dent or a weak follower spring. Most rifles will allow you to peek into the ejection port and see if the follower is all the way back. Some rifles have brightly-colored plastic followers that are easy to see. If the rifle denies access from above, remove the inner magazine tube and shake the gun vigorously with the muzzle down. That should deliver any rounds hidden within. To wipe out both tubes, it's a good idea to use an oiled patch in a *slotted tip* rather than a jag, so that it won't become stuck in the tubes. You'll have to force the follower back into the inner tube when cleaning it, but that's no problem.

Cleaning Procedures and Equipment

Autoloading rifles demand more attention to keep their actions free of gunk. By their very nature, they tend to accumulate more powder residue. When the action opens, there is usually a small amount of pressure present in the barrel, even if the bullet has passed the muzzle and is well on its way. Southpaw shooters like myself have become accustomed to the

split barrel if a thick coating of heavy grease piles up ahead of the bullet and can't get out of the way fast enough. That first shot afield isn't as serious a matter to the rimfire nimrod after rabbits or squirrels as it is to a big game hunter seeking a trophy grizzly, but all the same you can virtually assure that first shot landing in the group by wiping the bore with a patch impregnated with one of the degreasers, such as Zip Aerosol Degunge.

After a period of inactivity, it is smart to wipe out the bore of your favorite .22 before shooting it again, whether cleaned or not, to remove airborne dust particles that collect and make the first few shots highly abrasive and wearing. Any gun used on a boat or even at a seaside cottage is going to require constant attention to prevent the salt air from eating it alive!

Highly finished, deeply lustrous blued steel is beautiful to behold, and the strongest metal from which we can create fine firearms. The vile insidious enemy of the finest alloy steel is a red plague that turns the glass smooth surface into a gargoyle of hideous pits and scars. The culprit is simple *rust,* or ferric hydroxide

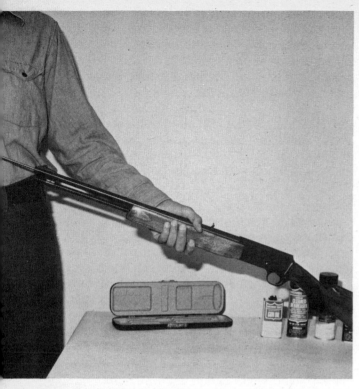

Some rifles, such as this Browning BAR-22, must be cleaned from the muzzle end. Care should be taken to clean no more often than required and also to avoid abrading the muzzle by dragging the rod against the rifling. Using a steel rather than brass or aluminum rod is also less damaging to the rifling.

sting of unburned powder, because we cheek the stock on the wrong side and catch everything sprayed out of the ejection port. Not all of that stuff gets out of the action. A lot of it collects around the breechblock, extractor, firing pin, mainspring, trigger mechanism etc., until one fine day everything grinds to a screeching halt, and the "automatic" isn't auto any longer! Better to anticipate the situation by cleaning every now and then. If the action is readily disassembled, take it down and scrub out everything with a toothbrush soaked in solvent. If not, you can use one of the blast-spray cleaners such as Birchwood Casey's Gun Scrubber, but use it with discretion! Hold the action in such a way that the solvent with its load of crud drains out of the ejection port, not down into the stock. In fact, it would be preferable to remove the stock if possible!

(Right) Cleaning from the rear is far less likely to wear the lands because the cleaning rod contacts the edges of the chamber first. Furthermore, wear to the lands near the chamber is not as damaging to accuracy as those at the muzzle.

(Below) Most bolt action rifles, such as this Remington 541-S, can be cleaned from the breech end by removing the bolt from the action.

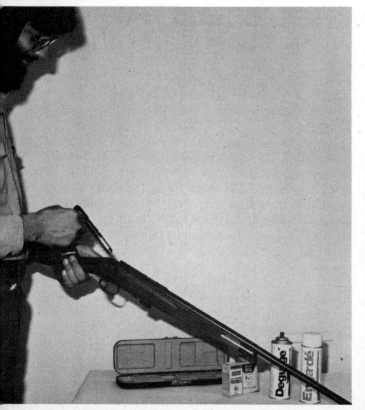

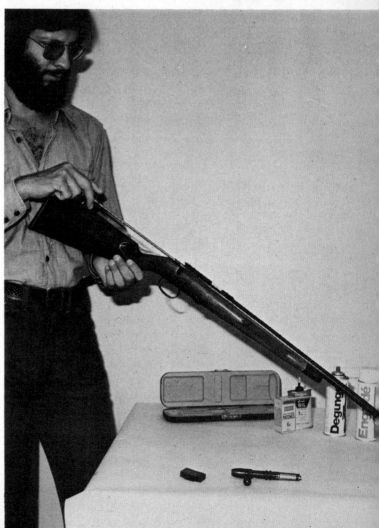

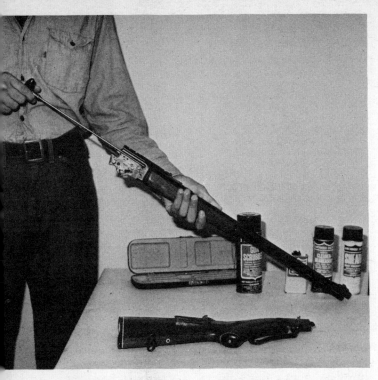

The Marlin 39 can be cleaned from the breech end when disassembled into two units—by removing the breech-block, and either removing or just pushing the spring-loaded ejector aside.

Sometimes a particular brand of ammo will lead the bore of your gun to the point where bullets can't even find the paper at 25 yards. It takes hours of scrubbing with a brass brush and solvent to remove such an accumulation of lead. It's far easier to plug the chamber end and pour in metallic mercury (quicksilver), then plug the muzzle and roll the mercury back and forth for about half an hour. That'll get the lead out!

Owners of the .22 Winchester Magnum Rim Fire or 5mm Remington are in the same boat as centerfire shooters when it comes to cleaning. There is no "protective coating" left by the bigbore-style jacketed bullets used in these high intensity smallbore rimfires. They require cleaning not only to remove firing residue, but also to control the fine copper wash that collects in the bore. Allowed to accumulate, this metallic coating promotes corrosion and can build into a lumpy coating that mysteriously destroys accuracy. If your gun suddenly becomes temperamental and starts sailing wild shots all over the target, try scrubbing out the bore with a brass brush saturated with a good solvent. The active agent in most of these solvents is ammonium oleate. Moist red litmus paper suspended over the surface of the fluid will reveal the remaining potency of the solvent. The ammonia gas dissipates when the bottle is left uncapped, so keep the lid on to preserve effectiveness.

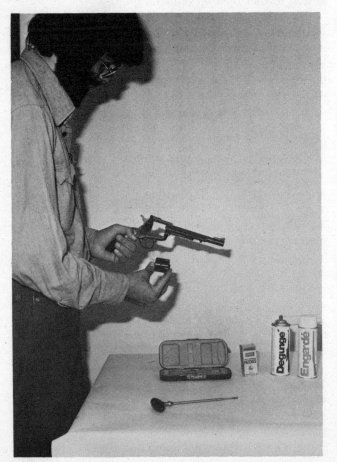

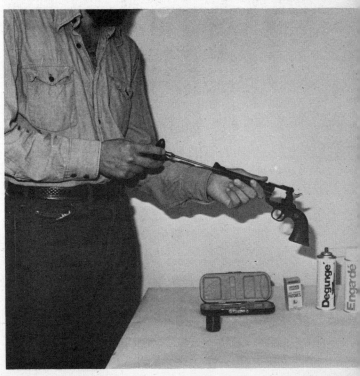

(Left) Single action revolvers, such as this Ruger New Model Super Single Six, can be readily taken down for cleaning by removing the cylinder.
(Below) The barrel of a single action revolver must be cleaned from the muzzle end. Again, take care not to drag the cleaning rod against the rifling at the muzzle.

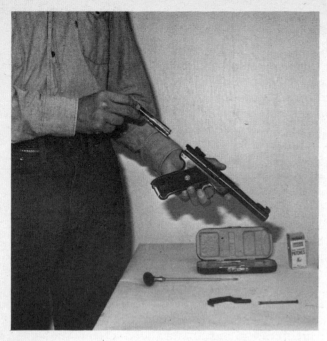

Autoloading pistols, such as this Ruger Mark I, can be dismantled or field stripped, by removing the bolt and/or barrel . . .

This allows cleaning the barrel from the breech end, thus preserving the high accuracy for which these guns are famous.

If you have neglected the bore of a .22 Magnum and suddenly find yourself with a stubborn case of metal fouling, you can remove it by plugging the chamber with a rubber stopper, and pouring the bore full of 28 percent ammonia. Allow to stand for no more than half an hour, then rinse with hot water and follow with the bristle brush. Finally, oil well. If left too long, the ammonia will attack the steel itself. J-B Non-Imbedding Bore Cleaner is a fine abrasive that can be used on a tight-fitting patch to follow up the ammonia treatment, smoothing up and scrubbing out any remaining copper deposits.

In normal cleaning don't attempt to remove every vestige of metal fouling. A light copper color atop the lands is normal and harmless. The amount of scouring required to remove it would be more damaging than the fouling itself. Excessive use of a cleaning rod can be as harmful as neglect. A certain amount of wear is inevitable. Contrary to common belief, a stainless steel cleaning rod is less harmful to the rifling than a "soft" rod. Aluminum or brass rods might logically seem less harmful, but they accumulate particles of carbon and other abrasive agents in their soft surfaces, then become in effect, "laps," that scrub away hard steel. The harder and stiffer the cleaning rod the better. A rod that bends under pressure pushes against the sides of the bore. Whenever possible, clean from the breech end. Slight wear around the perimeter of the chamber has little effect upon accuracy. That same funneling at the muzzle could totally destroy accuracy.

Firearms cleaning and rust prevention have become infinitely more reliable and simple in recent years with the introduction of space-age inhibitors that are preferentially absorbed by metals, actually displacing water films. Many preparations also function as cleaners and inhibit further buildup of metal fouling.

For years, I searched in vain for something that would remove rust without destroying the finish on a gun. These days, there are any number of excellent synthetic oils that perform such service merely as an afterthought! These are mentioned in the following product reviews. For removing rust from a polished surface such as the bolt or breechblock, nothing beats Happich Simichrome Polish, imported from Germany by Competition Chemicals, of Iowa Falls, Iowa. Unless the rust has had an opportunity to really dig in, you may not be able to detect where it was after using Simichrome.

Time was, if a gun was headed for the frigid climes of Alaska or Canada, the action was left dry, save for a dash of powdered graphite. Today, nearly all of the light lubricants are designed to refrain from congealing at temperatures far below those that the most avid hunter would care to endure! Even so, use lubricants in moderation! Don't douse the action and barrel with spray. Use the snorkle that comes with most modern-day spray cans, and direct the stream in short spurts only to those areas where it is needed.

One company that produces these space age chemical protectants calls itself, "Totally Dependable Products," of Zieglerville, Pennsylvania. If that name sounds like bragging, perhaps it's justified. TDP designed their SS1 solvent primarily for black powder shooters, who must contend with stubborn fouling that

A lineup of Totally Dependable Products, which includes just about everything needed in space-age lubricants and metal protection from corrosion. SS1 is excellent for removing light rust without damage to the blued surface.

Break Free CLP is a highly penetrating lubricant that cleans by burrowing under dirt and fouling, freeing it from the metal so that fouling just wipes away. Break-Free CLP has high corrosion resistance and resists the adhesion of further fouling.

usually yields only to a water-based cleaner. Up to now, I have always found the traditional hot, soapy water to be the best cleaner for cap-'n'-ball revolvers and muzzle loading rifles. Finally, SS1 has unchained muzzle loaders from the hot water tap! SS1 cleaner, and its companion SS2 lubricant were used to good advantage by the 1976 United States International Muzzle Loading Team during its win in France, and again in 1977.

Though basically a cleaner, SS1 has high resistance to corrosion as well. SS1 floats light rust off of a blued steel surface with no damage to the bluing or the raw steel underneath.

SS2 shares most of the benefits of SS1, but is four times more lubricant. Both are effective lubricants down to −60 degrees Fahrenheit, are harmless to metals, wood and plastics, and contain no silicones. They do contain microscopic, anti-static lubricating particles that adhere to all metal surfaces. The "creep" factor is so high, that SS2 can be aerosol sprayed into a gun muzzle, and it will spread over the entire bore to protect it against corrosion. At the 1977 National Sporting Goods Association show in Chicago, TDP president Bruce Weeber, chose a unique method of demonstrating the corrosion resistance of SS2. An aquarium filled with salt water held a Colt pistol sprayed with SS2, while a motor agitated the fluid through every nook and cranny. Yet after 100 hours no rust had appeared!

An even better rust remover (again without damage to bluing) is TDP's "Super Penetrant" SS-P. If you want to get a *creepy* feeling, just spray some of this stuff on a piece of clean steel and hold it where it reflects the light, so you can watch the SS-P "walk" across the surface. SS-P is great for loosening rust-frozen screws in guns. Totally Dependable Products also markets a wood conditioner called "Stock Slick." Saturating the barrel channel and action area reportedly ends forever the problem of shifting points of impact resulting from moisture absorption by the wood. When sprayed on the wood, Stock Slick foams up and penetrates the pores. After a period of 20 minutes or so, you wipe it off and enjoy the soft glow that it imparts. I tried Stock Slick on a number of my own rifles and can report that it makes mediocre wood look good and good grain look great! Stock Slick also has an antistatic agent that discourages ever-present dust from settling on your newly polished stock.

For some 17 years, Zip Aerosol products, (2130 Deering Ct., Canoga Park, California 91304) have been effectively used in industry, government, even the space program. During the Vietnam conflict, Zip oils kept cranky M-16's on the firing line. However, it was only

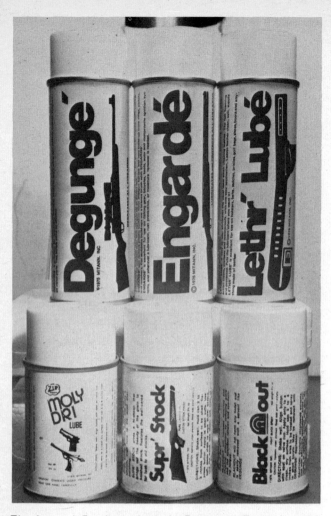

Zip Aerosol Products include Degunge, Engarde, and Lethr Lube, etc. All are products of modern technology without any trace of petroleum. The Black Out spray is a quick way to blacken sights without the usual mess of the "smoke pot."

Schultea's Gun String is a highly portable cleaning item that consists of a metal weight to drop through the bore, followed by a nylon string, which pulls through a knitted scrubber to clean the bore. The tiny package fits easily into the pocket or pack on the trail, always ready for emergencies.

recently that Zip has packaged their products, Degunge, Engarde, and Lethr Lube, in both 8- and 16-ounce spray cans, for sale to sportsmen. Degunge is a fast-dissolving degreaser and high-potency cleaner for all firearms uses. Sprayed into a badly-fouled receiver, it quickly flushes away dirt and gummed lubricant, leaving it dry and clean, ready to be sprayed with Engarde, a high grade lubricant and moisture-displacing rust preventive, fortified with acid neutralizers and waxes. Engarde cleans, lubricates and protects. Zip Lethr Lube is a foaming leather treatment, formulated to penetrate and restore life to old leather. It contains neat's-foot oil fortified with Z2, which allows it to wet out evenly without creating dark and light spots on the leather. The foaming action prevents runs and messy drips during application. The Zip trio is available by mail and represents a "best-of-breed" selection of modern chemical cleaner/preservatives!

Another space-age spin-off product of remarkable talents, called "Break-Free CLP," has just completed a series of tests by the armed services, in fast-firing automatic weapons large and small. In one of the tests, several automatic weapons were treated with Break-Free CLP and fired over 34,000 rounds without a malfunction. At the end of the test, the usually stubborn carbon deposits practically wiped from the metal because of residual film left by Break-Free CLP. The new formula which includes specially treated Teflon, performs all three functions of cleaning, lubrication and protection from corrosion for steel or nonferrous alloy parts. It cleans by burrowing under firing residue, lead, or bullet alloy and lifting them free. Independent laboratory tests showed Break-Free CLP treated surfaces resisted corrosion for over 900 hours in a humidity chamber and over 100 hours in a 5 percent salt spray chamber. If Break Free CLP isn't available in your locality yet, it can be obtained by mail order in 15.85-ounce ozone-safe aerosol cans from San/Bar Corporation, Chemicals Division, P.O. Box 11787, Santa Ana, California 92711.

A unique industrial lubricant called, "Tri-Flon," has surfaced recently in compact 9-gram spray cans. Tri-Flon is a synthesized multi-purpose lubricant containing Teflon, in sub-micron-sized particles. The tiny particles of Teflon are marble-shaped, acting like millions of tiny ball bearings. They run into the microscopic valleys and cracks present in even the most highly finished steel, evening it out to a micro-smooth friction-free surface. The boundary film is said by the maker to be so durable that it reduces the need for reapplication up to 90 percent. Tri-Flon displaces dirt, dust, and abrasive particles that account for most wear with ordinary lubricants. It is also highly penetrant, for freeing frozen screws. I found Tri-Flon enabled me to work a very tight slide back onto the frame of a .22/45 after some accurizing work. After the slide had worked-in a bit, I found it unnecessary to lap it in as usual. After considerable shooting, I was unable to find any spots where the bluing was worn through along the rails of the new slide, despite the tight fit. If Tri-Flon isn't available to you locally, it can be obtained by mail order from MK-V, P.O. Box 5337, Orange, California 92667.

One of the newer products developed for use in firearms, is "Gun Sav'r" (product #630) from Chem-Pak, Winchester, Virginia. Gun Sav'r retains its lubricating properties from −25 to +125 degrees Fahrenheit. Gun Sav'r impregnates metal with molybdenum disulfide, imparting a permanent lubricating base highly useful on high-abrasion parts in autoloading actions. Gun Sav'r is a moisture-displacing oil, that affords long-term protection from corrosion, and also functions as a release agent, freeing bore fouling and reducing leading. Nothing in the formula is harmful to rifle or pistol stocks. Because Chem-Pak intends Gun Sav'r for use in firearms, they were particularly interested in its effect upon primers in handguns. Lee Jurras, founder of Super Vel, mentioned that he had complaints from some police departments about rounds that refused to fire. Tests with a popular penetrant oil disclosed that it could disable primers especially if officers sprayed their guns indiscriminantly. Chem-Pak conducted a test using Gun Sav'r and "Brand X," which looked suspiciously like the one that caused Super Vel's problems. Of 300 rounds of .38 Special reloads, 100 were set aside as controls. The remaining 200 were evenly divided into two groups, one with Gun Sav'r sprayed directly on the primers and the other with Brand X. After 9 days, 25 rounds from each group were test fired. One of the cartridges in the Brand X group misfired. All of the Gun Sav'r treated rounds fired. After an additional 15 days of repeated spraying, the balance of the cartridges were fired. Again all Gun Sav'r treated rounds fired, however, there were 14 misfires and 3 hangfires among the Brand X group. All of the control rounds fired without incident. It would be virtually impossible for any normal usage to subject ammunition to this much oil exposure, so it could be reasonably said that it is highly unlikely that Gun Sav'r would ever cause primer problems. Centerfire difficulties stem from infiltration of the oil around the primer pocket, where it kills the priming mixture. Rimfires have no opening around the primer, and the union between bullet and case is usually very tight, with the added protection of the outside lubrication to help seal the crimp.

An interesting quick-cleaning device is Schultea's Gun String, 67 Burress, Houston, Texas 77022. It consists of a small weight attached to a nylon string, in turn attached to a bulky knitted pull-through, about a yard long, which can be saturated with an all-purpose cleaner/lubricant. Rolled up less than palm-size, you can carry it in its plastic pouch in the pocket when on the trail, for emergency or merely end-of-the-day cleanups. A smidgin of mud, snow or rain can be quickly purged from the bore by just pulling the Schultea Gun String through a few times. One bit of advice in the instructions troubles me, however. Schultea recommends leaving the Gun String in the bore during storage. My experience with leaving any absorbent material in contact with steel has been totally disastrous. I recall wrapping a new revolver in a square of silicone-impregnated cloth once, only to return some time later and find it spotted with rust everywhere that the cloth touched metal. Perhaps with the Gun String soaked in a space-age rust preventive, it might be OK, but the oil might evaporate out, allowing moisture to seep in and be held in intimate contact with the bore.

A number of old line companies have been in the business of producing top-grade gun cleaning supplies for so long that we take them for granted. Such names as Hoppe's, Outers, Marble, Birchwood Casey, and Williams have a familiar ring.

Although best known for their bore solvent, Hoppe's also offers jointed cleaning rods, cleaning kits with rod, oil, solvent, patches, brushes, grease, etc.

Outers Laboratories, Inc. continues their time-honored Gunslick line, epitomized by a life-long friend of mine, the graphite grease in the tiny silver tube that smooths out rifle and revolver actions and will impregnate the bore with graphite, discouraging leading. Outers' Gunslick Gun Grease has the body to protect rifled bores through long periods of storage. Outers produces the deluxe "Imperial Line" of sectioned stainless steel cleaning rods in plush-lined steel cases, by far the finest available. The most versatile is the .22 to .270 rifle rod, which can be used for handguns as well, even Buntline barrel lengths. Bronze thrust bearings in the handles make these rods easy-turning so that they don't resist the twist of the rifling. Outers also makes lower-cost steel, aluminum and brass jointed and one-piece rods that need make no apologies for quality.

Outers also produces their famed "polarized" gun oil, plus a variety of other bore solvents and oils. Outers' gun cleaning kits include all necessary solvents and oils, plus cleaning rod, jags, and phosphor bronze brushes.

Marble still makes their three-section brass cleaning rods, with the unique swivel tip that joins to any section, resulting in a pistol, rifle or shotgun rod, as required. Several jags and slotted ends are included, to adapt to various bore sizes from .22 to 12 gauge. Their cleaning kit includes Marble's non-freeze gun oil and bore solvent.

Birchwood Casey makes such a diversity of gun finishing and gun care products that it would take a book just to describe them adequately. Among their unique concepts is the "Sheath Take Along Anti Rust Gun Cloth," in handy, individual 2½ x 3-inch foil packs. On a hunting or camping trip, use the Sheath-impregnated "Gun Cloth" to wipe down your rimfire rifle or pistol.

The fine old name, "Marble's" still evokes expectations of quality products — you won't be disappointed. Their line includes oil and solvent for guns.

Birchwood Casey offers the widest array of gun care products yet, with their unique "Gun Scrubber" at the head of the line. With snorkel attached, it drives out accumulated residue from hard-to-reach areas of autoloading actions, and others too.

Then tear an appropriate-sized corner off to run through the bore with a cleaning rod, to clean and protect. Sheath polarized moisture-displacing rust preventive and lubricant is also available in a 6-ounce spray can. Birchwood Casey's "Gun Scrubber" provides an easy answer to those autoloading rifles that sometimes get so caked with powder residue that they finally refuse to function. With snorkel attached, the 16-ounce spray can directs a high-velocity jet of powerful solvent into every nook and cranny, degreasing, and driving out caked powder fouling. Allow the action to drain thoroughly, then relubricate with Sheath or Birchwood Casey Synthetic Gun Oil. Sheath is highly effective in removing light rust from blued finishes without damage to the bluing itself. What's more, it stops the rust cold!

Several years back when sub-calibers were very big, .17 caliber rifles were subject to mysterious lapses of accuracy. The culprit was finally isolated as simple bore fouling from jacketed bullets. One of the few products that effectively removed that metal fouling and restored accuracy was Birchwood Casey's Heavy-Duty Bore Solvent. It works just as well for cleaning up lead-laden .22 bores!

Williams Guide Line Products, noted for their fine open and scope sights, also produces a fast-acting bore cleaner and high viscosity, highly penetrating gun oil.

Guns and leather goods go together like ham-'n'-

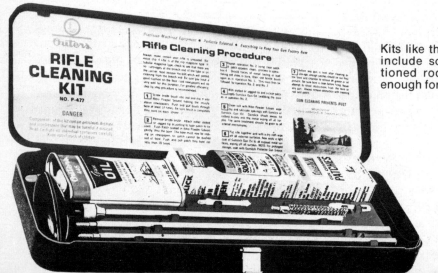

Kits like this Outers Rifle Cleaning Kit normally include solvent, patches, oil, plus steel sectioned rod, in a stamped steel case rugged enough for the trail.

eggs! Holsters, belts and boots all need constant attention to remain live and supple. From one of the foremost holster makers in the world, Safariland, comes a Professional Leather Maintenance Kit, with a plastic bottle of leather dressing for coating new or near-new leather products or for resurfacing old leather goods. Safariland Leather Conditioner soaks in deep to restore life to tired, dried-out boots and holster rigs. The maker recommends that leather and dressing be warmed to 90 degrees by placing in direct sunlight for some time before applying.

Storage & Security

So you're keeping your rimfire handguns and rifles in top shape by proper cleaning and lubrication, and protecting them from the elements. However, you didn't go to all of that trouble just to supply a burglar with readily saleable loot! All too often that becomes the bottom line.

There is no sure cure for the burgeoning burglary problem but there are steps that you can take to reduce the risk. Your first and foremost guardian is simple anonymity. Keep your position as a gun-owner in low profile. Keep your guns out of sight. It is sad to have to keep beautiful rifles concealed rather than on display as we once did in the good old days. Having them hidden takes much away from the joy of ownership. You can't enjoy the sight of the guns yourself, and you can't show them off to visitors. Many of the regular visitors to your house are better not advised of the presence of guns. TV repairmen, telephone, gas company, and electricity company service men are all likely perfectly honest, but they also talk to friends about those beautiful rifles that they saw in your house. When your neighbor drives up in a new Cadillac, restrain yourself from countering with, "Oh, that's nothing, I've got a rare Colt that's worth almost as much!" Of course, your neighbor's not going to sneak over and steal it! But how about his friends at the office, to whom he may mention it in passing, or even friends of his friends. Somehow, the information seems to spread like ripples fanning out from a pebble dropped in a pool of water. At the same time, caution your own children not to mention that you own firearms. Their friends, or friends of friends could decide that they need your guns more than you do! Even relatives are not above suspicion. In discussing this subject with a friend of mine who is a captain at a local PD, he said that teenage relatives are among the most likely suspects in any given burglary. They are in a position to know the victim's habits—when he is away from home, where the loot is kept, easiest points of entry into the home.

The captain also noted that chameleon-like, burglars have adapted to the changing life styles in the United States. With many, if not most, wives now working days, just like their husbands, burglaries during daylight hours have skyrocketed. Prime time is between 9:00 and 11:00 AM, after parents are at work and kiddies in school, and before anyone returns for lunch. The burglars are likely as not to drive boldly up to the front door, in a van or truck marked with "Joe's TV," or other appropriate sign, often of the magnetic variety that can be simply pulled off and hidden inside after leaving the scene. Then even if an observant neighbor reports the visit, police will be searching in vain for a truck with "Joe's TV" on the side.

A fine way to signal potential burglars that the coast is clear is to leave a note pinned to the door for the mailman, milkman, etc. saying just when you'll be back from shopping, work, or whatever.

If you're going away for a trip, by all means request that your mail be held for you at the post office, unless you have a door slot where the mail falls inside and is not visible from outside. Rather than stopping newspapers, better to have a neighbor pick them up each day. Not to intimate that the news boy is going to tell anyone that you're away, but you never know. The fewer people that you tell, the better! You may have to leave Fido with a local kennel. There is another possible information leak. You can reduce that risk by using a kennel somewhat removed from your immediate area, and giving a fictitious address. I know it goes against the grain to be so devious, but remember you are protecting some of your most valuable possessions.

If you can possibly arrange for a trusted friend or relative to live at your home while you are gone, that is an even better solution to the many problems involved. In any event, be certain to continue the lawn service, so that a weedy, overgrown appearance won't advertise your absence. Have at least two lights on timers to turn on with dusk and off at your customary bedtime. Tell your close neighbors about the lights, as well as having them keep an eye on the place. Once a neighbor of mine did his good deed for the day. When he observed that I had left a light burning, while away on vacation, he disconnected the circuit-breakers to save me electricity. He also turned off the freezer, spoiling about $300 worth of meat and frozen vegetables.

If you plan to be gone just for an evening, to the show, etc., always leave lights burning. A radio playing with a "talk show," loud enough to hear from outside, but not loud enough to be clearly distinguishable, is highly discouraging. So also is a large, *mean* dog! The dog must have free run of the house, so that he or she can be at the door to greet any potential intruder.

If you expect to be gone away from home for an extended period, touring the world on the Queen Mary perhaps (that could *really* take a long time!), it might be wise to pack your guns in a footlocker and place them in bonded storage for the duration.

Normal precautions around the home help discourage break-ins, such as keeping the shrubbery trimmed so that it won't provide concealment for someone making a forced entry, using double-cylinder (keyed inside

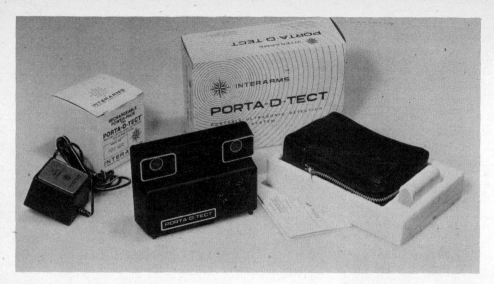

The Porta-D-Tect ultrasonic portable alarm is one practical approach to alerting the neighbors, or yourself to the presence of a burglar in the house.

The Robless Security Safe is a hexagonal steel cabinet with a lazy Susan divided into compartments. It is locked with two different keyed locks. It is compact enough to fit into most closets, where it can be camouflaged with clothing, etc. If a burglar should gain entry into the Robless Security Safe, he would get just two guns, because the balance are protected by the dividers in the lazy Susan, which is locked in place and very difficult to pick.

and out) deadbolts on all outside doors, using solid-core outside doors, having lockable window latches, etc. Even barred windows are becoming fashionable these days. In Italy, I observed solid steel shutters, tightly closed even in the daytime. Could that be an omen of things to come here? We imported "unisex" from Italy, perhaps we may soon copy their shutters as well.

Have your phone disconnected when away. Burglars often call several times to be certain the house isn't occupied. If the phone's not working, it may keep them guessing a little longer. Leave shades and blinds in their normal condition. Drawing all the shades, all but shouts, "There's no one home!" Don't render assistance to the burglar by leaving tools handy for him to use in forcing a door or window. Keep ladders locked away in the garage, for the same reason. For reasons yet unknown, some people will leave the garage door or even the front door to the house wide open, because they're only going next door—or only going to be gone a "little while." That's long enough for a burglar to work his mischief!

Guns are so popular with criminals that a known gunowner becomes three times as likely as the average householder to become the victim of burglary. Don't look for any sympathy from the police. A close friend had a highly valuable antique firearms collection stolen from his house. The guns were recovered unharmed. However, by the time he was able to reclaim his property from the police, the valuable heirlooms were scratched and scarred beyond recognition. To the average cop, *a gun is a gun is a gun!*

220

Tread Corporation offers a horizontal chest with counter-balanced steel lid and full-length piano hinge.

Tread Corporation offers the simple steel box, the Tread-lok Security Chest, of welded 12-gauge steel, with 12-gun built-in rack. It's rigs like this one that deter burglars.

Does your key ring have one of those handy-dandy metal tags with your name and address on it? If they become lost, the finder just drops them in a mail box and they fly home to you. Or he can drop in when you're at work and help himself to the goodies. Better to remove that tag and kiss the keys goodby in the event of loss. Then hurry to a locksmith to have all of your tumblers changed, just in case! Another "no no," is leaving your house keys attached to your car keys while your car is in a public parking lot or at the local car wash. Some enterprising individual need only make an impression of your house key—check your license plate number with the Department of Motor Vehicles to get your home address, then—I'll leave the rest to your imagination.

Home burglar alarms are definitely worthwhile. Costs range from about $100 to into thousands, but you should be able to strike a happy medium. Alarms are designed primarily to discourage casual teenage burglars. The professionals can usually work around them. Don't display an alarm bell outside where it is easily seen. It tips the potential burglar that he must cope with an alarm, and it makes the chore of defeating it easy. Alarm boxes are often advertised as tamper-proof, meaning that any attempt to open them will set off the alarm. A simple solution consists of filling the box with pressurized foam, which sets up quickly, freezing the bell clapper. Or the box can be filled with shaving foam, which muffles the alarm bell for a time—long enough to ransack the house. The alarm box can be hidden inside of the attic near a vent, where it is not visible, yet where its message will broadcast loud and clear! Be sure that any alarm system has a battery backup to the house current. Any halfway smart burglar will disconnect the circuit breakers before entering.

An interesting concept comes from Interarms of Alexandria, Virginia, in their Porta-D-Tect ultrasonic portable alarm, that weighs only 10½ ounces including its own 9-volt alkaline battery. The Porta-D-Tect broadcasts its own 45-degree ultrasonic cone. If anything moves within that area, the alarm emits a 106-decible alarm signal. This is more for warning the householder if anyone enters at night. It can be set up to trigger a much louder horn or bell on the outside, however.

Thousands of stolen guns are recovered every year. The Los Angeles County Sheriff's office dumps a good many of them into the blue Pacific! If you can't positively identify your own guns, you can expect them to end up in the drink or perhaps cut up with a welding torch. Describing the pretty curly grain in the stock isn't going to satisfy the police. They said *positive* identification, by serial number, or by a mark that you have placed thereon. There are a number of practical marking systems that you can use. One example is the "Stop Thief" system that includes a hard Carboly steel pointed stylus for engraving your driver's license number, Social Security number, etc. on metal surfaces, plus record book to inventory valuables, and Stop Thief decals to place upon windows of your house and vehicle, notifying potential burglars that items inside are marked for identification, thus more difficult to fence. Vibrator engraving tools result in deeper more difficult to remove markings. There is a trick to using a vibrator-engraver. You have to "tune" it with the speed adjusting dial until the sound and the action of the engraver are smooth. If the tool is jumping around in your hand instead of gliding over the metal, it isn't properly adjusted.Neither the vibrator nor hard-pointed stylus will mark very well on casehardened surfaces. It is well to choose some spot not too noticeable unless you are a master engraver and can make it look as if it belonged. On the bottom of the barrel under the forend is a good spot. Or you can engrave the bottom of the receiver where it is covered by the stock. Anyplace where the markings can be easily found, but won't deface the gun. Or you can have your guns engraved by a professional, adding to their appearance as well as security.

If you have a 35mm camera with a fairly good lens, you can take a series of photos of your various guns, as close as the lens will allow, until the entire frame of the viewfinder is taken up with the gun. Even if you only get the drugstore style double enlargements, the photos will provide positive identification. On the back of each print, write the make, model, and caliber, as well as the serial number. Keep these some place other than your home, preferably in a safety deposit box. In any case, you should have a complete listing of your firearms, and other valuables also, including serial numbers, if any, in a safe location away from your home, in the event of major disaster, fire, flood or burglary.

There is yet another method for making the burglar's life more difficult. Just remove vital parts from your guns and store them in a safety deposit box. As a matter of course, I pull all of the bolts from my smallbore and bigbore rifles, cylinders from revolvers, slides from autoloaders, etc., and store them at my bank. It's a shame that we are driven to such extremes by law-breakers and lawmakers, but we have to deal with the situation as it exists, not as we might wish it to be!

Despite all of the precautions that you may take, the chances of your attracting the attention of a burglar are high. It is well nigh impossible to keep him out of your house, unless your home is built like a fort of window-less concrete and steel, but you may be able to deny him access to what he wants most—your guns! There are numerous safe-like steel cabinets currently available to protect your guns, but the most compact unit yet is the "Robless Revolving Security Safe," which stacks your rifles upright on a lazy Susan, storing 14 rifles or shotguns up to 54 inches in length on just 2 square feet of floor space!

The Robless Security Safe consists of a steel cabinet in the shape of a hexagon when viewed from above. Inside is a revolving platform with seven vertical welded steel walls separating the compartments. The idea is to protect most of the guns even if the thief manages to defeat the two Ace-keyed locks in the door and gain access to the first compartment. The Lazy Susan won't rotate unless yet another lock is released and it is so inaccessible that only a talented lock picker could hope to open it. The Robless Safe can be ordered with a variety of options, including several that include shelves to hold cameras, pistols and other valuables. Because it requires only a 2-foot wide space, the Robless can be fitted into most clothes closets and readily concealed to further confound the burglar. Lacking a handy closet, you can order the optional Colonial-style wood cabinet that completely surrounds the steel cabinet disguising it as a china closet. The 310-pound (empty) weight of the cabinet should be enough to prevent its being carried away, but it can also be bolted to the floor! Burglar alarms can be attached to go off when the cabinet is tampered with. For information, write Robless Revolving Security Safes, 4246 Whittier Blvd., Los Angeles, California 90023.

Tread Corporation, P.O. Box 5497, Roanoke, Virginia 24012, offers a simple steel box, the Treadlok Security Chest T-600, 2 feet wide, 17 inches deep, and 63 inches tall, with built-in 12-gun rack, of 12-gauge welded construction. The door is folded in on both sides and the top for stiffness, and hung on three sturdy concealed hinges. A vertical locking bolt is held by a high security padlock at the bottom, in a difficult to reach spot, to discourage attempts at cutting or sawing. A similar safe, the Model 101, made in a horizontal

Weatherby also offers a variety of semi-hard gun cases of high-impact styrene, with thick polyurethane padding inside to protect the guns. They are offered in one- and two-gun sizes, long and short lengths.

configuration, is also available from Tread Corp.

Provo Steel & Supply Company of Provo, Utah, makes the nearest thing to an industrial safe for home storage of firearms. It is constructed of ¼-inch steel plate all around save for the door, which is ⅜-inch steel plate, reinforced full-circle. Lid Lockup is by 12 heavy-bolt plungers, like a real bank vault, secured by a commercial combination lock. Weight varies from 750 to 1,100 pounds—a bit much for the burglar to tote away on his back.

Security Products, P.O. Box 456, West, Texas 76691, makes a variety of upright and horizontal gun safes, all 10-gauge or heavier welded steel construction, and they offer the unique service of building custom safes to order out of any desired plate steel from 10-gauge to full ½-inch, which weighs an imposing 20.4 pounds per square foot!

Saf-T-Case, P.O. Box 5472, Irving Texas 75062, offers a rugged looking upright gun safe only 2 feet wide that holds 10 to 12 guns. Also of interest, Saf-T-Case makes a sturdy welded aluminum, foam-lined two-gun shipping/carrying case, with piano hinge, rubber gromet sealed lid and four-latch lockable closure. It costs the price of a new rifle, but when you have to check your guns in at the baggage ramp of your local airport, you'll be ever so grateful to have them snugly protected.

The most beautiful deluxe hard gun case of all time comes from Weatherby Inc. Smoothly-styled of silver-anodized aluminum, it boasts full-length piano hinge and full-circle rubber gasket to make it waterproof and floatable. Four rugged latches secure the lid. A tumbler lock or precision combination lock protects the contents. Weatherby aluminum gun cases are available in one- and two-gun sizes. Some cases rely

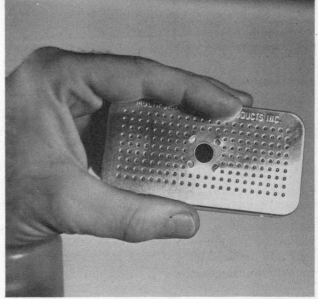

Given maximum security for your guns, you still have to combat the invisible killer that comes in the night and turns beautiful blue into wretched rust. Desiccants from Hydrosorbent Company suck moisture out of the air before it can damage steel surfaces. Shown here is the medium-sized desiccant container called the "Compact Unit," made of aluminum that will last a lifetime. The desiccant can be reactivated without end.

upon tying the two guns into place. Often before a trip is over, one or both have pulled loose, and they're rattling around like dice in a cup. Not so with the Weatherby case, which has a deep layer of polyurethane foam, cut out for two scoped rifles, with ample padding between so that never the twain shall meet! Weatherby aluminum cases have the look of expensive luggage, and don't telegraph to everyone that they contain guns. Weatherby Gun Guard Cases are molded of heavy-duty high-impact styrene, with thick polyurethane padding. Lightweight and rugged, they offer ample protection at budget cost.

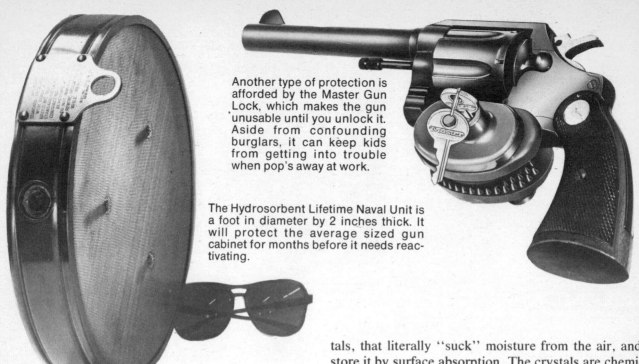

Another type of protection is afforded by the Master Gun Lock, which makes the gun unusable until you unlock it. Aside from confounding burglars, it can keep kids from getting into trouble when pop's away at work.

The Hydrosorbent Lifetime Naval Unit is a foot in diameter by 2 inches thick. It will protect the average sized gun cabinet for months before it needs reactivating.

Storage Rust—How To Avoid It

Regardless of the kind of gun cabinet or case you use to house your rimfire rifles and handguns, you should avail yourself of another inexpensive, highly important form of protection—namely, desiccants to remove and hold moisture in suspension. Any closed space tends to hold moisture in contact with your guns. Lack of air circulation is a prime cause of corrosion. However, an enclosed space is also the easiest to protect, especially so if you can seal the door edges with a weatherstrip or rubber molding. With the space secured against further invasion by moisture, you remove whatever was trapped inside when you closed the door by placing a package of desiccant, "crystals" of suitable size to handle the area involved.

The handiest of such items to come to my attention are sold by Hydrosorbent Company, P.O. Box 675, Rye, New York 10580. Hydrosorbent markets a variety of units to handle every situation, from 2 x 3-inch packets for use in pistol and rifle cases, to "Hydrosorbent Lifetime Naval Unit," a foot in diameter by 2 inches thick, which will protect the average-sized gun cabinet for months. The least expensive way to protect a large area is with the "Bagged Unit," which will protect up to 14 cubic feet of air space. Perhaps a little more durable and handy are the 2 x 4 x ½-inch aluminum "Compact Units," which will protect 3 cubic feet of enclosed air space. All of these various sized units are filled with the highest quality U.S. government spec silica gel crystals, that literally "suck" moisture from the air, and store it by surface absorption. The crystals are chemically inert, thus cannot harm any surface that they contact, although I recommend isolating the silica gel packets from the metal parts of your gun just to be safe. When the crystals have become saturated, a blue marker will turn pink, signaling that they should be reactivated by placing in an ordinary household oven at 200 to 300 degrees for ½ to 3 hours, until the marker returns to blue. The high quality silica gel packs sold by Hydrosorbent can be reactivated for a lifetime. There's nothing to wear out. They constitute a one-time reasonable investment that beats any insurance that you can buy!

Young children in the house call for another brand of gun security. Contrary to popular belief, an autoloading pistol can actually be safer around children than a revolver. It is hard for immature muscles to pull the slide back. Also, the clip can be removed and locked away in another location. When you return home, the loaded magazine can be returned to the gun and the chamber left empty. It requires but an instant to arm the gun.

It's not so easy to disassemble a revolver, but there is a cure. The Safariland Keyless Gunloc snaps into place in the guard, denying access to the trigger. To remove it, you must push in on a recessed button with one finger, against pressure far beyond the ability of any small-fry! Spring pressure is adjustable via an Allen wrench.

The Safariland Keyless Gunloc won't fit most rifles or shotguns, because the trigger guards are too thick. However, the Gun Lock from Master works equally well on rifles and shotguns. A positive ratchet lock attaches quickly, but will release only upon the use of a key that opens the pin tumbler lock. Any number of locks can be had keyed alike.